TRIBAL LAW
IN A NUTSHELL®

MATTHEW L.M. FLETCHER
Harry Burns Hutchins Collegiate Professor of
Law and Professor of American Culture
University of Michigan

WEST ACADEMIC

860 Blue Gentian Road, Suite 350
Eagan, MN 55121
1-877-888-1330

Published in the United States of America

ISBN: 979-8-31770-374-5

PREFACE

Tribal law in the United States refers to the constitutes, codes, ordinances, regulations, and judicial decisions created by sovereign tribal nations to govern individuals and entities within their jurisdiction and on tribal lands. It is distinct from federal Indian law, which focuses on the relationship between tribal, federal, and state governments. Tribal governments, frequently structured similarly to the federal system, develop and apply their own laws on matters like crimes, tribal membership, and resource management.

Federal Indian law and policy, for all its horrors, has always acknowledged that tribal nations possess inherent sovereignty, meaning they have the power to govern themselves. Tribal nations, which predate the existence of the United States by innumerable millennia, did exercise self-government until waves of colonizing nations and their constituencies destroyed Indigenous governance. Though tribal nations often muddled through the genocidal eradication of tribal polities and dispossessed Indigenous Peoples of nearly all their resources and undermined their cultures, tribal self-government never disappeared. In the last half century or so, as federal Indian affairs policy shifted explicitly toward tribal self-determination, tribal nations have jump started their governance capacities and, in doing so, their cultures and traditions.

This project is a memorialization of the last few decades of modern tribal self-government. Of the 575 federally recognized tribal nations in the United States (and there will be more in the future), more than 400 of them have developed or begun to develop tribal justice systems. This project attempts to summarize much of that work, primarily through the words and actions of tribal courts and tribal legislatures.

Finding tribal law is not easy, but it is far easier than it was a few decades ago. Early tribal court reporters dating back to the 1970s, the Tribal Court Reporter and the Indian Law Reporter, published many tribal court decisions on paper. The Indian Law Reporter is now available on HeinOnline in digitized form. Nowadays, Westlaw and Lexis Nexis host thousands of tribal court opinions. Since 2015, the National Indian Law Library of the Native American Rights Fund has collected new tribal court opinions on the Tribal Courts page of its Indian Law Bulletins website. The UCLA Law Library hosts links to several other important sources of tribal court opinions: the Northwest Intertribal Court System, Frank Pommersheim's archive of tribal court decisions hosted by the University of South Dakota School of Law Library, and the Hualapai Tribe's court of appeals. Numerous tribes and intertribal courts make their decisions available on tribal websites, including without limitation: Cherokee Nation, Choctaw Nation, Fond du Lac Band of Lake Superior Chippewa Indians, Gun Lake Tribe, Fort

Peck Tribes, Ho-Chunk Nation, Little River Band of Ottawa Indians, Little Traverse Bay Bands of Odawa Indians, Mashpee Wampanoag Tribe, Penobscot Nation, Pokagon Band of Potawatomi Indians, Puyallup Tribe, Rincon Band of Luiseño Indians, Sault Ste. Marie Tribe of Chippewa Indians, Sisseton Wahpeton Oyate, and Southwest Intertribal Court of Appeals. The Michigan Tribal-State-Federal Judicial Forum recently published a selection of Michigan tribal court decisions designed to show the scope and reach of tribal law. Michigan Tribal-State-Federal Judicial Forum, Anishinaabe Law: A Tribal Law Handbook for Michigan Legal Practitioners (2024).

This project owes an enormous debt to numerous people, but here I recognize merely four. First, *miigwetch* to Ninth Circuit Judge William C. Canby, the visionary who published *American Indian Law in a Nutshell* in 1980, just as he was appointed to the federal bench. Judge Canby's *Nutshell*, regularly updated with the eighth edition in print as of 2025, was then and remains now an enormously useful overview of Federal Indian Law that everyone who practices in the field relies upon heavily. As in-house counsel for four different tribal nations in the late 1990s and early 2000s, I kept Judge Canby's *Nutshell* within arms reach at all times. This project is by no means intended to be (or actually is) a replacement in any way for Canby's *Nutshell*, but is designed to be a humble companion to that work.

Second, I say *miigwetch* to Frank Pommersheim, judge for multiple tribal nations over many decades and stalwart legal scholar and advocate in both the federal Indian law and tribal law spaces. I once wrote that Judge-slash-Professor Pommersheim was my true Indian law professor. His writings as a legal scholar and as a tribal judge are voluminous, influential, pragmatic, and moral. Shortly after I entered the academy in 2004, Frank told me that tribal law is the real Indian law. I have carried that dictum with me ever since.

Third, I say *miigwetch* to John Petoskey, a citizen of the Grand Traverse Band of Ottawa and Chippewa Indians and the tribe's long-time general counsel. I worked for John for nearly four years as one of his minions and it was the most educational experience I could ever have hoped for as a neophyte lawyer and budding legal scholar. John did the grunt work that modern tribal governance demands, writing more than 90 percent of the Grand Traverse Band's tribal code, but he also masterminded critical federal court cases with his exceptionally broad knowledge of federal Indian law, often letting others take credit for the successes of the tribe.

Finally, I say *miigwetch* to Wenona Singel, law professor, tribal judge, and citizen of the Little Traverse Bay Bands of Odawa Indians, and my lovely partner in life. Wenona sees through all the baloney and states what appears to be obvious, but in fact is subtly genius. She has written numerous appellate opinions for Little T and for GTB, work that appears throughout this project. In this instance, she recently asked me why I had not yet bothered to submit a proposal to develop a tribal law nutshell. And so here we are.

MATTHEW L.M. FLETCHER

December 2025

OUTLINE

TABLE OF CASES

References are to Pages

TRIBAL LAW
IN A NUTSHELL®

CHAPTER 1

INTRODUCTION TO TRIBAL NATIONS

A. EARLY HISTORY OF TRIBAL LAW

Tribal nations are sovereign governmental entities with a unique status in American law. While there are currently 575 federally recognized tribal entities eligible to receive services from the United States, 89 Fed.Reg. 944 (Jan. 8, 2024), untold thousands of tribal political communities existed in a wide variety of forms and organizations prior to first contact with European colonizers. Estimates vary, but leading scholars assert that anywhere from 10 million to 100 hundred million people lived in the western hemisphere at the time of first contact with European colonizers, with a consensus estimate of approximately 50–55 million people.

The tribal nations of what is now the eastern shore of the United States came into contact with the Europeans early in the 16th century. Early colonizers were amazed to find vast food production fields, curated forests, and Indigenous villages of every size and complexity. However, over the next decades and centuries, the civilizations of the Indigenous Peoples of this place were nearly eradicated by the diseases brought by the colonizers, especially smallpox. Colonizers brought settlers, but they fared little better. Virtually every initial effort to settle and colonize the eastern shores of what is now the United States failed horribly due to starvation, disease, and, occasionally, violence. But European elites sent wave after wave of settlers to this place, eventually displacing the severely depleted populations and polities of Indigenous People. Over centuries, the armies and settlers of the Spanish, British, French, Dutch, and other European nations took control of the east coast, eventually establishing the famed colonies that would become the United States in 1776.

While the American Revolution was ostensibly a war designed to free American colonizers from the British yoke, Indigenous Peoples remained crucial to the politics of the era. The Declaration of Independence condemned individual Indian people as "merciless Indian savages" supposedly enabled by the British Crown to torment American colonizers. Individual Indians that constituted tribal nations were again referenced in Article IX of the Articles of Confederation that granted Congress the power of "regulating the trade and managing all affairs with the Indians, not members of any of the states; provided that the legislative right of any state, within its own limits, be not infringed or violated." The United States Constitution again referenced individual Indians in Article I's apportionment and representation clauses as "Indians not taxed." Const. Art. I, § 2, cl. 3, amended by Const. Amend. XIV, § 2. Tribal nations were first acknowledged in the Commerce Clause that delegated the power to regulate commerce with "Indian tribes." Const. Art. I, sec. 8, cl. 3. Early on, the United States Supreme Court labeled tribal nations as "domestic dependent nations." Cherokee Nation v. Georgia, 30 U.S. 1, 17

(1831) (Marshall, C.J.). That name remains in the vocabulary of the Court. See Michigan v. Bay Mills Indian Community, 572 U.S. 782, 788 (2014) ("Indian tribes are 'domestic dependent nations' that exercise 'inherent sovereign authority.' ") (quoting Oklahoma Tax Comm'n v. Citizen Band Potawatomi Tribe of Okla., 498 U.S. 505, 509 (1991)).

Even though tribal nations are heavily influenced, even dominated at times, by the federal government, at bottom, tribal nations are not creatures of the United States. Tribal sovereignty derives from American Indian people. Tribal nations are governed in accordance with tribal laws and are generally not constrained by federal laws except by tribal consent or Congressional fiat, principles recognized in the blackletter law of federal Indian law. Restatement of the Law of American Indians §§ 13, 15. Federal law also recognizes that United States Constitution does not regulate tribal powers. Id. § 16. State laws have no force in Indian country absent Congressional authorization. Id. §§ 29–34.

Modern tribal governments vary significantly in terms of available resources, land bases, population, histories, cultures, and every other factor, but almost all tribal nations have several critical commonalities. First, nearly all tribal governments are federal government contractors, accepting federal appropriations through self-determination or self-governance contracts with the federal government to provide governmental services to reservation constituents under the Indian Self-Determination and Education Assistance Act of 1975 and its amendments. 25 U.S.C. § 5301 et seq. (Public Law 638). These tribal bureaucracies, often in tandem with federal agencies such as the Bureau of Indian Affairs and the Indian Health Service, administer services such as health care, education, housing, law enforcement, and most other governmental services. Some tribal government bureaucracies are very small, like those of the Alaska Native villages, while others are enormous, like the Cherokee Nation and the Navajo Nation. Second, tribal governments tend to dominate reservation economies, either through natural resources exploitation, gaming or other commercial enterprises, and tribal government operations. Tribes are both economic actors and regulators. Restatement of the Law of American Indians §§ 46–50. Third, tribes exercise inherent governmental powers, sometimes constrained by federal laws or the tribal government's capacity to govern, but in general, tribal power in Indian country is plenary. Id. §§ 14, 17–27. In Indian country at least (and beyond in limited circumstances), tribal governments have robust powers, making tribal law a worthy area of discussion and analysis.

While tribal nations adopt much of their laws in the context of the federal-tribal contracting relationship or relations with nonmembers and nonmember businesses, the origins of tribal law are embedded in Indigenous languages, lands, and cultural teachings. This chapter ties the creation stories to the fundamental laws and the early written constitutions and statutes of several tribal nations.

B. CREATION STORIES AND FUNDAMENTAL LAWS

The creation stories of the Indigenous peoples of the United States help to establish the worldview of individual Indians. That worldview is the natural law, or the unwritten constitutions, of modern tribal nations. This natural law is sometimes considered to be the fundamental law of tribal nations. It is essential to acknowledge the role that creation stories play in the formation of these laws.

Consider the creation story of the Anishinaabeg—the Odawa, Ojibwe, and the Bode'wadmi nations of the Great Lakes. *Gizhie Manidoo* lowered the Anishinaabeg onto *Anishinaabewaki* (the world of the Anishinaabeg) through *bagone giizhik* (the hole in the sky). The Anishinaabeg landed on the earth with their feet and toes pointed downward so as to lessen their impact on the creatures already there, for the Anishinaabeg were the last and least important creatures to enter Anishinaabewaki. *Enawendewin* (we are all related) is a lifeway principle that acknowledges the status of the Anishinaabeg in relation to the rest of creation. The Anishinaabeg are not on earth to exercise dominion, but to know their place and to act to protect the harmony of creation. As a consequence, the Anishinaabeg choose to life live in the correct way, or *mino-bimaadiziwin*. E.g., Payment v. Election Commission, 2022 Sault Ste. Marie Chippewa App. LEXIS 1, at *9 (Sault Ste. Marie Tribe of Chippewa Indians Ct.App.2022); Raphael v. Election Board, No. 13-2189-CV-CV, slip op. at 6–7 (Grand Traverse

Band of Ottawa and Chippewa Indians Tribal Judiciary 2014); Wright v. Nottawaseppi Huron Band of Potawatomi, 2022 Nottawaseppi Huron Band Supreme LEXIS 1 at *6 (Nottawaseppi Huron Band of Potawatomi S.Ct.2022). The Anishinaabeg derive from *enawendewin* and *mino-bimaadiziwin* a set of principles often known as the *Niizhwaaswi Nokomis Gikinoo'amaagoowinaag*, or Seven Grandmother Teachings (or the non-gendered Seven Sacred Gifts):

1. Zaagidiwin—Love
2. Debwewin—Truth
3. Aakodewewin—Bravery
4. Dibaadendiziwin—Humility
5. Nibwaakawin—Wisdom
6. Gwayakwaadiziwin—Honesty
7. Minwaadendamowin—Respect

Spurr v. Election Board, 2012 Nottawaseppi Huron Band Sup. LEXIS 4 (Nottawaseppi Huron Band of the Potawatomi S.Ct.2012).

Anishinaabe tribal laws follow from those fundamental principles. For example, the child welfare code of the Nottawaseppi Huron Band of the Potawatomi codifies these and related principles:

> The Nottawaseppi Huron Band of the Potawatomi believes all children deserve the following: a mother (*gashe*); a father (*noos*); identity with the traditional way of life (*mno*

> *bmadzewen*); to learn and speak their language (*Bodewewadmi*); to have a family (*mezodan*); know their relatives (*nwemagen*); to know the traditional laws, customs, and ceremonies of the people; a knowledge and understanding of the seven grandfather teachings; *Bwakawen* (wisdom), *Debanawen* (love), *Kejitwawenindowen* (respect), *Wedasewen* (bravery), *Gwekwadzewen* (honesty), *Edbesendowen* (humility), and *Debwewin* (truth); and the ability to live according to the practice of the traditional laws, customs, and ceremonies that govern their people.

Nottawaseppi Huron Band of the Potawatomi Children's Code, § 7.5–1(C).

The Navajo Nation long has led American tribal nations in developing a traditional common law rooted in creation stories. Navajo laws originate from the Holy Beings who placed the Diné at a sacred place and established Diné fundamental laws, referred to as *Diné Bi Beenahaz'áanii.* 1 Navajo Nation Code §§ 201–06. Sections 201 through 205 detail Diné traditional law, customary law, and natural law. Section 206 establishes Diné Common Law:

> The Diné Common Law declares and teaches that:
>
> A. The knowledge, wisdom, and practices of the people must be developed and exercised in harmony with the values and principles of the *Diné Bi Beenahaz'áanii;* and in turn, the

> written laws of the Navajo Nation must be developed and interpreted in harmony with Diné Common Law; and
>
> B. The values and principles of Diné Common Law must be recognized, respected, honored and trusted as the motivational guidance for the people and their leaders in order to cope with the complexities of the changing world, the need to compete in business to make a living and the establishment and maintenance of decent standards of living; and
>
> C. The values and principles of Diné Common Law must be used to harness and utilize the unlimited interwoven Diné knowledge, with our absorbed knowledge from other peoples. This knowledge is our tool in exercising and exhibiting self-assurance and self-reliance in enjoying the beauty of happiness and harmony.

Tribal lawmakers have begun examining the connection between the culture and tribal laws. Sourcing tribal laws from creation stories is becoming common in Indian country. For example, the Creator of Salish and Kalispel tribal nations placed Coyote and Fox on the earth first, establishing the lifeways of harmony and interconnectedness for others to follow, including humans. The Great Mysterious (*Ma'xema'hēō'e*) of the Cheyenne Nation ordered their four great servants to search for earth and humans; on their fifth trip, they discovered a giant feminine entity in the formless darkness of the void about give birth. Yakama tribal leader Meninock described the creation story of their tribal nation during a trial for violating a state law on fishing:

> God created this Indian country and it was like He spread out a big blanket. He put the Indians on it. They were created here in this country, truly and honestly, and that was the time this river started to run. Then God created fish in this river and put deer in these mountains and made laws through which has come the increase of fish and game. Then the Creator gave us Indians life; we awakened and as soon as we saw the game and the fish we knew they were made for us. . . . I was not brought from a foreign country and did not come here. I was put here by the Creator.

Testimony of Chief Meninock (Yakima) During a 1915 Trial for Violating a Washington State Code on Salmon Fishing, in Great Documents in American Indian History, 297–98 (Wayne Moquin & Charles Van Doren eds., 1973), quoted in Rebecca Tsosie, Land, Culture, and Community: Reflections on Native Sovereignty and Property in America, 34 Ind.L.Rev. 1291 (2001).

In general, tribal nations tie their laws to the sacred homelands of Indigenous nations. The land is the law. The law is represented in the language. The people learn the law through the stories.

C. EARLY WRITTEN CONSTITUTIONS AND LAWS

The earliest known Indigenous constitution is the *Gayanashagowa*, the Great Law of Peace of the Haudenosaunee nations (originally the Mohawk, Oneida, Cayuga, Onondaga, and Seneca, later on the Tuscarora, nations). The Gayanashagowa dates back several centuries (12th century) and was written in the form of wampum belts. The Peacemaker instructed the original five nations to cease their fighting and join together in a confederacy. The law required the Haudenosaunee nations to share their external sovereignty, for example, the power to declare war or to enter into treaties with other nations, with the greater confederation. Clan Mothers held the primary leadership positions, with others serving as speakers when in the longhouse. The individual nations retained control over their internal or domestic relations, for example, familial relations, petty crimes, property disputes, and so on. The confederacy held until the American Revolution, when the nations split apart by joining separate sides of the conflict. Today, each of the Haudenosaunee nations has adopted their own separate laws, but the Gayanashagowa remains significant.

The Choctaw and Cherokee constitutions of 1826 and 1827, respectively, were the first instances of American tribal nations adopting written constitutions designed to adapt to the colonizing presence of the United States. The Cherokee Nation adopted its constitution to establish a national government with three branches. Of note, the constitution also created the Cherokee Supreme Court, famously the first supreme court in the state, as the State of Georgia had not yet created a formal appellate court. During that time, the Cherokee Nation also enacted a criminal code that ended the traditional blood feud method of resolving disputes. The Cherokee Nation also established a police force, the Cherokee Light Horse, and a national newspaper, the Cherokee Phoenix. All of these efforts were designed to push back against the efforts of the State of Georgia to undermine the political integrity of the Cherokee Nation.

The Cherokee Constitution was a key component of a series of cases arising out of the Cherokee Nation's territory from 1830 to 1832. Those cases, Georgia v. Tassel, 1 Dud. 229 (Ga. 1830), Cherokee Nation v. Georgia, 30 U.S. 1 (1831), and Worcester v. Georgia, 31 U.S. 515 (1832), form a trilogy of critically important cases not only to the American Indian law canon, but to the history of the United States.

The historic Cherokee Nation lands extended throughout what is now Georgia, Tennessee, North Carolina, and Alabama. The tribe executed the Treaty of Hopewell in 1785 that formally established the boundaries of the Cherokee Nation's reservation. 7 Stat. 18 (1785). See also Treaty of Holston, Treaty with the Cherokee, 7 Stat. 39 (1791). Subsequent treaties shrunk the Cherokee land base, but the core remained extant in Georgia, as did the federal-tribal relationship. That relationship, then known as the duty of protection (now commonly called the general trust responsibility), established as a matter of international customary law that the United States had agreed to preserve the territorial and sovereign authority of the Cherokee Nation. Into the 1820s, the Cherokees controlled a large land base in the northwest corner of Georgia. In many respects, the Cherokee people were thriving economically in their homelands. Consider for example that the Cherokees were exporting food to the people of Georgia. Conversely, Georgia's economy, based on inefficient agriculture and slavery, was foundering. Unfortunately, the Cherokees engaged in the slave labor economy as well.

President Andrew Jackson came to the presidency in 1828 at time when there was significant national debate over the future of American Indian affairs. Jackson was an ardent states' rights, anti-Indian force who promised to "remove" tribal nations to the lands west of the Mississippi River. In 1830, with Jackson's support, Congress enacted the Indian Removal Act, which authorized the President to enter into treaties that provided for the removal of tribal nations in the east to the west. 4 Stat. 111 (1830).

The State of Georgia, which likely ratified the United States Constitution in 1789 in the hopes that the federal government would force the Cherokees out of its boundaries, used all of its political and legal tools in opposition to the Cherokee Nation. Throughout the 1820s, Georgia enacted laws designed to undermine the Cherokees. Those laws included prohibitions on anyone entering Cherokee territory without the consent of the State, bans on Indian people testifying against white people in court, and assertions of state jurisdiction inside tribal territory. All of these laws flatly violated federal laws and the Cherokee treaties with the United States. In 1790, Congress enacted the first of a series of laws that would become known as the Trade and Intercourse Acts. 1 Stat. 137. See also Holmes v. St. Croix Casino, 26 Indian L.Rep. 6089, 6091 (St. Croix Tribal App.Ct.1999) (summarizing the Trade and Intercourses Acts from 1790 to 1834). Those laws prohibited land sales, commerce, and other interactions between tribal nations and American citizens without federal approval upon pain of criminal punishment, effectively preempting the field of Indian affairs. (Remnants of those statutes remain on the books, for example, the Non-Intercourse Act, which prohibits the sale of certain restricted lands by Indian tribes without federal consent, 25 U.S.C. § 177, and the Indian Country Crimes Act, 18 U.S.C. § 1152.) For Georgia to enact a law arrogating to itself the power to regulate interactions with the Cherokees conflicted with federal law. Georgia did much of this to force a political confrontation with the federal government at a time when the President of the United States was a strong ally.

Since Georgia had prohibited Indian people from bring lawsuits or testifying in state court against white persons, the Cherokee Nation chose to sue Georgia before the Supreme Court directly. Article III of the United States Constitution allows for states and foreign nations to initiate a suit under the

Court's "original jurisdiction." Const. Art. III, § 2. William Wirt, former Attorney General for the United States (and political opponent to President Jackson), petitioned directly to the Court, which then set a date for a hearing. The State of Georgia refused to accept the jurisdiction of the Supreme Court to hear a case involving the state. State laws prohibited state officials from appearing before the Court, even to the defend the state. And so, the Supreme Court heard arguments from only the Cherokee Nation while state officials angrily condemned the proceedings from afar.

That case, Cherokee Nation v. Georgia, 30 U.S. 1 (1831), decided little. The Supreme Court was deeply split three ways. Chief Justice John Marshall wrote the lead opinion, but only spoke on behalf of one other Justice. His lead opinion announced the judgment of the Court, which was that the Cherokee Nation had no standing to bring a suit under the Court's original jurisdiction. The Chief Justice pointed to the Commerce Clause of the Constitution, which provides that Congress may regulate commerce "with foreign nations, and among the several states, and with the Indian tribes." Const. Art. I, § 8, cl. 3. Marshall concluded that the Cherokee Nation was indeed a "nation" because the United States had ratified multiple treaties with the Cherokees; the President only negotiates treaties with sovereign nations. However, Marshall concluded that the Cherokee Nation, located within the borders of the State of Georgia, was not a "foreign" nation, but instead was a "domestic dependent nation." *Cherokee Nation*, 30 U.S. at 15 (Marshall, C.J.). Marshall further concluded that the Cherokee Nation was not a state like Georgia, since the Cherokees had not been invited to the Constitutional Convention nor asked to ratify the Constitution. In short, since the Cherokee Nation was not a foreign nation nor a state, it could not invoke the Supreme Court's original jurisdiction.

Two other Justices wrote separately and agreed with Marshall's conclusion that the Cherokee Nation did not have standing. These Justices would have held that the Cherokee Nation was no nation at all, the treaties negotiated by the President and ratified by the Senate were mere ruses to persuade the Cherokees to give up their lands. Justice Johnson, an appointee of President Jackson, labeled the Cherokee Nation and other tribal nations mere "petty kraal[s] of Indians." Id. at 25 (Johnson, J.). The remaining participating Justices dissented, agreeing with the lead opinion that tribal nations were sovereign nations, but insisting the Court go further and hold that the Cherokee Nation had standing. Ultimately, though, the Court voted 4–2 to dismiss the Cherokee Nation's original jurisdiction action, leaving unsettled the tribal-state sovereignty dispute.

Meanwhile, another flashpoint involved the State of Georgia's prosecution of George Tassel (also known as Corn Tassels). Georgia arrested Tassel, who was ostensibly a Cherokee Nation citizen, for murder in Cherokee Indian country. Any crime committed within the territory of the Cherokee Nation should have been investigated by the Light Horse and prosecuted in Cherokee courts. Georgia's intervention in Cherokee territory was a kind of declaration of war. Quickly, even with Wirt's efforts, the Georgia judiciary rejected Tassel's objections to its jurisdiction. Wirt petitioned the United States Supreme Court for relief. The Court agreed to review the case, setting up a showdown to determine whether Georgia's laws intending to undermine the sovereignty of the Cherokee Nation were valid. The Court never heard the case. Georgia convicted Tassel and executed him before his case could be argued.

Before George Tassel's execution, the Cherokee Nation hoped the United States Supreme Court would settle the matter of its sovereignty dispute with the State of Georgia by using Tassel's case as vehicle to render a decision. Tassel's execution changed the Cherokee Nation's strategy.

The next year, in Worcester v. Georgia, 31 U.S. 515 (1832), the United States Supreme Court finally decided the dispute in favor of the Cherokee Nation, even though the tribe was not even a party to the case. Once again, Georgia arrested a person inside of Cherokee territory, this time a non-Indian Christian missionary who was serving as the federal postmaster in New Echota. Samuel Worcester was an activist who published (with 11 others) an attack on Georgia's law prohibiting persons from entering Cherokee Indian country without a state license. Georgia arrested Worcester and his allies, convicted them of violating the state law they were protesting, and sentenced them to four years of hard labor. This time, Georgia could not moot the case by executing the convicted. Once again, William Wirt, now representing Worcester, sought review in the United States Supreme Court. Once again, Georgia refused to appear.

Chief Justice Marshall, writing for a clear 6–1 majority, held that Georgia's law had "no force" in Indian country. *Worcester*, 31 U.S. at 561. The Supremacy Clause of the Constitution provides that state laws that are in conflict with federal laws, including treaties, are preempted and therefore unenforceable. Const. Art. IV, para. 2. The majority opinion cemented the earlier holding from the *Cherokee Nation* decision that Indian tribes who are signatories to Senate-ratified treaties are nations. The Chief Justice never used the phrase "domestic dependent nation" in this opinion, instead referring to tribal nations as "distinct political communities." *Worcester*, 31 U.S. at 557. The Court also noted that those Indian treaties are treaties as understood under the Supremacy Clause and therefore are laws sufficient to preempt conflicting state laws.

Most importantly, the Court incorporated into federal common law the notion from international customary law that described the relationship between the United States and tribal nations as a "duty of protection" accepted by the more powerful nation. The Court wrote that the various Cherokee treaties had established a duty of protection upon the United States: "This treaty, thus explicitly recognizing the national character of the Cherokees and their right of self-government, thus guarantying their lands, assuming the duty of protection, and of course pledging the faith of the United States for that protection, has been frequently renewed, and is now in full force." Id. at 556. Critical to the duty of protection was the recognition by the federal government that tribal nations retain their internal sovereignty and whose sovereignty remains extant even within the borders of the United States:

> [T]he settled doctrine of the law of nations is that a weaker power does not surrender its independence—its right to self-government—by associating with a stronger and taking its protection. A weak State, in order to provide for its safety, may place itself under the protection of one more powerful without stripping itself of the right of government and ceasing to be a State.

Id. at 560–61. As a domestic sovereign under the protection of the federal government, therefore, the Cherokee Nation possessed the right to govern itself within its own borders free from the interference of the State of Georgia. See generally Colville Tribal Enterprise Corp. v. Orr, 1998 WL 35315175, at *2 (Colville Tribal Ct.App.1998) ("The United States Supreme Court under its first Chief Justice, John Marshall, argued that while in fact Indian tribes within United States borders could no longer be classed as truly independent foreign nations, they had proved capable in law and fact of self-government within the borders guaranteed them by treaty * * *."). Even if that were not the case, the state laws conflicted with the federal Trade and Intercourse Acts.

In sum, the Cherokee Trilogy of cases stands for numerous important propositions that remain unchallenged to this day. First, federally acknowledged tribal nations within the United States retain considerable inherent sovereignty to govern their own lands, their own citizens, and the activities within their territories. Second, the United States owes a duty of protection to those same tribal nations. Third, absent some authorization from Congress, states do not possess the power to regulate persons or activities within tribal territories.

D. TREATIES

On November 23, 2004, dozens of American Indian tribal nations and Canadian First Nations entered into the Tribal and First Nations Water Accord, the first formal treaty between tribal nations of the 21st Century. The Accord signifies a commitment to collaborate on the preservation and restoration of the Great Lakes ecosystem, focusing on reducing pollution, managing aquatic invasive species, protecting habitats, and preventing future water contamination. The accord also establishes a commitment to a government-to-government relationship, ensuring that the rights and sovereignty of Tribal and First Nations governments are respected and that they participate fully in water protection efforts. The State of Michigan and the federal Environmental Protection Agency have reached agreements furthering the purpose of the Accord.

Intertribal treaties of this sort predate the arrival of the European colonizing nations by centuries. Perhaps the most well known early intertribal treaty is the one that formed the Haudenosaunee Confederacy sometime around the 1500s, or perhaps earlier. Other famed intertribal confederacies include the Three Fires Confederacy of Great Lakes Anishinaabe, the Miami and Illinois Confederacies of the Ohio River Valley and the western Great Lakes, and the Powhatan Confederacy of what is now Virginia. Many tribal nations we know today once belonged to these intertribal confederacies. The Muscogee (Creek) Nation, the Cherokee Nation, the Hopi Tribe, and other tribal nations began as confederacies that later coalesced (not always willingly) into the modern tribal governments we see today.

As sovereign entities, the tribal nations of the United States and Canada have legal standing to enter into formal treaties with other sovereign entities. Tribal nations had long-standing relationships (and conflicts) with the individuals, entities, and governments that would eventually form the United States. These relationships often became memorialized into written treaty terms ratified by both tribal nations and the United States Senate. These Indian treaties are the supreme law of the land, according to the Supremacy Clause of the United States Constitution. Const. Art. VI.

Under tribal understandings, these written instruments were far more important, often creating kinship and other unique relationships, to

Indigenous people than they were for the American colonizers. Tribal nations usually understood the establishment of a government-to-government relationship between tribal nations and the United States (like other colonizing nations before it) as the creation or enhancement of a kinship relationship between the nations. Often, in order for American citizens to trade with tribal nations, they would have to be invited into the commercial markets of tribal nations. Since trade routes and commercial markets were owned and controlled by prominent tribal families, marriages between prominent young people often followed Indian treaty ratification. Consider, for example, the marriage of Henry Schoolcraft and Bamewawagezhikaquay (Jane Johnston), the daughter of a prominent *Anishinaabekwe* (Anishinaabe woman), Ozhaguscodaywayquay, who controlled important hunting grounds and trade routes in what is now the upper peninsula of Michigan. Ozhaguscodaywayquay herself had married John Johnston, a white man who had used the marriage as permission to enter the Ojibwe commercial markets. Henry Schoolcraft used his kinship relations with this prominent family in his rise to be the Michigan Indian Agent and lead American treaty negotiator of the 1836 Treaty of Washington, 7 Stat. 491, which led to the cession of about one-third of the lands that constitute what is now the State of Michigan.

The saga of Henry Schoolcraft is also instructive of how American colonizers viewed Indian treaties, not as the creation of true kinship, but as purely transactional documents that could and would be exploited, and usually outright violated, in the quest for more lands, resources, and power. In the lead-up to the 1836 treaty negotiation, Schoolcraft persuaded the lower peninsula Odawa tribal nations to travel to Washington to negotiate a small land sale, but he surreptitiously brought along lesser tribal leaders and young persons from the upper peninsula Ojibwe territories as well. Why did he do this? He had been instructed by his superiors, President Andrew Jackson and War Secretary Lewis Cass, to negotiate the cession of the lower peninsula lands from the Odawa nations. He knew the Odawa nations had no interest in doing this and would likely go to war instead of sign that treaty, a war he also knew would be extremely costly to the United States in terms of soldiers and finances. He also knew his federal government career would be over. As predicted, the lead Odawa speaker, or *ogema*, Aishquagonabe, opened the negotiation with a guarantee that the Odawa nations would not sign a major land cession treaty. The Odawa nations' choice of Aishquagonabe, a leading Anishinaabe warrior, or *ogitchidaa*, to open the negotiations was message enough; after all, he wore scalps he had collected from American soldiers in the War of 1812. But Schoolcraft noted to the Odawa negotiators that he expected them to sign a major land cession. And if they did not, he would ask the upper peninsula Ojibwe participants to do so. From the point of view of the United States Senate, Schoolcraft implied, Indians were Indians. The Senate would ratify a land cession regardless. From his familial relationships, Schoolcraft knew how to exploit and manipulate the Anishinaabe *ogemaag*.

And so, he did. Schoolcraft got his treaty and saved his career.

Treaty negotiations like the one leading to the 1836 Treaty of Washington were unique, yet typical. The United States usually came to negotiating table with an eye toward acquiring lands and resources from tribal nations. Indigenous leaders came to the negotiating table with a goal of preserving their tribal nations, lands, cultures, religions, and their children's futures. Most Indian treaties executed between tribal nations and the United States were sparse, minimalist agreements. Most of them involved lands and resources exchanged for undefined promises of protection.

It was the United States that introduced the legal concept of protection into treaties with tribal nations. Under customary international law of the 18th and 19th centuries, smaller sovereign nations could agree to come under the protection of larger, more powerful nations. Tribal treaty negotiators might or might not have understood the colonizer's legal theory of the duty of protection, but they understood a related and parallel theory undergirding Indian treaties—kinship, both literal and figurative.

E. FEDERAL ASSIMILATION POLICIES

Tribal nations brought the understanding that a treaty was a sacred arrangement between nations. Tribal leaders understood political entities as familial relationships. For most, if not all, tribal nations, to enter into a formal treaty was a sacred act requiring special ceremonies. An executed treaty therefore created a familial relationship between nations. What the Americans would have understood as a duty of protection, the tribal nations usually understood as family ties.

Consider the Anishinaabe sacred story, or *aadizookaan*, of Maudjee-kawiss, who served as guardian of the outer boundaries of *Anishinaabewaki*, the lands of the Anishinaabeg. Maudjee-kawiss traveled to the lands of the Bear Nation. From a distance, they observed the leader of the Bear Nation speaking to the people, pointing to images on a sash. The sash held the histories and stories of the Bear Nation, serving as a constant reminder to the leaders of their obligations and beliefs. Maudjee-kawiss went to the Bear Nation and stole the sash, killing a leading *ogitchidaa* (warrior) of the Bear Nation in the process. Eventually, the people of the Bear Nation caught Maudjee-kawiss. Some of them wanted vengeance, but the majority called for healing. Instead of punishing Maudjee-kawiss, even though he had wronged the family of the deceased *ogitchidaa*, that family adopted Maudjee-kawiss. They then invited Maudjee-kawiss to be their new *ogitchidaa* and a citizen. In the end, Maudjee-kawiss accepted the proposal, acknowledging their obligations to both the Anishinaabeg and the Bear Nation.

With this philosophy, it is understandable that tribal nations often deferred to their American relatives for a time after the establishment of a sovereign-to-sovereign relationship. This would cost them dearly. For example, in accordance with treaty terms in which the Americans guaranteed educational opportunities to tribal nations, tribal leaders would entrust their children to the federal government's Indian education initiatives. But the United States quickly abused that trust. Throughout Indian country, tribal leaders and families soon learned that federal education initiatives either involved military boot camp-style remedial education or oppressive religious instruction. Federal Indian education quickly became mandatory, explicitly designed to destroy Indigenous cultures, language, and government. Loosely beginning in the mid to late 19th century, the United States forced generations of Indigenous children into boarding schools, either secular military academies or religious schools. Most of these boarding schools remained in operation into the Depression era. A few continued to operate until the 1980s. The devastating impact of these boarding schools on tribal nations reverberates today. Most Indigenous people do not know their language or culture. Many moved away from their homelands, unable to return. Poverty reigns. Generations of Indian people never learned their traditional child rearing practices, leading directly to state intervention into their homes in the mid-20th century and beyond. By the 1970s, the states and their religious allies had removed 25–35 percent of all Native children in the United States, placing the vast majority of them in non-Indian homes. See 25 U.S.C. §§ 1901(4)–(5).

1. THE FEDERALIZATION OF INDIAN COUNTRY CRIMINAL JURISDICTION

Tribal nations depended heavily on kinship and community ties to prevent criminal violence. Virtually every Indigenous community has an analog to the Anishinaabe principles of *mino-bimaadiziwin* and *inaawendewin* that demand individuals understand their obligations to each other and to the world. The Lakota nations certainly do, as the story of Crow Dog and Spotted Tail (below) shows. See also Miller v. Crow Creek Sioux Tribe, 12 Indian L.Rep. 6008, 6010 (Northern Plains Intertribal Ct.App. 1984) ("Customarily among the Sioux, behavior—law and order in today's language—of tribal members was governed by relationship and kinship. Unfortunately, the colonizers' arrival and interventions undermined tribal cultures and imposed their own.") (quoting Ella Deloria, Speaking of Indians 17 (1944) (Dakota Press 1979)). Unfortunately, the colonizers' arrival and interventions undermined tribal cultures and imposed their own.

In the 1880s, federal Indian policy turned dramatically toward oppressive federal control of Indian reservation life. The first major turning point came as a result of a politically charged murder in the Dakota Territory. One prominent Lakota leader, Crow Dog, killed a political rival, Spotted Tail. After the murder, representatives of the two families met for several days to discuss punishment and reparations. They finally concluded that Crow Dog's family would pay $600, eight horses, and a blanket to the victim's family

The United States Attorney was not satisfied with this outcome and brought an indictment against Crow Dog. The government secured a conviction and death sentence. The Supreme Court, however, vacated the conviction for lack of federal court jurisdiction. Ex parte Crow Dog, 109 U.S. 556 (1883). The Court made two key holdings. First, the Court held that it would unfair to Indian people to be held to the standards of their "superiors of a different race," explicitly asserting that Indian people were in a "state of pupilage" requiring federal "guardianship." Id. at 568–71. Second, the Court invoked the duty of protection. Since protection does not mean the termination of tribal self-government, then for the United States to interfere with the criminal prosecution of an Indian for the killing of another Indian would be a "departure" from self-government requiring "a clear expression of the intention of Congress" to prosecute such crimes. Id. at 572. The Court had found no such thing.

At the urging of the Executive branch, Congress quickly went to work to provide that clear expression. In 1885, Congress enacted the Major Crimes Act, authorizing federal criminal jurisdiction over felonies committed by or against Indians. 18 U.S.C. § 1153. Almost immediately, the government prosecuted Pekwutl (or Pekwututl or Pactah Billy), also known as Kagama, for the murder of Iyouse, or Jefferson Dowd. They quarreled over an allotment selection illegally made by Kagama to the detriment of Iyouse on lands just outside the boundaries of the Hoopa Valley Reservation in Northern California. Once again, as in the *Crow Dog* case, the colonizer's interventions into the internal affairs of tribal nations led to violent conflict.

The government appealed and the prosecution of Kagama reached the Supreme Court, which held that Congress possessed the power to enact a federal criminal jurisdiction statute governing Indians inside of Indian country. United States v. Kagama, 118 U.S. 375 (1886). The Court did the unexpected, at least from the federal government's perspective. The Court rejected all of the federal government's arguments, but still adopted a theory that granted the United States vast powers in Indian affairs. The government pointed first to the Commerce Clause of the Constitution, which delegates powers to Congress to regulate commerce with Indian tribes. Const. Art. I, § 8, cl. 3. The Court held that the Commerce Clause could not justify a criminal code like the Major Crimes Act. The government then pointed to the Territory and Property Clause, which grants Congress the power to regulate activities on the territory and property of the United States. Const. Art. IV, § 3, cl. 2. The Court pointed out that California was a state, not a territory. Additionally, though the Court did not explicate on this point, the land upon which the murder occurred was located just off the Hoopa Valley Reservation, perhaps not federal property (unless it was a trust allotment). Finally, the Court rejected the government's claims that the Treaty Power authorized Congress to enact the Major Crimes Act. Had the case involved a reservation created by treaty, or a tribe acknowledged by treaty, then perhaps the Court would have gone the other way on that point. But the Hoopa reservation was created by Executive Order authorized by an Act of Congress, not by treaty. In fact, the Executive branch had executed 19 treaties with California tribes, but the Senate had refused to ratify them.

Instead, the Court used an alternate theory—the duty of protection itself—to acknowledge enormous, plenary power over Indian affairs vested in Congress. See Hunt v. Hunt, 16 Indian L.Rep. 6039, 6040 (Fort McDermitt Paiute-Shoshone Tribal Ct.1988) ("The power of the federal government over Indians, tribes and Indian affairs (known as 'plenary power') is vast and has rarely been successfully challenged."). Every tribal nation acknowledged by the federal government located within the boundaries of the United States or its territories was and is under the federal duty of protection. The Court asserted that since Indian people were the "deadliest enemies" of the states and their citizens, that they were weak and dependent on the United States for their food, shelter, and their very lives. *Kagama*, 118 U.S. at 383–85. The Court concluded, based on these (demonstrably false) factual observations, that Indian people were "the wards of the nation." A charitable way of putting this holding was that Congressional power did not come from the text of the Constitution, but instead from the duty of protection. Restatement of the Law of American Indians § 7(e).

Kagama was retried, but prevailed. He showed that the crime was committed off the reservation, outside the jurisdiction of the federal government. He supposedly walked home from San Francisco after his acquittal, more than 300 miles.

2. FORCED ALLOTMENT OF INDIAN RESERVATIONS

Tribal nations also quickly learned to not trust the government on matters of Indian lands. By the 1880s, the United States had adopted an aggressive and experimental policy of privatizing Indian reservations by "allotting" them to individual Indian heads of households. The Department of the Interior would then sell off any "surplus" lands on the federal public lands market. Tribal leaders, on occasion, would consent to the allotment of Indian lands, persuaded by their federal government advisors that private property ownership was a solution to poverty and other ills caused by colonization. Tribal leaders tragically learned that "allotment" was a complicated feint designed to break up the Indian reservation land mass, as described by Indian affairs leaders, including President Theodore Roosevelt, and allow even more access to tribal lands and resources for non-Indians. Allotment usually destroyed the integrity of Indian reservations and the tribal governments that served them. Many Indian families benefitted from selecting an allotment, their descendants possibly still owning the family's original parcel, but many, many more did not.

Consider the case of the Kiowa and Comanche Nations that executed the 1867 Treaty of Medicine Lodge with the United States. 15 Stat. 581 (1867). The treaty "set apart" the reservation "for the absolute and undisturbed use and occupation" of the tribal nations. The treaty also stated that there could be no additional land cessions by the tribes unless three-fourths of adult males consented. Two decades later, Congress adopted the allotment program as the preferred national Indian affairs policy. In 1892, the government sent a commission to the tribes to seek consent for an allotment plan. Some tribal member men agreed, some did not. The tribal leadership and the federal allotment commission disagreed on whether there was the requisite consent. The government proceeded with a legislative proposal to Congress anyway. In 1900, Congress ratified the allotment plan over tribal leaders' objections.

Lone Wolf the Younger sued the Secretary of the Interior. The case reached the Supreme Court in 1903. The government conceded that the commission may have used "fraudulent misrepresentation" to secure consent tribal member men." Lone Wolf v. Hitchcock, 187 U.S. 556, 561 (1903). The federal government argued that whether consent was valid was irrelevant because Congress had determined that Indian people were "absolutely incapable of protecting [themselves]." Appellees Brief at 16, Lone Wolf v. Hitchcock, 187 U.S. 553 (1903) (No. 275). The Court agreed, holding that because Indian people were under the "guardianship" of Congress, the federal government had virtually absolute authority over tribal lands and resources. *Lone Wolf*, 187 U.S. at 555.

Allotment was a source of terrible disruption to Indigenous Peoples. The colonizer's emphasis on transforming Indian people into farmers undermined their diverse and flexible lifeways developed to ensure sustainable livelihoods. Indigenous lifeways had already been undercut by the creation of the reservation system, which had dramatically cut back on the land base of Indigenous homelands. Often pressed into lands unlikely to be useful for mass agriculture, Indian people struggled to adapt to the siloed activities of farming. Most allotted lands moved into non-Indian ownership within a few decades. The land loss destabilized already weakened tribal governments. The focus on farming severely impaired Indigenous lifeways.

Allotment also terribly impacted Indigenous gender relationships. In many Indigenous governance and property rights regimes, women possessed significant rights and duties. Women often enjoyed political rights to men and superior property rights. The colonizer's preference for farming and confinement on a small parcel of land disproportionately affected women's property interests by forcing conformity into the male-centric society of the colonizer.

3. BUREAUCRATIC OPPRESSION, PRE- AND POST-REORGANIZATION

The Department of the Interior's Office of Indian Affairs (originally located within the Department of

War in 1824 and later renamed the Bureau of Indian Affairs in 1947) dominated reservation governance throughout most of Indian country well into the mid to late 20th century. From the treaty era until the enactment of the Indian Reorganization Act in 1934, 25 U.S.C. § 5101 et seq., traditional tribal government structures remained in place. For the most part, these were structures that elevated tribal leaders who negotiated and signed Indian treaties with the United States. But when the colonizer stripped many Native families of their children, eradicated communal land ownership, and undermined tribal culture and religion, traditional leadership in most reservation communities became a sham.

The Office of Indian Affairs frequently dominated Indian reservation governance. Federal officials and Indian agents had access to federal funds they could use to influence, persuade, or coerce tribal nations to do their bidding. Most federal actions were local actions, often taken without Congressional authorization or even Secretarial-level approval. For example, in the 1880s, while Congress was dramatically asserting legislative power in Indian country, the Indian Office established Courts of Indian Offenses, Indian police, and Law and Order Codes on numerous reservations. In re Saunooke, 2008 N.C. Cherokee Ct. LEXIS 1, at *10 (Eastern Band of Cherokee Tribal Ct.2008) ("The CFR Courts are the offspring of the Courts of Indian Offenses, first provided for in the Indian Department Appropriations Act of 1888, 25 Stat. 217, 233."). Federal officials installed Indian people they could control into judicial and police positions. They forced tribal governments to adopt Law and Order Codes designed to impose American-style retributive criminal justice into reservation life. Many of these codes criminalized or otherwise undercut the exercise of tribal religions. Note that the massacre of Wounded Knee, likely fueled by federal bureaucratic and military fear of the power of Indigenous religious activities, occurred in 1890. The Indian Office did all of this without Congressional authorization, though Congress did legislatively acquiesce to the establishment of these colonizing justice systems by appropriating funds for their continuation. In many tribal communities, Indian people adapted to these new justice systems and were able to undermine the intent of the colonizer's bureaucrats to eradicate Indigenous cultures.

F. INDIAN REORGANIZATION ACT

In 1934, Congress passed the Indian Reorganization Act. 25 U.S.C. § 5101, et seq. The Act encouraged tribal nations to "reorganize" into constitutional, representative democracies, giving tribes the opportunity to opt-in through an election conducted by the Secretary of the Interior, usually called Secretarial elections. 25 U.S.C. § 5123. An early draft of the law developed by Felix S. Cohen of the Department of the Interior would have allowed tribal nations to also assume control of reservation governance using Congressional appropriations, but Congress struck that provision from the bill after lobbying from the Office of Indian Affairs. Congress retained a provision extending Indian preference in employment to Indian people within the Indian Affairs Office, however. 25 U.S.C. § 5117. About two-thirds of then-federally acknowledged tribal nations voted to adopt a written constitution under the Act.

The IRA is the key federal statute governing the vast majority of tribal nations in the United States, though the impact on traditional and customary Indigenous governance has been stark. See Housing Authority of Sac and Fox Nation v. Walker, 1 Am. Tribal Law 534, 537 (Sac and Fox Nation S.Ct.1998) ("In the Indian Reorganization (Wheeler-Howard) Act of 1934 (IRA), Congress reversed a long-standing policy of weakening and dissolving the governments of the Indian tribes in this country, and authorized the reestablishment of some form of tribal self-government."). Section 16 allowed Indian voters to opt in or opt out of establishing a written tribal constitution, a controversial process for many tribal nations. Federal control over the new tribal governments was a given. The Hopi Tribe, for example, was an entity created by the IRA under the influence of the federal government out of 12 self-governing villages speaking three separate languages. Few "Hopi" citizens voted in the Secretarial election, a political choice that in the villages' cultures was effectively a "no" vote, but the United States declared the election valid and helped to establish a national Hopi government. The Hopi Appellate Court later detailed how the Hopi government came into being:

> Prior to the formation of the Hopi Tribal Council, the Hopi and Tewa Villages were

autonomous city-states that did not answer to any central authority or federated body. Before and after the passage of the United States federal government's Indian Reorganization Act of 1934, federal agents lobbied hard for the villages to adopt either distinct village constitutions or a central "tribal" constitution. The concept of a central, representative law-making body was new and unprecedented. After significant consultation with village leaders, the federal agent realized that it would not be politically possible to get most villages to adopt IRA-style constitutions.

In the end they had to significantly alter even the central tribal constitution from the IRA tribal constitution boilerplate before the villages would support it. Numerous concessions were made in the allocation of powers between the Tribe and the villages and between traditional leaders and their village populations, including 1) recognizing the authority of the Kikmongwis to certify representatives to Council, Hopi Const., Art. IV, § 4; 2) the preservation of the leadership powers of the Kikmongwi absent the proper adoption of village constitutions that might allocate some or all of his powers to the members of the village, Hopi Const., Art. III, §§ 3 & 4; and 3) the explicit reservation of dispute resolution power to the villages over certain subject matter areas, Hopi Const., Art. III, § 2. Absent from these explicit recognitions or reservations of village and/or Kikmongwi

> powers is the power to remove certified representatives to the Tribal Council.

In re Village Authority to Remove Tribal Council Representatives, 2008 WL 8929354, at *2 (Hopi App.Ct.2008), superseded by 11 Am. Tribal Law 80, 83–84 (Hopi App.Ct.2010). However, of the 12 villages, only six have ever sent representatives to the national Hopi council. Even though the tribal constitution drafters took pains to render a passable constitution, many in the Hopi Tribe polity reject it.

G. TERMINATION

Congress ended all Indian affairs appropriations during World War II, halting implementation of the new tribal constitutions. By the end of the war, national politics had turned against tribal sovereignty in a dramatic fashion. From 1954 until the early 1970s, Congress enacted a series of laws that terminated the federal-tribal trust relationship for hundreds of tribal nations, liquidating the governmental and commercial assets of those tribes, and confiscating many of the homelands of terminated tribes, usually without the consent of the tribes at issue. Congress would later restore many of these tribes to federally acknowledged status, but termination was an unmitigated disaster. Most terminated tribes never really recovered their governmental and economic strengths.

The first tribe Congress terminated was the Menominee Tribe in 1954. As the government confiscated and liquidated the tribe's economic assets, the State of Wisconsin began to assert regulatory authority over tribal member hunting and fishing activities, culminating in the prosecution of a tribal member. The Wisconsin Supreme Court held that the Menominee Termination Act of 1954 also abrogated the tribe's treaty rights to hunt and fish. State v. Sanapaw, 124 N.W.2d 41 (Wis.1963). Theorizing that the abrogation of its treaty-guaranteed hunting and fishing rights was equivalent to a taking of a vested property interest under the Fifth Amendment to the Constitution, the tribe sued for money damages against the United States. The government prevailed in the Court of Claims, 388 F.2d 998 (Ct.Cl.1967), but when the tribe petitioned for Supreme Court review, the United States switched its position. Before the Court, the federal government argued that the Menominee Termination Act, which was silent as to hunting and fishing rights, had not terminated those rights. Therefore, the government claimed, there was no taking of a vested property interest. The Supreme Court agreed. See Menominee Tribe of Indians v. United States, 391 U.S. 404 (1968).

In 1973, Congress restored the federal-tribal relationship with the Menominee Tribe. Over the next few decades, Congress restored the federal-tribal relationship to most of the tribal nations, but not all. Some terminated tribes were simply extinguished or merged into other tribal entities. The last termination proposal, involving the Colville Confederated Tribes, was soundly defeated in a tribal election in the early 1970s.

Even non-terminated tribes suffered during this era. In the late 1940s and early 1950s, Congress allowed numerous states to assume criminal jurisdiction over Indian country in their territories. The most far-reaching of those statutes, colloquially referred to as Public Law 280, mandated that five states—California, Minnesota, Nebraska, Oregon, and Wisconsin (Alaska was added in 1959)—to assume primary jurisdiction in Indian country. 18 U.S.C. § 1162. (A civil jurisdiction analog was codified at 28 U.S.C. § 1360.) The extension of state jurisdiction into Indian country again destabilized tribal governance. For many decades, the federal government illegally denied tribal justice system funds to tribes located in Public Law 280 states, reasoning that state courts and law enforcement had primary control. Perhaps ironically, Public Law 280 was an unfunded mandate, so when the United States vacated the field in those states, it usually left a jurisdictional void if state and local governments did not have the resources or political will to take on Indian country law enforcement.

Perhaps worse, during the 1950–1953 tenure of Indian Affairs Commissioner Dillon S. Myer, the federal government initiated a series of programs designed to eradicate non-terminated tribal nations completely. Myer accused attorneys representing tribal nations of fomenting dissent within Indigenous communities, especially on the question of termination, which he believed was the proper national policy, and sought to control tribal attorney contracts. Myer came to the Bureau of Indian Affairs as the outgoing head of the War Relocation

Authority, an Orwellian governmental entity charged with managing the internment of Japanese-Americans into concentration camps during World War II. Myer oversaw direct interventions into tribal governance and the day-to-day lives of Indigenous Peoples in reservation communities. Felix S. Cohen, drawing from official governmental records, reported that BIA officials instituted curfews, restrictions on cultural and religious practices, and attempted to expand BIA law enforcement control over reservation Indians. Ironically consistent with his initiatives during Japanese internment, Myer initiated the Urban Relocation Program that would remove Indian people from their homelands and dump them into urban areas dominated demographically by non-Indians. Myer stopped funding public schools that served Indian children and closed about 60 hospitals serving Indian patients. See generally Felix S. Cohen, The Erosion of Indian Rights, 1950–1953: A Case Study in Bureaucracy, 62 Yale L.J. 348 (1953).

In 1968, several years after the Kennedy and Johnson Administrations declined to proceed with termination policies, Congress passed the Indian Civil Rights Act. 25 U.S.C. § 1301 et seq. Congress intended the Indian Bill of Rights, as it was called, or ICRA, to fill a gap supposedly left with the Supreme Court's decision in Talton v. Mayes, 163 U.S. 376 (1896), that held the United States Constitution does not apply to tribal government activities. Section 2 of the Act enumerated a series of individual rights that persons under tribal jurisdiction possess, loosely based on the Bill of Rights under the Constitution. 25 U.S.C. § 1302(a). In 1978, the Supreme Court held that tribal governments alone possessed the power to enforce the individual rights of persons under tribal jurisdiction. Santa Clara Pueblo v. Martinez, 436 U.S. 49 (1978). The lone exception to that holding was that Congress expressly authorized the federal courts to review habeas petitions brought by persons under tribal detention. 25 U.S.C. § 1303.

In general, the termination era, which ran from the end of World War II until the 1970s, when Congress turned toward a national policy favoring tribal self-determination, was disastrous for tribal nations and Indigenous Peoples in the United States. Ironically, since ICRA was designed to assert more federal control over tribal governance and to coerce tribal nations into conformity with federal and state prerogatives, ICRA would become a source of great tribal initiative and power in the decades to come.

H. TRIBAL SELF-DETERMINATION

In 1975, Congress enacted the Indian Self-Determination and Education Assistance Act, formally declaring that national policy favored tribal nations' self-government. 25 U.S.C. § 5301. The Act, also known as Public Law 638, required the Bureau of Indian Affairs (and later the Indian Health Service and the Department of Housing and Urban Development) to contract with tribal governments regarding the provision of services on the reservation. Other than in the case a few tribal nations, most notably the Navajo Nation, the Bureau handled all reservation governance matters funded by the United States. Under Public Law 638, tribal nations could select from a menu (of sorts) of tribal government services provided by federal agencies with Congressional appropriations, for example, job training, law enforcement, tribal courts, enrollment, family services, health care, and so on. Tribal governments could then make an offer to the federal agency to administer those items themselves. With narrow exceptions, the federal agency was obligated to accept the tribes' offers. Tribal governments became federal government contractors, providing federal services to their own people. This is often called "638 contracting". In 1994, Congress authorized tribal nations with a solid record of 638 contracting and with demonstrated governmental capacity to offer to administer all federally funded services. These tribes became known as self-governance tribes.

As a general matter, the self-determination policy has been an enormous, if qualified, success. The Navajo Nation Supreme Court noted that self-determination allows for the development of tribal law:

> Our laws, although indigenous and extra-Constitutional, are American domestic laws that will endure for future generations through the Federal policy of Indian self-determination. Our laws reflect our indigenous cultures and practices. They are vital to the survival of our culture, which is not only a Navajo heritage, but a heritage of the American people.

EXC, Inc. v. Kayenta District Court, 9 Am. Tribal Law 176, 190 (Navajo Nation S.Ct.2010). Tribal self-government is a core feature of tribal politics. E.g., *In re Navajo Nation Election Administration's Determination of Insufficiency Regarding Two Initiative Petitions*, 8 Am. Tribal Law 240, 244 (Navajo Nation S.Ct.2009) ("'Self-governance is premised on the principle that '*Diné bi nahat'á* is the foundation of the *Diné bi naat'á* (government).' * * * Self-governance thus is expressed not only in the right of Navajo individuals, but also in self-governance at the national (or tribal) level. This inherent right is retained by the People. This 'reserved' right cannot be denied or disparaged except by a vote of the People.") (citations and footnote omitted).

Beginning in the 1970s, Congress enacted dozens of laws designed to enhance the capacity and authority of tribal nations to self-govern. Important statutes include without limitation the American Indian Religious Freedom Act, 42 U.S.C. § 1996, the Indian Child Welfare Act, 25 U.S.C. § 1901 et seq., the Indian Gaming Regulatory Act, 25 U.S.C. § 2701 et seq., the Native American Housing Assistance and Self-Determination Act, 25 U.S.C. § 4101 et seq., and the Native American Graves Protection and Repatriation Act. 25 U.S.C. § 3001 et seq. Congress has also "fixed" or partially abrogated limitations on inherent tribal sovereignty that the Supreme Court has announced in criminal jurisdiction area. Notably, Congress (1) restored tribal inherent powers to prosecute nonmember Indians, 25 U.S.C. § 1301(2), abrogating Duro v. Reina, 495 U.S. 676 (1990); (2) required federal courts to recognize tribal court domestic violence convictions, 18 U.S.C. § 117(a);

United States v. Bryant, 579 U.S. 140 (2016); (3) enhanced tribal criminal sentencing powers, 25 U.S.C. § 1302(b), and (4) restored inherent tribal powers to prosecute non-Indians for certain crimes, 25 U.S.C. § 1304.

Even so, self-determination is a difficult and complicated process. Federal agencies and bureaucrats from the beginning of the era and even now can slow the process down considerably. For the first few decades of the era, federal bureaucrats were notorious for refusing to contract with tribes under Public Law 638 for arbitrary reasons and for imposing restrictions on contracting, both of which ran afoul of the intent of Congress. Tribal political actors also can undermine their own tribes' efforts, as attested to by the Navajo Nation Supreme Court:

> The Navajo Nation Council has persisted in applying state and federal doctrines verbatim over the bedrock principles of our civilization in arguing their positions in this case. Frankly, this Court is exhausted by our seemingly never-ending exercise in reminding the Council that we are a unique sovereign governance system within the diverse American governmental framework, based on our own unique civilization, and on our own terms.

Nelson v. Initiative Committee to Reduce Navajo National Council, 9 Am. Tribal Law 204, 209 (Navajo Nation S.Ct.2010).

I. ACKNOWLEDGEMENT OR RECOGNITION OF TRIBAL SOVEREIGNTY

Tribal nations do not need a foreign government to acknowledge their sovereignty in order to possess and employ governmental power, they need their own tribal citizens to do so. Throughout the history of the United States, dozens and sometimes hundreds of tribal nations existed as viable governing entities without the acknowledgement of the federal government. Indian tribes were nations before they entered into a formal government-to-government relationship with the United States. Indian tribes were nations after they did so. Indian tribes were nations even if the United States terminates the formal government-to-government relationship.

Federal recognition, or federal acknowledgment, is the formal acceptance of a duty of protection by the United States to a given tribal nation. Today, there are 575 federally recognized Indian tribes in the United States. There are several mechanisms by which a tribal nation can become formally acknowledged by the United States. 108 Stat. 4791. First, the United States can enter into a negotiation with a tribal nation concluding with a Senate-ratified treaty. Second, Congress can enact a statute acknowledging, reaffirming, restoring, or otherwise recognizing the sovereignty of a tribal nation. Restatement of the Law of American Indians § 2(a)(2). Third, the Department of the Interior can acknowledge or recognize a tribal nation's sovereignty through a process and standards codified in 25 C.F.R. Part 83. Fourth, although this is largely hypothetical, a tribal, state, or federal court can acknowledge an Indian tribe's sovereignty. See 25 U.S.C. § 5310, note. More likely, a court may acknowledge aspects of a non-recognized tribe's sovereignty or property rights under a federal common law test articulated in Montoya v. United States, 180 U.S. 261, 265 (1901). E.g., Gristede's Foods, Inc. v. Unkechuage Nation, 660 F.Supp.2d 442 (E.D.N.Y.2009) (recognizing the sovereign immunity of a tribe meeting the *Montoya* common law definition).

Tribal nations vary dramatically in their formation and composition. The Navajo Nation, for example, consists of hundreds of one-autonomous villages that organized, with significant pressure from the federal government, into a tribal nation that covers a land base about the size of Ireland. Other tribal nations consist of small family groups, such as the Augustine Band of Cahuilla Indians in southern California, owning a one-square mile land base. The federal governments sometimes coerced tribal nations that were once considered enemies onto a single parcel of reservation land, such as the tribes located in the Wind River Reservation, which is now the home of the Northern Arapaho Tribe and the Eastern Shoshone Tribe. Other tribal nations formed as bands out of much larger tribal communities, such as the 16 tribal nations (and additional eight First Nations in Canada) that formed from the Lakota, Nakota, and Dakota tribal groups spread throughout the northern Great Plains. On rare occasions, tribal nations subdivide into separate nations, such as the

Sault Ste. Marie Tribe of Chippewa Indians, which separated from the Bay Mills Indian Community, and the Lac Vieux Desert Band of Lake Superior Chippewa Indians, which separated from the Keweenaw Bay Indian Community.

Tribal nations must sometimes confront matters that arise when a political subdivision of the larger tribe seeks autonomy from the tribal nation. In Thlopthlocco Tribal Town v. Anderson, 2022 Muscogee Creek Nation Supreme LEXIS 1 (Muscogee (Creek) Nation S.Ct.2022), the court rejected the claims of the tribal town seeking significant autonomy from the tribal nation. The court noted that the Creek Nation originated as a confederation of tribal nations located in what is now northwest Mexico. The Nation relocated to what is now the southeastern United States before removal to the Indian Territory (now Oklahoma). There was no central or national government at that time, which each governing unit, called *Italwa* or *Talwa* (translating into English loosely as "town") and operating autonomously. The United States pressured the towns to adopt a centralized government in order for the federal government to deal more easily with the Creeks, succeeding in doing so only after the American Civil War. Under the Oklahoma Indian Welfare Act of 1936, the federal government recognized the Thlopthlocco Tribal Town as a "recognized band," a term of art specific to that statute, leading the town to adopt its own constitution. But that did not mean the town's source of governmental power was separate from the tribal nation. As the tribal court noted, under federal law, the town was sovereign, but under tribal law, the town was a political subdivision of the tribal nation.

The key issue in the *Thlopthlocco* case involved whether the town enjoyed sovereign immunity as a tribal town. The court held that it did, concluding, "The [town] is a federally recognized band of the Muscogee (Creek) Nation. The [town] is also something more under Muscogee tribal law. This finding does not diminish the [town's] rights, but expands them. The [town] is entitled to sovereign immunity in the Court's of the Muscogee (Creek) Nation." Id. at *22. The power of the Muscogee tribal judiciary to recognize the sovereignty of a tribal town is representative of the power of tribal nations to acknowledge tribal sovereignty.

More recently acknowledged tribal nations may find themselves in internal conflicts about the validity of governing bodies. In Raphael v. Grand Traverse Band of Ottawa and Chippewa Indians, 1996 Grand Traverse Band App. LEXIS 4 (Grand Traverse Band of Ottawa and Chippewa Indians Tribal Ct.1996), the Grand Traverse Band of Ottawa and Chippewa Indians tribal court rejected the legal validity of a land assignment issued by a nonprofit entity called Leelanau Indians, Inc. that had once stepped in the shoes of the tribal government during the tribe's effort to achieve federal recognition. The tribal government, the entity actually acknowledged by the federal government, had issued a conflicting land assignment, necessitating the invalidation of the assignment issued by the nonprofit group.

J. THE SPECIAL CASE OF THE FIVE TRIBES OF OKLAHOMA

Five tribal nations forcibly removed from the southeastern United States in the 1830s to what is now the State of Oklahoma shared a parallel history that differed in many salient respects from the rest of tribal nations. The United States largely allowed these tribes—the Cherokee Nation, the Chickasaw Nation, the Choctaw Nation, the Creek Nation (later the Muscogee (Creek) Nation and now the Muscogee Nation), and the Seminole Nation—significant self-governance throughout the 19th century, or at least self-government with far less interference than that of nearly every other tribal nation.

Prior to removal in the 1830s, the United States tended to grant the status of "civilized" to the five tribes, eventually leading to the moniker, "Five Civilized Tribes." As tribal nations located in the Deep South where slavery dominated the regional economies, many tribal citizens participated in the slave trade. Additionally, the Five Tribes frequently "adopted" significant numbers of non-Indians into their citizenry, a fairly unusual choice amongst the body of American tribal nations. These choices led to three critically important United States Supreme Court decisions that would dramatically impact tribal nations throughout the United States.

In first case, United States v. Rogers, 45 U.S. 567 (1846), involved an effort by a Cherokee Nation citizen who had been adopted into tribal membership but who was not Indigenous by ancestry to avoid federal prosecution for murder of another non-Indian man. The Supreme Court held that Cherokee citizenship did not immunize Rogers from federal criminal law because he was a still a "white man." The Court's analysis, authored by Chief Justice Roger Taney (who also authored the notorious and anti-canonical *Dred Scott* decision), assumed that the federal government possessed plenary authority over the internal political activities of tribal nations despite clear treaty language to the contrary. *Rogers* is still cited for the proposition under federal law that a person is not an "Indian" unless they have some degree of Indian ancestry, though *Rogers* says no such thing and did not involve an "Indian status" assessment. E.g., United States v. Zepeda, 792 F.3d 1103, 1118 (9th Cir.2015) (en banc) (Kozinski, J., concurring) (accusing the en banc majority of relying on *Rogers*, which is a "pre-civil war precedent laden with dubious racial undertones"). Some tribal courts have pointed to *Rogers* as well. E.g., Seymour v. Colville Confederated Tribes, 2001 WL 36243309, at *2 n.6 (Colville Confederated Tribes Ct.App.2001). Others have roundly questioned the so-called *Rogers* "test", suggesting that the federal judiciary (the Ninth Circuit in particular), is "making itself a pretzel over this common-law definition." Jackson v. Fort Peck Tribes, 18 Am. Tribal Law 87, 91 (Fort Peck Ct.App.2024).

In the second key case, Parks v. Ross, 52 U.S. 362 (1850), the Supreme Court rejected a claim for money damages against the principal chief of the Cherokee Nation, John Ross. Ross had been the named recipient of federal funds appropriated for the purpose of covering costs associated with removal.

The estate of a deceased Cherokee citizen, Samuel Parks, who opposed the Ross government (and may have paid for his life as a result), sued for damages. The Supreme Court rejected the suit, invoking what would now be called tribal sovereign immunity:

> * * * The Cherokees are in many respects a foreign and independent nation. They are governed by their own laws and officers, chosen by themselves. And though in a state of pupilage and under the guardianship of the United States, this government has delegated no power to the courts of this district to arrest the public representatives or agents of Indian nations who may be casually within their local jurisdiction and compel them to pay the debts of their nation, either to an individual of their own nation, or a citizen of the United States.

Id. at 374. *Parks* is the first United States Supreme Court decision acknowledging that tribal nations and their officials enjoy sovereign immunity in foreign jurisdictions (that is, state and federal courts). The measured separatism (to borrow a phrase from Charles F. Wilkinson) of tribal nations acknowledged in Worcester v. Georgia, 31 U.S. 515 (1832), remained potent then and now.

In the third major case, Talton v. Mayes, 163 U.S. 376 (1896), the Supreme Court rejected a habeas petition from a Cherokee citizen sentenced to death by the Cherokee Nation for capital murder. Bob Talton (who likely was an adopted non-Indian citizen) murdered another Cherokee citizen on reservation lands and was sentenced by the tribal court to die. He claimed in his habeas petition that he was entitled to a grand jury under the Fifth Amendment to the United States Constitution and that jury should consist of at least six persons, according to a federal statute applicable to federal court. The Court rejected the claim, noting that the Cherokee Nation's sovereignty predates the Fifth Amendment and nothing Congress had enacted to that point limited tribal powers:

> * * * [A]s the powers of local self-government enjoyed by the Cherokee Nation existed prior to the Constitution, they are not operated upon by the Fifth Amendment, which, as we have said, had for its sole object to control the powers conferred by the Constitution on the national government. The fact that the Indian tribes are subject to the dominant authority of Congress, and that their powers of local self-government are also operated upon and restrained by the general provisions of the Constitution of the United States, completely answers the argument of inconvenience which was pressed in the discussion at bar.

Id. at 384.

The self-governance of the five tribes temporarily ended in a series of statutes enacted in the 1890s and 1900s that dramatically undermined tribal self-government. For a time, the federal government directly took control of the five tribes' governments. Notably, the President of the United States possessed the power to select the principal chiefs of the tribes, a power exercised well into the 1970s.

The Oklahoma tribes were initially excluded from the Indian Reorganization Act of 1934, but Congress passed the Oklahoma Indian Welfare Act of 1936 that allowed the government to treat Oklahoma tribes largely the same way. 25 U.S.C. § 5201 et seq. Even so, Oklahoma tribes remained firmly under the thumb of the federal government until the 1970s. For example, the Department of the Interior continued to acknowledge only the Presidentially appointed principal chief over the tribally elected national council until at least 1976. Harjo v. Kleppe, 420 F.Supp. 1110 (D.D.C.1976). Additionally, the United States presumed, along with the State of Oklahoma, that the five tribes' reservations had been terminated upon the extension of statehood to Oklahoma in 1907. The Supreme Court held in 2020 that that presumption was incorrect. McGirt v. Oklahoma, 591 U.S. 894 (2020).

K. THE SPECIAL CASE OF ALASKA NATIVES

The history of the Alaska Native tribal nations proceeded along a much different path than that of the tribal nations in the lower 48 states. In 1867, the United States purchased the territory of Alaska from Russia. Though the treaty that memorialized the purchase noted that Indigenous peoples resided on the lands, the United States did little for over 100 years to deal with Alaska Native tribal nations.

Without ever dealing seriously with the land ownership rights of the Alaska Native tribal nations and peoples, the United States colonized the

Territory of Alaska. The federal government acknowledged a limited number of tribal nations and created a limited number of reservations, but did little as American citizens in the territory viciously discriminated against Alaska Native people for decades. Perhaps the worst moment came in 1955 when the Supreme Court, at the behest of the Department of Justice, held that Alaska Native tribal nations and individuals had no compensable property interest in any of the lands or resources of the territory. Tee-Hit-Indians v. United States, 348 U.S. 272 (1955).

In 1971, Congress passed the Alaska Native Claims Settlement Act. 43 U.S.C. § 1601 et seq. The settlement act paid $963 million and reserved 44 million acres for Alaska Native uses. The Act created hundreds of regional and local Alaska Native Corporations to serve as recipients of the funds and lands. Alaska tribal nations received all but nothing, the Act ignoring them, with many policymakers assuming that the settlement act had terminated the tribes. Congress formally recognized the corporations' selections of land in 1980 with the passage of the Alaska National Interests Lands Consolidation Act. 43 U.S.C. § 1631 et seq. The State of Alaska and, for many years, the federal government refused to treat the 229 (save one, the Metlakatla tribe) Alaska tribal nations as federally acknowledged tribal governments.

ANCSA established what are now over 300 regional and village corporations. Congress granted ownership of the settlement funds and land transfers to these Alaska Native Corporations, or ANCs. They are for-profit entities charged with maximizing the assets made available to them. The vesting of these assets in the ANCs stripped the Alaska tribal nations of their assets and land bases. Further, in Alaska v. Native Village of Venetie, 522 U.S. 520 (1997), the United States Supreme Court held that the ANC land did not constitute Indian country, further eroding Alaska tribal governance powers and isolating tribal nations further. Shortly after the *Venetie* decision, however, the Alaska Supreme Court recognized continued and inherent tribal governance powers in Alaska, even on non-Indian land, sourced in tribal membership, which is based in consent. In John v. Baker, 982 P.2d 738 (Alaska 1999), the court acknowledged the sovereign immunity of Alaska tribal villages as a function of inherent tribal sovereignty. See also State v. Central Council of Tlingit and Haida Indian Tribes of Alaska, 371 P.3d 255 (Alaska 2016) (acknowledging tribal inherent authority to set child support obligations); Simmonds v. Parks, 329 P.3d 995 (Alaska 2014) (requiring litigants to exhaust tribal remedies).

In 1993, the Bureau of Indian Affairs published a list of tribal governments eligible to receive federal services that included the Alaska Native tribal governments. After a political furor, Congress ratified that list, effectively and permanently restoring the federal acknowledgment status of the Alaska Native tribal governments. Pub. L. 103–454, Nov. 2, 1994, 108 Stat. 4791. Alaska's tribal nations are playing catch-up in the era of self-determination, having been denied access to resources and technical assistance from the federal government for decades and continually having to fight the politics of state government.

CHAPTER 2
TRIBAL GOVERNMENTS

Tribal nations have governed themselves long before the arrival of European and American colonial governments. Indigenous governance philosophies tended to allow for the broad sharing of power. Unlike the governments of the colonizers, Indigenous feudal-style governments that established stark hierarchies rooted in race and gender differences were rare. Also, unlike the governments of the colonizers, the leaders of Indigenous tribal nations less often established a monopoly on violence. State violence was usually unnecessary to maintain law and order. The fear of a Hobbesian state of nature that dominated western philosophies (and still does), where life in the absence of an all-powerful government was "solitary, poor, nasty, brutish, and short" due to the belief that humans were (and are) inherently selfish, competitive, and violent, was usually unknown to Indigenous Peoples. Indigenous Peoples tended to presume that humans humbly knew their place in the world, that harmony was the state of nature in the absence of government, and the primary obligation of humans in the world was to act to preserve harmony through cooperation and respect, rather than to seek dominion over all places and things.

The arrival of the colonizing nations was apocalyptic for tribal nations. Europeans brought diseases that nearly eradicated the populations of tribal nations. Even before the arrival of formal colonizing institutions, tribal nations suffering from the dramatic loss of population were forced to modify their cultural and governance institutions, even their philosophies and religions. Explorers, traders, governmental officials, settlers, trading companies, and others brought their violent, colonizing mentality to the territories of tribal nations. They were often accompanied by religious missionaries that created additional social disruptions within tribal communities.

Even so, for centuries, formal interactions between tribal nations and European and American governments were peaceful, sovereign-to-sovereign negotiations. But in most instances, the relative bargaining power of tribal nations and the colonizers was, of course, wildly skewed in favor of the colonizing nations. The very structure of a treaty negotiation, with the colonizing nations' officials speaking on behalf of a unitary (or something close to unitary) sovereign, such as a king, emperor, pope, president, or chief executive officer, often required tribal nations to counter with representatives of a sovereign individual or institution of their own. The colonizing government usually would not recognize the power of tribal negotiators unless they were few and male. The colonizers were always represented by men, who negotiated and memorialized any agreement in the language of the colonizer and ruthlessly exploited the weakened state of tribal nations. These clashes of cultures alone had monumental impacts on the governance of tribal nations, usually by forcing tribal nations to consolidate leadership in a small, elite group of (usually) men. The consequences of these encounters are felt today

A. TRADITIONAL GOVERNMENTS

Unlike the stereotypes most American learn about Indian people, tribal nations and Indigenous Peoples firmly believed in government, law and order, and property rights. The powers to enforce those interests, however, tended to be spread out over diverse institutions, rather than consolidated with a small, powerful elite. Tight social connections between individuals, families, and tribal institutions served to ensure compliance with tribal laws and governmental decisions. For specific purposes and for limited times, tribal nations delegated significant government powers to individual leaders or small groups of leaders, for example, to lead the negotiation of a treaty or to manage an acute resource scarcity. For general purposes, such as establishing hunting or farming territories, tribal nations typically spread out those decisions among the greater population of the tribal community, investing power in groups such as villages, families, clans, or specialized councils. See generally Rave v. Reynolds, 23 Indian L.Rep. 6150, 6157 (Winnebago S.Ct.1996) ("The traditions of most Indian tribes in the United States, including the Ho-Chunk people, part of whom compose the Winnebago Tribe of Nebraska, encouraged participatory and consensual resolution of disputes, maximizing the opportunity for airing grievances (i.e., hearing), participation, and resolution in the interest of healing the participants and preventing friction within the tribal community."). Limitations on political participation, endemic in western style democracies, was unheard of in many Indigenous nations. E.g., Bennett v. Navajo Board of Election Supervisors, 18 Indian L.Rep. 6009, 6011 (Navajo Nation S.Ct.1990) ("In Navajo tradition, government and governing was a matter of consensus of the people, and Navajos had a participatory democracy. It was, in fact, one of the purest democracies in human history. Long before the United States of America extended the privilege and right to vote to those who did not own property and to women, all Navajos participated in public decisions.").

Now, traditional tribal governments are few and far between in the modern era. They tend to be small, insular communities that either successful staved off much of the impact of colonialism or they were distant enough from the domination of the colonizers to retain significant aspects of their traditional governments. Some Pueblos in the desert southwest, many Alaskan Native villages, a smattering of Great Lakes Haudenosaunee and Anishinaabe nations, and scattered tribal nations in other states still govern in their traditional ways. But these tribes are few and even they must alter their governing practices as they deal with the United States and state and local governments.

Traditional governments tended to spread power out over different institutions. Many tribal nations followed a clan system of social organization. E.g., Ben v. Burbank, 24 Indian L.Rep. 6001, 6002 (Navajo Nation S.Ct.1996) ("The Navajo law builds on relationships. It works because of them. [The] people's conduct is guided by family and clan relationships. Therefore, a clan is a legal 'institution.' ") (quoting Robert Yazzie).

Consider the Anishinaabe tribal nations. They organized under a clan system of usually seven clans, or *dodemaag* (the plural of *dodem*, the Anishinaabe word for clan). Each clan was named after an animal or a supernatural creature. Typical clans included the loon, crane, eagle, bear, deer, fish, muskrat, marten, badger, turtle, and thunderbird clans. Each clan had a kind of personality that gave root to its individual and specific obligations to the tribal nation. For example, the marten or badger clans were known for their martial abilities and tended to be responsible for the external security of the tribal nations. The bear clan was responsible for internal security, like modern day police, but also had a countervailing obligation to the broader health and welfare of the community. Winged clans tended to serve in more leadership positions, though that did not automatically translate to actual power. Members of a clan selected to represent the clan in bigger tribal political meetings, what we might call a tribal council now, served as equal to the other clans. Each clan representative was obligated to speak in accordance with the obligations and interests of their clan. In this way, power was diffuse. Virtually every political position would be heard and respected equally. Decisions would be made by consensus after considerable discussion.

With the advent of federal assimilation policies, heightened during the 1880s with the enactment of the Major Crimes Act in 1885, 18 U.S.C. § 1153, and the General Allotment Act in 1887, 24 Stat. 388 (1887), federal government officials asserted more power to govern reservations than ever before. Federal officials routinely undermined traditional tribal governments. In several notorious instances, such as that of the Five Tribes of Oklahoma, the Navajo Nation, the Hopi Tribe, and the Minnesota Chippewa Tribe, federal officials extended their power so far as to actually create tribal governments in the image that was suitable for federal administration. Many others suffered egregious neglect from federal officials.

B. IRA-STYLE GOVERNMENTS

In 1934, Congress enacted the Indian Reorganization Act or IRA. 25 U.S.C. § 5101 et seq. Section 16 of the IRA authorized (and the Department of the Interior encouraged or occasionally coerced) tribal nations to adopt a written constitution establishing an American-style government largely modeled on municipalities. 25 U.S.C. § 5123. In the wake of the Act, about two-thirds of tribal nations voted to adopt a written constitution. Despite the best intentions of reformers like Felix S. Cohen, local federal bureaucrats often took control of the tribal constitutional drafting process. Since the IRA required Secretarial approval of all initial tribal constitutions, federal officials had outsized control over the final form of the tribal constitutions. In the end, most IRA-era constitutions were very similar, leading many to describe them as "model IRA" or "boilerplate" constitutions. They radically differed from traditional tribal governments, effectively replacing traditional governments. See generally Thorstenson v. Cudmore, 18 Indian L.Rep. 6051, 6052–54 (Cheyenne River Sioux Tribal Ct.App.1991) (summarizing the issues created by IRA-era constitutions); Lane-Oriero v. Lummi Indian Business Council, 21 Indian L.Rep. 6143, 6145 (Lummi Tribal Ct.1994) ("When functions which were traditionally performed by the elders were splintered and reassigned to others, by the restructuring of the tribal government under the Indian Reorganization Act, there was a major alteration in the way in which the tribe functioned. It became difficult to determine which portions of traditional government, public dispute resolution, and internal standards of conduct survived the change.").

IRA-era constitutions established a tribal council consisting of officials elected in elections conducted by the Secretary of the Interior, so-called Secretarial elections. The tribal councils served as the executive, legislative, and frequently the judicial branch of government, all in one. Tribal governments, whatever their structure, had little real power. Tribal governments, even to this day, typically have no substantial tax base to generate revenue to fund governmental programs. See Michigan v. Bay Mills Indian Community, 572 U.S. 782, 813 (2014) (Sotomayor, J., concurring); In re Atkinson Trading Co., Inc., 1 Am. Tribal Law 451, 462 (Navajo Nation S.Ct.1997) ("Unlike the states, the Navajo Nation just recently began building its tax base."). This left the new tribal councils completely dependent on federal funding. Since federal Indian affairs funding during the 1930s was not sufficient, stopping completely during World War II, tribal councils had no real capacity to govern. Federal bureaucrats that used their influence to undermine traditional tribal governments before 1934 simply kept on doing so long after 1934.

Ironically, the IRA itself undercut the Congressional policy favoring tribal self-government that the statute was intended to promote. Since the first tribal constitution was invalid absent Secretarial approval, 25 U.S.C. § 5123(d), federal bureaucrats had control over the final constitutional text. Nearly all IRA-era constitutions, and almost all tribal constitutions that followed over the next several decades, included provisions that required Secretarial approval for important tribal government actions. Many tribal constitutions provided that if the tribal council adopted an ordinance that would apply to non-Indians, it was invalid and unenforceable unless it was approved by the Interior Department. E.g., Merrion v. Jicarilla Apache Tribe, 455 U.S. 130 (1983) (interpreting a tribal constitutional provision authorizing taxation of non-Indians so long as the Secretary of the Interior approved the tax). Some tribal constitutions dictated an actual process that that the tribe must follow when seeking Secretarial approval. E.g., Hannahville Indian Community Constitution, art. V, § 5 (1936).

In 1953, former federal Indian affairs lawyer Felix S. Cohen documented the intensity of federal intervention into the lives of tribal citizens, simply quoting federal bureaucrats' own self-serving reports about their activities in Indian country. See Felix S. Cohen, The Erosion of Indian Rights, 1950–1953: A Case Study in Bureaucracy, 62 Yale L.J. 348 (1953). Cohen believed that the federal government, in general, was generally supportive of tribal self-government from 1930 to 1950 (excepting the period during World War II when federal Indian affairs budgets were zeroed out). But by 1950, the Interior Department began intensely interfering. In some tribal elections, the government used federal funds to back favored candidates for tribal office. In others, the government used coercion. The government began to interfere with the selection of tribal attorneys, with 40 tribes complaining that the Secretary of the Interior was questioning attorney contracts. One tribe that criticized wasteful expenditures of the Bureau of Indian Affairs had its funds frozen until it withdrew the criticism. The list of abuses went on.

To the extent that federal officials did deal with post-IRA tribal governments in a government-to-government fashion, federal officials elevated and favored Indigenous men who rose to high level tribal political positions. It is no accident that one of the most influential national tribal advocacy groups of the mid-20th century was the National Tribal Chair*men*'s Association.

C. MODERN-ERA GOVERNMENTS

Congress finally gave teeth to tribal self-determination in the 1970s when it authorized tribal governments to administer federal Indian affairs programs. 25 U.S.C. § 5301 et seq. Each year, tribal nations and federal agencies negotiate "638 contracts," effectively annual funding agreements. E.g., Rusk v. Fallon Paiute-Shoshone Tribes, 1998 WL 35297248, at *2 (Nev. Inter-Tribal Ct.App.1998) ("Under the [Public Law 638] the tribes assume functions performed by the federal government for the tribes, thereby allowing the tribes to avail themselves of the opportunity to control the benefits and services available to tribal members through this source of federal funding. The services and benefits are made through self determination contracts with the Bureau of Indian Affairs."). These negotiations are, in important respects, analogous to sovereign-to-sovereign treaty negotiations. See EXC, Inc. v. Kayenta Dist. Court, 9 Am. Tribal Law 176, 189 (Navajo Nation S.Ct.2010). The key difference is that the tribal nations possess much of the bargaining power, as federal law requires the federal agency to accept the terms offered by tribal nations in most instances. The self-determination acts like Public Law 638 largely shifted the balance of power in Indian country back to tribal governments:

> When the U.S. Constitution was ratified, Indian Nations were in the process of being discovered. Under the Indian Self-Determination Act, Indian Nations take their place fully in the network of governmental

> systems of the United States. Enactment of the Indian Self-Determination Act, P.L. 93–638 (January 4, 1975), was a significant milestone in recognizing the government-to-government relationship between the United States and sovereign tribal nations. In addition, P.L. 93–638 has given tribes the opportunity and responsibility to establish their own governments and assume functions previously performed directly or indirectly under the federal trust relationship through contracts with the Bureau of Indian Affairs (BIA). A substantial portion of the operations of Navajo Nation law enforcement, this Court, and the eleven Navajo Nation trial courts are funded and performed pursuant to P.L. 93–638 contracts. Fundamental features of these contracts are the reliance of the Federal Government on tribal governments to perform governmental functions previously under that government's responsibility. In addition, the governmental functions are performed according to tribal laws whose development is funded by the Federal Government.

EXC, 9 Am. Tribal Law at 189 (footnote omitted). Insufficient and inefficient federal funding still hamstrings Indian country, however, to this day.

As a consequence of these self-determination acts, tribal governments became federal government contractors. The administration of federal Indian affairs programs required tribal nations to develop capacity quickly. The bureaucratic work of federal contracting is demanding and comes on top of the actual work of delivering governmental services. In the first decade of 638 contracting, the Bureau of Indian Affairs adopted and applied onerous federal procurement policies that few tribal nations could comply with. The Indian Health Service refused to contract with tribal nations at all. Congress made technical amendments in the 1980s and 1990s to improve tribal contracting. Ultimately, self-determination contracting fits relatively easily with the IRA-era tribal governmental structures adopted by tribal nations, even after the significant and often coercive influence of the federal government. Much like the 19th century treaty negotiations, federal agency officials meet with appointed tribal officials in sovereign-to-sovereign negotiations. Now, instead of high-level officials, federal and tribal bureaucrats work out the details, leaving elected or appointed officials to approve the final product. The self-determination process all but guarantees that tribal governments retain and strengthen the hierarchies established in the IRA-era constitutions. Traditional tribal governance structures and philosophies often slid into the underground of tribal society. Many tribal nations, however, have infused their work with tribal culture.

The hierarchies established and cemented as a consequence of federal self-determination policy that now permeate tribal nations have enormous positive and negative consequences. Billions of dollars now flow from Congress through the Bureau of Indian Affairs and Indian Health Service to tribal nations, money that mostly would have not reached tribal governments prior to the self-determination era. But tribal nations engaged in self-determination conform to federally preferred governmental structures. As the Menominee Tribal Court explained, tribal nations govern from a top-down, delegated hierarchy:

> A tribal government acts, exerts its power and conducts its affairs in the same general way that the federal and state governments do; it creates or establishes commissions, agencies, and boards, delegating to them powers necessary to carry on the day-to-day functions of government. Any action by these administrative or regulatory agencies has the same force and character as if taken by the tribal governing body itself.

Menominee Tribal Housing Authority v. Tucker, 18 Indian L.Rep. 6131, 6135 (Menominee Tribal Ct.1991).

Because tribal nations are both sovereign governments and federal government contractors, there will occasionally be conflict over those dual roles. For example, see In re Executive Authority, 10 Okla. Trib. 454, 2007 WL 9192749 (Cheyenne-Arapaho S.Ct.2007), where the court was faced with an emergency tribal budgeting crisis. The tribe's chief executive officer sought to expend federal funds to keep the government functioning during the crisis over the opposition of the tribal legislature. The court, faced with the possibility of forcing the government to shut down, acknowledged the authority of the governor to continue to expend funds to continue "essential governmental services," but with the possibility of judicial review over which "services" were "essential":

> At the outset, we explicitly hold that Article VII, Section 4(b) does not preclude Governor Flyingman from exercising appropriate executive authority to ensure the provision of services for which the Tribes have contracted with the federal government pursuant to [Public Law 638], and other similar contracting regimes. Moreover, we further conclude that in the emergency situation now before us, the Governor may continue to seek federal assistance through "638 contract" and other similar mechanisms, and that he may as a matter of tribal law contract with the United States (if the United States is willing) for the provision of future services to tribal members with federal funds. Just as would be the case absent any emergency, the Governor may exercise his normal executive powers to ensure the Tribes' compliance with such contracts, though we emphasize that such gubernatorial power does not authorize the Governor to violate the separation-of-powers structure established by the tribal Constitution.
>
> In the present emergency, the Governor has requested that we explicitly authorize him to expend tribal funds on "essential governmental services" as he defines such services. That request is granted insofar as its "essential governmental services" component is concerned, but denied insofar as its "as determined solely

> by the Governor" component is concerned. From the date and time of the filing of this Opinion and Order, the Governor may (and in some instances must) cause tribal funds to be expended on "essential government services," but the identity of such services (and personnel) shall be subject to judicial review as provided by this Opinion and Order.

Id., 2007 WL 9192749, at *7 (emphases omitted).

D. TRIBAL GOVERNMENT OFFICIALS

The large majority of tribal nations now elect leadership. While numerous tribal nations still rely on leaders appointed through traditional means, elected officials are the norm in Indian country. Elected officials tend to serve at the top of tribal governmental (and economic) hierarchies. Federal self-determination policy originated and reinforces those hierarchical structures by privileging tribal leaders in sovereign-to-sovereign interactions.

Unlike state and federal elected officials, however, tribal elected officials are unusually accountable to the electorate. Many tribal polities are very small, with just a few hundred or thousand people. Most of those tribal citizens have strong family or personal relationships with their elected officials. Outside political influences such as campaign funding and lobbying range from limited to nonexistent. Outside economic influences, however, can be powerfully influential, especially given the oft-desperate economic straits many tribal nations feel. Even so, tribal elected officials are well known for favoring traditional governing philosophies. The close nature of federal funding of tribal governmental programs and tribal leadership usually means that the most important entity on the reservation is the tribal government.

Because of the conflicting elements of modern tribal government, that is, the tribal nation as federal government contractor while at the same time pursuing policies and services that are consistent with traditional philosophies, means that interesting and difficult legal issues arise.

1. JUDICIAL REVIEW OF POLITICAL DECISIONS

Consider matters involving the separation of powers between tribal government branches. Tribal constitutions established tribal councils to fulfill the legislative function and sometimes the executive function of government, too. IRA-era constitutions often did not even create a tribal judiciary, but left the creation of a judiciary to the tribal council through simple legislation. Since the tribal council could repeal the existence of the court at any time, such a structure undermined or threatened the independence of judiciaries. Many tribes have changed their laws to ensure judicial independence in the last several decades. Even where there is a clear separation between the legislative, executive, and judicial branches, unique conflicts arise. Recall that many traditional tribal governments spread power out in an even more diffuse manner than a two or three branch-style government. It is often difficult for elected officials charged by their constituents to govern in light of traditional philosophies to compartmentalize government in this way.

Tribal courts have held that judicial review of political disputes, such as election disputes, enrollment matters, and tribal ethics matters, properly rests in the tribal court absent valid legislation stripping courts of that power. E.g., Mississippi Band of Choctaw Indians v. Smith, 28 Indian L.Rep. 6184, 6187 (Mississippi Band of Choctaw Indians S.Ct.2001) ("[I]t is axiomatic that an essential element of the highest court of any jurisdiction is the ability to engage in constitutional adjudication.") (citing Marbury v. Madison, 5 U.S. 137 (1805)); Committee for Better Tribal Government v. Southern Ute Election Board, 17 Indian L.Rep. 6095, 6096 (Southern Ute Tribal Ct.1990) ("[A]bsent legislation specifically denying this court jurisdiction to address violations of guaranteed rights, the tribal court is the proper forum to hear alleged violations of the tribe's constitution and code, as well as the Indian Civil Rights Act."). But see, e.g., Lac du Flambeau Band of Lake Superior Chippewa Indians v. One 200–250 Foot Small Mesh Gillnet, 16 Indian L.Rep. 6095 (Lac du Flambeau Band of Lake Superior Chippewa Indians App.Ct.1989) (rejecting the power of judicial review after locating no authorization in the tribal constitution or tribal laws allowing judicial review of tribal council enactments). Of course, tribal court review of decisions committed to the tribal council under tribal law, for example, is inappropriate. E.g., Standing Rock Group for Accountability v. Defender,

29 Indian L.Rep. 6014, 6017 (Standing Rock Sioux Tribal Ct.2001) ("Tribal Council spending decisions * * * are political choices and not appropriate fodder for judicial review.").

In Terry-Carpenter v. Las Vegas Paiute Tribal Council, 29 Indian L.Rep. 6041 (Las Vegas Paiute Ct.App.2002), aff'd in relevant part, 30 Indian L.Rep. 6150 (Las Vegas Paiute S.Ct.2003), the court traced the tribal court's power of judicial review to the tribe's ratification of a written constitution. There, the tribal council had enacted a resolution designed to authorize the disenrollment of a tribal citizen, but the court concluded that the resolution violated the tribal constitution. The tribal council argued that the court had no power of judicial review over enrollment matters. The court held that the existence of a written tribal constitution that contained a bill of rights required judicial review over tribal legislative acts:

> The very theory of a written constitution presupposes that the Paiute people of the Las Vegas Tribe of Paiute Indians delegated a limited and structured power to their tribal government, in this case the Tribal Council. Clearly, this theory is evidenced by the Preamble to the Constitution and Bylaws of the Las Vegas Tribe of Paiute Indians. The limitations on those delegated powers are evident in the very first article of the Constitution and Bylaws of the Las Vegas Tribe of Paiute Indians—a Bill of Rights. This Bill of Rights expressly guarantees that:

> All members of the Las Vegas Tribe of Paiute Indians shall have equal rights, equal protection, and equal opportunity to participate in the economic resources, tribal assets, and activities of the Tribe. No member shall be denied any rights or privileges enjoyed by other citizens of the United States, including but not limited to freedom of religion, speech, and conscience, due process of law, and all other rights reserved to individuals under Section 202, Title II of the Act of April 11, 1968 (82 Stat. 77).
>
> Clearly, if the Tribal Council hypothetically adopted a civil or criminal statute that deprived tribal members of their right to freedom of speech, for example, by outlawing criticism of the policies of the Tribal Council, the tribal court could not be required to enforce such a law without considering its constitutionality. This is because an act of the Tribal Council contrary to or in excess of the power delegated to it in the Tribal Constitution is simply not a valid law.

Id. at 6043. The court further concluded that the tribal council's effort to incorporate limitations on tribal court jurisdiction rooted in federal court traditions was antithetical to "the value of tribal harmony. * * * [S]mall Indian communities, such as the Las Vegas Paiutes, often found effective traditional means to heal disputes within the community so that they did [not] fester and get out of hand." Id. (citing Rave v. Reynolds, 23 Indian L.Rep. 6150 (Winnebago S.Ct.1996)).

In Muscogee (Creek) Nation National Council v. Scott, 2022 Muscogee Creek Nation Supreme LEXIS 2 (Muscogee (Creek) Nation S.Ct.2022), the court struck down a tribal statute that authorized the National Council to initiate impeachment proceedings on its own volition. There, a National Council Representative was accused of self-dealing and fined $50,000 by the National Council. The tribal constitution allowed for impeachment or removal of elected officials, but only upon the execution of a signed petition of 20 percent of voters from the Representative's district or from the Nation's voters. The court asserted that to allow the National Council to amend the constitution's plain terms by simple legislation could be disastrous:

> * * * [O]ur Courts have previously found that "[t]he written Constitution of the Muscogee (Creek) Nation is the highest expression of the sovereign will of the people. The very life and spirit of the government centers around this written Constitution. It is the deliberate and affirmative utterance of the sovereign majority." "The Constitution must be strictly interpreted and where the Constitution speaks in plain language with reference to a particular matter, the Court must not place a different meaning on the words." "It is very probable that there will be inconveniences from following the Muscogee (Creek) Nation Constitution as it is written. If the Courts, Legislature or Principal Chief add to the plain language under the color of construction, then boundaries to governmental power have been distorted. To allow such to

happen would inflict a wound upon the Constitution that nothing can heal. One step taken to enlarge the powers of government opens the door to another until all respect for the fundamental law is lost and the powers of government are just what those in authority please to call them." "A Constitution, by its very nature, serves as a limitation on the power of the government. Without judicial interpretation, however, it may be construed to have as many different meanings as it has readers. Once a case or controversy concerning the meaning of a constitutional provision reaches the courts, then the courts become the final arbiter as to the constitutionality of governmental actions as they relate to the constitution which empowers them. In other words, if the legislature does not provide for firm constraints on official action, then the courts must do so."

Id. at *9–10 (footnotes and citations omitted). See also White v. Sisseton-Wahpeton Oyate, No. APP-17-026-012 (Sisseton-Wahpeton Oyate S.Ct.2017) (rejecting due process challenge to tribal constitutional provision for removal of tribal council member).

Inter-branch conflicts in tribal governments do occur. In Standing Bear v. Pratt, No. SCO-2016-1 (Osage Nation S.Ct.2017), the court was confronted with a difficult conflict between the tribal executive and legislative branches of government. The Osage Congress had enacted a series of budget appropriation bills that included some provisions that the Osage President deemed unconstitutional. The President signed the bills anyway in order to keep the government funded, but brought suit to challenge the portions of the bills they deemed unconstitutional. The court pointed to first principles, that is, tribal customary law, to assess the dispute:

> In conducting our review, we first consider 𐓡𐓘.𐓷𐓸𐓘^, a unique Osage value that guides us as we attempt to balance the roles and responsibilities of each branch of government in a manner that respects the efforts of those who prepared this Constitution as well as the interests of Osage constituency to whom we are all accountable.
>
> The Osage Constitution was adopted to unite our Nation under the values of "Justice, Fairness, Compassion and Respect for the Protection of Child, Elder, All Fellow Beings and Self," creating three co-equal branches of government, with no single branch holding more power than the other and each branch accountable to the whole. * * * Within this framework, we must evaluate constitutional provisions by reviewing the document as a whole, considering each provision as it relates to the others and giving each word its plain meaning when read in context to avoid absurd or inconsistent results.

Id. (citing Redcorn v. Red Eagle, SPC-2013-01 at 3–4 (Osage Nation S.Ct.2013)). See also Citizen Potawatomi Nation Business Council v. Barrett, 29

Indian L.Rep. 6061 (Citizen Potawatomi Nation S.Ct.2001) (affirming trial court order declaring council resolution forbidding payment of tribal chairman's salary); Porter v. Lowe, 24 Indian L.Rep. 6119 (Ho-Chunk Nation Trial Ct.1996) (enjoining tribal chief executive's reorganization of the tribal government in the absence of general or business council authorization).

A tribal court may be confronted with a challenge to its jurisdiction analogous to the federal judiciary's political question doctrine. In Village of Mishongnovi v. Humeystewa, 1 Am. Tribal Law 295 (Hopi Ct.App.1998), the court addressed a conflict between a cultural preservation board and a village government. At Hopi, there are 12 self-governing village governments that form a federation of sorts linked to a national Hopi tribal government. The court rejected an argument that it possessed no jurisdiction over the issue, that it should be addressed by the village government alone. The court applied the United State Supreme Court's political question doctrine test under Baker v. Carr, 369 U.S. 186 (1962), and concluded that the tribal constitution did not expressly reserve such questions to any particular branch of government:

> In essence, respondents argue that Article III, Section 3 of the Hopi Constitution reserves "to the villagers themselves" the power to decide which rival faction is the rightful village authority. Applying the first factor enumerated in *Baker v. Carr*, we do not find that Article III, Section 3 is a "textually demonstrable

> constitutional commitment" of this issue to a "coordinate branch of government." It is not at all clear from this or any other provision of the Hopi Constitution that the village or the Tribal Council alone may hear a challenge to the legality of the actions of individuals claiming to be a village's governing body. Because the Hopi Constitution does not explicitly give another entity of the Hopi government exclusive jurisdiction over this type of dispute, we hold that the political question doctrine does not preclude the Tribal Court from resolving the issues raised in this case.

Village of Mishongnovi, 1 Am. Tribal Law at 305 (footnote omitted).

In Chapoose v. Ute Indian Tribe of the Uintah-Ouray Reservation, 13 Indian L.Rep. 6023 (Ute Tribe Ct.1986), the tribal legislature enacted legislation purporting to strip the tribal court of jurisdiction to review enrollment decisions. The court noted that under the tribal constitution, the tribe's Business Committee (the legislature) possessed authority to establish tribal courts. The Business Committee's attempt to strip the tribal court of jurisdiction over 19 enrollment appeals and appoint the Business Committee as the appellate body for enrollment appeals, however, would violate the due process clause of the Indian Civil Rights Act:

> * * * Plaintiffs in this action have named the tribal Business Committee as defendant. It is inconceivable that a forum would provide an acceptable minimum level of fundamental

> fairness where the decision-maker is also the defendant. The court holds that any attempt by the tribal Business Committee to vest in themselves the power to judicially review a case in which they are themselves the defendants would, at least under the circumstances presented by this case, be a denial of due process of law and therefore void.

Id. at 6025. The tribal court further rejected the Business Committee's claim that the issue was a nonjusticiable political question.

In Shenandoah v. Halbritter, 28 Indian L.Rep. 6036 ([N.Y.] Oneida Nation Ct.2001), the court dismissed an action alleging

> a litany of allegedly unauthorized and illegal actions taken by defendant Halbritter together with the Men's Council and Clan Mothers—e.g., wrongfully "convicting" plaintiffs of "treasonous" activities and sanctioning them by denying essential services, causing them to lose their voices as Nation citizens, terminating their distributions, suspending them from employment with the Nation, and enacting and implementing a program to improve housing which will assertedly cause some of them to be illegally evicted from their homes.

Id. at 6037. The tribal ordinance establishing the tribal court provided that any questions that were "inherently political in nature" were outside the scope of the court's jurisdiction. Id. The court held that to allow the suit to proceed against the tribal officials in their official capacity would "would conflict with the Nation's recognized powers of self-government as a sovereign Indian nation." Id.

In Little River Band of Ottawa Indians Tribal Council v. Romanelli, 2023 MI Ottawa Trib. LEXIS 9 (Little River Band of Ottawa Indians Tribal Ct.2023), the court held that the tribal council's decision made in closed session to authorize a lawsuit was void. Under tribal law, the council can meet in closed session to discuss litigation strategy, but the decision to authorize the filing of a lawsuit was one that required a vote of the council in open session. The court criticized the practice of the council taking official action in closed session:

> Voting in closed session is antithetical to the purpose of a representative form of government. This is an incredibly troubling aspect of this case. To be informed voters and active political citizens, tribal members must have notice of what is occurring within the Tribe. Voting in closed session tribal members of certain critical aspects of a representative government: it mutes their vote and their collective voice by stripping them of their ability to know which elected council member voted on which issue and which way they voted.

Id. at *19–20.

The original public understanding of tribal constitutions is of critical importance to modern day constitutional questions in tribal nations. Unlike the American Constitution, the drafting of which was dominated by wealthy white men, usually slave-owners and Indian killers, tribal citizens drafted modern tribal constitutions. Also, many of the people who worked on framing or amending tribal constitutions remain alive, providing additional sources of authority for constitutional interpretation. E.g., Turtle Mountain Judicial Board v. Turtle Mountain Band of Chippewa Indians, No. 04-007, slip op. at 15 (Turtle Mountain Band of Chippewa Indians Ct.App.2004) (relying on letter from Gene DeLorme to Paul W. Picotte, Bureau of Indian Affairs, May 17, 1995, that described the tribe's legal justification for amendments to the tribe's constitution that required Secretarial approval).

2. TRIBAL ELECTIONS

Tribal elections are relatively new to most tribal nations, which rarely selected leaders in this manner prior to the reorganization. For example, the Anishinaabe tribal nations' leaders were selected by respected elders who led by persuasion and influence, not by simple majority vote:

> Historic leadership among the Anishnabeg was provided by elders who had demonstrated to their village members that they looked out for the best interests of the people. These "*ogima*" (leaders) were generous, and people followed them because they respected their judgment in civil and political matters. The *ogima* of the Anishnabeg were also articulate speakers who could motivate the people to action or issue impassioned pleas on behalf of a fellow villager

> if necessary. They led by influence and example rather than by controlling wealth and political machines.

Fisher v. Pigeon, 24 Indian L.Rep. 6258, 6259 (Saginaw Chippewa Tribal Ct.1996) (quoting George L. Cornell, The Chippewa, in People of the Three Fires: The Ottawa, Potawatomi, and Ojibway 75, 83 (1986)).

Tribal elections are now independently administered elections held by tribal nations to elect their own leaders and decide on governance issues. Because tribal nations are sovereign, they set their own distinct laws, rules, and processes for these elections, which are separate from federal, state, and local elections in the United States. For many decades after the enactment of the IRA in 1934, the Secretary of the Interior possessed the power to administer tribal elections, the so-called Secretarial elections. Secretarial elections are still conducted for a dwindling number of tribes and done so in accordance with 25 C.F.R. Part 81 and tribal law. Secretarial elections must still be conducted in accordance with tribal custom and tradition, if applicable. E.g., Kavena v. Hopi Indian Tribal Court, 16 Indian L.Rep. 6063 (Hopi Tribe App.Ct.1989) (affirming injunction of Secretarial election in one Hopi village for violation of customary law).

Most tribes have assumed control over their own elections in recent decades, but several factors lead to an enormous amount of litigation over tribal elections. First, tribal governments are new to the administration of elections, so their election rules are often fairly informal and prone to challenge. Second, most tribal populations are very small, so a small number of votes can sway an election outcome. Third, access to tribal justice is relatively inexpensive, meaning anyone can afford to bring an election challenge. Many tribes' elections end with election challenges decided in tribal court. E.g., Garcia v. Tohono O'Odham Council, 16 Indian L.Rep. 6151 (Tohono O'Odham Ct.App.1989) (rejecting claim that the political question doctrine rendered election disputes nonjusticiable).

Rios v. Election Board, 2022 Nottawaseppi Huron Band Sup. LEXIS 3 (Nottawaseppi Huron Band of the Potawatomi S.Ct.2022), is illustrative of the complex constitutional issues that can arise. There, the court addressed difficult issues of political speech in small, insular tribal communities. During a tribal community meeting, a tribal leader allegedly made prejudicial statements that affected the outcome of an election. The loser of the election complained to the tribal election board, which ordered a new election. The tribal court overruled the election board's order and the tribal appellate court affirmed, writing:

> The principle of *kejitwawenindowen*, or respect, should form the basis for the way that Tribal relatives treat one another in nearly all matters, but particularly where one is leading or governing. Words, tones, context, body language, timing, action, and intent all play a part in how one gives or receives respect. Different people may have different

> understandings of what this means. However, it is usually clear to most when *kejitwawenindowen* isn't being given. Harsh words, gossip, and fighting over election processes that are non-Bode'wadmi inspired means that the individuals, groups, and/or processes are stressed by something that is not being carried out with *kejitwawenindowen* as well as other Grandfather Teachings, thereby not allowing *mno-bmadzewen* to flourish. It is up to individuals to look at themselves and their conduct first, then the group together, and, finally, the process itself.

Id. at *26. The appellate court found that the tribal leader's political speech was consistent with the principle of *kejitwawenindowen* and therefore did not prejudice the election. Note that under the First Amendment, which does not apply to tribal communities, the tribal leader's speech would likely be absolutely protected. This tribal community recognized the possibility that political speech could harm the broader community and further recognized an implicit limit on that speech.

Similarly, in Payment v. Election Commission, 2022 Sault Ste. Marie Chippewa App. LEXIS 1 (Sault Ste. Marie Tribe of Chippewa Indians Ct.App.2022), the court rejected a decision by the commission to sanction a non-candidate tribal citizen for a controversial advertisement placed in a local newspaper. The court held that the commission had violated the citizen's due process rights. The court applied traditional Anishinaabe principles in determining what "due process" meant under tribal law:

> As Anishinaabe people, and in carrying out duties delegated from one authority to another, we would be remiss if we did not seek out our Ojibway teachings to inform this Court's due process jurisprudence. Indeed, the notion of due process emanates from the concept of achieving harmony in life, to live in balance with all of creation, otherwise known to the Anishinaabe as *mino-bimaadiziwin*. * * * Our Anishinaabe teachings of *nibwaakaawin* (wisdom—use of good sense), *zaagi'idiwin* (practice absolute kindness), *minadendmowin* (respect—act without harm), as well as *ayaangwaamizi* (careful and cautious consideration) must guide this Court's decision-making.

Id. at *9.

Tribal courts also confront issues related to the qualifications of tribal electoral candidates. Tribal courts have recognized that tribal citizens possess a right to engage in political participation, including running for office. However, tribal laws placing restrictions on candidates and voting rights, such as age, residency, and other restrictions are valid so long as they are "reasonable and forward some important governmental interest." Bennett v. Navajo Board of Election Supervisors, 18 Indian L.Rep. 6009, 6011 (Navajo Nation S.Ct.1990). See also Gray v. Hoopa Valley Tribal Election Board, 26 Indian L.Rep. 6138 (Hoopa Valley Tribal Ct.1999) (confirming ineligibility of candidate for tribal office due to debts owed by the candidate to the tribal government); Bird Bear v. Three Affiliated Tribes Election Board, 26 Indian L.Rep. 6046 (Three Affiliated Tribes of the Fort Berthold Reservation Trial Ct.1999) (same).

In McCoy v. Board of Elections, 16 Am. Tribal Law 13 (Eastern Band of Cherokee Indians S.Ct.2019), the court rejected a decision to disqualify a candidate who was alleged to have defrauded the tribe more than two decades earlier but was not found liable or guilty. The court found that the election board's decision to disqualify the candidate violated the "fundamental fairness" of the process:

> [F]undamental fairness requires that the Board employ standards that are sufficiently clear, fair, and consistently applied with respect to (1) the evidence the Board considers or refrains from considering; (2) the quantum of evidence necessary to support its findings of fact; (3) the burden or showing that the Board must meet to support its conclusions and ultimate determination that a candidate should not be certified for defrauding the Tribe under the Election Code and the Charter; and (4) the burden or showing that an applicant, like Ms. McCoy, must make to overcome the Board's determination that the applicant should be disqualified as a candidate for Tribal office for allegedly defrauding the Tribe. The record raises significant issues with respect to all the above.

Id. at 26. Other tribal courts similarly have focused on the principle of "fundamental fairness" in address tribal election disputes. E.g., Bailey v. Election Board, 2008 WL 6196206, at *11 (Grand Traverse Band of Ottawa and Chippewa Indians Tribal Judiciary 2008) ("The procedural protections, which include fundamental fairness, are based on what the individual situation demands. * * * Fundamental fairness includes: (1) consideration of the private interest at stake; (2) the risk of an erroneous deprivation of such interest through the procedures used; (3) the probable value of additional or substitute procedures; and (4) the interest of the state or government, including the function involved and the fiscal or administrative burdens imposed by substitute procedures."); Honyaoma v. Nuvamsa, 7 Am. Tribal Law 320, 328 (Hopi Tribe App.Ct.2008) ("[O]ur Hopi law would require at a minimum the application of fundamental fairness in the review proceeding-prior notice and an opportunity to be heard."); Office of Navajo Nation President and Vice-President v. Navajo Nation Council, 9 Am. Tribal Law 46, 65–66 (Navajo Nation S.Ct.2010) ("We state today that logic and fundamental fairness demands that there be consistency and harmonious linkage between the recitals and the statute enacted. Words are sacred, and the Navajo People have the right to keep the Navajo Nation Council to the whole of its words, not simply a portion thereof.").

In general, the burden of challenging decisions by a tribal election board or commission is very high. Challengers rarely succeed. E.g., Sekaquaptewa v. Hopi Tribal Election Board, 13 Indian L.Rep. 6009 (Hopi Tribal Ct.1986); Fulton v. Redhouse, 18 Indian L.Rep. 6025 (Navajo Nation S.Ct.1991); Haskie v.

Navajo Board of Election Supervisors, 18 Indian L.Rep. 6026 (Navajo Nation S.Ct.1991); Moran v. Rosebud Sioux Tribal Election Committee, 19 Indian L.Rep. 6014 (Rosebud Sioux Tribal Ct.1991); Murphy v. Standing Rock Sioux Election Commission, 17 Indian L.Rep. 6069 (Standing Rock Sioux Tribal Ct.1990); Williams v. McAdams, 18 Indian L.Rep. 6161 (Wichita Tribe Ct. of Indian Appeals 1991). Only in extraordinary circumstances will tribal courts declare election results invalid and/or order a new election to be conducted. E.g., Apache Election Board v. Wildes, 18 Indian L.Rep. 6033 (Apache Tribe Ct. of Indian Appeals 1990) (election board illegally removed candidate's name from ballot); *Bailey*, 2008 WL 6196206 (election board adjudicated challenge to candidate's politicking activities without notice to the candidate); Gwin v. Bolman, 25 Indian L.Rep. 6121 (Three Affiliated Tribes of the Fort Berthold Reservation Dist.Ct.1998) (ordering election board not to hold recall and general election at same time).

Some tribes deny jurisdiction to tribal courts under constitutional or statutory law providing that the decision of the tribal election board is final. E.g., Darden v. Chitimacha Election Board, 28 Indian L.Rep. 6043 (Chitimacha Indian Tribal Ct.App.2001) (tribal statute); Const. of the Grand Traverse Band of Ottawa and Chippewa Indians, art. VII, § 5(a).

Finally, consider one of the worst problems in Indian country, the problem of holdover councils arising from intractable political disputes. Occasionally, depending especially on a given tribe's election laws and rules, elected leaders who lose an election can simply decline to leave office. They point to their powers under tribal statutes or constitutional provisions, or allege significant election irregularities, or point to traditional leadership prerogatives that conflict with tribal statutes, or simply hold on to the reins of power because there is no entity that can force them out.

Perhaps the first modern era holdover council controversy arose at the Saginaw Chippewa Indian Tribe in the 1990s. While the issue dragged on for years, the leading case arising from that dispute was Chamberlain v. Peters, 27 Indian L. Rep. 6085 (Saginaw Chippewa Indian Tribe of Mich.App. Ct.2000). The holdover council, known as the Chamberlain council, refused to leave office because it believed that its election in 1996 granted it a mandate to commence the reform of the membership rolls, a mandate it had not yet fulfilled. Tribal laws also allowed the sitting council to invalidate an election. The tribal appellate court held that the holdover council did not possess authority to remain in office after the expiration of its term, focusing on the text of the tribal constitution. Members of the competing parties, known as the Peters council, formed what they called an "interim" government. The court also held that this "interim" council was invalid, given that there was no authority in the tribal constitution for interim councils. After the *Chamberlain* court reached its decision, it pointed out that where no party takes tribal law and tribal justice systems seriously, the potential for these political disputes to happen is serious. The court asked the parties to engage in mutually respectful behavior, which seemed to calm the proceedings:

> In part, our closing comments here are an admission, as is more often the case, that the parties are each at fault and each to be acclaimed. We would only urge that each accept responsibility for the errors each has committed and each accept the responsibility to work cooperatively in the future. Traditions of generosity, respect, integrity and cooperation compel each party to do what good grace and a proper way of life would dictate, well beyond what a Court may order. The rest remains to a higher source.

Id. at 6097.

Some tribal constitutions allow for holdover councils in extraordinary circumstances. For example, the Grand Traverse Band of Ottawa and Chippewa Indians' constitution allows for holdovers in the event of the removal of a council member or other vacancy. See Barrientoz v. Election Board, 2006 WL 6285478, at *3 (Grand Traverse Band of Ottawa and Chippewa Indians Tribal Judiciary 2006) ("Article III § 2(b) of the GTB Constitution contemplates 'hold over' Councilors in the event a seat becomes vacant or a Councilor is removed from office. Both circumstances would require that 'Council members remain in office until their successors are elected.' * * * The powers would be the full powers of the office of Tribal Council until such time as a successor is elected.").

Since tribal judges tend to be appointed for terms of years (and because many tribal court dockets, especially appellate court dockets, are light), tribal judges occasionally serve beyond their terms. Generally, tribal courts allow tribal judges to serve as holdovers unless tribal law forbids it. E.g., In the Service of Office of Justices, 6 Okla. Trib. 573, 1998 WL 34067270, *3 (Cherokee Nation Judicial Appeals Trib.1998) ("[A] judge has a right and duty to hold over and exercise the duties and functions of the office until his successor is duly selected and qualified, even where there is no explicit constitutional nor statutory provision regarding holdover."). Of course, holdover judges' tenure as holdovers must be temporary.

3. REMOVAL OR IMPEACHMENT OF TRIBAL ELECTED OFFICIALS

Removal or impeachment of tribal elected officials is rare, but virtually all tribal constitutions provide a process for the removal of elected officials. Typically, tribal elected officials can only be removed for criminal acts or incapacity. One tribal court panel, however, mused that tribal constitutions enacted in accordance with the Indian Reorganization Act, 25 U.S.C. § 5123, may "in reality promote the removal, rather than strengthen and protect the rights of tribal council members." Pavizo v. Fort McDermitt Tribal Council, 20 Indian L.Rep. 6020, 6021 (Western Nevada Agency Ct. Indian Appeals 1993).

Since removals or impeachments rarely happen, tribal courts struggle with the cases as they arise.

For example, in Eastern Band of Cherokee Indians on behalf of Enrolled Members v. Lambert, 15 Am. Tribal Law 55 (Eastern Band of Cherokee Indians S.Ct.2018), the court assumed jurisdiction over a sitting tribal chief's suit designed to prevent his summary suspension from office after being impeached but before being removed. The tribe's Attorney General intervened in the suit to defend the tribal council's decision to suspend the tribal chief but by doing so the appellate court held, their intervention abrogated tribal immunity. One judge dissented, finding no law authorizing the Attorney General to intervene:

> * * * Under Cherokee Code § 114–2(a), the AG has the duty to "prosecute or provide for the prosecution and defend or provide for the defense in all actions" in which the client—the EBCI tribal government—"shall be interested, or a party." Again, nothing in this statement permits the AG, in his official capacity or on behalf of the tribal membership, to bring suit as the Tribe against the Principal Chief and Tribal Council, thereby imposing his own views on the client.

Id. at 72–73 (Pipestem, C.J., dissenting).

Consider In re McSauby, 1997 WL 34691849 (Grand Traverse Band of Ottawa and Chippewa Indians Tribal Judiciary 1997). There, the tribal constitution placed the authority to remove elected officials in the hands of the tribal judiciary sitting en banc. After a hearing in which the tribal court ordered the tribal government to provide paid counsel to the respondent, the tribal judiciary removed a tribal council member for self-dealing in real estate issues involving the tribe. The court concluded:

> The tribal community has every right to expect that tribal officials and employees will avoid conflicts-of-interest. Tribal members have a right to loyal service and fulfillment of confidence placed in officials and employees. Tribal officials have a fiduciary responsibility to tribal membership. Good government will require that even the appearance of a conflict-of-interest be avoided. In that regard, the Tribal Council is urged to seriously consider the adoption of a code of ethics for tribal official and employee conduct to provide additional guidance beyond that offered in this Opinion.

Id. at *5. Cf. Grievance Committee of the Sac and Fox Nation v. Rhoads, 7 Am. Tribal Law 661, 664 (Sac and Fox Nation S.Ct.2007) (tribal chief had right to counsel at own expense during removal process).

For a case addressing the specific duties imposed on tribal leaders under tribal common law, see In re Certified Question II (Navajo Nation v. MacDonald), 16 Indian L.Rep. 6086 (Navajo Nation S.Ct.1989). There, the court imposed upon Navajo leaders a form of fiduciary duty specific to Diné common law:

> The Navajo traditional concept of fiduciary trust of a leader (*naat'aanii*) is just as relevant here. After the epic battles were fought by the Hero Twins, the Navajo people set on the path of

> becoming a strong nation. It became necessary to select *naat'aaniis* by a consensus of the people.
>
> A *naat'aanii* was not a powerful politician nor was he a mighty chief. A *naat'aanii* was chosen based upon his ability to help the people survive and whatever authority he had was based upon that ability and the trust placed in him by the people. If a *naat'aanii* lost the trust of his people, the people simply ceased to follow him or even listen to his words. The *naat'aanii* indeed was expected to be honest, faithful and truthful in dealing with his people.

Id. at 6092. The court confirmed that a sitting elected official can be removed by the tribal council if that person is indicted for serious felonies involving questions of public trust.

Occasionally, tribal elected officials are subject to petitions for removal by their constituents. Tribal constitutions and tribal codes determine the process by which an elected official can be subject to recall. In Kinnart v. Morrow (2023), a decision of a specially constituted hearing board of the Sault Ste. Marie Tribe of Chippewa Indians, the tribal code called for the establishment of a hearing board to assess allegations that an elected official had violated tribal law, once recall petitioners had gathered a sufficient number of signatures to initiate the process. Once the signatures were collected, the hearing board concluded that the alleged violations of tribal law were insufficient to justify removal. The board drew from Anishinaabe traditions to guide its analysis:

> In the traditional Anishinaabe governance structure, each of the clans, through individual representation, selected *ogimaag* (chiefs or leaders) to implement the Bands governance system and to represent the interests of the clan at the national council. As a result, the traditional form of governance, or sovereignty for the Anishinaabe is defined by the concept *gaa-ezhi-ogimaawaadizid* (to act in a way that recognizes those I am responsible for). * * * Therefore, this Hearing Board recognizes the role of the tribal citizenry in choosing their *ogimaag* (chiefs, leaders), through their *doodem* (clan) responsibilities as a fundamental component of traditional Anishinaabe governance in accordance with the principle of *inawendiwin* (reciprocal relationships). These connective reciprocal relationships contributed to the overall social organization and governance of the Anishinaabe, enabled inter-community cooperation and political coordination as well as the advancement of leadership in fulfillment of the principle of *mino-bimaadiziwin*. In addition, the traditional law principle of sovereignty, as expressed through the concept *gaa-ezhi-ogimaawaadizi* is applicable in determining how the Board of Directors, as *ogimaag* (tribal leaders), must act in a way of recognizing the rights of the people, which includes the protection of their right to removal.

Id., slip op. at 6 (citing Hoffman v. Board of Directors, 2022 Sault Ste. Marie Chippewa App. LEXIS 5, at *8

(Sault Ste. Marie Tribe of Chippewa Indians Ct.App.2022)).

In the absence of the application of tribal common law, however, ICRA or tribal constitutional or statutory provisions require tribal courts to ensure that due process is provided. E.g., Coalition for Fair Government II v. Lowe, 23 Indian L.Rep. 6181 (Ho-Chunk Nation Trial Ct.1996) (enjoining special election to remove council member due to violations of due process toward tribal officers); Hicks v. Carerra, 22 Indian L.Rep. 6065 (Nev. Inter-tribal Ct.App.1995) (finding notice and hearing requirements were met).

Contemporary tribal governments are dynamic and unique entities. They are rooted in contradiction, with structures often rooted in colonialism but infused with Indigenous tradition. Tribal governments in their current incarnation are only several decades old, some only a few years old. Most tribal government structures originate with the "model" tribal governmental structures impressed upon tribes by the federal government beginning in the 1930s. Few tribes employ governmental structures their ancestors would have recognized, though tribal nations endeavor to restore structures that are cognizant of Indigenous cultures, religions, and philosophies. Tribal nation governments are effectively locked in as long as tribes depend on federal money to provide services under various self-determination acts. The overlay of federal structures and Indigenous philosophies guarantees difficulty, but tribal leaders should think of contemporary tribal governments as temporary but necessary inconveniences. As Justice Holly T. Bird wrote in the coda to an election dispute decision:

> The world around us is in a state of stress and unrest. We live in a time when our *penojen* (children) are growing up with the fear of uncertainty that comes with a pandemic, climate change, political unrest, and war. These times have come and gone for our Indigenous people throughout our time here on *Segmekwe*, our Mother Earth. Through it all we have been resilient and adaptive. We also carry trauma and huge scars that sometimes feed our fears and reactions. It is more important than ever that we provide a structure and way of life for our *penojen* that reflect who we are and who we want to be as Indigenous people. The values of *mno-bmadzwen* are more than just words that we post on our websites or on paper. Or that we speak about when calling out another person. "For the Anishinaabe, the concept of achieving harmony in life, to live in balance with all of creation is expressed by the term *mino-bimaadiziwin*." * * * *Mno-bmadzwen* reflects a way of living and how we treat one another so that we may all live in harmony together. It is a uniquely tribal concept that considers the individual as no different from the whole, and the whole as no different from the Universe. How each individual community chooses to create lifeways based on *mno-bmadzwen* is

> important to their future as Indigenous people and to all that feel its effect.
>
> Tribal elections are a messy process, made more complicated by personal emotion, motive, and lack of reason. The people of [the Nottawaseppi Huron Band of the Potawatomi] are all relatives so the ramifications of conflict can be far-reaching and damaging to the entire Tribe. We have all seen how our Tribal elections have largely followed the processes mandated by the larger U.S. society that surrounds us. There are some good things about the process, and also some things that don't work for our Indigenous nations and ways of being. As we figure out what processes work best for our people in our adaptation to modern Tribal governance, it is important that our leaders and potential leaders provide an example of how to treat one another so that *mno-bmadzwen* is present for all. "The principles of *mino-bimaadiziwin* should be utilized to interpret and develop *Anishinaabe-inaakonigewin*." "The principles of *mino-bimaadiziwin* as a fundamental law of the Anishinaabe are achieved through the application of the seven sacred laws of creation—the Seven Grandfather Teachings."

Rios v. Election Board, 2022 Nottawaseppi Huron Band Sup. LEXIS 3, at **22–24 (Nottawaseppi Huron Band of the Potawatomi S.Ct.2022) (quoting Cholewka v. Grand Traverse Band of Ottawa and Chippewa Indians Tribal Council, No. 2013-16-AP (Grand Traverse Band of Ottawa and Chippewa

Indians App.Ct. 2014), and Kekek Jason Stark, Anishinaabe Inaakonigewin: Principle for Intergenerational Preservation of Mino-Bimaadiziwin, 82 Mont.L.Rev. 293, 295 (2021)) (footnote omitted).

CHAPTER 3

TRIBAL JUSTICE SYSTEMS

More than 400 contemporary tribal nations have established tribal justice systems. Tribal justice systems typically but not always include courts and judges, prosecutors, presenting officers, defenders, police and other public safety personnel, and jails. Prior to colonization, tribal justice systems existed but tended toward restorative and healing in line with Indigenous political philosophies. Now, tribal justice systems derive from tribal courts established by federal colonizers, though many tribes are moving toward restoration of their traditional dispute resolution structures.

A. OVERVIEW OF MODERN OF TRIBAL JUDICIAL PHILOSOPHIES

Despite the superficial similarities of tribal justice systems to state and federal courts, the differences are legion. The dockets of contemporary tribal justice systems tend to be much smaller than those in federal and state courts. This gives tribal judges more opportunity to engage with the parties in every case. The costs of initiating litigation are much smaller as well. Many tribal courts have streamlined court rules of procedure, evidence, and forms. The unstated public policy of state and federal court litigation, going back to the colonizer's English origins, is that the complexity of court procedures are designed to weed out the claims of the under-resourced. Tribal justice systems usually seek to make the court system more accessible to all. Many cases are litigated more informally, without the presence of lawyers or with the assistance of lay advocates. Most tribal citizens cannot afford legal counsel. Smaller docket sizes also undercut the apparent need to fully fund tribal courts, however.

Tribal court can philosophies differ from state and federal judicial philosophies. Tribal courts have expressed the goal of seeking "justice" rather than rote application of tribal law. E.g., Sage v. Lodge Grass School District No. 27, 13 Indian L.Rep. 6035, 6040 (Crow Ct.App.1986) ("Tribal courts, in both their present form and their 'traditional' predecessors, however, have been centrally concerned with the overall concept of *justice* and have oftentimes managed to be free of the obsession with technicalities that has so often plagued non-tribal court systems.") (emphasis in original); Ben v. Burbank, 24 Indian L.Rep. 6001, 6001 (Navajo Nation S.Ct.1996) ("Our law contains a common rule based upon the principle that *courts are to be just and do justice*.") (emphasis added, quoting Zions First National Bank v. Joe, 4 Navajo Rep. 92, 93 (1983)); Rios v. Nottawaseppi Huron Band of the Potawatomi Election Board, 2022 Nottawaseppi Huron Band Sup. LEXIS 3, at *3 (Nottawaseppi Huron Band of the Potawatomi S.Ct.2022) ("To begin, we first respectfully acknowledge our gratitude for being given the responsibility of helping to make decisions for the people of NHBP. We also recognize our solemn duty to continue *Gaagige-inaakonigwein*, or Anishinaabe law, for the future of all generations. By doing so, we uplift the concepts of achieving harmony and living in balance with all of creation under the principles of Mno-Bmadzewen. Through this we hope to bring forth that which defines the people of the Tribe as Anishinaabe and achieve *justice* under the law as rooted in Anishinaabe ways of thinking and being.") (emphasis added); Puyallup Tribe v. Blaze Construction, 21 Indian L.Rep. 6146, 6148 (Puyallup Tribal Ct.1987) ("Concepts of equity will be followed to the extent they create *justice*. * * * [T]his court will look to the substance of the actions to determine a *just result*.") (emphasis added). Like federal and state judges, tribal judges are impartial, but tend to interpret ambiguities in the law differently, often to the benefit of the individual over the government. Federal courts have acknowledged that tribal courts are effective at guaranteeing civil rights protections. E.g., FMC Corporation v. Shoshone-Bannock Tribes, 942 F.3d 916, 944 (9th Cir.2019); Norton v. Ute Indian Tribe of the Uintah and Ouray Reservation, 863 F.3d 1236, 1250 (10th Cir.2017).

Tribal courts also must address when tribal custom and tradition, also referred to as tribal common law or tribal customary law, applies. In Hopi Indian Credit Assn. v. Thomas, 25 Indian L.Rep. 6168 (Hopi Tribe App.Ct.1996), the court adopted a rule for determining the process and substance of applying Hopi customary law:

> If applicable, Hopi custom, tradition and culture must be considered before the application of foreign law. Because Hopi custom, tradition and culture are generally unwritten and can change over time, the party who wishes

> to use unwritten custom, tradition or culture in a trial court may be required to provide sufficient evidence for the trial court to find the alleged custom, tradition or culture does exist and that it is legally relevant to the case at hand. A trial court may also take judicial notice of a custom, tradition or culture, but the relevancy must always be demonstrated.

Id. at 6169. The court articulated a robust pleading standard for parties to raise Hopi customary law:

> The proponent of Hopi customs, traditions and culture must then (1) plead them to the court with sufficient evidence so as to establish the existence of such a custom, tradition or culture, and then (2) show that the recognized custom, tradition, or culture is relevant to the issue before the court.

Id. The court added that a judge may "dispense with proof of the existence of a Hopi custom, tradition or culture if it finds the custom, tradition or culture to be generally known and accepted within the Hopi Tribe." Id.

In a later decision in the same matter, the appellate court noted that the written and unwritten laws of the Hopi Tribe are controlling in any suit in the tribal court, with federal law, Arizona law, and "The Common Law" merely persuasive authorities. See Hopi Indian Credit Assn. v. Thomas, 27 Indian L.Rep. 6039, 6050 (Hopi Tribe App.Ct.1998).

In Stepetin v. Nisqually Indian Community, 2 NICS App. 224 (Nisqually Tribal Ct.App.1993), the dissenting judge argued that tribal statutes originating in non-Indian legal traditions should be construed and interpreted in light of tribal common law:

> * * * Tribal statutes which have been adopted in derogation to tribal tradition should be regarded with caution. Just because tribal communities have sometimes given paper recognition to non-Indian practices and Anglo-American law principles in their laws does not necessarily mean that such apparent adoption of non-Indian legal concepts and practices should be taken at face value.
>
> * * * The courts have also taken over some of the functions originally performed by the tribal elders in providing a forum to resolve disputes in the community and in sanctioning members for conduct the community will not tolerate. In performing any of these functions the court must be fundamentally fair and evenly address the needs of the tribal community in order to maintain legitimacy and respect.

Id. at 232–33 (Irvin, C.J., concurring and dissenting).

Contemporary tribal judges are a mix of lawyers and non-lawyers, tribal citizens and noncitizens, and Indigenous elders. E.g., Eastern Band of Cherokee Indians v. Crowe, 9 Am. Tribal Law 27, 35 (Cherokee Ct. of the Eastern Band of Cherokee Indians 2010) ("This Court is staffed with highly professional, bar licensed judges, who have attended some of the finest law schools in the country and who have a wide variety of professional and academic achievements and a wealth of jurisprudential experience."). For many years, because tribal nations rarely could afford licensed attorneys as judges, observers assumed that tribal judges were incompetent and biased. Until the 2000s, when the New York Times reported on the thousands of non-lawyer judges working in rural state courts (think magistrates, justices of the peace, and family court referees), the United States Department of Justice frequently opposed Congressional efforts to expand tribal court authority. Now, it is routine for tribal courts to assign complex litigation to law-trained judges with specific expertise in the legal issue in question and to assign law judges to cases where the amount in controversy is small or involves an interest domestic or property issue, to name a few examples. Tribal appellate panels often are a mix of different types of professionals and tribal citizens and non-citizens. On occasion, if necessary, tribal appellate courts will vacate the decision of a lay judge and reassign a case on remand to a law-trained judge. E.g., Monette v. Schlenvogt, 32 Indian L.Rep. 6074, 6075 (Turtle Mountain Band of Chippewa Indians Ct.App.2005).

Tribal judges tend to be appointed by tribal political branches of government for a term of years, though many tribes do conduct judicial elections. Most tribes retain a full time chief trial judge, who also doubles as a tribal department head for the court system, and panels or rosters of part-time judges to assist the chief trial judge, to serve as conflicts or subject matter judges, and as appellate judges. Part-time judges are necessary supplements to appointed judges. See Conway v. Conway, 26 Indian L.Rep. 6146, 6147 (Puyallup Ct.App.1999) ("Pro tem judges play a critical role in tribal court since they are frequently utilized by small tribes at remote locations to ensure that every appearance of fairness, as well as actual fairness, is provided within the limited resources available to tribal courts."). Since tribal dockets are often small and tribal budgets are even smaller, tribes have occasionally banded their sovereignties together (so to speak) into inter-tribal court systems. Past and present intertribal courts include the Nevada Intertribal Court System, the Northern Plains Intertribal Court System, the Northwest Intertribal Court System, the Southern California Intertribal Court System, and the Southwest Intertribal Court of Appeals. Each of these intertribal court systems establishes a roster of available judges, prosecutors, and other advocates for the participating tribes. The administrative arms of the court systems serve as court staff.

Most tribal justice systems, which include judges, prosecutors, defenders, presenting attorneys, and court staff, are funded at least in part by the federal government through Public Law 638. As per usual, the federal funding is always insufficient, forcing tribes to accept either severely underfunded courts or to supplement the federal money with tribal money.

In recent decades, tribal nations have begun to make available the tribal constitutions, codes, regulations, ordinances, court rules, and judicial decisions online and in print. The National Indian Law Library, housed at the Native American Rights

Fund, collects tribal laws in a massive database available online and by request in hard copy from the library. Moreover, many thousands of tribal court decisions are now available on Westlaw and LexisNexis, and often on other online databases. The legacy tribal court reporter, the Indian Law Reporter, that published many hundreds of tribal court decisions in print from the 1980s through the 2000s, is also available online through academic libraries. Still, many smaller, resource-poor tribes have little in the way of resources to make their laws available online. Some tribes, worried about the influence of outsiders, do not make their laws available at all.

B. HISTORY OF THE DEVELOPMENT OF TRIBAL JUSTICE SYSTEMS

The earliest precursors of modern tribal courts are the courts of the Cherokee Nation (and neighboring tribal nations) prior to forcible removal in the 1830s. The Cherokee Nation Supreme Court, for example, is the first high court in the State of Georgia. The Cherokee Nation also established a police force, called the Light Horse or Lighthorse. These justice systems were intended as adaptive structures designed to show to federal and state policymakers that Indigenous peoples need not be removed to the west. They failed on that front, but the Five Tribes of Oklahoma quickly reestablished those justice systems in Indian Territory (now the State of Oklahoma) after removal.

The Five Nations' courts remained viable court systems throughout the remainder of the 19th

Century. The United States Supreme Court impliedly acknowledged the powers of those court systems as late as 1896, when the Court held that a Cherokee Nation conviction for a capital crime was beyond plenary federal court review. Talton v. Mayes, 163 U.S. 376 (1896). That decision affirmed, as a practical matter, the power of tribal nations to sentence tribal citizens to death. Congress, however, terminated the Indian Territory tribal courts in 1898. 30 Stat. 495.

For much of the rest of Indian country, tribal nations continued to employ their traditional dispute resolution mechanisms. Tribal councils, often of elders or other traditional leaders, would meet to resolve intramural disputes. These mechanisms tended to be non-adversarial, family-oriented affairs. For example, during the annual Green Corn ceremonies of the Creek and Miccosukee tribal nations, elders would gather to address inter-personal conflicts between tribal citizens. In Anishinaabe communities, an entire tribal village would gather in a lodge to address serious criminal activities following a pipe ceremony. In Haudensaunee and other communities, domestic violence perpetrators might be subject to ridicule and even physical violence from the female members of the community. Indigenous elders often held the knowledge and experience needed to solve intratribal matters:

> * * * Traditionally, disputes within the tribe were resolved by the elders, who were the governing authority for tribal families and the

> tribe. An elder earned his or her power by maintaining a life of integrity and adhering to traditional teachings; protection of ones' reputation and position demanded a virtuous lifestyle. There was a standard within the tribal community as to what was "wise" and "virtuous."

Lane-Oriero v. Lummi Indian Business Council, 21 Indian L.Rep. 6143, 6145 (Lummi Tribal Ct.1994).

Formal (yet less formal than state and federal courts) court systems came to Indian country in 1880s as the Bureau of Indian Affairs decided to implement Courts of Indian Offenses in many reservation communities (without Congressional direction or authorization). These courts enforced Law and Order Codes imposed on tribal councils by those same federal bureaucrats. Local federal officials appointed Indian people over whom they had control as judges and police to enforce the Law and Order Codes. The federal bureaucrats intended these courts and codes as tools of cultural assimilation, notoriously including limitations on and even criminalization of Indigenous religious practices in the codes. Indian people were able to lessen the intended impact of the Courts of Indian Offenses, however.

Though Congress never explicitly authorized the BIA to establish the Courts of Indian Offenses and promulgate the codes, it would later appropriate funds to continue their operation and development, effectively approving them. Later incarnations of federal regulations establishing uniform Law and

Order Codes and authorizing the Courts of Indian Offenses were published the Code of Federal Regulations, leading many to refer to them going forward as "CFR Courts." The current incarnation of the Law and Order Code is located at 25 C.F.R. Part 11, though few tribes continued to rely on their CFR Courts, opting instead to either take over those courts under federal self-determination contracts or establishing entirely new court systems.

CFR Courts did serve as the primary court systems for tribal nations throughout most of the 20th century. However, starting with the Navajo Nation in the 1950s, tribal nations began to establish their own justice systems, often by assuming control over the CFR Courts. In Williams v. Lee, 358 U.S. 217 (1959), the United States Supreme Court noted that the Navajo Nation had taken control over its CFR Court from the BIA, leading to the adoption of its own law and order code. Federal self-determination contracting beginning in 1975 jump-started this process, along with the United States Supreme Court's decision in Santa Clara Pueblo v. Martinez, 436 U.S. 49 (1978). That case held that the civil rights protections of the Indian Civil Rights Act of 1968, sometimes referred to as the Indian Bill of Rights, now codified as amended at 25 U.S.C. § 1302(a), could only be enforced in tribal forums. Congressional support for the administration of tribal courts has been halting and intermittent, but Congress has done nothing to cut back on tribal court powers for the last half-century.

There are now less than two dozen tribal nations that rely on CFR courts. Since CFR courts are federal entities, with employees and prosecutions managed by federal appointed officials and funded by Congress, what sovereignty those courts are exercising can be a thorny question. CFR courts have described themselves as tribal instrumentalities:

> The Courts of Indian Offenses, although established pursuant to regulations in 25 C.F.R., partially administered by the Bureau of Indian Affairs, and funded from federal sources, are essentially tribal entities. The court is not a federal court established pursuant to either article I or article III of the U.S. Constitution, nor is it simply an administrative arm of the Bureau of Indian Affairs. The Courts of Indian Offenses act as tribal courts since they are exercising the sovereign authority of the tribe for which the court sits. The governmental power being asserted is that of the individual Indian tribe, not that of the federal government. It is from the inherent power of the Indian nations to make laws, and be ruled by them that is the source of the court's power.

Ponca Tribal Election Board v. Snake, 17 Indian L.Rep. 6085, 6088 (Ponca Tribe Ct. of Indian Appeals 1988); see also Gallegos v. French, 18 Indian L.Rep. 6151, 6156 (Delaware Tribe of Western Okla. Ct. of Indian Appeals 1991) ("While at the turn of the century, the Courts of Indian Offenses were used by the federal government simply to enforce the policies of the Interior Department, today's modern C.F.R.

Courts are actually very similar to most tribal courts. The judges are not subject to direction or control by field officers of the Bureau of Indian Affairs, nor are the judges influenced by BIA employees' directives or opinions in making their decisions. To the contrary, the intrusion of field employees of the Bureau of Indian Affairs into the decisionmaking processes of the judges of the Court of Indian Offenses is strictly prohibited by federal regulation. 25 C.F.R. § 11.21.").

Despite this logic, the issue came to a head in a recent United States Supreme Court case, Denezpi v. United States, 596 U.S. 591 (2022). There, the CFR court for the Ute Mountain Ute tribal nation prosecuted Denezpi for assault and battery, a crime under both the tribal criminal code and the federal law and order code used by CFR courts. Later, the United States prosecuted Denezpi for the same crime. Normally, it is understood that a federal prosecution subsequent to a tribal prosecution does not invoke the federal constitution's prohibition on exposing criminal defendants to double jeopardy because tribal and federal sovereigns are separate (and tribal governmental powers largely are not constrained by the United States Constitution). See United States v. Wheeler, 435 U.S. 313 (1978). However, because the CFR court is a federal instrumentality, the separation was far from clear. Even so, the Court affirmed the federal conviction of Denezpi.

C. CONTEMPORARY TRIBAL JUSTICE SYSTEMS

Tribal courts today seem very similar to state and federal courts. The differences are in the details. Congress typically underfunds tribal governance, so most tribal courts have suffered from dramatic resource limitations since their inception. However, tribal courts tend to have much smaller dockets than state courts, allowing for a more personalized experience for litigants, criminal and civil.

The few tribal courts that existed in the 1960s came under the scrutiny of Congress during the lead up to the enactment of the Indian Civil Rights Act. Lacking resources but still insisting on respecting traditions, tribal courts of that era were very informal. Tribal judges were not lawyers, there was little in the way of written procedures, and the old Law and Order Codes remained law. In some respects, that generation of tribal courts replicated many of the injustices of the courts that were under the control of the BIA. Armed with a fair amount of largely anecdotal evidence about procedural abuses of tribal courts, Congress adopted the Indian Bill of Rights, now codified at 25 U.S.C. § 1302(a), in 1968. Congress also gutted the sentencing powers of tribal courts, limiting jail time for tribal convictions to six months. Congress in 1986, as a strange consequence of the War on Drugs, ratcheted that limit up to a full year in 1986. In 2010, Congress reaffirmed tribal sentencing authority to three years, so long as tribal convictions met stringent criteria. 25 U.S.C. § 1302(b).

In the 1970s, the American Bar Foundation published a study on tribal courts condemning them for a wide variety of issues. See Samuel J. Bracker, American Indian Tribal Courts: The Cost of Separate Justice (1978); see also Samuel J. Brakel, American Indian Tribal Courts: Separate? "Yes," Equal? "Probably Not," 62 A.B.A.J. 1002 (1976). The study, which relied heavily on anecdotal evidence (and a healthy helping of ethnocentrism) condemned tribal courts for the informality of procedures, which generated the perception that fundamental fairness was at risk. The study asserted that tribal judges, who were largely non-law trained, were incompetent and biased (no such commentary was extended to non-lawyer state judges). The study also asserted that tribal judges, appointed by the tribal legislatures, lacked independence from the political branches of government.

The National American Indian Court Judges Association (NAICJA) countered with a study of its own, headed by David Getches, that surveyed tribal courts directly. See National American Indian Court Judges Association, Indian Courts and the Future: Report of the NAICJA Long Range Planning Project (David H. Getches & H. Orville N. Olney eds., 1978). The surveys showed that lack of federal funding condemned most tribal courts to limited jurisdiction and effectiveness. The Getches/NAICJA report showed that most tribal judges were not licensed attorneys and that some tribal legislatures did continue to interfere with tribal court functions. Cf. Gillette v. Hall, 26 Indian L.Rep. 6028 (Three Affiliated Tribes of the Fort Berthold Reservation

Dist.Ct.1998) (dismissing as unripe a tribal judge challenge to the power of the tribal chairman to suspend the tribal judge for usurping the role of the tribal council by issuing an ex parte temporary restraining order over the chairman).

D. THE DEVELOPMENT OF TRIBAL JUDICIAL INDEPENDENCE

In the decades that followed these competing reports, tribal governments responded to the concerns about separation of powers and lack of funding. Federal funding for tribal justice systems under the 1970s era self-determination acts set a minimal baseline that many tribal nations have been able to supplement with revenue from commercial enterprises such as natural resources extraction and gaming operations. Some tribal courts are well funded and, coupled with smaller dockets, employ court systems that are the envy of courts nationally. Many other tribal nations have few resources and must still rely on limited federal funding. These court systems target their operations on needs established by tribal leaders, such as child welfare, and usually do not take the lead on Indian country law enforcement. Many tribal courts start this way.

IRA-era tribal constitutions typically granted authority to tribal legislatures to establish tribal courts and to define the scope of tribal court jurisdiction. Because the tribal council structurally has control over the tribal courts in that system, tribal courts are reluctant to assert jurisdiction over tribal council actions. E.g., Lane-Oriero v. Lummi

Indian Business Council, 21 Indian L.Rep. 6143 (Lummi Tribal Ct.1994) (rejecting jurisdiction over claim seeking review of recall petitions).

Tribal response to the separation of powers concerns were two-fold. First, it is now common for tribal nations to have adopted tribal constitutional provisions that guarantee an independent judiciary, or at the very least, statutes that do so. Some tribes have even criminalized interference with the judicial function. Likely even more effective is the increased and continued professionalization of tribal judiciaries. Indian country has moved from the 1960s and 1970s era where few tribal judges were lawyers to an era where it is far more common for tribes to appoint attorneys as judges. Lawyers are bound to their own codes of ethics obliging them to reject outside interference in judicial functions. Moreover, there is a very strong market for Indian lawyers, protecting tribal judges from outside influence on their judicial work.

Two cases demonstrate the development of tribal judicial independence. The first case, Moran v. Council of the Confederated Salish & Kootenai Tribes, 22 Indian L. Rep. 6149 (Confederated Salish & Kootenai Tribes Ct.App.1995), involved an executive clemency order amending a criminal sentence by the Confederated Salish & Kootenai Tribes. The tribal judge sued the council, challenging the authority of the tribal council to issue an executive clemency order. The council responded by demanding that the judge be recused from any case involving the tribe as a party and, allegedly, began an investigation of the tribal judge and the court system to seek justification for the removal of judge in retaliation for the filing of the suit. The court there reaffirmed the independence of the tribal judiciary, affirming the judiciary's power to issue an injunction stopping the council from proceeding with those actions. The court did vacate the lower court's injunction, which was exceptionally broad, and remanded for further proceedings.

The second case (or rather, a trilogy of cases), White v. Poarch Band of Creek Indians, were decided more than a decade later. White v. Poarch Band of Creek Indians, No. SC-10-02 (Poarch Band of Creek Indians Tribal S.Ct.2010) (*White I*); White v. Poarch Band of Creek Indians, No. SC-11-01 (Poarch Band of Creek Indians Tribal S.Ct.2011) (*White II*); White v. Poarch Band of Creek Indians, No. SC-12-01 (Poarch Band of Creek Indians Tribal S.Ct.2013) (*White III*). Those cases involved the tribal chair's termination of a tribal judge's contract. The tribal judge was not a lawyer and the tribe had chosen politically to require its judges to be licensed attorneys going forward. The judge sued for wrongful termination and, after several years of litigation, won a large judgment from the tribal court. In the third incarnation of the case, the court concluded that the tribes' sovereign immunity, a creature of tribal statutory and common law, must give way to its constitutional commitment to judicial independence:

> We hold that the Constitution of the Poarch Band of Creek Indians abrogates tribal official immunity from suit where tribal government

action violates the separation of powers between the tribal policy-making branch of government and the tribal judiciary. The Poarch Band Constitution expressly establishes * * * a firm separation of powers between the tribal policymaking branches of government and the tribal court. The Constitution provides that the tribal council has the power to:

> [E]stablish a civil and criminal law enforcement code and judicial system governing the conduct of the Indian residents within the reservation lands of the Poarch Band of Creek Indians by a *separate and independent judicial system whose powers and duties shall not be encroached upon by another branch of tribal government*, except as may be provided for by the Constitution and any amendments thereto[.]

Poarch Band of Creek Indians Tribal Constitution art. IV, § 4(K) (1985) (emphasis added). * * * And, while we have held that tribal sovereign immunity is grounded in the reservation of tribal sovereignty contained in the tribal constitution, see English v. Poarch Band of Creek Indians, No. SC-08-01, at 4–5 (Poarch Band of Creek Indians Tribal S.Ct.2008) (per curiam) ("This immunity from suit derives from the 'inherent and aboriginal sovereignty' that the People of the Poarch Band of Creek Indians acknowledged and reserved in ratifying the tribal constitution.") * * *, Poarch Band immunity from suit is not governed by the

> constitution, but through tribal statute and tribal judge-made common law. * * * The express constitutional protection of judicial independence provided for in article IV, § 4(K) must control over statutory and common law principles, even principles as weighty as tribal sovereign immunity. * * *

White III, slip op. at 4.

Tribal judicial independence is now well protected throughout much of Indian country. The growth of tribal resources and governmental capacity allows tribes to retain professional judges, most of whom are licensed attorneys. Many tribal governments still value non-lawyer tribal judges (always tribal citizens and usually tribal elders) in certain roles, most notably in appellate cases or special cases involving tribal customs such as child welfare or citizenship cases. Judicial removals (or threats of removal) for political reasons are rare in the 21st century.

Removals for cause do happen on occasion. Tribal courts extend generous procedural protections to judges subjected to removal proceedings. In LaRance v. Hopi Tribe, 10 Am. Tribal Law 345 (Hopi App.Ct. 2010), the court held that any removal proceedings must be conducted fairly in an adjudicative process:

> We interpret [Hopi Ordinance 21,] Section 1.5.1 to require an impeachment style adjudicatory hearing before a judge can be removed for a number of compelling reasons. First, judges, and in this case, the Chief Judge of the entire Hopi judicial system, should be

insulated from both executive and legislative interference to be free to make judgments in cases based upon legal principles and facts and not based upon whether he or she might be removed for doing so. Anything less than an adjudicatory process for removal makes it far too easy for the Chairman's/Vice Chairman's Office and/or the Council to tamper with how the judges decide their cases. Second, members of past Hopi Tribal Councils have expressed a commitment to judicial independence in the passage of Hopi Resolutions H–3–81 and H–14–69, and these resolutions have never been rescinded. Third, past Councils have demonstrated that they value and can oversee adjudicatory hearing processes to remove high government officials for serious neglect of duty under Article V, Section 2 of the Hopi Constitution, and have done so in at least four instances. For these reasons, we find that the trial judge below erred in characterizing Section 1.5.1 as requiring anything less than an impeachment hearing with an adjudicatory process.

Id. at 354. See also McKinney v. Business Council of the Shoshone-Paiute Tribes, 20 Indian L.Rep. 6064 ([Duck Valley] Shoshone-Paiute Tribal Ct.1993).

Separation of powers between the political and judicial branches of government runs both ways. In Willis v. Tribal Council, 2001 WL 36210379 (Little River Band of Ottawa Indians Ct.App.2001), the court rejected the power of the trial judge to engage in their own investigation of tribal elected officials during the pendency of a case involving the tribal council. Writing for the court, influential Anishinaabe tribal judge Michael Petoskey wrote:

> Judges should never conduct investigations on their own into any matter pending before them. To do so is to taint their ability to remain objective and to maintain the impartiality of the Court. Judicial institutions are designed to be reactive in nature as opposed to being pro-active. The Judiciary must involve itself only in community concerns and disputes which are appropriately raised before it. It cannot police the community for issues to bring to itself. Likewise, it can not compromise its impartially by conducting its own investigations. The only exception to this hard and fast rule is to allow for an investigation of an ethics charge by the Judicial Commission Chairperson.

Id. at *1. See also Mosier v. Squaxin Island Tribe, 6 NICS App. 162, 165–66 (Squaxin Island Tribal Ct.App.2004) ("[Rules of Conduct for Judges] Section 4.16.050A, entitled 'Independence', states, 'A tribal judge shall not engage in outside activity which would be inconsistent with the Tribal Court's status as an independent government branch. In particular, the judge shall not participate in legislative or administrative activities of the tribal government.' ") (emphasis omitted). Cf. Wells v. Blaine, 21 Indian L.Rep. 6129, 6129 (Northern Plains Intertribal Ct.App.1994) ("This court is reluctant to tamper with official acts of the [Crow Creek Tribal Council members] when they are acting in their status as council members. . . .").

Judicial independence requires that the judiciary and the political branches of tribal government interact to some extent, for example, in tribal court personnel matters. In Tribal Council v. Tribal Court Administrator, 2003 WL 25838644 (Grand Traverse Band of Ottawa and Chippewa Indians Tribal Judiciary 2003), the tribal council sued the tribal court administrator over Indian preference in hiring, insisting that the tribal court follow the tribe's personnel hiring policies. The court and the council reached a memorandum of understanding, mediated by visiting judge Frank Pommersheim, in which the tribal court agreed to follow the tribe's personnel policies in principle.

E. TRIBAL LAW ENFORCEMENT

Tribal nations provide law enforcement to protect tribal sovereignty, ensure public safety, and maintain justice and order within their communities, addressing issues like high rates of violence against Indigenous Peoples. Tribal law enforcement also supports self-governance and allows tribes to enforce their own laws in a culturally competent manner, building trust and working collaboratively with community members to improve public safety.

Tribal law enforcement is one of the most complex areas of American Indian law. As a consequence of both the importance of the law enforcement function and the ravages of colonization, tribal police are heavily scrutinized and regulated. Many tribal nations struggle with hiring, training, and retaining qualified police officers who are also culturally competent to conduct police work in Indian country. Occasionally, tribal police are undertrained, forcing tribal judges to engage in searching inquiries of search warrant applications. E.g., Eastern Band of Cherokee Indians v. Rattler, 5 Cher.Rep. 17, 2006 WL 6499919, at *10 (Cherokee Ct. of the Eastern Band of Cherokee Indians 2006) (addressing issued related to a tribal police officer's admission that he had "no training in how to draft applications for search warrants."). Overall, however, tribal police officers are competent. E.g., Oglala Sioux Tribe v. United States, 674 F.Supp.3d 635, 676 n.43 (D.S.D. 2023) ("Those involved in tribal law enforcement who testified during the February hearing were certainly competent and nothing in this decision should be read as questioning tribal police's competence."). They are, after all, certified by state and/or federal police officer certification entities.

Traditional Indigenous law enforcement looked nothing like modern day tribal law enforcement. At one time, law enforcement functions were performed traditionally by entities such as the *mukwa doodem* (bear clan) of the Anishinaabeg, for example, or ceremonially during certain times of the year, such as the Creek Green Corn Ceremony. Most tribal law enforcement was performed by families rather than a tribal sovereign. Often, Indigenous law enforcers had additional medicinal and healing obligation as well. See generally Kekek Jason Stark, Indian Policing: Agents of Assimilation, 73 Case W. Reserve L.Rev. 683, 685–710 (2023).

The earliest formal tribal police departments were likely the Lighthorse of the southeastern tribal nations such as the Cherokee and Creek Nations. Most other tribal nations did not have a vertical, coercive law enforcement entity until the Department of the Interior formed Courts of Indian Offenses and promulgated Law and Order Codes beginning in the 1880s. Federal officials typically appointed tribal citizens to serve as Indian police. Indian police also typically served as prosecutors. The thinking, of course, was that Indian people would be more receptive to law and order if that regime was enforced by their own people. Even so, Indian police were part and parcel of a federal program to assimilate Indian people into American culture and destroy traditional tribal governmental structures. Indian police gave way to the Bureau of Indian Affairs (BIA) police in the 20th century, performing the same functions.

The advent of the self-determination era of the 1970s allowed tribal nations the option of taking over the law enforcement functions of the BIA through the federal contracting process. At first, most tribes did not take advantage of this authority, discouraged and hamstrung by federal bureaucrats. Congressional appropriations under the self-determination laws have never come close to the amounts needed to patrol Indian country effectively, either in its vast landed reservations or in smaller tribal communities. Potential liability, jail space (and health care for inmates), training, and equipping police are some of the largest expenses any government can assume. Worse, in states where Congress chose to extend state criminal jurisdiction into Indian country under Public Law 280 and similar laws, federal officials unilaterally determined that federal funding of tribal law enforcement was unnecessary. That policy continued until recent years.

The Congressional hearings of the 1960s that led to the enactment of the Indian Civil Rights Act of 1968 were replete with complaints from Indian reservation residents about the inefficiencies and human rights abuses perpetrated by BIA and state police officers. In fact, far more persons complained about local, state, and federal law enforcement than did so about tribal courts, but Congress chose to do nothing to regulate or reform their activities, choosing instead to focus only on tribal courts.

In recent decades, however, more and more tribal nations have chosen to assume the law enforcement function, even with limited federal resources. Federal contracting rules imposed on tribal communities require that tribal police be trained and equipped the same as state and local governments, or the BIA police. Tribes certainly can and do hire tribal citizens as law enforcement officials, but their limited resources and oft-distant locales make it difficult for tribes to retain experienced officers.

The good news is that tribal police are federal government contractors protected by the Federal Tort Claims Act. 28 U.S.C. § 1346(b), § 1402(b), § 2401(b), and §§ 2671–2680. The United States Department of Justice will defend tribal police officers from suits so long as the officer was acting in accordance with a tribal self-determination contract.

That said, tribal courts may still exercise jurisdiction over similar claims against tribal law enforcement officials in tribal courts. E.g., Welch v. Eastern Band of Cherokee Indians, 6 Cher.Rep. 20, 2007 WL 7079613, at *3 (Cherokee Ct. of the Eastern Band of Cherokee Indians 2007) ("The Federal Tort Claims Act does not preclude this Court's exercise of subject matter jurisdiction over these claims.").

All of this means that tribal nations are effectively barred from developing and restoring traditional and culturally appropriate police. Tribal police, funded and regulated through a combination of federal and tribal structures, more than resemble the coercive and often violent character of state and local law enforcement. There are certainly costs to introducing the coercive and violent method of policing prevalent in state and local jurisdictions into Indian country. Cf. Navajo Nation v. Platero, 19 Indian L.Rep. 6049, 6051 (Navajo Nation S.Ct.1991) ("Police officers have a certain trust of the people. When they lose sight of their obligations to serve and protect, the safety of the public is compromised, and the public trust is tarnished. The Navajo public definitely expects its police officers to hold themselves to the highest degree of professionalism.").

Tribal police (or BIA police) are almost always the first responders to reservation crime. Tribal police investigate crime in the same ways as their state and local colleagues, with interrogative questioning and interventionist stops of reservation residents. Tribal police are frequent defendants in civil rights suits resulting from policing violence and other abuses.

E.g., D'Ambra v. Maikshilo, 12 Am. Tribal Law 207, 208 (Mohegan Gaming Disputes Ct.2011) (assessing complaints against tribal police for "abusive treatment"); Rusk v. Fallon Paiute-Shoshone Tribes, 1998 WL 35297248 (Nev. Inter-Tribal Ct.App.1998) (allowing complaint against tribal police for various torts to proceed).

Tribal law enforcement relations with state and local governments have been fraught, to say the least. Indian country criminal jurisdiction is intensely complicated, rooted in territorial, personal, and subject matter jurisdiction that often makes law enforcement too complicated to serve as an effective deterrent or response to crime. See generally Indian Law and Order Commission, A Roadmap for Making Native America Safer 1–32 (Nov. 2013) (detailing jurisdictional "chaos" in Indian country). Cooperation between jurisdictions is critical to blurring the jurisdictional lines for the purpose of making Indian country safer. See generally id. at 99–115 (detailing Indian country criminal law enforcement cross-jurisdictional cooperation). Some state and local jurisdictions either outright refuse to cooperate or use cooperative agreements to control tribal law enforcement.

Federal, state, and local law enforcement and prosecutors long have considered tribal police to be incompetent and inefficient despite tribal police being trained in the same techniques and principles. In many jurisdictions, especially in Public Law 280 and similar states with primary law enforcement jurisdiction authority in Indian country, tribal law enforcement had faced harassment from local law enforcement; in one case, a county sheriff stopped tribal police for displaying light bars, accusing them of the crime of impersonating police officers. Cabazon Band of Mission Indians v. Smith, 388 F.3d 691, 693 (9th Cir.2004) ("Prior to commencement of this suit, the County of Riverside Sheriff's Department repeatedly stopped the Tribe's police officers' vehicles on public highways between the sections of the Tribe's reservation. The Tribe's officers were cited for displaying emergency light bars in violation of the Vehicle Code because the tribal police vehicles were not designated 'authorized emergency vehicles' within the meaning of Vehicle Code section 165.").

In spite of the expense and complexity of Indian country law enforcement, many tribal nations are resolute in developing tribally controlled law enforcement. E.g., Eastern Band of Cherokee Indians v. Torres, 4 Cher.Rep. 9, 2005 WL 6437828, at *4 (Eastern Band of Cherokee Indians S.Ct.2005) ("[T]he Cherokees 'have and exhibit the same interest in the enforcement of the law and in the protection of personal and property rights as the United States citizen resident therein. In some sense they have the higher interest, because they are owners of the soil, and constitute the more fixed and permanent population.' ") (quoting Carter v. United States, 1 Indian Terr. 342, 37 S.W. 204 (Indian Terr. 1896)).

F. RESTORATIVE JUSTICE PRACTICES

Indigenous law enforcement traditions rooted in restorative justice are beginning to reappear in many tribal jurisdictions in the form of peacemaking, circle sentencing, healing to wellness courts, and resiliency courts. On occasion, state and local governments have adopted aspects of these restorative justice mechanisms, where appropriate and effective.

Peacemaking originated in the Navajo Nation justice system. Diné people that attended law school and returned to the Navajo reservation realized quickly that the American justice system was a top-down, violent structure that created conflict and disharmony within Navajo communities. Robert Yazzie, "Life Comes From It": Navajo Justice Concepts, 24 N.M.L.Rev. 175, 177–80 (1994). In response, the Navajo judiciary established a peacemaking system designed to allow the courts to route relevant cases into a non-adversarial process for "talking things out" rather than the winner-takes-all adversarial process. Navajo peacemaking has expanded into other branches of government as well into private circles. E.g., Yazzie v. Catron, 19 Indian L.Rep. 6125, 6127 (Navajo Nation S.Ct.1992) ("Like many land disputes, particularly among family members, it has been both complicated and emotional. It would have been better addressed in a non-adversarial proceeding more consistent with Navajo tradition, such as is available in the Peacemaker Court."); Williams v. Yazzie, 19 Indian L.Rep. 6116, 6117 (Navajo Nation S.Ct.1992) (asserting that a small claims issue not involving money damages, such as a dispute over a cow, should be resolved by the Navajo Peacemaker Courts).

The Navajo judiciary has adopted restorative justice principles in probation revocation cases, as well. In Haungooah v. Greyeyes, 11 Am. Tribal Law 171 (Navajo Nation S.Ct.2013), the court invoked the Navajo principle of *Diné bi beenahaz'áanii* to reverse a trial court revoking probation for an unhoused tribal citizen:

> Petitioner in this case was homeless. A fact of reservation life is that many of our people live in very constrained financial circumstances, relying on their families and extended families for shelter and assistance. Here, petitioner is a non-member Indian whose family, formerly residing in the Kayenta area, entirely left the reservation, leaving him without shelter and support in winter months. We take judicial notice that no alcohol abuse treatment centers are located in the Western Agency area, making services unreachable for those without long-distance resources. The record is clear that Petitioner's desperate homeless situation was known to PPS. Guided by *Diné bi beenahaz'áanii*, which emphasizes restorative justice, the prosecution and PPS here had the discretion and responsibility to find a solution for Petitioner other than seek reinstatement of his original jail sentence. *Diné bi beenahaz'áanii* imposes a duty on our government to provide avenues for restoration. Diné justice "throws no one away." *Diné bi beenahaz'áanii* gives our

> judicial system greater options and responsibilities than strictly applying punishments. In any system, one does not place unreasonable burdens on a defendant. In a restorative justice system, a close eye should be kept on the defendant with an obligation to help defendants obtain services, even beyond the locality if necessary. Such assistance gives a community hope by ensuring rehabilitative services so that offending members can be treated rather than merely punished or expelled. It is a fundamental right of our people to expect that their governmental agencies pursue restorative measures, especially where dire living circumstances are beyond a defendant's control, as in this case.

Id. at 176 (footnote omitted). See also Martine-Alonzo v. Jose, 13 Am. Tribal Law 481, 485 (Navajo Nation S.Ct.2016) ("The New Mexico deferred sentencing system is consistent with the restorative justice principles embodied in *Diné bi beenahaz'áanii.*").

Dozens of other tribal nations have borrowed from Navajo to establish their own peacemaking courts. Many Alaska tribal nations have adopted circle sentencing, with similar principles as peacemaking, in the criminal context as well. One tribal court expressed a legal interest in non-adversarial models of conflict resolution, focusing on avoiding the punishment model of justice in favor of healing. In re I.W., 2018 Nottawaseppi Huron Band Tribal LEXIS 1, at *9 (Nottawaseppi Huron Band of the Potawatomi Tr.Ct.2018) ("The principles involved with the traditional Indigenous approach to conflict resolution may also be utilized in cases where individuals have violated the law to promote the healing of the victim, the defendant, and the community. Although most Tribal Justice Systems are not punishment-focused like the American legal system, accountability of the defendant is a foundational requirement for healing to begin.").

Tribal healing to wellness courts originated in the borrowing of state and local drug court principles. Drug courts used the coercive power of the government to force nonviolent drug offenders into getting clean or face criminal prosecution. A critical feature—and weakness—of these drug courts was the zero tolerance policy, where one positive drug test could lead to significant jail time. Tribal healing to wellness courts largely reject this coercive element in favor of culturally appropriate treatment. *Waabshki-Miigwaan* (white feather), the healing to wellness court of the Little Traverse Bay Bands of Odawa Indians, is a good example. Judges in the *Waabshki-Miigwaan* program assume the role of mentor rather than enforcer.

In recent years, tribal communities have begun to establish resilience or healing-to-wellness courts to modify and perhaps replace family courts. See generally Carrie E. Garrow, Changing Family Courts to Help Heal and Build Resilient Families, 2018 BYU L.Rev. 1277. These courts bring into child welfare proceedings the principles learned from peacemaking and healing to wellness courts as preventative tools designed to stop the break-up of Indian families.

Some state and local governments have adopted aspects of tribal resilience and healing-to-wellness courts in Indian Child Welfare Act cases. Cf. *In re I.W.*, 2018 Nottawaseppi Huron Band Tribal LEXIS 1, at *9 ("The American legal system is realizing the long-term value to all involved, including the community, of these traditional Indigenous principles of striving towards accountability, consensus, and healing in justice systems, with these principles frequently referred to as 'restorative justice.' ").

CHAPTER 4

TRIBAL POLICE POWERS

Tribal police powers are important for protecting public safety, upholding tribal sovereignty, addressing the specific needs of tribal communities, and providing culturally relevant law enforcement within reservations. These powers allow tribes to govern themselves, investigate crimes, and enforce laws like hunting and fishing regulations and community rules, often serving as the primary responders to incidents on tribal lands. Within lands owned and controlled by an Indian tribe and its citizens, a tribal nation possesses plenary power to govern and may exercise police powers to regulate the activities of persons within its jurisdiction. Tribal governmental power also extends to tribal citizens beyond tribal lands and to nonmembers, often depending on consent.

Tribal police powers are governed primarily by tribal constitutions, codes, and common law, but they are also impacted by federal statutes, such as the Indian Civil Rights Act, 25 U.S.C. § 1302(a), and by federal court decisions. "Inherent police powers can neither be abdicated, bargained away and are inalienable." San Xavier Dist. Council of the Tohono O'Odham Nation v. Francisco, 1988 Tohono O'Odham Jud. LEXIS 3, at *4 (Tohono O'Odham Judicial Ct.1988). See also Sells v. Espil, 17 Indian L.Rep. 6102, 6110 (Navajo Nation S.Ct.1990) (defining "police powers").

Tribal police powers are necessary for the protection of tribal citizens and all persons under tribal jurisdiction. As the Cherokee Court of the Eastern Band of Cherokee Indians wrote, "The power of any legitimate sovereign nation to act is necessarily derived from the consent of the governed. Accordingly, one of *the* most important, if not the most important responsibilities of government is the protection of its citizenry and all those living within the confines of its homeland." In re H.B., 16 Am. Tribal Law 42, 46–47 (2019) (emphasis in original). In the words of the appellate court of the Wind River Indian Reservation, "Tribal Court jurisdiction over tort actions is a means of controlling economic activity and work place safety within its jurisdiction." Marathan Oil Co. v. Johnston, 2006 WL 6926419, at *4 (Shoshone and Arapaho Tribal App.Ct.2006).

Though Congress possesses a duty of protection in regard to tribal nations and Indigenous Peoples, the federal judiciary has repeatedly intervened in reservation governance to immunize many nonmembers from tribal authority, significantly limiting tribal powers over nonmembers, at least on paper. In the real world, nonmembers routinely consent to tribal jurisdiction, often leaving only undesirable outliers to fight tribal powers in court. Congress has not broadly legislated to recognize inherent tribal authority over all persons regardless of race. However, Congressional statements of policy do: "The Congress finds and declares that—tribal justice systems are an essential part of tribal government and serves as important forums for ensuring public health and safety and the political integrity of tribal governments." 25 U.S.C. § 3601(5).

A. TRIBAL CITIZENSHIP OR MEMBERSHIP

Tribal nations have power to decide their own citizenship criteria. Restatement of the Law of American Indians § 18. Historically, Indigenous belonging was deeply cultural, rooted in kinship and shared philosophies. Federal colonizers intervened into tribal citizenship matters for many decades until Congress declared the tribal self-determination era in the 1970s. Federal bureaucrats still have outsized influence in tribal citizenship matters but they have little or no authority to do so.

Federal intervention into tribal citizenship matters began in earnest during treaty times. Many Indian treaties required the United States to pay annuities to tribal citizens per capita (and sometimes by blood quantum), which enabled federal bureaucrats to create the first tribal citizenship rolls in the mid to late nineteenth century. Occasionally, when tribal nations would prevail in money damages suits against the United States (often for failure to pay treaty annuities), Congress would require the awards to be paid out per capita as well. Congress and Interior Department officials began enacting federal statutes and rules declaring Indian eligibility for discrete federal governmental services, such as health care, to depend on blood quantum and, later, formal enrollment in an Indian tribe. During the Indian reorganization era, when many tribal constitutions came into existence, federal intervention in tribal membership criteria was often oppressive. E.g., Bryant v. Saginaw Chippewa Tribal Clerk, 32 Indian L.Rep. 6090, 6092 (Saginaw Chippewa Indian Tribe App.Ct.2005) ("In spite of the fact that the Tribe had devised its own text regarding who would be included into the Tribe, Assistant Commissioner Zimmerman insisted on a different characterization of the membership requirements.").

Modern day tribal membership or citizenship is, in the words of Anishinaabe tribal judge Michael Petoskey, "everything":

> Tribal membership for Indian people is more than mere citizenship in an Indian tribe. It is the essence of one's identity, belonging to community, connection to one's heritage and an affirmation of their human being place in this life and world. In short, it is not an overstatement to say that it is everything. In fact, it would be an understatement to say anything less. Tribal membership completes the circle for the member's physical, mental, emotional and spiritual aspects of human life.

Wabsis v. Enrollment Commission, 2006 MI Ottawa Trib. LEXIS 1, at *3–4 (Little River Band of Ottawa Indians Ct.App.2006).

1. TRIBAL ENROLLMENT CRITERIA

Tribal constitutions enacted in accordance with the Indian Reorganization Act of 1934, which required Interior Department approval, 25 U.S.C. § 5123(d), codified stringent tribal citizenship criteria based on ancestry. The federal goal here was to specify and often limit the number of Indian people to whom the United States owed a duty of protection, usually referred as the trust responsibility. Some tribal nations have adopted much more open criteria. Tribal constitutional citizenship criteria might also be traced to lineal descendancy, meaning that any person who could trace their ancestry to a person listed on an appropriate roll or census would be eligible for enrollment. Other persons could be eligible for enrollment if adopted by a tribe through a political process or through marriage.

The watershed United States Supreme Court decision in Santa Clara Pueblo v. Martinez, 436 U.S. 49 (1978), confirmed that tribal nations possess exclusive authority to determine their citizenship criteria, subject only to overriding Congressional enactments. That case arose under the equal protection clause of the Indian Civil Rights Act, 25 U.S.C. § 1302(a)(8). Julia Martinez sued her tribal nation on behalf of her children, who were not eligible for enrollment based on a 1936 tribal ordinance that created a gender-based and discriminatory citizenship rule. The *Martinez* Court held that federal courts did not possess subject matter jurisdiction over actions to enforce ICRA, effectively leaving tribal forums as the exclusive forums for enforcing the law. That the 1936 ordinance derive from Interior Department interventions into tribal governance is important but was not relevant to the Court. After many years of internal political activity, the Pueblo of Santa Clara changed its citizenship criteria to reflect its culture and traditions rather than blood quantum or other colonizer-influenced criteria.

The *Martinez* decision left tribal nations with clearer authority to make their own citizenship decisions, though the federal government still possessed authority to approve initial tribal constitutions, meaning that newly recognized tribal nations still had to negotiate with their colonizer over belonging. For example, federal officials demanded that the Grand Traverse Band of Ottawa and Chippewa Indians, federally acknowledged in 1980 under an administrative process, limit its membership criteria based on blood quantum and geography, threatening to revoke the tribe's acknowledgment if it did not comply:

> The present Constitution of the Grand Traverse Band of Ottawa and Chippewa Indians was adopted on March 29, 1988, by its members, and was approved by the Secretary of Interior. It is undisputed that the Constitution was drafted and amended several times prior to adoption under strict guidelines imposed by the Bureau of Indian Affairs. The Secretary of Interior had authority to approve or disapprove the proposed Constitution under 25 U.S.C. § 476(a)(2) [now § 5123(a)(2)]. Many provisions of the Constitution of the Grand Traverse Band of Ottawa and Chippewa Indians were modified prior to its adoption in order to gain the approval and recognition of the United States government, including the membership provisions of the Constitution. Although it is

> certainly true that the Tribe's Constitution was ultimately adopted and approved by the members of the Grand Traverse Band, this Court cannot ignore the circumstances under which the current Constitution was adopted and the influence the United States government also exerted on its creation.

In re Menefee, 2004 WL 5714978, at *5 (Grand Traverse Band of Ottawa and Chippewa Indians Tribal Ct.2004).

Ancestry, demonstrated either by a blood quantum or lineal descendancy eligibility regime, remains the paradigmatic characteristic of tribal enrollment. E.g., Cutler v. Enrollment Office, 2004 WL 5760774, at *2 (Little Traverse Bay Bands of Odawa Indians Tribal Ct.2004). A half century after the beginning of the tribal self-determination era, many tribal nations are reconsidering blood quantum as the primary means of determining citizenship. For many Indian people, blood quantum is genocidal, designed by federal bureaucrats to slowly eradicate tribal nations through intermarriage. For others, blood quantum is a valid, if difficult, measure of Indianness and belonging. The fact that tribal nations provide services to their citizens (and others) as federal government contractors usually means that tribal nations have little choice but to follow federal and tribal blood quantum requirements. Depending on political winds, tribal nations can ratchet up or down the degree of Indian blood needed for enrollment. E.g., *Cutler*, 2004 WL 5760774, at *2 ("Changing membership requirements from time to time creates the unfortunate reality that some members of individual families might become enrolled members while other members of the same family do not. It hardly seems fair to those ultimately denied membership. For this very humane consideration, membership requirements should not be changing through time."). Interestingly, at least two Ojibwe tribal nations in the western Great Lakes area that retain minimum blood quantum requirements have exercised their sovereign authority to declare that all tribal citizens possess 100 percent Indian blood, rebooting their tribal citizenship criteria for the time being.

2. ENROLLMENT CONTROVERSIES

Disputes over tribal citizenship are legion. Some disputes involve the proofs required to show lineage, either as a function of blood quantum or as descendancy. For many Indian people, the sources of their lineage include personal records or oral histories. Some tribes accept these records and testimonies, but some do not. For many other Indian people, their lineage records are in the possession of the federal government, state agencies, or private historians. Where records are held by the tribal government, enrollment decisions can be made relatively easily, but where outsiders possess those records, matters become more complex. In Hoffman v. Colville Confederated Tribes, 23 Indian L. Rep. 6163 (Colville Confederated Tribes Ct.App.1997), for example, a petitioner attempted to force the tribal enrollment office to boost his blood quantum based on a plethora of state and federal records showing a higher blood quantum for his ancestors than what tribal records showed. The court rejected the showing following a clear and convincing evidence standard, holding that the petitioner could not show that there was evidence underlying the records that backed their statements. The fact that the records contained contradictory evidence was damning to the petitioner's case. In Powless v. Enrollment Committee, 9 Am. Tribal Law 147 (Ho-Chunk Nation Trial Ct.2010), another case involving the facts of an enrollment petition, the court vacated the enrollment committee's reliance on a DNA test to reject an enrollment petition, reasoning that the committee must demonstrate the scientific reliability of the test before relying upon it.

Tribal nations also tend to follow a rule preferred by the federal colonizer, the prohibition of dual enrollment in more than one tribe. In Cooke v. Yurok Tribe, 2005 WL 6458622, *2 (Yurok Tribal Ct.App. 2005), the court enforced a provision in the tribal constitution that barred enrollment to anyone otherwise eligible if (1) they had ancestors (living or dead) enrolled in another tribe and (2) they had no parent enrolled at Yurok. See also DeVerney v. Grand Traverse Band of Ottawa and Chippewa Indians, 2001 WL 36194134 (Grand Traverse Band of Ottawa and Chippewa Indians App.Ct.2001) (affirming decision of enrollment office that tribal citizens were erroneously enrolled at the time they were enrolled with another tribe).

Tribal nations may establish or vest any entity they choose to administer and/or enforce enrollment matters. Many tribes vest the power in a tribal agency, such as an enrollment committee, commission, or department. Other tribes vest the power with the tribal council or a mixture of tribal entities and branches of government. The Mohegan Tribe vests much of the power with its Council of Elders. See Mohegan Tribe v. Mohegan Tribal Court, 8 Am. Tribal Law 213 (Council of Elders of the Mohegan Tribe):

> The [Council of Elders, or] COE is composed of Tribal members aged 55 and older directly elected by the Tribal membership to carry out judicial functions, certain legislative functions, and certain executive functions in regard to their areas of cultural oversight. The COE carries out these functions in accordance with Mohegan custom and tradition and does not view any of the functions as delegable, from initial enactment of the Enrollment and Membership Ordinances to rendering a decision as to the constitutionality of any aspect of the process. In the final analysis, the COE is accountable to the Tribal membership and the Tribal membership is accountable to the COE. This civil system for adjudicating alleged misconduct within the Tribe is a manner consistent with Mohegan custom and tradition is the appropriate tribal forum for adjudicating the sort of due process claims raised in the instant case.

Id. at 222. Some tribes vest exclusive jurisdiction to decide enrollment matters in the tribal council, prohibiting judicial review. E.g., Paul v. Southern Ute Indian Tribe, 24 Indian L.Rep. 6038 (Southwest Intertribal Ct.App. 1997).

One tribe modified its enrollment criteria to allow more persons to enroll, then reversed course six months later before the petitioners had completed their enrollment. In Shoshone Business Council v. Skillings, 20 Indian L.Rep. 6001 (Shoshone & Arapaho Tribal Ct.App.1992), the court confirmed that those individuals had a right to be enrolled. The dispute involved the power of the tribal general council (a body composed of all voting citizens) and the power of the tribal business council (the tribal legislature). The tribe did not have a written constitution, but tribal law had established the general council as the "supreme governing body" of the tribe, known as the Eastern Shoshone Tribe of the Wind River Reservation. Id. at 6002. The next year, the court held the business council in criminal contempt for failure to comply with the order. Shoshone Business Council v. Skillings, 21 Indian L.Rep. 6050 (Shoshone & Arapaho Tribal Ct.App. 1992). Some of the petitioners sought a federal court order requiring the Secretary of the Interior to take action to complete the enrollment process, but the suit failed. Ordinance 59 Assn. v. United States Dept. of the Interior Secretary, 163 F.3d 1150 (10th Cir.1998).

3. DISENROLLMENT AND ENROLLMENT MORATORIA

Several tribal nations have acted to limit enrollment as well, either through disenrollment actions or placing moratoria on enrollment decisions. Few of these tribes have established court systems that would allow judicial review of disenrollment actions. The Saginaw Chippewa Indian Tribe, however, has adjudicated many disenrollment actions. In Snowden v. Saginaw Chippewa Indian Tribe, 32 Indian L.Rep. 6047 (Saginaw Chippewa Indian Tribe Ct.App.2005), the court rejected the authority of the tribal council to disenroll members where the government had claimed inherent authority independent of the text of the tribal constitution:

> No, the Tribe may not disenroll people for whatever "good" reasons it might identify. No, the Constitution does not (and cannot) condone any constitutional failure of justice that would potentially endorse (constitutional) fraud and mistake in obtaining membership. Beyond such quite limited constitutional authority to disenroll on grounds of fraud or mistake, there are no other implied grounds for disenrollment.

Id. at 6050. Later, after the council adopted a statute authorizing disenrollment actions, the tribe's courts allowed the tribe to proceed. E.g., Alberts v. Saginaw Chippewa Indian Tribe of Michigan, No. 13-CA-1058 (Saginaw Chippewa Indian Tribe of Michigan App. Ct.2015); Kequom v. Atwell, No. 12-CA-1051 (Saginaw Chippewa Indian Tribe of Michigan App.

Ct.2013); Graveratte v. Saginaw Chippewa Tribe of Michigan, Nos. 09-CA-1040, 09-CA-1041 (Saginaw Chippewa Indian Tribe of Michigan App.Ct.2010); and Gardner v. Cantu, No. 08-CA-1027 (Saginaw Chippewa Indian Tribe of Michigan App.Ct.2008).

Similarly, the Confederated Tribes of the Grand Ronde Reservation modified the tribe's citizenship criteria to be more restrictive in the early 21st century, leading the tribe to engage in large disenrollment actions. In one of the more compelling cases striking down disenrollment efforts by a tribal nation, the court in Alexander v. Confederated Tribes of the Grand Ronde Reservation, 13 Am. Tribal Law 353 (Confederated Tribes of the Grand Ronde Reservation Ct.App.2008), the court applied the equitable doctrine of laches against the tribe's effort to disenroll members of the tribe after the government changed the enrollment criteria, Noting that the purported disenrollees had been enrolled for nearly three decades, the court concluded:

> The only reasonable conclusion that can be drawn from the facts in this case is that Petitioners have been prejudiced by the 27 year delay, including the faded memories and deaths of relevant witnesses, and a passage of such an amount of time that makes discovering evidence difficult or impossible. Moreover, Petitioners reasonably relied on the Tribe's 27 year lack of action and did change their positions and conditions such that it would be nearly impossible and very injurious to undo, including the impact on such crucial issues as cultural and

> personal identity. Petitioners would also suffer the loss of some well-known benefits of tribal citizenship such as tribal and Indian Health Service medical and dental care, tribal housing, tribal employment opportunities, and per capita distributions of revenues and more.
>
> In light of the undisputed facts regarding the 27 year unreasonable delay in the Tribe bringing this action and the reasonably anticipated prejudice and harm that Petitioners would suffer if the Tribe were allowed to proceed with this disenrollment action, we hold that laches prevents the Tribe and Enrollment Committee/ Board from so proceeding.

Id. at 363.

In later cases, the Grand Ronde courts accepted the argument from the tribe that its actions to remove citizens from the rolls were merely error corrections, not prohibited disenrollments. In Swan v. Confederated Tribes of the Grand Ronde Reservation, 13 Am. Tribal Law 80 (Confederated Tribes of the Grand Ronde Reservation Tribal Ct.2015), the court distinguished between improper disenrollment and mere errors:

> As a general matter, linguistic tension between "an action to correct a prior enrollment error" and "a disenrollment action" theoretically exists. And there may in time be a case before this Court where the facts stretch the linguistic tether of a claimed action to correct a prior enrollment error so far as to snap it from its

> Constitutional moorings. However, the actions below are reasonably viewed as correcting an error of the Petitioners common ancestors being ineligible at the time of enrollment at CTGR, and as such the actions of the relevant Tribal parties are authorized by the Constitution and Tribal Ordinance. Upon similar grounds, the Tribal Ordinance is Constitutional, and the actions of the Tribal actors in relation to the Tribal Ordinance to process Petitioners for proposed disenrollment based on enrollment in error are legally authorized.

Id. at 87. See also Crocker v. Tribal Council, 13 Am. Tribal Law 369 (Confederated Tribes of the Grand Ronde Community Ct.App.2016) (rejecting equitable relief for person enrolled by error).

Error corrections are common reasons to disenroll tribal citizens. For example, in Cholewka v. Tribal Council, No. 2013-16-AP (Grand Traverse Band of Ottawa and Chippewa Indians App.Ct.2014), the tribal council took action to disenroll several tribal members who did not possess the required blood quantum. They had been enrolled in accordance with a special tribal council resolution despite their insufficient blood quantum in the 1990s. After relatives of the newly enrolled members sued for enrollment, claiming they had the same blood quantum and deserved enrollment under an equal protection theory, the tribal council eventually chose to disenroll the citizens enrolled by the council. The disenrollees challenged the action, briefly winning a tribal court of appeals decision that found they had shown enough facts in their favor to justify a trial. Cholewka v. Tribal Council, 8 Am. Tribal Law 174 (Grand Traverse Band of Ottawa and Chippewa Indians App.Ct.2009). But they lost at trial, a decision upheld by the appellate court, which lamented the outcome:

> Disenrollment is a dirty word in Indian country, and rightfully so. In too many instances of disenrollment that observers read about in the news it is tribes and tribal leaders playing politics and exhibiting greed and malice toward one another. This is not one of those stories. This is a story of people in power trying to govern in the best way they knew how running up against the realities of tribal constitutional law, federal Indian law, and the Bureau of Indian Affairs. It is hard to find a bad guy in all of this mess, and we firmly believe that all the parties and affected individuals acted in accordance with *Mino-Bimaadziwin*. We are, after all, all Anishinaabe. Even so, the law compels the outcome we reach today. There are no winners here.

Cholewka v. Tribal Council, No. 2013-16-AP, slip op. at 2 (Grand Traverse Band of Ottawa and Chippewa Indians App.Ct.2014).

In Stoplman v. St. Croix Chippewa Indians of Wisconsin Tribal Council, Nos. 16-CV-500, 501, 502, 504, and 504 (St. Croix Tribal Ct.2016), the court halted the disenrollment of several tribal citizens who had been enrolled by tribal council action. Tribal law required a unanimous vote from the council to enroll applicants. Six months after the vote, two council members claimed to not have voted in favor, leading the tribe to seek disenrollment more months later. Applying principles of equity, the court applied the deadline for appealing denials of membership to the tribal council members seeking review of the approval of the applicants, noting, "[T]he tribe has a right to disenroll individuals who have been erroneously enrolled, but citizens of the St. Croix Chippewa Indians of Wisconsin must be entitled to a sense of security in their tribal membership." Id., slip op. at 5. After an extensive hearing, the tribal court further found that all of the newly enrolled persons had received tribal identification cases, hunting, fishing, and gathering permits, and per capita payments. The court concluded, "The action to vacate the enrollment of the five petitioners is unconscionable and violates the basic tenets of justice and fairness." Id., slip op. at 18. The court also concluded that the preponderance of the evidence supported the conclusion that the persons targeted for disenrollment actually possessed the requisite blood quantum needed for enrollment. The court noted in dicta that it appeared that the enrollment office acted in a slipshod manner in these cases for "political reasons." Id., slip op. at 14.

Another tribe chose to engage in a mass disenrollment by providing the barest of procedural protections to those targeted. In Roberts v. Kelly, 12 NICS App. 33 (Nooksack Tribal Ct.App.2014), the tribe established new rules shortening the period of time a potential disenrollee has to prepare for a hearing if the disenrollee is served personally, denying access to counsel, and other procedures to which the potential disenrollees objected. The court struck those provisions down as violative of due process rights. Id. at 41 (holding that "prohibiting a potential disenrollee from being represented at the proceeding violates due process and that allowing representation will not unduly burden the Tribe" and stating "[t]here is simply no Tribal interest served by granting the Council the discretion to decide to provide a person less than 21 days notice based on its belief the person has sufficient time to arrange a telephonic appearance, particularly when there is no mechanism for a person to challenge that belief").

One tribe chose to reboot its citizenship by amending its constitution to deny eligibility to any person born before 2019, but protecting any currently enrolled citizen from disenrollment. In Wright v. Nottawaseppi Huron Band of the Potawatomi, 2022 Nottawaseppi Huron Band Supreme LEXIS 1 (Nottawaseppi Huron Band of the Potawatomi S.Ct.2022), the court allowed a suit brought by enrollment petitioners just before the constitutional amendment went into effect and remanded the case. The court lamented how the colonizer's practices and policies had impacted modern Bodewadmi citizenship decisions:

> Bodéwadmi people understand that *Mno Bmadzewen* begins with kinship. "For the Anishinaabe, the idea of kinship relations is contained in the concept indinawemaaganidog. This concept is defined as all my relations." [Kekek Jason Stark, Anishinaabe Inakonigewin:

Principles for the Intergenerational Preservation of Mino-Bimaadiziwin, 82 Mont. L. Rev. 293, 319 (2021)] (citations omitted). "Anishnaabe *inawendiwin* is a way of relating to spirit and to one another that honors the interconnectedness of all our relations—*kina enwemgik.*" Nicholas J. Reo, *Inawendiwin* and Relational Accountability in Anishnaabeg Studies: The Crux of the Biscuit, 39(1) J. Ethnobiology 65, 68 (2019). *Ndénwemagnek* is a Bodéwadmi concept that is defined as "all my relations." *Ggaténmamen Gdankobthegnanek* is a Bodéwadmi concept that is defined as "we are honoring our ancestors." Anishinaabe connectedness is instilled at childhood, where they "learn governance, power, decision making and our political cultures" as channeled through their observations as children. Leanne Simpson, Dancing on Our Turtle's Back: Stories of Nishnaabeg Re-Creation, Resurgence and a New Emergence 122 (2011). "The value of social harmony was instilled in an individual from birth. . . ." Donald Joseph Auger, The Northern Ojibwe and Their Family Law 118 (2001) (unpublished dissertation, Osgoode Hall Law School).

In significant ways, colonization complicates modern American tribal membership and citizenship questions. At one time, Anishinaabe belonging was rooted in the *doodem* tradition. Heidi Bohaker, Doodem and Council Fire: Anishinaabe Governance through Alliance 57 (2020); [Lawrence W. Gross, *Bimaadiziwin*, or

> the "Good Life," as a Unifying Concept of Anishinaabe Religion, 26:1 Am. Indian Culture & Research J. 15, 20 (2002)]. Now, the membership criteria of the Nottawaseppi Huron Band of the Potawatomi originates with the Taggart Roll of 1904, which was created to establish a list of Bodéwadmi persons eligible to receive a judgment award arising from a lawsuit filed under the leadership of Phineas Pamptopee. See Bureau of Indian Affairs, Proposed Finding for Federal Acknowledgment of Huron Potawatomi, Inc., 60 Fed.Reg. 28,426, 28,427 (May 31, 1995) (referencing the "1904 Taggart Roll, compiled by the Bureau of Indian Affairs in connection with the issuance of Potawatomi annuity payments under Federal treaties"). The clan tradition is no longer explicitly a part of the NHBP tribal membership criteria. It is axiomatic and tragic that any list of Bodéwadmi persons is likely to exclude at least some biological and clan relatives. It is especially difficult given that the NHBP is dedicated to *Mno Bmadzewen* and *Ndénwemagnek*.

Id. at *6–9 (footnote omitted).

Rarely, a tribal nation might amend its enrollment criteria, potentially affecting the rights of petitioners for enrollment whose petitions had not yet been processed. For example, the *Wright* court remanded to the trial for a determination of the impact of a constitutional amendment. In Ballini v. Confederated Tribes of the Grand Ronde

Community, 4 Am. Tribal Law 107 (Confederated Tribes of the Grand Ronde Community Ct. App. 2003), the court held that it could "be unfair to change the rules that apply to those applicants who submitted their applications before the effective date of the new amendment." Id. at 111. See also Twyon v. Confederated Tribes of the Grand Ronde Community, 30 Indian L.Rep. 6053, 6054 (Confederated Tribes of the Grand Ronde Community Tribal Ct.2001) ("The general rule is that, absent some affirmative evidence of a contrary intent, a change in the law or a new law is presumed to operate prospectively only."). Ultimately, however, the *Ballini* court held that the pre-amendment applicants had no vested interest in tribal enrollment and rejected their claims. *Ballini*, 4 Am. Tribal Law at 120–21.

In the case of the tribal nations whose citizens' ancestors engaged in slavery during the 18th and 19th centuries, most notably the Five Tribes of Oklahoma, tribal citizenship is not necessarily tied to Indian blood. In the post-Civil War treaties between the United States and the Five Tribes, the tribes agreed to allow the so-called "Freedmen" and their descendants to enjoy tribal citizenship. However, many tribal leaders and citizens opposed citizenship of the Freedmen descendants then and now on grounds not worth discussing here. Litigation over the citizenship rights of the Freedmen descendants has raged for the last half century as the Five Tribes frequently (but not always) fight to keep the Freedmen descendants off their rolls. E.g., Effect of Cherokee Nation v. Nash, 16 Am. Tribal Law 268

(Cherokee Nation S.Ct.2021) (recognizing the impact of the federal court decision, Cherokee Nation v. Nash, 267 F.Supp.3d 86 (D.D.C.2017), acknowledging the citizenship rights of the Cherokee Freedmen); Citizenship Board v. Grayson, 2025 Muscogee Creek Nation Supreme LEXIS 3 (Muscogee (Creek) Nation S.Ct.2025) (recognizing the citizenship rights of the Creek Freedmen descendants). See also Seminole Nation of Oklahoma v. Norton, 206 F.R.D. 1 (D.D.C. 2001) (refusing to validate tribal election excluding the Seminole Freedmen descendants from voting); Seminole Nation of Oklahoma v. Norton, 223 F. Supp. 2d 122 (D.D.C. 2002) (same).

Disputes over tribal enrollment are directly tied to the colonizer's coercive influence over tribal nations going back a century and more, but they are also tied to the reality that tribal nations act as federal government contractors. As federal contractors, tribal nations are obligated to spend federal money in accordance with federal prerogatives. The federal government has made clear that it recognizes a duty of protection to members and citizens of federally recognized tribal nations. For the most part, the United States defers to tribal citizenship criteria, allowing some tribes to use restrictive blood quantum rules keep their numbers in the low hundreds or thousands, or to employ lineal descendancy rules that allow for population growth to tens or hundreds of thousands. But above all, with a few exceptions, the colonizer insists that the beneficiaries of the federal-tribal relationship possess some degree of Indian blood. The sad part of that story is that many tribal nations have internalized racial-based membership and citizenship rules into local politics, making reform especially difficult.

B. JURISDICTION OVER NONMEMBERS

A critical consequence of federal colonization and assimilation efforts was the introduction of many thousands of nonmembers into Indian country. Nonmembers own much of the land within Indian country. They work and engage in commercial activities in Indian country. And they commit crimes in Indian country. This section surveys the history and legal groundwork for tribal regulation of nonmember activity.

Prior to American governmental intervention into tribal governance, tribal nations required outsiders to earn access into their political and economic affairs and activities. See generally Matthew L.M. Fletcher and Leah Jurss, Tribal Jurisdiction—A Historical Bargain, 76 Md.L.Rev. 593 (2017). From the earliest days of the American republic, the goal of the United States was to acquire the lands west of the original 13 states from Indigenous peoples. International customary law gave colonizing nations two mechanisms to dispossess Indigenous peoples of their lands and resources, conquest or purchase. E.g., Johnson v. McIntosh, 21 U.S. 543 (1823). In almost every circumstance, even where military conflict occurred, the United States chose commerce. Early American leaders enabled Indian traders to infiltrate

Indian country, creating enormous disruption within tribal nations. As colonization and assimilation progressed, more and more nonmembers entered tribal homelands. Perhaps the most impactful federal step was allotment, whereby Congress enabled and encouraged nonmembers to settle within Indian country by confiscating Indian reservation lands and distributing them to non-Indians.

By the advent of the tribal self-determination era, Congress had undermined the stability of many Indian reservation boundaries, leaving newly enabled tribal governments overwhelmed by nonmember land holdings and activities. Even as Congress and the Department of the Interior haltingly supported tribal governments, nonmembers appealed to the federal judiciary for the right to be free from tribal regulation. A watershed decision early in the self-determination era from the United States Supreme Court, Montana v. United States, 450 U.S. 544 (1981), all but granted nonmembers immunity from tribal governmental powers for decades.

Montana involved the attempted regulation of fishing activities within the Crow Nation's reservation. Nonmembers sought to fish free of regulation on nonmember-owned lands within the reservation, refusing to purchase tribal fishing licenses. The State of Montana intervened as nonmembers faced prosecution by the United States for poaching in Indian country, leading to a high-stakes treaty rights suit over whether the tribe retained ownership interest in the Little Big Horn

River, which ran through the reservation. Based in part on ahistorical testimony adopted as fact by an ethnocentric federal district court judge that Crow Nation citizens did not eat fish, the United States Supreme Court held that the tribe did not own the river. The Court crafted a common law-style rule that tribes do not possess the power to regulate nonmember activities on nonmember-owned land within reservation boundaries absent two exceptions, (1) consent of the nonmember or (2) substantial impact on the tribe's political integrity, economic security, or health and welfare of the tribe and its citizens. *Montana*, 450 U.S. at 560–61. One tribal court criticized *Montana*, arguing, "Following the logic in the [*Montana*] case, one would have to conclude that, among other things, Indians must hunt only with bows and arrows and live only in tipis; that we must travel on foot, canoe or horse and forego the questionable pleasures of television, radio and other modern conveniences. Of course these are preposterous notions; Indians live in the present." Miller v. Crow Creek Sioux Tribe, 12 Indian L.Rep. 6008, 6009 (Northern Plains Intertribal Ct.App. 1984). Another tribal court noted that *Montana* "departs—without constitutional or congressional authorization—from the previous 150 years of federal Indian law which presumed tribal authority within Indian Country unless expressly limited by Congress." Grand Portage Band of Chippewa v. Melby, 28 Indian L.Rep. 6156, 6157 n.13 (Grand Portage Band of Chippewa Indians Tribal Ct.App. 2000).

A few years after *Montana*, the United States Supreme Court held that nonmembers challenging tribal jurisdiction must exhaust their remedies in tribal court first. National Farmers Union Ins. Cos. v. Crow Tribe of Indians, 471 U.S. 545 (1985). See also Iowa Mutual Ins. Co. v. LaPlante, 480 U.S. 9 (1987) (requiring appellate court exhaustion as well); Sage v. Lodge Grass School District No. 27, 13 Indian L.Rep. 6035 (Crow Ct.App.1986) (confirming tribal jurisdiction over school district in postscript to *National Farmers Union*). The Court held that nonmembers were beneficiaries of a federal court cause of action to bring suit to challenge the powers and jurisdiction of tribal governments and tribal courts, but that these federal court challenges were not direct appeals from tribal court judgments. Consequently, relatively few cases originating in tribal jurisdictions lead to federal judicial review of a tribe's jurisdiction. Most of these cases are resolved in tribal courts, often favoring nonmembers on the merits. E.g., Qwest Corp. v. Bailey, 36 Indian L.Rep. 6020 (Nez Perce Tribal Ct.App.2008) (dismissing suit against nonmember utility company, following *Montana* analysis).

Occasionally however, a case ranges over *four* adjudicative tribunals, as in the case of First Specialty Insurance Corporation v. Confederated Tribes of the Grand Ronde Reservation, 16 Am. Tribal Law 390 (Confederated Tribes of Grand Ronde Community Tribal Ct.App.2006). There, the tribe terminated an investment consulting contract with a nonmember-owned business and brought suit in an Oregon state court for breach. Since the contract called for the parties to resolve disputes with arbitration, the state court dismissed the action, forcing arbitration. The nonmember company prevailed before the arbitrator, who awarded attorney fees to the prevailing party. The tribe then brought suit in tribal court to foreclose the attorney fee award, arguing that it was immune from the enforcement of the arbitration award. In the tribal court action, the nonmember company asserted that federal law prohibited tribal court jurisdiction over the matter. After the tribal appellate court confirmed jurisdiction and immunized the tribe from the attorney fee award, id. at 402 ("The parties have not cited any provision in the tribal or federal constitutions or laws that prevent us from exercising subject matter jurisdiction over the 1992 Agreement, and we are aware of none"), the nonmember brought suit in federal court to challenge the tribal court's jurisdiction. There, the tribe prevailed again. First Specialty Ins. Corp. v. Confederated Tribes of Grand Ronde Community of Oregon, 2007 WL 3283699 (D.Or.2007).

1. COMMERCIAL RELATIONSHIPS

Despite federal judicial rules governing the scope of tribal jurisdiction over nonmembers, tribal governments and judiciaries handle and conclude the vast majority of these cases, most of which arise under consensual commercial relationships. The large majority of nonmembers living in or conducting activities on Indian reservations consent to tribal jurisdiction; most nonmembers are employees or business partners and patrons, or even live on tribal properties under a formal lease. E.g., Foster v. Flyingman, 11 Okla. Trib. 727, 2009 WL 10269896 (Cheyenne and Arapaho S.Ct.2009) (assuming jurisdiction over a dispute between a nonmember contractor and the tribe); Ho-Chunk Nation, Business Department v. Indiana Recycling & Renewable Fuels, LLC, 14 Am. Tribal Law 361 (Ho-Chunk Nation Trial Ct.2011) (assuming jurisdiction over settlement agreement between tribe and nonmember business); Lopez v. Benecke, 28 Indian L.Rep. 6178 (Pueblo of Pojoaque Tribal Ct.2001) (assuming jurisdiction over a nonmember mobile home tenant renting tribal trust property).

Montana, through its progeny, is an important federal judicial decision affecting tribal justice systems, but on its face governs only federal and state courts. Tribal judges have, from the moment of its announcement, attempted to understand it and (to extent necessary under tribal law) faithfully employ it. Consider, for example, Keith v. Allread, 10 Indian L.Rep. 6003 (Navajo Nation Chinle Dist.Ct.1981). There, the court asserted jurisdiction over a nonmember's objections to a civil suit alleging negligence resulting in damage to a tribal citizen's personal property. The nonmember's defense was that a tribal court cannot assert jurisdiction over the nonmember because of his race, essentially claiming a race-based immunity to tribal court jurisdiction. The court calmly responded by pointing to *Montana*, holding, "There is no substantive right under federal law not to be sued in tribal court, at least not after the clear pronouncement of the United States Supreme Court in *Montana* . . . ." Id. at 6004. Since that moment, tribal courts and tribal regulatory bodies throughout the country have asserted jurisdiction over many thousands of nonmembers (almost all of whom have consented to tribal jurisdiction in some form), though if one reads through the federal court reporters, one might begin to believe that these cases are the height of polemic and debate in national Indian affairs.

The few cases that do populate the federal courts often involve outliers, typically callous lawbreakers attempting to flout governmental regulation, *any* governmental regulation. Examples include sexual predators, Dollar General Corp. v. Mississippi Band of Choctaw Indians, 579 U.S. 545 (2016), aff'g by equally divided court, 746 F.3d 167 (5th Cir.2014); racist bankers, Plains Commerce Bank v. Long Family Land and Cattle Co., 554 U.S. 316 (2008); and child endangering drunk drivers, United States v. Cooley, 593 U.S. 345 (2021).

The *Plains Commerce Bank* case is worth exploring further. There, the Supreme Court held 5–4 that the tribal court did not possess jurisdiction over a tribal member-owned company's contract and tort claims against a nonmember-owned bank for actions arising on nonmember-owned land within the Cheyenne River Sioux Tribe's reservation. Whittled down to its essence, the Court held that a tribal court cannot assume jurisdiction over a tort claim rooted in unwritten tribal custom and tradition against a nonmember that had no knowledge or understanding of such a claim. Despite winning at the Supreme Court, the nonmember bank did not really prevail at all. The tribal appellate court, in an opinion from Justice Frank Pommersheim, had explained years earlier that the tribal common law claim was merely one of several separate and independent causes of action rooted in state and federal law. The nonmember bank appealed only the tribal common law cause of action, but no other, "presumably foreclose[ing] any federal appeal under the exhaustion doctrine of any other issue involved in this case save the" tribal common law claim. Bank of Hoven [Plains Commerce Bank] v. Long Family Land and Cattle Co., 32 Indian L.Rep. 6001, 6002 (Cheyenne River Sioux Tribal Ct.App.2004). Judge Pommersheim was correct, it appears, because ultimately the parties reached agreement years later in a confidential settlement that would not have been necessary if the *Plains Commerce* Court had properly understood its role or the law. Much like the nonmember in *Keith v. Allread*, the nonmember bank claimed immunity from tribal jurisdiction from jurisdiction based on the race of the bank's ownership. *See Bank of Hoven*, 32 Indian L. Rep. at 6004, 6006 (noting that the bank's counsel had asserted a "race card" and that the bank's counsel made "jarring and inappropriate" and "most offensive and unprofessional" comments during oral argument).

Most tribal court jurisdiction cases are not so dramatic. Nonmembers challenging tribal adjudicatory authority typically challenge the tribal court's personal jurisdiction over them. For example, in Cabazon Band of Mission Indians v. Lexington Insurance Co., No. CBMI 2020-0103 (Cabazon

Reservation Ct.App.2021), the tribe sued its insurance company over COVID-related business losses, where the insurance company base was in a different state. The company challenged the court's personal jurisdiction under the Indian Civil Rights Act's due process clause, 25 U.S.C. § 1302(a)(8), and the tribe's inherent jurisdiction under *Montana*. Normally, tribal courts are not obligated to follow federal precedents on these questions, but the tribal choice of law statute provided that federal law governed questions of "extraterritorial jurisdiction." Cabazon Code § 9–102(a) ("The Reservation Court shall also exercise such extraterritorial jurisdiction *as may be authorized under federal law.*") (emphasis added). On the personal jurisdiction matter, the court applied and interpreted the tribe's long-arm statute in light of federal precedents like International Shoe Co. v. Washington, 326 U.S. 310 (1945), and its modern progeny. The insurance company argued that its agents had never set foot on the Cabazon Reservation and that the insurance policy, which had been brokered by a third party, was not executed on the reservation. The court concluded that since the property at issue was located on the reservation, which the insurer knew was the case, that the court's assertion of personal jurisdiction was fundamentally fair under due process principles. On the *Montana* issue, the court concluded that Lexington had expressly consented to tribal jurisdiction by agreeing to insure the tribe's reservation property. The insurance company appealed the outcome to federal court after exhausting its tribal court remedies under *National Farmers Union*, but the Ninth Circuit confirmed tribal court jurisdiction over the matter. Lexington Ins. Co. v. Mueller, 2024 WL 5001815 (9th Cir.2024) (unreported), cert. denied, 145 S.Ct. 2703 (2025). For similar cases, see Port Gamble S'Klallam Tribe v. Lexington Ins. Co., 19 NICS App. 12 (Port Gamble S'Klallam Tribal Ct.App.2021); Suquamish Indian Tribe v. Lexington Ins. Co., No. 200601-C (Suquamish Tribal Ct.App.2021). See also Lexington Ins. Co. v. Smith, 94 F.4th 870 (9th Cir.2024) (confirming the Suquamish tribal court's jurisdiction over the insurance company), cert. denied, 145 S.Ct. 2701 (2025). Other tribal courts have similarly found jurisdiction over nonmember insurance companies insuring on-reservation property and activities. E.g., McDonald v. Harlan Racine & Guaranty National Ins. Co., 15 Indian L.Rep. 6003 (Confederated Salish & Kootenai Tribal Ct.1988) (automobile accident claim).

The Navajo Nation has been especially active in asserting jurisdiction over nonmembers. The tribe's key treaty, the 1868 Treaty of Fort Sumner, also known as the "old law," contains strong language affirming the power of the tribe to regulate nonmember activity. Sells v. Espil, 17 Indian L.Rep. 6102, 6106–09 (Navajo Nation S.Ct.1990). The Navajo reservation is the size of Ireland and the vast majority of people residing and working within the reservation are tribal citizens and nonmember Indians. Additionally, the Nation was the key beneficiary of the first modern United States Supreme Court decision affirming tribal court jurisdiction, Williams v. Lee, 358 U.S. 217 (1959), so the assertion of jurisdiction is reasonable. The

Navajo tribal courts have asserted jurisdiction over multinational corporations in products liability cases, e.g., Fort Motor Co. v. Kayenta Dist. Ct., 7 Am. Tribal Law 652 (Navajo Nation S.Ct.2008); Nelson v. Pfizer, Inc., 4 Am. Tribal Law 680 (Navajo Nation S.Ct.2003); companies engaged in business on Navajo roads, e.g., EXC, Inc. v. Kayenta Dist. Court, 9 Am. Tribal Law 176 (Navajo Nation S.Ct.2010); trading posts and hotels conducting business on nonmember-owned fee lands within the reservation boundaries, e.g., In re Atkinson Trading Co., Inc., 1 Am. Tribal Law 451 (Navajo Nation S.Ct.1997); brokerage contracts with a tribal citizen contract partner, *Sells*, 17 Indian L.Rep. 6102; and religious entities accused of sexual abuse of Navajo children, e.g., Doe BF v. Diocese of Gallup, 10 Am. Tribal Law 72 (Navajo Nation S.Ct.2010). The tribal courts exercise discretion in assuming jurisdiction over suits between nonmembers where a federal court possesses concurrent jurisdiction. E.g., PacifiCorp v. Mobil Oil Corp., 4 Am. Tribal Law 694 (Navajo Nation S.Ct.2003). In most of these cases, the Nation itself is not a party, though if the nonmember seek federal judicial review of the tribal court's jurisdiction, the tribe participates in order to protect its sovereignty. Federal court decisions have only inconsistently confirmed the jurisdiction of the Navajo courts in these cases, however. E.g., Atkinson Trading Co., Inc. v. Shirley, 532 U.S. 645 (2001) (rejecting jurisdiction in *Atkinson Trading*, 1 Am. Tribal Law 451); Jensen v. EXC, Inc. (9th Cir.2024) (rejecting tribal jurisdiction in *EXC*, 9 Am. Tribal Law 176).

Other tribal courts have found jurisdiction over nonmember commercial suits where the nonmembers have consented to tribal jurisdiction, even impliedly, under a personal jurisdiction-type analysis. In Guggolz v. Farmer's Union Oil Co., 2007 WL 7274883 (Standing Rock Sioux Tribal Ct.2007), the court assumed jurisdiction over a slip-and-fall action where "the defendant was on the Reservation to deal with Indians and non-Indians alike who came to deal with it. The parking lot was clearly part and parcel, there to facilitate those dealings." Id. at *2. See also Confederated Tribes of the Colville Reservation v. Stock West, Inc., 14 Indian L.Rep. 6025, 6027–28 (Colville Confederated Tribes Tribal Ct.1987) (asserting jurisdiction over nonmembers who consented to tribal jurisdiction in contract with tribes); Marathon Oil Co. v. Johnston, 2006 WL 6926419, at *4 (Shoshone and Arapaho App.Ct.2006) ("Tribal law authorizes the Tribal Court through the Shoshone and Arapaho Law and Order Code to hear tort actions arising out of an injury on tribal lands pursuant to the Tribe's inherent sovereign authority to control economic activity with its land."). In Clark v. Richter, 2 Am. Tribal Law 179 (Fort Peck Ct.App. 2000), the court assumed jurisdiction over a medical malpractice action where "a member of the Fort Peck Tribes, su[ed] a non-Indian doctor[ ] for damages resulting from an alleged injury which took place on the grounds of the Poplar Community Hospital, Poplar, MT., and continued at another medical facility off the reservation." Id. at 187.

Tort claims are often more difficult to analyze. Nonmember tortfeasors that are mere visitors to tribal lands likely have not consented in writing to tribal jurisdiction, complicating the personal jurisdiction analysis. Land ownership can be a useful proxy for determining jurisdiction, though it is hardly dispositive. Vehicular accidents, for example, are complicated by the United States Supreme Court's decision in Strate v. A-1 Contractors, Inc., 520 U.S. 438 (1997), that held tribal courts do not have jurisdiction over car accidents occurring on reservation roads over which a state possesses an easement to manage and patrol the highway. Prior to *Strate*, it was common for tribal courts to assume jurisdiction over tort claims arising on reservation land against nonmembers. E.g., Sage v. Lodge Grass School District, 10 Indian L.Rep. 6019 (Crow Tribal Ct.1982), aff'd, Sage v. Lodge Grass School District No. 27, 13 Indian L.Rep. 6035 (Crow Ct.App.1986) (same case following decision in *National Farmers Union*, confirming tribal jurisdiction over school district); Sisseton Wahpeton Sioux Tribe v. Seaboy, 16 Indian L.Rep. 6118 (Northern Plains Intertribal Ct.App.1989) (affirming jurisdiction over a criminal drunk driving and child endangerment matter arising on a Bureau of Indian Affairs road); Sisseton Wahpeton Sioux Tribe v. Feather, 15 Indian L.Rep. 6027 (Northern Plains Intertribal Ct.App.1988) (same); Fredericks v. Continental Western Ins. Co., 20 Indian L.Rep. 6009 (Northern Plains Intertribal Ct.App.1992), abrogated by *Strate*.

A nonmember can subject themselves to tribal jurisdiction to suit by invoking tribal jurisdiction as a plaintiff. In Smith v. Salish Kootenai College, 4 Am. Tribal Law 90 (Confederated Salish and Kootenai

Tribes Ct.App.2003), the court confirmed jurisdiction over a nonmember Indian who was a student at a tribal college on the reservation who was involved in an auto accident. The court concluded that the nonmember student had consented to tribal jurisdiction both by enrolling in school and by bringing a suit in tribal court:

> Our examination of *Montana*'s "first exception" results in a determination that Appellant Smith has a "consensual relation" with the Tribes within the meaning of that exception. Smith chose to enroll in the college for the purpose of being educated and trained to be a heavy equipment operator and to obtain his commercial driver's license ("CDL"). Thus he voluntarily engaged in a consensual relationship with the SKC, a tribal entity within the exterior boundaries of the Flathead Reservation. Appellant Smith acknowledges that he, "was driving the truck as part of his educational requirements as a student at Salish-Kootenai College." * * * All three occupants of the dump truck were enrolled at SKC and studying to become heavy equipment operators. * * * As part of Appellant Smith's requirements to graduate, he had to obtain a CDL and become knowledgeable in operating heavy equipment such as the dump truck that was involved in the accident. * * * The requirements for the CDL involved both course work and operation of heavy equipment. The course work, included classes, conducted on the SKC campus, such as truck driving laws and regulations, heavy

> machinery operation, and safety instruction.
> * * *
>
> Further, the record establishes a direct nexus between the voluntary, consensual relationship between Smith and SKC and the civil complaint filed by Smith. His allegations against the college are a direct outcome of the relationship of student-college that he chose to establish.

Id. at 97 (citations to court record omitted). The Ninth Circuit sitting en banc also confirmed tribal jurisdiction. Smith v. Salish Kootenai College, 434 F.3d 1127 (9th Cir.2004) (en banc).

Tribal jurisdictional provisions contained in tribal constitutional or statutory provisions often provides for expansive jurisdiction over tribally-owned or controlled lands, even outside the reservation. For example, in Niagara Aerospace Museum v. Seneca Niagara Falls Gaming Corp., No. 0179-05-01 (Seneca Nation Ct.App.2007), the Seneca Nation Court of Appeals affirmed jurisdiction over a nonmember leasehold located outside the tribe's reservation on land owned in restricted fee by the tribe. The museum had not paid its rent and was being evicted by the tribe's business entity. Had the museum's case been appealed to federal court to challenge the tribe's jurisdiction, the court likely would have pointed out that the nonmember museum's lease contained a consent provision that would have met the *Montana* consent requirement.

On occasion, tribal courts have assumed jurisdiction over state officials, though federal courts have been very reluctant to confirm tribal jurisdiction. E.g., Nevada v. Hicks, 533 U.S. 353 (2001) (Section 1983 claim against state law enforcement officials); MacArthur v. San Juan County, 497 F.3d 1057 (10th Cir. 2007) (rejecting jurisdiction over state health service officials). Tribal courts have construed agreements with state governments and tribal actors narrowly to defeat jurisdiction. E.g., Dorman v. Eastern Band of Cherokee Indians, 7 Cher.Rep. 5, 2008 WL 7610174, at *4 (Cherokee Ct. of the Eastern Band of Cherokee Indians 2008).

2. JURISDICTION ARISING FROM THE TRIBAL POWER TO EXCLUDE

Independent of the *Montana* rubric, tribal governments also possess the power to exclude persons from their properties, which assumes that tribes also possess the power to condition entry onto tribal lands. Restatement of the Law of American Indians § 22; Merrion v. Jicarilla Apache Tribe, 455 U.S. 130 (1982). E.g., People v. Sorrell, No. BR 17-01 (Sault Ste. Marie Tribe of Chippewa Indians Tribal Ct.2017) ("Barring, or exclusion, has been used by tribes for centuries, not only as a form of punishment, but also as a means for a Tribe to protect its people and property. The inherent and sovereign authority of tribes to banish or bar individuals, whether members of the tribe or not, is well-established, and it is a privilege, not a right for all."); Lopez v. Benecke, 28 Indian L.Rep. 6178, 6181 (Pueblo of Pojoaque Tribal Ct.2001) ("The Court finds that Pueblo of Pojoaque customs and legal history, as a sovereign, give the Pueblo a legal right to exclude anyone from its exterior boundaries. This legal right allows the Pueblo of Pojoaque to exclude individuals who endanger the health, safety and welfare of the community. This legal right also protects the Pueblo's ability to determine for itself its customs, traditions and way of life.").

In Colorado River Indian Tribes v. Water Wheel Camp Recreation Area, Inc., No. 08-0003 (Colorado River Indian Tribe Ct.App.2009), the Colorado River Indian Tribes appellate court affirmed the tribe's power to evict a holdover tenant from its lands. The nonmember-owned campground was the successor to a lease of land owned by the federal government in trust for the benefit of the tribe. The campground stopped paying rent years before the lease expired, then refused to leave the land once the lease expired. The tribe brought an eviction action in tribal court. The nonmember agreed for sake of argument its execution of the lease meant that it had consented to tribal jurisdiction under *Montana*, but then claimed that consent ended once the lease expired. From the nonmember's perspective, once the consent issue was gone, the only way the tribe could assert jurisdiction over it was if the nonmember's activities had a catastrophic impact on the tribe. The court disagreed, holding that the nonmember's consent did not expire at the termination of the lease period. Water Wheel brought a claim in federal court to challenge the tribal court's jurisdiction. The Ninth Circuit ultimately held that *Montana* did not apply at all. Since the nonmember was located on tribal lands (lands held in trust for Indian tribes by the federal government are considered tribal lands), the tribe possessed the power to exclude the nonmember from that land. Under that analysis, *Montana* was irrelevant. See Water Wheel Camp Recreational Area, Inc. v. LaRance, 642 F.3d 802 (9th Cir.2011).

Tribal courts have approved of the *Water Wheel* analysis as "more informed and respectful" of tribal inherent powers. Neptune Leasing, Inc. v. Mountain States Petroleum Corp., 11 Am. Tribal Law 162, 168 (Navajo Nation S.Ct.2013).

C. TAXATION

A core feature of governance is the power to tax. Tribal nations possess an inherent sovereign power to tax as a fundamental aspect of their self-government. This power is used to raise revenue for essential governmental services, manage territory, and regulate economic activity within their jurisdiction. However, the scope of this power is complex and varies depending on who is being taxed, the nature of the transaction, and the type of land involved.

Tribal courts have frequently held that tribal nations retain the inherent power of all governments to tax. E.g., Thompson v. Cheyenne River Sioux Tribe, 13 Indian L.Rep. 6005 (Cheyenne River Sioux Tribal Ct.App.1985); Public Service Co. of New Mexico v. Chairman, Tax Protest Panel, 18 Indian L.Rep. 6097 (Jicarilla Apache Tribal Ct.1991); Conoco, Inc. v. Ponca Tax Commission, 21 Indian L.Rep. 6119 (Ponca Indian Tribal Tax Ct.1994). Federal constitutional doctrines relating to the power of taxation generally do not apply. E.g., Cortez Pipeline Co. v. Santa Ana Tax Administration Division, 14 Indian L.Rep. 6015, 6019 (Santa Ana Pueblo Tribal Ct.1986) (rejecting challenge to tribal taxation statute under the federal Commerce Clause). Tribal courts may also apply the Indian Civil Rights Act in determining whether a tribal tax discriminates against certain classifications of persons or entities. E.g., Conroy v. Bear Runner, 16 Indian L.Rep. 6037 (Oglala Sioux Tribal Ct.App. 1994) (striking down tribal tax enforced only against tribal employees and not others doing business on the reservation).

The tribal power to tax is limited by several factors. First, the reservation tax base is severely restricted by the poverty of tribal citizens, limited economic activity, and by federal and tribal control over most reservation lands. Second, the United States Supreme Court has held that the *Montana* analysis applies to tribal taxation of nonmembers. In recent decades, tribal nations have reached intergovernmental agreements on the sharing of tax revenue with state and local governments.

Like nations generally, tribal nations possess the power to tax income, property, and other activities of persons and entities under tribal jurisdiction. Restatement of the Law of American Indians § 21. See also Blaze Construction, Inc. v. Navajo Tax Commission, 2 Am. Tribal Law 487, 491 (Navajo Nation S.Ct.1999) ("The Navajo Nation's Business Activity Tax helps to pay for essential government operations and services for Navajos and non-Navajos on the Navajo Nation."). Tribal nations typically do impose sales and use taxes on commercial activities within their reservation lands. Much of the revenue from these taxes is collected from nonmembers. E.g., Mohegan Tribe of Indians of Connecticut v. Big Bubba's BBQ, LLC, 12 Am. Tribal Law 405 (Mohegan Tribal Gaming Disputes Ct.2014) (reviewing challenge to tribal sales tax enforcement efforts); Estate of Jorgenson v. DHS Drilling Co., 11 Am. Tribal Law 136 (Shoshone and Arapaho Tribal Ct.2011) ("[T]he activities of Encana and DHS have a substantial effect on the economic security and the political integrity of the Tribes. Tribal revenue from mineral royalties and severance taxes is substantial. This revenue allows the Tribes to provide important governmental services throughout the Reservation.").

For more than a century, tribal nations have been collecting taxes from nonmember commercial activities on tribal lands, typically arising from mining and agricultural leases. In Buster v. Wright, 135 F. 947 (8th Cir.1905), the Eighth Circuit affirmed the power of the tribal impose taxes on a nonmember grazing business and the power of the federal government to enforce the tribal tax. For much of the 20th century, the federal government had to approve tribal tax ordinances involving nonmembers due to Secretarial approval requirements contained in many tribal constitutions. In Merrion v. Jicarilla Apache Tribe, 455 U.S. 130 (1982), the United States Supreme Court affirmed the inherent tribal power to tax, but appeared to condition that tribal power on the fact that the tribal tax required federal approval before it would be valid. A few years later, in Kerr-McGee Corp. v. Navajo Tribe, 471 U.S. 195 (1985), the Court again confirm the power to tax. That case involved a tribe that did not adopt a written constitution and did not need Secretarial approval for its tax ordinances. Because those cases involve some form of written consent from the nonmembers, the tribal power to tax is rarely controversial. For example, in Mustang Fuel Corp. v. Cheyenne-Arapaho Tax Commission, 4 Okla. Trib. 1, 1994 WL 1047927 (Cheyenne-Arapaho Tribes S.Ct.1994), the court held, "The Cheyenne-Arapaho Tribes * * * properly may exercise tribal power to tax the activities of those who avail themselves of the substantial privilege of doing business on and taking valuable resources from Indian lands, including non-Indians and non-Indian entities." Id. at *16. Cf. Conoco, Inc. v. Ponca Tax Commission, 21 Indian L.Rep. 6119, 6120–23 (Ponca Indian Tribal Tax Ct.1994) (affirming tribal power to tax nonmember activities on trust land).

However, where nonmembers did not reach agreement with a tribal nation on taxes, tribal powers are often limited. In general, when the nonmember business activity occurs on tribal lands, the tribal nation may assess the tax. Restatement of the Law of American Indians § 30. When the nonmember activity occurs on nonmember lands, the tribe must show that it meets the *Montana* criteria. In Matter of Atkinson Trading, Inc., 1 Am. Tribal Law 451 (Navajo Nation S.Ct.1997), the court held that a nonmember owned hotel on nonmember land surrounded by tribal lands must pay an occupancy tax to the tribe. The tribe provided expensive public safety services such as law enforcement, fire, and ambulance to the hotel and its patrons. The nonmember sought federal court review of the tribe's powers, culminating in a United States Supreme Court decision, Atkinson Trading Co., Inc. v. Shirley, 532 U.S. 645 (2001). The Court applied the *Montana* analysis, concluding that the nonmember had not consented merely by accepting services. The Court also found that the tribe's political integrity, economic security, and health and welfare of the tribe and its citizens was not sufficiently impacted by the hotel's activities.

Worse, perhaps, for tribal nations was the United States Supreme Court's decision in Cotton Petroleum Corp. v. New Mexico, 490 U.S. 163 (1989). There, the state imposed taxes on a nonmember business that already paid taxes to the tribal nation, creating a double taxation problem for the tribe and its business partner. The Court held that states may tax on-reservation activities of nonmembers even though that tax might duplicate the tribal tax, interfering with the tribe's powers to tax and regulate its own lands.

Tribal sovereignty may work to preclude state and local taxation on Indian-owned property real property. In Pease v. Yellowstone County, 21 Indian L.Rep. 6109 (Crow Tribal Ct.App.1994), a tribal citizen sought to invoke tribal court jurisdiction to enjoin the country from taxing real property on the reservation. A split panel of the tribal appellate court agreed, invoking the inherent tribal sovereignty theory. Finding no federal law prohibiting tribal court jurisdiction, the court proceeded. The court also reasoned that tribal court jurisdiction may be the only forum where tribal citizens can seek to protect self-governance:

> To rule in [the county']s favor would require this court to ignore the Crow Allotment Act and ignore a tradition of independence that has historically existed between the Crow people and the United States government. It would also require ignoring a policy of self-determination observed by Congress and the President since 1968 and ignoring the amending of P.L. 280 to require consent of Indian tribes prior to any assuming of state jurisdiction. It would require applying the principles of assimilation repudiated by the policy of self-determination and the repeal of the allotment process that occurred in 1934.

Id. at 6110. The Ninth Circuit ultimately excused the county from tribal jurisdiction. Yellowstone County v. Pease, 96 F.3d 1169 (9th Cir.1996).

The case of Rose v. Adams, 27 Indian L.Rep. 6057 (Crow Ct.App.2000), evidences the problems with nonmember immunities from tribal taxation (and regulation more generally). In *Rose*, the tribe imposed taxes on several nonmember business engaged in recreation and tourism, but with a faux-Indian cultural overlay. The nonmembers themselves admitted that "their business operations are enhanced by their location within an Indian reservation and that they use the 'Indian mystique' for marketing purposes" and that "some of the tourist opportunities are tribally related or have tribal aspects, e.g., the Auke Bay at the Big Horn Canyon Recreation area, the Little Big Horn Battlefield and the annual Crow Fair, one of the largest powwows in the country." Id. at 6064. Moreover, tribal witnesses testified that nonmember customers "routinely trespass on Indian trust property along the banks of the Big Horn River." Id. One of the nonmembers leased trust land for a dude ranch. The court confirmed the authority of the tribe to tax these activities, but the trend in nonmember challenges to tribal authority to tax nonmembers who do not consent is troubling.

For decades, tribal nations have reached agreements with state and local governments on the collection of taxes and the fair distribution of tax revenue. The United States Supreme Court's decision in Oklahoma Tax Commission v. Citizen Band Potawatomi Indian Tribe of Oklahoma, 498 U.S. 505 (1991), helped to encourage tribes and states to the bargaining table. There, the Court held that the state was entitled to tax revenue for on-reservation, nonmember activities—and that the tribe was obligated to collect and remit those taxes to the state. However, the Court also held that the tribe was immune from state tax collection activities, meaning that the state had a right with no remedy. The Court's admonition to both parties was to seek agreement on how to collect and share tax revenue. On occasion, the tax agreements that followed were cancelled by the state, leading to disputes that can reach the Supreme Court. E.g., Wagnon v. Prairie

Band Potawatomi Nation, 546 U.S. 95 (2005) (validating state taxes on tribal gas station sales after the state governor unilaterally terminated a tax agreement with the tribe).

D. UTILITY AND RAILROAD REGULATION

For many, many years, the federal government granted to nonmember-owned companies easements and rights-of-way in Indian reservations, notably railroads and utility companies, to exploit reservation resources, often without tribal consent. While some tribal nations now retain control over easements, many legacy railroads and utilities remain on tribal lands. These businesses often claim immunity from tribal regulatory and adjudicatory jurisdiction. Tribal nations long have attempted to assert jurisdiction over nonmember-owned utilities that provide services on tribal lands, but with middling success as federal courts routinely excused the utilities from tribal jurisdiction. Compare Crow Tribe of Indians v. Gregori, 25 Indian L.Rep. 6087 (Crow Ct.App.1998) (asserting jurisdiction over electric cooperative); Harris v. Big Horn County Electric Cooperative, 14 Indian L.Rep. 6023 (Crow Tribal Ct. 1986) (same); Oglala Sioux Tribe v. Alltell Communications, 38 Indian L.Rep. 6033 (Oglala Sioux Nation S.Ct.2010) (same); Rosebud Housing Authority v. LaCreek Electric Coop., Inc., 13 Indian L.Rep. 6030 (Rosebud Sioux Tribal Ct.1986) (same); Three Affiliated Tribes Tax Commission v. Reservation Telephone Cooperative, 28 Indian L.Rep. 6049 (Three Affiliated Tribes of the Fort Berthold Reservation Tribal Ct.2000) (same), with

Big Horn County Elec. Co-op., Inc. v. Adams, 219 F.3d 944 (9th Cir.2000) (excusing nonmember utility from tribal jurisdiction); Burlington Northern R. Co. v. Red Wolf, 196 F.3d 1059 (9th Cir.1999) (excusing nonmember railroad from tribal jurisdiction). Cf. El Paso Natural Gas Co. v. Neztsosie, 526 U.S. 473 (1999) (holding tribal courts have no jurisdiction over tort claims arising from uranium mining).

In recent years, however, because the Ninth Circuit has articulated a legal theory that recognizes broad tribal authority over nonmember activities on tribally owned and controlled lands, the tide seems to have turned, at least on tribal lands. For example, in Big Man v. Big Horn County Electric Cooperative, Inc., No. AP-2013-001 (Absaalooke App.Ct.2017), the court concluded that the tribal court possessed jurisdiction over the utility company for three reasons. First, the court held that the commercial relationship between Big Man and the utility company memorialized the consent of the utility company to tribal authority. Second, the court held that the utility company's threat to shut off electricity to Big Man's home during the middle of winter in the northern Great Plains was conduct that threatened the health and welfare of the Crow Nation and its citizens. Third, the power of the tribe to exclude nonmembers from tribal lands comes with it the concomitant power to regulate those nonmembers as part of the license for entering tribal lands. The federal courts later confirmed tribal jurisdiction over the utility company. Big Horn County Electric Cooperative, Inc. v. Big Man, 526 F.Supp.3d 756 (D.Mont.2021), aff'd, 2022 WL 738623

(9th Cir.) (unreported), cert. denied, 143 S.Ct. 525 (2022). See also Blackfeet Tribal Business Council v. East Glacier Water & Sewer District, 11 Indian L.Rep. 6021 (Blackfeet Tribal Ct.1984) (finding tribal jurisdiction to enjoin utility from shutting off water and sewer to tribal members).

The Navajo Nation asserts treaty rights under the 1868 Treaty of Fort Sumner to assume jurisdiction over nonmember activities. For example, in Thinn v. Navajo Generating Station, 7 Am. Tribal Law 558 (Navajo Nation S.Ct.2007), the court explained:

> Under the Treaty of 1868, the Nation has authority to regulate non-Indian activity on trust lands. * * * This power is absolute, and does not require the Nation to fulfill the exceptions announced by the United States Supreme Court in Montana v. United States * * *. The Nation therefore has jurisdiction, unless it has validly waived that jurisdiction in the provisions of a lease.

Id. at 561–62.

Notwithstanding *Big Man* and *Thinn*, though, tribal nations may still struggle to regulate or tax nonmember utility activities on nonmember-owned fee lands. In recent decades, more tribal nations have taken steps to establish their own utility companies, avoiding complicated jurisdictional questions. E.g., Echevarria v. Tulalip Utilities Authority, 8 Am. Tribal Law 424 (Tulalip Tribes Ct.App.2010) (assuming jurisdiction over suit against tribal utility company). See also Margaret Schaff, Regulation of

Electric Utilities on Indian Reservations: Tribal Governments' Oversight of Renewable Energy Development and Utility Providers and Authority to Create Tribal Utilities, 41 Energy L.J. 211 (2020).

E. CIVIL OFFENSES

Tribal nations possess robust authority over members all reservation lands. Restatement of the Law of American Indians § 14. Tribal nations also possess authority over nonmembers on tribal lands and limited authority over nonmembers on nonmember lands. Id. § 27. As civil offenses are not an exercise of a tribal nation's criminal law enforcement authority, tribal nations may assess a civil infraction ticket on non-Indians and nonmembers. E.g., Eastern Band of Cherokee Indians v. Hicks, 3 Cher.Rep. 91, 2004 WL 5806991 (Cherokee Ct. of the Eastern Band of Cherokee Indians 2004) (confirming tribal jurisdiction over non-Indian's civil offense for impaired driving); Confederated Salish & Kootenai Tribes v. Brueckman, 14 Indian L.Rep. 6044 (Confederated Salish & Kootenai Tribes of the Flathead Reservation Tribal Ct.1987) (same, but for on-reservation hunting and fishing violations); Kloker v. Fort Peck Tribes, 15 Am. Tribal Law 292 (Fort Peck Ct.App.2018) (same, after a rejecting a challenge to the tribe's reservation boundaries on the Milk River).

The issuance of civil offense or civil infraction tickets on tribal citizens requires procedural fairness, though perhaps not to the level required in criminal cases. In Socula v. Confederated Colville Tribes, 9

Am. Tribal Law 129 (Colville Tribal Ct.App.2010), the trial court relied on the personal knowledge of the tribal citizen defendant's home address (which was incorrect) to send official court notice of a hearing, despite the fact that the citizen had confirmed their updated address with the officer issuing the traffic ticket. The court reversed a default judgment against the defendant, writing, "[T]he Trial Court must be ever vigilant in protecting the rights of litigants before it, and proceed objectively and fairly in every case, no matter how minor. One way to ensure fair application of the law it to provide uniform procedures for litigants to follow." Id. at 132. Cf. Pokagon Band of Potawatomi Indians v. Engle, 2014 Pokagon Band Tribal LEXIS 1 (Pokagon Band of Potawatomi Indians Tribal Ct.2014) (denying defendant a trial in a civil offense matter in the absence of controlling tribal statutory law guaranteeing a trial).

Montana v. United States, 450 U.S. 544 (1981), looms large for tribes that have acquiesced to federal law restrictions on tribal powers. Federal law generally prohibits tribes from exercising criminal jurisdiction over non-Indians in the absence of Congressional authorization. Oliphant v. Suquamish Indian Tribe, 435 U.S. 191 (1978). For reasons that are largely historical accidents, the personal jurisdictional predicate for tribal civil regulatory powers controlled by the *Montana* analysis is member/nonmember status whereas the predicate for criminal jurisdiction Indian/non-Indian status. Tribes, then, are left to assert authority to impose civil penalties on non-Indian lawbreakers in light of the *Montana* analysis as a matter of federal Indian law.

Leading cases on the power of tribal nations to assess civil penalties on nonmembers arose from traffic offenses, civil forfeiture, personal protection orders, and temporary detention by tribal police. The leading example of tribal civil forfeiture of nonmember property is One Thousand Four Hundred Sixty-Three Dollars v. Muscogee (Creek) Nation, 9 Okla. Trib. 83, 2005 WL 6218811 (Muscogee (Creek) Nation S.Ct.2005). There, the Muscogee (Creek) Nation Supreme Court affirmed the confiscation of a nonmember's truck, cash, guns, and illegal drugs found within the truck by a tribal security officer at the tribe's casino. Though the court analyzed the case with federal law in mind, the court ultimately relied on tribal law:

> The Nation has a significant interest in the activities by any and all persons who enter the Nation's Indian country. The presence of illegal drugs and the need to rid the community of the drugs is of the utmost significance to the Nation, just as it is to all communities and all sovereigns.
>
> We hold that as a matter of tribal law jurisdiction was proper in this case based on the laws of the Muscogee (Creek) Nation alone. The Nation has exclusive jurisdiction to regulate the conduct of all persons on tribal land, particularly those that voluntarily come on to tribal land for the purpose of patronizing tribal businesses.

Id. at *4. The nonmember sought federal relief from the confiscation of the truck, cash, and guns (but not the drugs), but the Tenth Circuit held that once the tribe possessed the property, it was immune from any suit brought to recover the property. Miner Elec., Inc. v. Muscogee (Creek) Nation, 505 F.3d 1007 (10th Cir.2007).

Other tribes have adopted civil forfeiture statutes, but there are many examples of forfeitures being invalidated by tribal courts. E.g., Swinomish Tribal Community v. 2002 BMW, 17 Am. Tribal Law 235 (Swinomish Tribal Ct.2022) (holding that civil forfeiture violated excessive fines prohibition); Swinomish Tribal Community v. One 1978 Blue Plymouth Two Door Motor Vehicle, 1991 WL 11818233, at *3 (Swinomish Tribal Ct.1991) (finding tribal forfeiture law was void for vagueness); Tulalip Tribes v. 2008 White Ford Econoline Van, 11 Am. Tribal Law 199 (Tulalip Tribal Ct.App.2013) (remanding to determine whether forfeiture violated excessive fines prohibition). But see, e.g., James v. Real Property Known as 3705 Sinclair Drive, Ferndale, Washington, 30 Indian L.Rep. 6118 (Lummi Nation Tribal Ct.2003) (affirming civil forfeiture of tribal member's property associated with a drug investigation); Tulalip Tribes v. 1997 Oldsmobile Bravada, 36 Indian L.Rep. 6089 (Tulalip Tribal Ct.App.2009) (same).

In Begay v. Navajo Nation, 15 Indian L.Rep. 6032 (Navajo Nation S.Ct.), the court held that the forfeiture of an individual's vehicle for its use in illegal liquor bootlegging was invalid due to the failure of the tribe provide adequate notice, emphasizing Dinó common law.

> When conflicts arise, involved parties will go to an elder statesman, a medicine man, or a well-respected member of the community for advice on the problem and to ask that person to speak with the one they see as the cause of the conflict. The advisor will warn the accused of the action being contemplated and give notice of the upcoming group gathering. At the gathering, all parties directly or indirectly involved will be allowed to speak, after which a collective decision will be made. This is Navajo customary due process and it is carried out with fairness and respect. The heart of Navajo due process, thus, is notice and an opportunity to present and defend a position. Applying these concepts, we hold that the Tuba City District Court violated Mr. Begay's due process rights by granting the "Motion for Forfeiture" without notice to Mr. Begay or without allowing him an opportunity to be heard.

Id. at 6034.

Tribal courts split on tribal traffic offenses imposed on nonmembers, perhaps in part because many reservation roads are maintained and patrolled by state and local governments, but also because of the heightened standard in the *Montana* rubric to show an impact on the tribal citizenry. For example, in Skokomish Tribe v. Mosbarger, 7 NICS App. 90 (Skokomish Tribal Ct.App.2006), the court affirmed the tribal power to issue speeding tickets for drivers on state-controlled roads near a tribal school, involving the *Montana* analysis. However, in Skokomish Tribe v. Smith, 9 NICS App. 33 (Skokomish Tribal Ct.App.2009), the same court reversed a civil conviction for reckless driving where the tribe made no factual allegation that the nonmember driver's conduct threatened tribal citizens.

Until 2013, the tribal power to enforce personal protection orders on nonmembers was limited by the *Montana* analysis. However, Congress reaffirmed the inherent power of tribal nations to enforce their protection orders against nonmembers in Section 905 of the Violence Against Women Reauthorization Act of 2013, codified at 18 U.S.C. § 2265(e). In Spurr v. Spurr, 2018 Nottawaseppi Huron Band Supreme LEXIS 6 (Nottawaseppi Huron Band of the Potawatomi S.Ct.2018), the court invoked § 2265(e) to affirm a civil protection order against a nonmember who lived miles off the reservation who was harassing a tribal citizen from a distance (and occasionally on tribal lands as well). Tribal court jurisdiction over protection orders involving tribal citizens, on the other hand, has always been presumed. E.g., Mike v. Mike, 7 Am. Tribal Law 186, 190 (Ho-Chunk Nation Trial Ct.2007) (confirming authority to issue protection order brought under the customary law of the Ho-Chunk Nation).

Finally, in United States v. Cooley, 593 U.S. 345 (2021), the United States Supreme Court invoked the *Montana* analysis to confirm that tribal law enforcement has the authority to pull over and detain non-Indians who are in the act of committing a state or federal crime until state or federal authorities arrive. Tribal courts long had already been enforcing criminal law against nonmembers through the issuance of civil offense tickets. E.g., Pueblo of Pojoaque v. Garcia, 26 Indian L.Rep. 6131 (Pueblo of Pojoaque Tribal Ct.1999) (illegal dumping).

F. LAWS GOVERNING LAWYERS

Thousands of lawyers and lay advocates practice law in Indian country or practice under the authority of tribal governments every day, but tribal regulation of those practitioners is minimal. In general, lawyers are regulated by their licensing authorities (typically, state bar associations), courts, or through malpractice actions. In Indian country, virtually all regulation is conducted by tribal judges. Few tribal nations have established bar associations or bar exams to test applicants for admission to practice law. Lawyers typically are admitted to practice by tribal courts by waiving in, so long as they are licensed in another jurisdiction. Many tribes allow for non-lawyers to serve as lay advocates, a practical necessity given the dearth of private lawyers that represent individuals in and around Indian country.

Historically, the Secretary of the Interior had sole authority to approve contracts involving tribal nations, including attorney contracts, under federal law. In many instances, that meant that a tribal nation could not retain counsel without federal approval, which the government could deny when a tribe was preparing to sue the United States. Federal approval requirements ended formally in 2000, compare Indian Reorganization Act § 16(e) (requiring that "the choice of counsel and fixing of fees to be subject to the approval of the Secretary") with Pub. L. 106–179, § 3 (repealing § 16(e)). Though the Secretary only intermittently interfered in attorney contracts after the beginning of self-determination, attorney contracts remained subject to the approval process. E.g., Littlegeorge v. Lowe, 24 Indian L.Rep. 6099 (Ho-Chunk Nation Trial Ct.1996) (enjoining appointment of lawyer as tribal Attorney General until Interior Secretary approved the lawyer's contract under § 81). But see, e.g., Standing Rock Sioux Tribe v. American Tobacco Co., 27 Indian L.Rep. 6184 (Standing Rock Sioux Tribal Ct.2000) (holding that federal approval requirement likely violated the federal constitutional right to counsel and declining to enjoin attorney action under a non-approved contract). Likely because of the long history of federal control, tribal regulation of attorney conduct is behind the curve, the exception being the Navajo Nation, which established the Navajo Nation Bar Association in 1978. Boos v. Yazzie, 17 Indian L.Rep. 6115, 6116 (Navajo Nation S.Ct.1990).

Unethical lawyer conduct in such conditions can thrive. Jack Abramoff, perhaps the most notorious tribally-retained lawyer, did not practice in tribal courts, but his story is worth retelling. Abramoff was federally convicted in the mid-2000s for defrauded several tribal nations and bribing public officials for political favors. Abramoff orchestrated a scheme to bill tribes millions for lobbying services while secretly working against them and overbilling their accounts.

He also provided lavish gifts, including trips to golf resorts, to lawmakers and their aides in exchange for legislative support and campaign donations. The ensuing investigation by Senator John McCain exposed a vast web of corruption, leading to numerous indictments, convictions, and lobbying reforms. Because Abramoff worked under the cover of secrecy and information asymmetry between tribal clients, he got away with this fraud for years. Only when he started appearing in photo ops with federal and tribal leaders was Abramoff's duplicity discovered.

Tribal courts and tribal legislatures typically share powers to regulate attorney conduct. Many tribal legislatures, though far from all of them, have adopted statutory rules of professional conduct. Many tribal courts have adopted rules of professional conduct as court rules. However, once a lawyer is admitted, the tribal court has exclusive authority to directly regulate that lawyer, not the legislature. Consider In re Saunooke, 2008 N.C. Cherokee Ct. LEXIS 1 (Cherokee Ct. of the Eastern Band of Cherokee Indians 2008), the court rejected the authority of the tribal council to remove lawyers from the tribal bar. Under the tribal statute, lawyers must be licensed by the State of North Carolina in order to earn admission to the tribal bar, though the tribal council later allowed tribal citizens enrolled in other states to be admitted. Rejecting the tribal council's effort to remove Saunooke, the court concluded:

> The members of the Bar have an expectation that, while supervising and regulating them

> vigilantly, the Court will also protect them in their office of Attorneys and Counselors of the Court. As the Supreme Court of the United States has spoken, "it is the duty of the Court" to ensure that the exercise of its supervisory authority over the members of its Bar is accomplished in such a way "whereby the rights and independence of the bar may be as scrupulously guarded and maintained by the court, as the rights and dignity of the court itself." Ex Parte Secombe, 60 U.S. (19 How.) 9, 13, 15 L.Ed. 565, 566 (1857). To do any less would weaken the very foundation of Tribal government. Furthermore, the enrolled members of the Eastern Band of Cherokee Indians and indeed all people who have business before the Court have an expectation that they will not be deprived of the lawyer of their choosing by virtue of a whim of one of the political Branches.

Id. at *17–18.

In general, tribal nations possess jurisdiction over any lawyer engaged in legal practice on tribal lands. E.g., In the Matter of Sekayuptewa, 26 Indian L.Rep. 6170, 6177 (Hopi Tribe App.Ct.1997) (affirming criminal contempt conviction of lawyer who repeatedly failed to appear at noticed court hearings); In re De Los Santos, 11 Indian L.Rep. 6043, 6047 (Puyallup Tribal Ct.1984) (asserting jurisdiction of a non-Indian lawyer held in civil contempt, noting that any professional sanction against the lawyer could not be a criminal sanction).

Of course, tribal courts must ensure that lawyers receive due process prior to any sanction, discipline, or disqualification. E.g., In the Matter of Suspension of Bluespruce, 31 Indian L.Rep. 6105 (Cheyenne River Sioux Tribal Ct.App.2004).

As many tribal nations have not adopted formal rules of professional responsibility, tribal courts will apply the law of the state in which the conduct occurred or perhaps the law of the state jurisdiction where the lawyer is licensed. E.g., Gallaher v. Colville Confederated Tribes, 15 Am. Tribal Law 159, 162 (Colville Tribal Ct.App.2018) ("The Colville judiciary has never adopted rules of professional conduct for spokespersons (a/k/a legal ethics), however, the Colville Tribal Code at [Colville Tribal Code] § 1–2–11 allows this Court to look to state common law when there exists a circumstance where tribal law is lacking regarding a subject this Court is obligated to determine. We have set out in this Opinion rules of professional conduct for state bar members which have been adopted by the Supreme Courts of more than forty-eight states."); Cole v. Kaw Housing Authority, 4 Okla. Trib. 281, 1995 WL 1073446, at *4 (Kaw Nation S.Ct.1995) ("At this time, the Court finds no applicable law in the ordinances of the Nation, the United States, the customs or usages of this Tribe or any regulations of the Department of the Interior to provide guidance here. Accordingly, the Court then resorts to Oklahoma state law to provide guidance. Additionally, the Court finds that since counsel for both the Plaintiff and Defendant are members of the Oklahoma Bar Association, this Court may freely apply Oklahoma's rules for regulating lawyers in the Kaw Nation Tribal Court.").

Tribal attorneys have special obligations to their clients and to the tribal public akin to that of state or federal governmental attorneys. The leading case on governmental attorney regulation is In re Seanez, 9 Am. Tribal Law 329 (Navajo Nation S.Ct.2010); 9 Am. Tribal Law 377 (Navajo Nation S.Ct.2011). There, the Navajo Nation Supreme Court acting *sua sponte* disciplined the Chief Legislative Counsel (CLC) for the Navajo Nation Tribal Council. The court became aware that attorney had advised the legislative branch, following a series of politically controversial tribal supreme court decisions, that his client did not have to follow the court's orders. Because the attorney represented a branch of tribal government, the court established guiding principles for government lawyers:

> * * * A lawyer working for the People is a leader who should be further guided as follows:
>
> *Diné bá nijigháao, bá naat'áanii jílį́įgo éł bá dóó bił nidajilnishígíí Diné bibeenahaz'áanii bee bich'į̋' yájíłti' dóó bee nazhnitin dooleeł; azhą́shį́į doo ýidínéelnáada ndi, áko Diné binant'a'í dóó bá bee agha'diit'aahii jílį́įgo ei Diné t'áá náhwiist'áánt'éé bibeenahaz'áanii hoł nilį́įgo baan tsíjíkees dooleeł.*
>
> As a representative of the People, a leader for the People, and also for those you work with, you must advise and teach them of the laws of the Diné, even though they might not

> agree with the law; therefore, to be a leader and lawyer for the People, one must use and respect the laws of all the People.

9 Am. Tribal Law at 343–44. The court added at length that tribal government lawyers are not mere partisan advocates, they owe a duty toward the entire citizenry of the tribal nation:

> * * * Government lawyers in upper level positions such as the CLC who are directly engaged in governmental policymaking must deal daily with political pressures from his or her client in a setting where institutional opinions, unlike mere legal advice, serve as get-out-of-jail free cards for government action. There will be many times when policymakers will bear on their lawyers to arrive at results that support their positions, to exclude from the results laws or provisions conflicting with the policymaker's positions, or otherwise to come forward with reasons to justify defiance of those laws. Such political pressures do not relieve government lawyers of their duty "to exercise independent professional judgment and render candid advice" under Rule 2.1 of the Navajo Nation Rules of Professional Conduct. We note also that the ABA Committee on Ethics and Professional Responsibility has written, in Formal Op. 85–352 (1985) that "in the role of advisor, the lawyer should counsel the client as to whether the position is likely to be sustained by a court if challenged." This ABA opinion dovetails with 7 N.N.C. § 206 which requires

> that government cooperate with the courts and do not obstruct, interfere with, control, or influence court functions. Omitting likely issues to be faced in court, including the consequences of defiance of court orders, opens the door to unnecessary conflict and bears on the respect of the justice system as a whole, particularly when binding advice is issued extra-judicially through the assistance of government lawyers. Under all circumstances, it is the heightened duty of the government lawyer to be independent, candid, neutral rather than partisan because of their duty to the public trust, and most of all thorough in their analysis.

Id. at 344. The court ultimately disbarred the attorney and ordered that he pay a civil penalty of $72,612. Lawsuits by tribal attorneys against their former tribal clients are not unheard of. E.g., Hoopa Valley Tribe v. Bernardo, 15 NICS App. 26 (Hoopa Valley Tribal Ct.App.2017) (rejecting contractual waiver of immunity in attorney contract where same contract contained language reserving the tribe's immunity from suit and where plaintiff attorney had drafted the contract).

Occasionally, tribal constitutions provide procedures for the retention of counsel. These provisions likely are holdovers from the period of time where tribal attorney contracts were void unless approved by the Secretary of the Interior, a requirement that Congress repealed in 2000. For example, in Hoffman v. Business Committee, 9 Okla. Trib. 242, 2006 WL 6122518, at *3 (Cheyenne-

Arapaho Tribes S.Ct.2006), the court enforced a constitutional requirement that only the Tribal Council could retain counsel to represent the tribe, not the Business Committee.

Tribal politics can also interfere in governmental lawyer practice. In Ujke v. Ho-Chunk Nation, 26 Indian L.Rep. 6042 (Ho-Chunk Nation S.Ct.1999), the tribal chair retained counsel and negotiated an attorney contract. In accordance with federal law of the time and with tribal constitutional provisions, the contract was void unless approved by the Secretary of the Interior. The attorney contract was not fully approved (an amendment to the contract was not submitted). The tribal council refused to approve the contract. The appellate court confirmed that the contract was void under federal law. In Lomayesva v. Talayumptewa, No. 2-15-CR-0088 (Hopi Tribal Ct.2015), the court held that the tribal council must follow its own procedures and an attorney's retention agreement in order to terminate its relationship with in-house counsel.

In a cautionary tale involving the Little River Band of Ottawa Indians that involved several court systems, tribal counsel engaged in outrageous misconduct that ultimately led to the disbarment of the attorney. The tribal constitution provided for separate branches of government between the tribal council and tribal *ogema* (the chief executive). Each branch of government retained its own counsel. The conflict began when the tribal *ogema* attempted to terminate the contract of the legislative branch's legal counsel in 2008. Tribal Council v. Tribal

Ogema, No. 08 093 GC, 2009 MI Ottawa Trib. LEXIS 3 (Little River Band of Ottawa Indians Tribal Ct.2009). The court confirmed that the tribal *ogema* did indeed possess authority to terminate the attorney's contract (as did the tribal council).

The attorney then sued the tribe for breach of contract. The tribe argued that the contract termination was justified by the attorney's failure to become licensed by the State of Michigan (he was licensed in Illinois) and by his continued representation of a client in Wisconsin. The attorney claimed to be a whistleblower. The court found in favor of the tribe. Martin v. Little River Band of Ottawa Indians, Nos. 09-169 GC & 09-244 GC (Little River Band of Ottawa Indians Tribal Ct.2010). The attorney then filed another suit alleging new civil rights claims and adding the tribal judge as a defendant. That suit, too, was dismissed, with the court holding the attorney in contempt. Martin v. Little River Band of Ottawa Indians, No. 09-248 GC, 2010 MI Ottawa Trib. LEXIS 14 (Little River Band of Ottawa Indians Tribal Ct.2010). The court dismissed the claims against the presiding tribal judge on the basis of judicial immunity and sanctioned the attorney for bringing a frivolous action. The attorney filed another claim after that, focusing on his attorney contract, which he alleged required the tribe to pay him a severance sum to be determined by the tribal court. Again, the court dismissed the action, on the basis of tribal immunity and res judicata, and barred the attorney from bringing any additional suits. Martin v. Little River

Band of Ottawa Indians, No. 10-210 GC (Little River Band of Ottawa Indians Tribal Ct.2011).

The attorney also sued the tribe in state court, a suit that the attorney ultimately dismissed voluntarily. Martin v. LRBOI Tribal Council, No. 10-138845-CZ (Mich.Cir.Ct.2010). However, in its responsive pleading, the tribal government included as an exhibit a letter sent to the tribal government. The letter was ostensibly an effort to initiate a settlement but, in the letter, the attorney threatened to reveal attorney client privileged information about the tribe's off-reservation gaming development efforts to non-parties that opposed the tribe's efforts. Eventually, the Illinois Attorney Registration and Disciplinary Commission filed a complaint against the attorney, resulting in the voluntary withdrawal of the attorney from licensure in Illinois.

Tribal courts may impose obligations on attorneys practicing in Indian country that may appear different from that of state rules of professional responsibility. In Smith v. Kasper, 8 Am. Tribal Law 347 (Navajo Nation S.Ct.2009), for example, the court expressed disappointment that counsel in a domestic dispute involving potential violence and a child did not know where their clients were, nor had they communicated with their clients:

> Aside from the legal issues on appeal, the Court is concerned that legal counsels of the parties do not know the whereabouts of their clients, that they have not communicated with their clients for this appellate hearing, and especially that they do not know where the

minor child is at this time. *Héída hach'í' cho'oos'Í1111íid dóó hol yah 'aníichą́ą́go ei doo t' óó bijilkáá da dooleel.* [The Court is aware of the *bilagaana* doctrine of "parens patriae" or "parent of the nation." The Court deliberately does not use this Latin phrase because the *bilagaana* concept with its root in English common law is different. The protection provided by the Sovereign (King) is based simply on its role of as guardian. The root of the Navajo value is based on the moral responsibility of the animate government and the familial relationship (*ké*) between the government and its People.] It is an affirmative duty and responsibility of legal counsel to maintain contact and communication with their client. See Model Rules of Prof'l Conduct R. 1.4 (1984). In other words, lawyers cannot simply sit back and wait for the client to contact them. The Court instructed counsels to locate their clients to inform the Court of the child's location and safety. A child has come to us seeking refuge. The trial court saw the need to shield the child from harm. Like any relative, parent, or guardian, it will continue to be concerned and worry about whether the child is safe; *be' ewéé' bil yah aníícháígíí éi yikéé bíni'íí'á dóó yaa jé' ólná.* More than five weeks have passed since oral argument and counsels have yet to file their updates. The Court finds good cause to remand this matter to the Family Court.

Id. at 351–52 (footnotes omitted).

Admission to practice in tribal court is mandatory. See Corporation of the President of the Church of Jesus Christ of Latter-Day Saints v. Window Rock District Court, 15 Am. Tribal Law 362, 367 (Navajo Nation S.Ct.2018) ("Every court has the inherent ability to control the proceedings before it. A practitioner that is not otherwise the counsel of record in an action, particularly those not otherwise authorized to practice law in this jurisdiction, must obtain permission from the court by motion to be able to appear."). Most tribal nations allow licensed attorneys to waive in to practice in tribal courts, but a few require passage of a bar exam. E.g., Alderman v. Navajo Nation Bar Assn., 17 Indian L.Rep. 6077 (Navajo Nation S.Ct.1990) (establishing procedures for appeals of bar exam results). Tribal courts will sanction advocates for unauthorized practice of law. E.g., Matter of Dutcher, 16 Am. Tribal Law 150 (Navajo Nation S.Ct.2020) (sanctioning advocate for unauthorized practice). Dishonesty in an application to practice merits disbarment. E.g., In the Matter of Continued Admission of Zvenia, 28 Indian L.Rep. 6110 (Duckwater Shoshone Tribal Ct.2000) (disbarring individual who misrepresented his status as a lawyer to the tribal court); In re Continued Admission to the Muscogee (Creek) Nation Bar Assn. by Zvenia, 2019 Muscogee Creek Nation Supreme LEXIS 4 (Muscogee (Creek) Nation S.Ct.2019) (same); In re Unger, 4 Mash.Rep. 276, 2005 WL 5740560 (Mashantucket Pequot Tribal Ct.2005). A sham tribal judge who attempted to take over the Window Rock District Court based on a purported appointment from the tribal chairman that was a fraud was disbarred. See In re Bowman, 16 Indian L.Rep. 6085 (Navajo Nation S.Ct.1989). See also In re Certified Questions I (Navajo Nation v. MacDonald), 16 Indian L.Rep. 6098 (Navajo Nation S.Ct.1989) (holding that the Navajo chairman, who had been criminally indicted, had no independent authority to appoint tribal judges). One fraudster established a paper tribal court in the name of the Native Village of Karluk began issuing orders in personal legal matters until being discovered later. Compare In re Baldwin, 38 Indian L.Rep. 6030 (Native Village of Karluk Tribal Ct.2011) (issuing "order" in child welfare matter), with Koniag, Inc. v. Kanam, 699 Fed.Appx. 663 (9th Cir.2017) (rejecting authority of "tribal court" and questioning relationship between the Karluk Native Corporation and the Native Village of Karluk).

Tribal courts also impose reciprocal discipline on attorneys sanctioned by their licensing jurisdiction. E.g., In re Dixon, 2 Mash.Rep. 402, 1998 WL 35232491 (Mashantucket Pequot Tribal Ct.1998). Tribal courts must, of course, provide adequate due process to lawyers charged with misconduct. E.g., Brown v. Puyallup Tribal Court, 2009 Puyallup App. LEXIS 1 (Puyallup Tribal Ct.App.2009) (reversing the disbarment of a lawyer by a tribal judge who initiated disciplinary hearing with an order to show cause, interrogated the attorney personally, and relied on evidence obtained after the hearing).

Many tribal courts keep rosters of attorneys available to serve under appointment as criminal defense attorneys or for other needs. E.g., Boos v.

Yazzie, 17 Indian L.Rep. 6115, 6116 (Navajo Nation S.Ct.1990) ("The Navajo Nation courts have the power to appoint any active member of the [Navajo Nation Bar Association] to represent an indigent party, including a defendant charged with crimes in Navajo court."). Misconduct can lead to their removal or suspension from the list. E.g., In re Stewart, 1 Mash.Rep. 239, 1996 WL 34403080 (Mashantucket Pequot Tribal Ct.1996).

Because of the relative dearth of Indian country lawyers and the reality of close-knit tribal communities, conflicts of interest are not unusual. For example, in Gallaher v. Colville Confederated Tribes, 15 Am. Tribal Law 159 (Colville Tribal Ct.App.2018), a criminal defendant's public defender previously had served as the tribal judge. As judge, the lawyer had reviewed the complaint and issued a summons. After the defendant was convicted, the tribal appellate court reversed on the ground that the defendant was entitled to unconflicted counsel, even in the absence of a showing of prejudice. See also Joseph v. Marshall, 9 NICS App. 55, 60 n.2 (Hoopa Valley Tribal Ct.App.2010) (raising possibility that judge should have recused himself from case in which he issued a personal protection order against a respondent who was also running against him in a campaign for tribal judge).

The relative dearth of law firms experienced in tribal court matters also opens up the potential for conflicts. See In the Matter of Removal of McCauley, 30 Indian L.Rep. 6142, 6148–49 (Kaw Nation S.Ct.2003), where the court disqualified a law firm purported representing the tribal government in the instant suit while at the same time suing the tribal government in another case. The court concluded that such a conflict violated the Oklahoma rules of professional conduct and was the type of conflict that could not be waived by the clients:

> * * * It is clear that [Michael] Minnis has become personal counsel to the individual Removal Respondents while also claiming to be counsel for the Nation as a whole. A lawyer cannot represent both parties. * * * Minnis has an irreconcilable conflict of interest in representing both the Nation and individual members of the Executive Council in removal actions involving the Removal Respondents. Minnis' representation of the individual Removal Respondents limits its ability to represent the Nation as a whole. The representations are directly adverse to two clearly distinguishable clients. We hold that the Removal Respondents could not lawfully vote to waive the conflict on behalf of the Nation when each of those members had a personal interest in the outcome. No such resolution in the limited record before us exists anyway. If it did, such resolution would directly conflict with [tribal law].

Id.

Tribal in-house counsel and counsel for business partners and others adverse to tribal nations regularly seek and receive from their clients for consent to proceed in spite of the conflict after consultation. But not always. Consider In re Lile, 2025 Muscogee Creek Nation Supreme LEXIS 5 (Muscogee (Creek) Nation S.Ct.2025). There, a lawyer representing a criminal defendant was retained as counsel for the Muscogee (Creek) Nation's Office of Attorney General. The lawyer did not withdraw as counsel for the defendant while working for the tribe. Worse, the lawyer accessed confidential government information on behalf of the criminal defendant. Even worse, the lawyer made false statements to the tribunal regarding their intention to withdraw. Eventually, the lawyer resigned from the tribal office so as to continue representing the defendant. The court disqualified the lawyer and suspended them for 12 months. See also In re Ducheneau, 10 Indian L.Rep. 6061 (Standing Rock Sioux Tribal Ct.1983) (holding that the appointment of the previous tribal public defender to the position of tribal prosecutor created numerous conflicts of interest and enjoining the appointment).

Interestingly, there are numerous tribal court decisions declining to disqualify a lawyer in close cases involving previous employment or family relations. Cole v. Kaw Housing Authority, 4 Okla. Trib. 281, 1995 WL 1073446 (Kaw Nation Dist.Ct.1995) (declining to disqualify lawyer who had previously served as tribal judge in same jurisdiction); Plummer v. Brown, 16 Indian L.Rep. 6101 (Navajo Nation S.Ct.1989) (issuing writ of prohibition disqualifying trial judge who was brother-in-law of party); GNS, Inc. v. Blackhawk, 24 Indian L.Rep. 6262 (Winnebago S.Ct.1997) (declining to disqualify tribal judge that had once served, while in their capacity as a law professor, as an academic reference to an attorney representing one of the parties).

Many tribal courts allow (and encourage) lay advocates to represent parties in tribal court, primarily due the lack of affordable legal counsel available to individual Indians in Indian country. See Cole v. Kaw Housing Authority, 4 Okla. Trib. 281, 1995 WL 1073446, at *4 (Kaw Nation Dist.Ct.1995) ("Tribal courts in general are often located in rural and isolated areas, are not well funded, are often relatively new or newly reestablished, and do not have well-settled bodies of law and codes to guide them. Often, the number of lawyers and advocates licensed, available, willing and able to practice before tribal courts is small. Frequently, litigants can draw upon only a handful of lawyers and advocates familiar with 1) tribal court procedures; 2) tribal custom and law; and 3) federal tribal sovereignty."); Day v. Chief Judge of Tribal Court, 5 Am. Tribal Law 219, 224 (Hopi App.Ct.2004) (noting "the far reach of lay counsel to the Hopi public"). In some types of cases, such as small claims cases where attorney representation is often barred, lay advocates may also be barred. E.g., Cheyenne River Sioux Gas Co. v. Dupris, 32 Indian L.Rep. 6137, 6137 (Cheyenne River Sioux Tribal Ct.App.2005).

Lay advocates generally must comply with the same rules of conduct and practice required of licensed attorneys, though obviously they are not required to be licensed by a state bar or be graduates of an accredited law school. E.g., In re Suspension of Reum, 6 Am. Tribal Law 168 (Fort Peck Ct.App.2006) (affirming disciplinary action against lay advocate for misconduct); In re Robertson, 4 NICS App. 111, 118 (Hoopa Valley Tribal Ct.App.1996) (same); *Day*, 5 Am. Tribal Law at 226 ("[T]he Court's equal treatment of lay advocates and attorneys as bar members meant that any punishment, not just contempt, applies equally to both groups."). Many tribal courts will still require lay advocates to fulfill the same admission requirements, which may include the completion of a bar exam.

In one unusual case, a split Navajo Nation Court of Appeals (now known as the Navajo Nation Supreme Court) panel addressed long-standing issues related to distrust of lawyers, especially foreign lawyers, in Indian country. See In the Matter of Practice of Battles, 10 Indian L.Rep. 6022 (Navajo Nation Ct.App.1982). There, a non-Indian lay advocate who had passed the first Navajo bar exam in 1976, was disqualified from representing a criminal defendant by the trial court. The tribal code at that time prohibited "professional attorneys" from appearing in Navajo tribal courts unless the court adopted rules of professional responsibility (which had not yet occurred), though non-lawyer Navajo citizens could appear. The trial court concluded that the intent of the Navajo Tribal Council was to protect the Nation and its citizens from bad outside influences:

> The court concluded that these limitations were reasonable and they were made to

> strengthen Navajo sovereignty in the face of possible state takeover, and sovereignty was protected by the fact [that] members of the tribe would understand Navajo custom and tradition and nonmember professionals would have the skills necessary to learn those Navajo laws and customs. * * * It was assumed that non-Navajo nonprofessionals (i.e., professionals in the field of law) would not know Navajo customs and traditions or know how to learn them.

Id. at 6022–23 (citations omitted). The majority agreed that the council might have intended to exclude all non-Navajos, but noted that to do so would prohibit legal representation for Navajo citizens in many cases. The court instead concluded that the council's actions recognized the inherent authority of the tribal court to regulate legal representation in Navajo courts. That power and the fact that the lay advocate in the case had been practicing regularly in Navajo courts for at least five years led to the court's reversal of the disqualification order. The dissent argued that "[t]he council wanted problems taken care of by the Navajo People in their own ways, with as little outside intervention as possible." Id. at 6025 (Bluehouse, Acting C.J., dissenting).

Tribal courts are also more receptive to allowing parties to proceed pro se, although courts are split on whether pro se litigations should be held to the same standards as attorneys. Compare Northwest Collections, Inc. v. Pichette, 22 Indian L.Rep. 6047, 6049 (Confederated Salish & Kootenai Tribes Civil

Ct.App.1995) ("Northwest as a *pro se* litigant as a matter of law cannot be held to the same exacting standards as a member of the bar."), with Hoopa Valley Tribal Plant Management Dept. v. Smith, 5 NICS App. 132, 134 (Hoopa Valley Tribal Ct.App. 1999) ("[A] party who represents himself is bound by the same rules of procedure and substantive law as any attorney representing him would have been."). Cf. IDM Financial, LLC v. Napeahi, 5 NICS App. 78 (Tulalip Tribal Ct.App.1998) ("Although a judge should take reasonable steps to insure that fair proceedings occur and to ensure that all parties have an opportunity to present their evidence, a judge cannot assist a party in presenting his or her case.").

In Cheyenne River Sioux Tribe v. Howard, 32 Indian L.Rep. 6165 (Cheyenne River Sioux Tribe Ct.App.2005), the court worried in dicta about the potential unfairness of an uncounseled tribal citizen litigating against the tribal government:

> The case unfortunately demonstrates the legal imbalances created by the lack of any statutory right to appointed defense counsel in civil proceedings. Mr. Howard was fighting to remain in the only home he knew. Arrayed against him was not only the CRHA [Cheyenne River Housing Authority] but its well-educated, highly skilled and very professional legal counsel. Given his lack of resources and the unavailability of appointed counsel, Mr. Howard was required to defend himself in an unfamiliar legal arena, where the trial judge held him fairly strictly to normal professional rules of procedure

> with which he was obviously unfamiliar. The adversary system, which, for better or worse, is employed in a relaxed form in the CRST Tribal Court presumes the ability of each side to fully and fairly present its own case. Where, as here, a significant imbalance between the two parties exists in both professional legal ability and the knowledge of the legal system, injustice is more likely to occur. Some tribes have sought to remedy this imbalance of legal resources between the Tribe and its members by creating a tribal Public Defender, paid for by the Tribe, and charged with representing indigent tribal members who are defendants in either criminal or civil proceedings.

Id. at 6166–67 n.3.

CHAPTER 5

INDIAN COUNTRY CRIMINAL JURISDICTION

Indian country criminal jurisdiction is as complicated as any area of public law. Federal, tribal, and state and local governments share territorial jurisdiction over "Indian country," a legal term of art currently defined by 18 U.S.C. § 1151 and United States Supreme Court decisions that interpret that codification. Restatement of the Law of American Indians § 68. Some states possess criminal jurisdiction over Indian country pursuant to federal enactments and accompanying state laws. Id. § 71. Personal jurisdiction is governed by "Indian status," another legal term of art defined by tribal, federal, and state judicial decisions that establish a test to determine whether a defendant or a victim is "Indian." Id. § 69. Acts of federal, tribal, and state legislatures determine the subject matter jurisdiction of Indian country crime, namely by identifying the crimes to be prosecuted.

Tribal sentencing authority is also governed by federal statutory enactments. 25 U.S.C. § 1302(a)(7). Tribal criminal procedure is governed by tribal codes and judicial opinions, with federal statutory enactments setting a floor. 25 U.S.C. §§ 1302, 1304. See also Nevayaktewa v. Hopi Tribe, 26 Indian L.Rep. 6164, 6170 (Hopi Tribe App.Ct.1998) (applying federal precedents to hold that imperfect trial procedures did not violate the "fundamental fairness" of the process, rejecting a "substantive due process" argument). Tribal courts are faithful to the requirements of the Indian Bill of Rights. E.g., United States v. McGaughey, 10 Indian L.Rep. 6051, 6051 (Hoopa Valley Ct. of Indian Offenses 1983) (The "Indian Civil Rights Act of 1968, both in intent as demonstrated by a reading of the legislative history of the Act and by the specific language of the Act, was designed to promote the imposition in part of the existing dominant culture's notions of equal protection and due process as they apply to the 'criminal process.' Without commenting on either the 'acceptability' or the 'desirability' of such an approach, those factors, plus a reading of the cases interpreting the Act make Congress' intent and accomplishments clear."). Following federal law, tribal courts hold that the Indian country criminal jurisdiction regime meets constitutional standards. Hopi Tribe v. Lonewolf Scott, 14 Indian L.Rep. 6001, 6004 (Hopi Tribal Ct.1986) (relying on Morton v. Mancari, 417 U.S. 535 (1974), to reject an equal protection claim brought by nonmember Indians objecting to tribal criminal jurisdiction).

Congress has established a right to habeas for persons detained by tribal court order. 25 U.S.C. § 1303 ("The privilege of the writ of habeas corpus shall be available to any person, in a court of the United States, to test the legality of his detention by order of an Indian tribe.").

A. TRIBAL CRIMINAL JURISDICTION

1. HISTORICAL BACKGROUND OF TRIBAL CRIMINAL LAW

Prior to colonization, American Indian tribal nations enforced societal norms in a fashion that rarely involved confinement or physical punishment. Tribal governments did not usually assert a monopoly on violence. Most law enforcement was confined to family and kinship groups. Indigenous communities were often so tight-knit that simple shaming or temporary banishment was sufficient to punish and deter crime. Moreover, execution or banishment of tribal community members could harm families or entire communities that depended on every single individual. That said, many tribal nations followed practices of banishment, corporeal punishment, and even blood feuds.

Early in the American colonization project, some tribal nations adapted to their changed political circumstances and adopted Anglo-American style justice systems, most famously the Cherokee Nation. The Cherokee Nation of Georgia retained its territorial nationality even as American colonies turned into American states, putting enormous pressure on the federal and tribal governments to either eliminate or remove them. To blunt the political pressure they believed was driven by the "otherness" of the tribal nation, the Cherokees prohibited blood feuds and created a police force called the Lighthorse. The tribe established written laws and formal court system, establishing the first appellate court in the State of Georgia. Other tribes in the American southeast followed suit, to similar or lesser extent, in order to avoid removal. It failed to stop removal however, as the Cherokee, Chickasaw, Creek, Choctaw, Seminole, and other tribal nations succumbed to the political, economic, and military pressure for removal to the west.

The survivors of removal to the Indian Territory (now a part of the State of Oklahoma) quickly reestablished their formal law enforcement structures. The Cherokee and Muscogee (Creek) nations in particular kept detailed written records of their court proceedings. E.g., 5 Mvskoke Law Rep. (2006) (collecting historic tribal district court materials from 1832 to the end of the 19th century). Federal and state law had no force in Indian country, allowing space for tribal nations to assert plenary jurisdiction over their lands throughout the 19th century. Even as late as 1896, the United States Supreme Court disclaimed jurisdiction to review a capital conviction by the Cherokee Nation in a decision captioned Talton v. Mayes, 163 U.S. 376 (1896). Bob Talton, likely a white man who had been adopted into Cherokee Nation citizenship, brutally murdered another tribal member. He petitioned the Supreme Court for a writ of habeas corpus, claiming the tribal conviction was invalid under a federal law establishing rules for a grand jury. The Court held that the American Constitution, by its terms, did not govern the powers of tribal governments and rejected the appeal.

The Indian Territory justice systems were very much an outlier, as few to no tribal nations elsewhere established justice systems similar to the Cherokee or the Creek nations systems. E.g., Pueblo of Pojoaque v. Gutierrez, 30 Indian L.Rep. 6020, 6021 (Pueblo of Pojoaque Tribal Ct.2002) ("The Pueblo maintained its criminal-civil jurisdiction, law enforcement, and dispute resolution over its members within the exterior boundaries through its War Chief, Tribal Council, and Governor."). Tribal justice remained informal and dependent on kinship and family structures, although numerous tribes began adopting ordinances (influenced by federal Indian agents), such as the Ottawa Laws of 1850. These laws were established by bands of the Odawa tribal nations originating in southwest Michigan and northwest Ohio, once led by the *ogema* Pontiac, after removal by the federal government to Kansas. Devastated by removal, forced into stark prairie lands almost diametrically opposite from their wooded, well-watered homelands, they adopted rudimentary laws addressing their new circumstances. These laws protected white men from Indian depredations first (likely influenced by federal officials), then prohibited much of the traditional means of enforcing rights. The laws prohibited revenge, horse theft, bad stud, gambling, and whiskey.

Starting in the 1870s, federal Indian agents and superintendents began to establish Law and Order Codes and Courts of Indian Offenses (CIOs) to enforce those laws. Somewhat like the Ottawa Laws, the Law and Order Codes established basic crimes in the American style, including "crimes" like adultery. Written by reservation superintendents and imposed on tribal councils, these Codes also restricted or banned outright Indigenous behaviors that the federal officials disfavored, such as religious and cultural practices, most notably the Sun Dance. Federal officials typically would appoint Indian people they trusted and controlled as judges and police (who also served as prosecutors in a classic conflict of interest). Interestingly, Congress never instructed the federal Indian Office (Bureau of Indian Affairs) to establish these Codes or CIOs. (Later, the Department of the Interior would regularly promulgate and modify Law and Order Codes, as well as promulgate regulations on the administration of the CIOs published in the Code of Federal Regulations, leading many to refer to the CIOs as "CFR Courts.") Instead, federal officials simply created them by coercing tribal councils into adopting them, then later sought ratification for their actions by seeking—and receiving—federal appropriations to fund them.

There were few appeals of convictions under the Courts of Indian Offenses. However, at least one "appeal" of sorts reached the federal judiciary, United States v. Clapox, 35 F. 575 (D.Or.1888). There, the Umatilla Court of Indian Offenses prosecuted a tribal member woman for adultery. Even in the 1880s, when adultery was considered in American society to be a serious matter, it was not generally prosecuted as a crime. But the federally controlled reservation court convicted a woman anyway. While she was being held in a tribal jail, Clapox attempted to break her out. Prison escape being a federal offense, the federal court convicted Clapox of a federal crime and sentenced him to one month in federal prison.

Clapox argued that the attempted prison break was justified because the reservation court, established under the authority of the Office of Indian Affairs, had never been authorized by an Act of Congress. Clapox further argued that the procedure used by the reservation court was deficient. The federal district court rejected both arguments, relying on the *Kagama* reasoning adopting the duty of protection as an independent source of federal power to act. The court surmised that Indian reservations were akin to schools for children, where the Indian wards of the federal government would be subjected to federal laws as a tool for their assimilation and civilization. Id. at 577. If anyone's rights were violated, under *Clapox* those violations were excused. See generally Eastern Band of Cherokee Indians v. Torres, 4 Cher.Rep. 9, 2005 WL 6437828, at *8 & n.1 (Eastern Band of Cherokee Indians S.Ct.2005) (Philo, J., concurring) (describing the Courts of Indian Offenses as resulting in "a national policy of 'separate but unequal,' for Indian tribes, and their courts").

At times, tribal judges criticize notions of Anglo-American criminal laws. For example, a Navajo trial judge rejected the government's demand for restitution to be paid to the tribal government:

> In general Anglo-European history, the victims of crime lost their right to be paid back for crime by the offender. * * * Some Anglo

> historians argue that this was because of the need of European governments to build social unity and stop revenge, the desire of kings to take all powers to themselves and the practice of kings of taking money in the form of fines as payment to protect the wrongdoers from the vengeance of the victim. * * * This ridiculous trend, which thankfully is being slowly replaced by concern for the victim of crime, is totally the opposite from the traditional Navajo way.
>
> Under Navajo tradition, all offenses (with the exception of witchcraft) were punished by payments to the victim or the victim's immediate family and clan. * * * In this case, robbery with injury would be punished by a payment of "blood money" to the immediate family, plus a multiple payment for any property taken. * * * Theft would be punished by a multiple payment to the victim or immediate family group.

In re D.P., 11 Indian L.Rep. 6023, 6024 (Navajo Nation Crownpoint Dist.Ct.1982). State and federal public policies behind criminal law such as deterrence and retribution would be foreign to traditional Indigenous cultures.

2. FEDERAL LAW AND MODERN TRIBAL JURISDICTION

The Law and Order Codes and Courts of Indian Offenses dominated tribal criminal justice throughout the 20th century. Even after Congress enacted the Indian Reorganization Act of 1934 that allowed tribal nations to adopt their own constitutions, 25 U.S.C. § 5123, some tribes under federal coercive influence incorporated the CIOs into their new constitutions. By the mid-20th century, several dozen tribal communities had taken over more control over their court systems, attempting to re-incorporate tribal custom and tradition into these Anglo-American legal structures. These justice systems also incorporated incarceration as punishment. By the 1960s, Congress began to hear about human rights abuses by a handful of tribal judges. After a series of hearings over several years in which Senate Committee on Constitutional Rights took anecdotal testimony about federal, state, local, and tribal human rights abuses in Indian country (perpetrated mostly by state and local officials), Congress passed the Indian Civil Rights Act of 1968 (ICRA), 25 U.S.C. § 1301 et seq.

ICRA set federal minimum baselines for tribal governments in the exercise of their powers, primarily in the so-called Indian Bill of Rights, an enumerated list of individual rights akin to the federal Bill of Rights. The "Indian Bill of Rights" as currently amended is codified at 25 U.S.C. § 1302(a). ICRA limited tribal criminal sentences to six months in jail and a $500 fine (increased in 1986 and again in 2010, see discussion infra). ICRA also opened up federal courthouse doors to petitions for writs of habeas corpus from persons detained by virtue of tribal court orders. 25 U.S.C. § 1303. These provisions created pressure for tribal governments to formalize their court systems. In 1975, Congress passed the Indian Self-Determination and Education

Assistance Act, or Public Law 638, 25 U.S.C. § 5301 et seq., which further enabled tribes to assume control over Indian country justice. Public Law 638 also allowed tribes to take control over their own justice systems, including many CIOs, by then often called CFR Courts.

The United States Supreme Court's views on tribal criminal jurisdiction changed dramatically since it had decided *Talton v. Mayes* in 1896. In Oliphant v. Suquamish Indian Tribe, 435 U.S. 191 (1978), the Supreme Court held that tribal nations never possessed the power to prosecute non-Indians. The Court concluded from a lengthy review of federal Indian policy going back to the Founding that each federal branch of government, and even the tribes themselves, had always assumed that tribal nations could not prosecute non-Indians. This "unspoken assumption," id. at 203, was sufficient to deny tribal jurisdiction over Oliphant, a white man (and his acquaintance, Belgarde, who was alleged at the federal district court level to be a nonmember Indian), for reckless driving and assaulting tribal police officers.

Somewhat confusingly, less than two weeks later in United States v. Wheeler, 435 U.S. 313 (1978), the Supreme Court agreed that tribal powers to prosecute their own citizens was inherent and subject only to abrogation by the tribe itself or by an Act of Congress clearly expressing an intent to do so. *Wheeler*, which involved a federal prosecution of a crime subsequent to a tribal prosecution for the same crime, also stands for the proposition that tribal convictions do not implicate the Double Jeopardy Clause. The Court, as it had in *Talton*, recognized that tribal prosecutions were not governed by the United States Constitution.

Since that time, Congress has enhanced tribal criminal jurisdiction in piecemeal fashion, usually through amending ICRA. In 1991, the United States Supreme Court extended the *Oliphant* holding to nonmember Indians, Duro v. Reina, 495 U.S. 676 (1990), abrogating Salt River Pima-Maricopa Indian Community v. Duro, 11 Indian L.Rep. 6050 (Salt River Pima-Maricopa Indian Community Ct.1984). In line with tribal courts who viewed *Duro* as creating "a chaotic state of affairs" and a "jurisdictional void," Colville Confederated Tribes v. Stead, 21 Indian L.Rep. 6005, 6007 (Colville Tribal Ct.App.1993), Congress overrode that decision and reaffirmed tribal powers over all Indians, an act known colloquially as the *Duro* fix. See 25 U.S.C. § 1301(2). In 2004, the Supreme Court affirmed Congress's power to enhance tribal criminal jurisdiction powers. United States v. Lara, 541 U.S. 193 (2004). One tribal court held the *Duro* fix to have immediate application. E.g., *Stead*, 21 Indian L.Rep. at 6110 (affirming criminal conviction of nonmember Indian initiated one week after *Duro* fix enactment).

In the Violence Against Women Reauthorization Act of 2013, Congress reaffirmed the power of tribes to prosecute domestic violence and intimate partner violence against non-Indians. 25 U.S.C. § 1304. In 2022, Congress added more crimes by non-Indians over which tribes had jurisdiction, notably, child abuse, human trafficking, and assaults on police. Tribal legislatures and tribal courts must match tribal criminal codes with state and/or federal crimes in order to determine whether a tribe may prosecute a given crime under § 1304. E.g., Eastern Band of Cherokee Indians v. Johnson, 18 Am. Tribal Law 62, 73 (Cherokee Ct. of the Eastern Band of Cherokee Indians 2024) (assessing whether the tribal charge of obstruction of justice was similar enough to the federal statute, 25 U.S.C. § 13094(a)(9)).

In 1968, Congress limited tribal sentencing authority to six months and a $500 fine, eroding the likelihood of traditional tribal punishments. E.g., Winnebago Tribe of Nebraska v. Bigfire, 24 Indian L.Rep. 6232, 6239 (Winnebago Tribal Ct.1997) (detailing severe punishments for sexual assault under tribal traditional law), aff'd, 25 Indian L.Rep. 6229 (Winnebago Tribe of Neb.S.Ct.1998). In 1986, Congress extended that authority to a year and $5000. 25 U.S.C. § 1302(a)(7)(B). Given the limits on sentencing, some tribal courts imposed consecutive or stacked sentences in order to expand tribal powers. E.g., Colville Confederated Tribes v. St. Peter, 20 Indian L.Rep. 6108 (Colville Tribal Ct.App.1993).

Some tribal nations have even provided for pardoning power via statute. In Rosebud Sioux Tribe v. Horse Looking, 33 Indian L.Rep. 6092 (Rosebud Sioux Tribal Ct.2006), the court surveyed the laws of several tribes providing for a pardon power and its substantive and procedural scope. In that case, the tribal president sent a letter ostensibly pardoning a criminal defendant after the defendant had absconded. The court found no positive law authorizing the president to exercise a pardon power and held that the pardon was ineffective.

In the Tribal Law and Order Act of 2010 (TLOA), Congress authorized tribes meeting federal constitutional law criteria to sentence offenders to up to three years in jail and up to nine years of consecutive sentences. 25 U.S.C. § 1302(a)(7)(C). Tribal courts are just beginning to interpret the new federal authorities. Compare Desautel v. Colville Confederated Tribes, 13 Am. Indian Tribal Law 150, 151–52 (Colville Tribal Ct.App.2016) (rejecting tribal sentencing authority for more than one year where tribe had not adopted rules of evidence), with Picard v. Colville Confederated Tribes, 16 Am. Tribal Law 81, 86 (Colville Tribal Ct.App.2020) (affirming tribal sentencing authority for more than one year where tribe had fulfilled the federal requirements under ICRA and TLOA). Despite this authority, many tribal nations (mostly for financial reasons) do not exercise the full panoply of powers available to them. Especially when it comes to the more recent federal reaffirmations of tribal powers under VAWA and TLOA, relatively few tribal nations exercise this jurisdiction because the costs associated with compliance with the federal parameters are very high.

In the absence of the authority to impose lengthy prison or jail sentences and in the absence of criminal jurisdiction over non-Indians, tribal nations have turned to traditional punishments such as exclusion or banishment. Tribal legislatures and tribal courts must take care to be clear that an exclusion or banishment order issued against a nonmember or non-Indian is either a civil or criminal sanction. Federal Indian law provides that tribal courts cannot exercise criminal jurisdiction over non-Indians by race, Oliphant v. Suquamish Indian Tribe, 435 U.S. 191 (1978), but may exercise civil jurisdiction over nonmembers (Indian or non-Indian) under *Montana* and Merrion v. Jicarilla Apache Tribe, 455 U.S. 130 (1983). For example, in Crow Creek Sioux Tribe v. Buum, 10 Indian L.Rep. 6031 (Northern Plains Intertribal Ct.App.1983), the court held that a tribal court contempt citation leading the exclusion of a non-Indian person would be valid if the contempt order was civil in character, not criminal.

In sum, tribal criminal jurisdiction is a core element of tribal sovereignty. "The tribes . . . have complete inherent and exclusive criminal jurisdiction over Indians and Indian country unless there are federal statutes, treaties, or judicial decisions which limit the tribal court's jurisdiction." McCauley v. Pyramid Lake Paiute Tribe, 2005 WL 6344534, at *3 (Nev. Inter-Tribal Ct.App.2005). Other than the few tribes from which Congress has stripped jurisdiction, every tribe can choose to exercise that power. E.g., Squaxin Island Tribe v. Thomas, 10 Indian L.Rep. 6005, 6007 (Squaxin Island Tribe Ct.App.1982) (finding sufficient authority to enact criminal code in tribal constitution language authorizing council "to administer justice").

3. "INDIAN STATUS" DETERMINATIONS UNDER TRIBAL LAW

Outside of tribal criminal procedural matters, the most critical legal issue is Indian status. Indian country criminal jurisdiction depends heavily on whether the defendant or a victim is "Indian." Federal statutory law does not define "Indian," leaving tribal governments and/or tribal courts to determine Indian status. One does not have to be a citizen of a federally-recognized tribal nation to be considered an "Indian" for criminal jurisdiction purposes. E.g., Eastern Band of Cherokee Indians v. Lambert, 3 Cher.Rep. 62, 2003 WL 25902446, at *1 (Cherokee Ct. of the Eastern Band of Cherokee Indians 2003) (asserting jurisdiction over an unenrolled "first lineal descendant"); Muscogee (Creek) Nation v. Wilson, 2024 Muscogee Creek Nation Supreme LEXIS 1, at *15–16 (Muscogee (Creek) Nation S.Ct.2024) ("The Nation has clearly shown its willingness to extend 'benefits of tribal affiliation' to a limited class of individuals that are eligible for membership in a federally recognized Indian tribe. This is consistent with Mvskoke traditional common law that placed significant importance on the protection of minor children, even those who are not members of the Muscogee (Creek) Nation."). See also Taypayosatum v. Fort Peck Tribes, 16 Am. Tribal Law 224 (Fort Peck Ct.App. 2020) (asserting jurisdiction over Canadian First Nation member who had lived in the tribal community for many years); Swinomish Indian Tribal Community v. Sam, 15 Am. Tribal Law 375 (Swinomish Tribal Ct.2017) (same). Some tribal courts have allowed non-Indians to consent to tribal criminal jurisdiction. E.g., Eastern Band of Cherokee Indians v. Bowers, 6 Cher.Rep. 8, 2007 WL 7080171 (Cherokee Ct. of the Eastern Band of Cherokee Indians 2007).

What constitutes sufficient evidence that a person is an "Indian" is complex. In Mashantucket Pequot Tribe v. Boyd, 1 Mash.Rep. 234, 1996 WL 34403079 (Mashantucket Pequot Tribal Ct.1996), the court rejected criminal jurisdiction over a person who had applied for tribal membership but was not yet enrolled. In Jackson v. Fort Peck Tribes, 18 Am. Tribal Law 87 (Fort Peck Ct.App.2024), the court held that there was probable cause that the defendant was "Indian" because "has held out a Fort Peck member, Michael Jackson, as her father for most of her life and goes by his surname she claims that biologically she is the progeny of two non-Indians and although she has lived on the Fort Peck reservation and been a member of the Community her entire life." Id. at 91. In dicta, though, the court noted that because the tribal prosecution must show at trial that the defendant was "Indian" beyond a reasonable doubt, the answer might differ in that situation. Id. at 92 ("Had she proceeded to trial and offered some proof that another individual with no degree of Indian blood was her real father, the Tribes may have been hard pressed to rebut that beyond a reasonable doubt at trial."). Defendants can stipulate to Indian status. E.g., Rowe v. Fort Peck Tribes, 18 Am. Tribal Law 92 (Fort Peck Ct.App.2024).

Many tribal courts view Indian status as an element of a criminal offense, placing the burden on the prosecution to prove Indian status. E.g., McIntosh v. Muscogee (Creek) Nation, 7 Okla. Trib. 290, 2001 WL 34090536, at *3 (Muscogee (Creek) Nation S.Ct.2001) ("It may also be true that it was common knowledge that Appellant was an Indian person and a member of the Muscogee (Creek) Nation. Nonetheless, knowledge alone is not enough. Without proof contained in the record, a criminal charge may not be brought against any person in the Muscogee (Creek) Nation courts."). However, some tribal courts have held that Indian status is not an element of a crime that would require the prosecution to prove beyond a reasonable doubt that a person is Indian. E.g., Seymour v. Colville Confederated Tribes, 2001 WL 36243309, at *4 (Colville Tribal Ct. App.2001) ("Whether a defendant is an 'Indian' is not an element of an offense. In our Courts, elements of an offense have been recognized to be those facts offered to prove a defendant committed specific acts at a specific place, time and date which constitute criminal behavior."); McCauley v. Pyramid Lake Paiute Tribe, 2005 WL 6344534 (Nev. Inter-Tribal Ct.App.2005) ("[T]he use of the term 'any Indian' in Section 3.04.3304 of the Pyramid Lake Paiute Tribe Code, does not result in 'Indian status' becoming another element of the crime 'Driving Under the Influence.' It is a statutory recognition that only Indians are within the criminal jurisdiction of the Tribe.").

The special jurisdictional provisions allowing for tribal jurisdiction over non-Indians for certain crimes creates additional legal issues. In Eastern Band of Cherokee Indians v. Johnson, 18 Am. Tribal Law 62 (Cherokee Ct. of the Eastern Band of Cherokee Indians 2024), the court assumed jurisdiction of a non-Indian United States citizen charged with obstruction of justice related to drug crimes under 25 U.S.C. § 1304. Even in the absence of Congressional recognition of tribal authority, some tribes had been prosecuting non-Indians. In Eastern Band of Cherokee Indians v. Torres, 4 Cher. Rep. 9, 2005 WL 6437828 (Eastern Band of Cherokee Indian S.Ct. 2005), the court scoured through the United States Supreme Court decision in *Oliphant* and could find no prohibition on prosecuting a non-Indian, non-American citizen:

> The Court's restriction of its holding in *Oliphant* to "non-Indian citizens of the United States" has a significant historical basis, and is consistent with the Court's concerns of liberty, justice and fairness justifying the Court's ruling prohibiting the exercise of criminal jurisdiction over non-Indian citizens of the United States. The Court has traditionally recognized this distinction between citizens and non-citizens. Over a century ago, the Court indicated that the general "object" of Congressional statutes regarding Indian country was "to reserve to the courts of the United States [criminal] jurisdiction of all actions to which its own citizens are parties on either side." In re Mayfield, 141 U.S. 107, 115–116, 11 S.Ct. 939, 35 L.Ed. 635 (1891) (quoted in *Oliphant*, 435

> U.S. at 204, 98 S.Ct. at 1019, 55 L.Ed.2d at 219) * * *.

Id. at *3. See also Eastern Band of Cherokee Indians v. Martinez, 15 Am. Tribal Law 45, 49 (Eastern Band of Cherokee Indians S.Ct.2018) ("This Court stands by its analysis and decision in *Torres*—that it is based upon a proper interpretation of *Oliphant* and that the Tribe retains its inherent authority to protect the safety and liberty of its members.").

The most famous (if not leading) Indian status case is Means v. District Court of the Chinle Judicial District, 2 Am. Tribal Law 439 (Navajo Nation S.Ct. 1999). There, the Navajo Nation charged Russell Means with criminal threatening and battery of two of his in-laws. The court held that the tribe possessed jurisdiction over Means, a nonmember Indian who a citizen of the Oglala Sioux Tribe, under three theories. First, Congress has expressly reaffirmed the inherent tribal power to enforce criminal law against all "Indians," 25 U.S.C. § 1301(2), also known as the *Duro* fix. Second, the 1868 Treaty of Fort Sumner reserved the power to prosecute nonmember Indians:

> Using surrounding circumstances, history, and the "as the Indians understood it" canon of treaty construction, the issue of how to deal with "bad" Indians was the subject of specific discussions at Fort Sumner. Barboncito, the primary Navajo treaty negotiator, gave an opening speech where he outlined the hardships suffered by Navajos at the adjoining Bosque Redondo "reservation." He complained: "I think

> that all nations around here are against us (I mean Mexicans and Indians) the reason is that we are a working tribe of Indians, and if we had the means we could support ourselves far better than either Mexican or Indian. The Comanches are against us I know it for they came here and killed a good many of our men. In our own country we knew nothing about the Comanche." Link, Treaty Between the United States of America and the Navajo Tribe of Indians 3–4 (1968) (hereafter "Link"). General William T. Sherman said this in reply: "The Army will do the fighting, you must live at peace, if you go to your own country the Utes will be the nearest Indians to you, you must not trouble the Utes and the Utes must not trouble you. If, however, the Utes or Apaches come into your country with bows and arrows and guns you of course can drive them out but must not follow beyond the boundary line." Link at 5.

Id. at 448 (footnote omitted). Finally, the court applied Navajo common law governing in-laws, or *hadane*. The court concluded that by voluntarily forming family relationships with Navajos in Navajo country, Means had agreed to comply with tribal laws:

> * * * An individual who marries or has an intimate relationship with a Navajo is a *hadane* (in-law). The Navajo People have *adoone'e* or clans, and many of them are based upon the intermarriage of original Navajo clan members with people of other nations. The primary clan

> relation is traced through the mother, and some of the "foreign nation" clans include the "Flat Foot-Pima clan," the "Ute people clan," the "Zuni clan," the "Mexican clan," and the "Mescalero Apache clan." See, *Saad Ahaah Sinil*: Dual Language Navajo-English Dictionary, 3–4 (1986). The list of clans based upon other peoples is not exhaustive. A *hadane* or in-law assumes a clan relation to a Navajo when an intimate relationship forms, and when that relationship is conducted within the Navajo Nation, there are reciprocal obligations to and from family and clan members under Navajo common law. Among those obligations is the duty to avoid threatening or assaulting a relative by marriage (or any other person).

Id. at 450 (footnote omitted). Years later, the federal judiciary would reject Means' jurisdictional challenges to Navajo jurisdiction. Means v. Navajo Nation, 432 F.3d 924 (9th Cir.2005).

Another tribal court recognized criminal jurisdiction over a non-Indian person who resided on fee land within the tribe and was considered a kind of relative, known to that tribe as a "Moccasinits," as opposed to a "Ayokoo" or "ordinary * * * white man." Kaibab Band of Paiute Indians v. Johnson, 26 Indian L.Rep. 6100, 6101 (Kaibab-Paiute Tribal Ct.1999). The court defined those terms as follows:

> * * * The Kaibab Band word for descendants of those Mormons who originally invaded their lands and settled in Moccasin is "Moccasinits." Other Euro-American or Europeans who merely

> drive through the Kaibab Paiute Indian Reservation, and those who live on the reservation for only a short period of time, are referred to as "Ayokoo."
>
> In context, "Moccasinits" refers to the Kaibab concept that relations with an individual create reciprocal obligations.

Id. at 6104. Echoing United States Supreme Court statements on the importance of individual consent to tribal jurisdiction, the court concluded that the defendant, was subject to tribal jurisdiction for serious traffic offenses:

> Any Moccasinits or Ayokoo who assaults a Kaibab spouse, a Kaibab in an affectional relationship, or a relative of that person, should be subject to criminal penalties for the offenses. Any Moccasinits or Ayokoo who resides within the Kaibab Paiute Indian Reservation and is a lessee or permittee of the Band, or one of its members, should be subject to criminal penalties. Any Moccasinits or Ayokoo who is employed by the Kaibab Band, and receives wages or fees from it, should be subject to criminal statutes which deal with ethical violations, fraud, theft, etc., in relation to their employment.

Id. at 6104–05.

Finally, at least one tribal court has held that the initial burden of proof rests with a criminal defendant to show that they are *not* an Indian. The Hopi appellate court reached this conclusion, relying on the Ninth Circuit's decision in United States v. Hester, 719 F.2d 1041, 1042 (9th Cir.1983):

> To balance the interest of the parties, this Court believes that the burden should first fall on the defendant and then shifts to the prosecution once the defendant has made a threshold showing that he or she is not an Indian. Under this option, the defendant would have to raise the issue and then create a reasonable belief that he or she is not an Indian. Once the defendant fulfills this requirement, the burden will shift to the prosecution to prove beyond a reasonable doubt that the defendant is an Indian.

In re Certified Question, 3 Am. Tribal Law 423 (Hopi App.Ct.2001). However, the Tenth Circuit later rejected the *Hester* court's reasoning in United States v. Prentiss, 256 F.3d 971, 978 (10th Cir.2001) (en banc).

4. TRIBAL TERRITORIAL JURISDICTION

Federal law generally draws a line at "Indian country" for purposes of tribal criminal jurisdiction, making tribal territorial jurisdiction co-terminus with federal territorial jurisdiction. See Pueblo of Pojoaque v. Gutierrez, 30 Indian L.Rep. 6020, 6021 (Pueblo of Pojoaque Tribal Ct.2002) ("[T]he United States has criminal jurisdiction over all Indians within the exterior boundaries of the Pueblo of Pojoaque, and that this criminal jurisdiction is concurrent with the criminal jurisdiction of the Pueblo of Pojoaque.").

In some circumstances, that power can extend outside of Indian country. The leading case on that point is People of the Little River Band of Ottawa Indians v. Kelsey, 8 Am. Tribal Law 283 (Little River Band of Ottawa Indians Ct.App.2009). There, a tribal council member was convicted by the tribe of misdemeanor sexual assault of a tribal employee. The assault occurred at the tribe's community center, located within the historic territory of the tribe, but on fee land. Treating the location of the crime as outside of Indian country, the tribe argued that the assault was still a crime against the tribe by a tribal citizen. The tribal appellate court agreed. And on habeas, the Sixth Circuit also agreed in Kelsey v. Pope, 809 F.3d 849 (6th Cir.2016). The appellate courts adopted the theory that tribal jurisdiction is dependent on membership, which in turn with tribal citizens is dependent on consent because tribal citizenship is not birthright citizenship. In other words, individual Indians must affirmatively enroll with a tribe, effectively consenting to tribal laws wherever they extend. If a tribal citizen travels to Geneva, Switzerland for a meeting at the United Nations and attempts to, say, bribe one of their tribe's elected officials, then the tribe should have jurisdiction to prosecute that crime.

Kelsey was not a case of first impression in the federal courts. Tribes have been prosecuting tribal citizens for violations of tribal hunting and fishing regulations of off-reservation treaty rights for many decades. In 1974, Ninth Circuit decided Settler v. Lameer, 507 F.2d 231 (9th Cir.1974), affirming the power of Indian tribes to prosecute tribal members for off-reservation treaty fishing. Michigan tribal nations had been prosecuting off-reservation fishing violations for decades as well. E.g., Chippewa-Ottawa Tribes v. Peterson, 20 Indian L. Rep. 6142 (Chippewa-Ottawa Conservation Ct.1993) (Lake Huron); Chippewa-Ottawa Tribes v. Payment, 18 Indian L. Rep. 6141 (Chippewa-Ottawa Conservation Ct.1991) (same); Chippewa-Ottawa Tribes v. Sebastian, 17 Indian L.Rep. 6119 (Chippewa-Ottawa Conservation Ct.1990) (same); Chippewa-Ottawa Tribes v. Peterson, 16 Indian L. Rep. 6144 (Chippewa-Ottawa Tribes Conservation Ct.1989) (Lake Superior).

Some crimes cross jurisdictional lines, though tribal nations can assume jurisdiction over a crime that at least partially occurs within Indian country. For example, in Mellon v. Colville Confederated Tribes, 2005 WL 6462840 (Colville Tribal Ct.App. 2005), the court confirmed jurisdiction over the illegal use of tribal credit cards. Though the defendant used the cards off the reservation, the defendant procured those cards from the tribe's offices on the reservation. The court held, "Jurisdiction goes to the power of the Court to hear the matter because the defendant committed the actions that form the basis of the crimes charged within the jurisdictional boundaries of the Reservation." Id. at *4. See also Mellon v. Colville Confederated Tribes, 32 Indian L.Rep. 6021 (Colville Tribal Ct.App.2005) (same); Champagne v. People, 35 Indian L.Rep. 6003 (Little River Band of Ottawa Indians Tribal Ct.2006), aff'd, 35 Indian L. Rep. 6004,

6006 (Little River Band of Ottawa Indians Tribal Ct.App.2007) (same).

5. CROSS-JURISDICTIONAL AGREEMENTS

Because Indian country boundaries are often uncertain, tribal nations have regularly entered into cross-deputization or public safety cooperation agreements with federal, state, and local police. See United States v. Cooley, 593 U.S. 345, 355 (2021) (citing Matthew L.M. Fletcher, Kathryn E. Fort, & Wenona T. Singel, Indian Country Law Enforcement and Cooperative Public Safety Agreements, 89 Mich. Bar J., Feb. 2010, at 42). Tribal law enforcement will often be the first responders to crime in Indian country, then turning the case over to the proper jurisdiction after arrest or keeping the case for prosecution in tribal court. E.g., Mashantucket Pequot Tribe v. Sebastian, 4 Mash.Rep.112, 2003 WL 25586062, at *3 (Mashantucket Pequot Tribal Ct.2003). State and local police tend to step back when tribal police are responding to crime on tribal lands. E.g., Absentee Shawnee Tribe v. Ponkilla, 5 Okla. Trib. 312, 1997 WL 1146309, at *2 (Absentee Shawnee Tribal Ct.1997) (describing tribal police chief's testimony that "no other law enforcement agency * * * provides law enforcement services to Housing Authority homes [and t]hat the Sheriff's officers are cross-commissioned as tribal police officers, but their past practice is to not enter a Housing Authority crime scene without tribal police present").

Many cross-jurisdictional agreements arise from the negotiation of a Class III gaming compact under the Indian Gaming Regulatory Act, 25 U.S.C. § 2710. E.g., Mashantucket Pequot Tribe v. Sebastian, 4 Mash.Rep. 112, 2003 WL 25586062, at *3 (Mashantucket Pequot Tribal Ct.2003) (detailing tribal-state cross-deputization agreement).

In sum, federal law generally governs the scope of tribal criminal jurisdiction. The United States Supreme Court severely limited tribal criminal jurisdiction over non-Indians. Congress has restored a small amount of that jurisdiction, but few tribes are able to comply with the obligations required to exercise that power. Tribal sentencing authority is also limited.

B. TRIBAL CRIMINAL PROCEDURE

Tribal criminal procedure, once informal, is now dominated by federal criminal procedure doctrines, though numerous tribal justice systems have incorporated tribal traditions in a manner designed to blunt the sharp edges of policing and incarceration. E.g., Seymour v. Colville Confederated Tribes, 2001 WL 36243309, at *2 n.6 (Colville Confederated Tribes Ct.App.2001) ("The U.S. Supreme Court continues to press non-Indian standards on tribal courts in their interpretations of tribal jurisdiction. It is the tribal judiciaries' responsibility to be ever vigilant in ensuring that *tribal* law is developed, based on our cultural mores and standards, and not just the pan-Indianism view of the Supreme Court. We must accept the limits of the Supreme Court in the most conservative way possible.") (emphasis in original); Navajo Nation v. Kelly, 6 Am. Tribal Law 772, 777 (Navajo Nation S.Ct.2006) ("Merely because the Navajo Bill of Rights uses the same term does not mean that the Court should simply adopt and apply federal interpretations. * * * Though the Court considers federal interpretations, the Court ultimately must interpret the Bill of Rights consistent with *Diné bi beenahaz'áanii.*") (citation omitted).

Tribal courts often must engage in a reconsideration of criminal legal theory in adjudicating tribal criminal cases. In Teeman v. Burns Paiute Indian Tribe, 25 Indian L.Rep. 6197 (Burns Paiute Tribal Ct.App.1997), the court reversed a trial level decision rejecting the defense of self-defense because the tribal laws enacted by the tribal legislature had not mentioned it. The trial court held that it possessed no authority to adopt judge-made legal doctrines in the absence of explicit tribal legislative authority. The appellate court noted that the trial judge's reasoning meant that "absent a statutory provision for self-defense, all crimes against a person would be strict liability crimes, and there would be no exculpatory factors or circumstances which would offer justification or excuse for those crimes." Id. at 6198. After engaging in a lengthy historical review of the origins of self-defense as a legal theory in American and English common law, the court pointed to the obligation of tribal courts to guarantee due process under the Indian Civil Rights Act, 25 U.S.C. § 1302(a)(8). The court offered the following commentary in conclusion:

If ever a case in its infancy cried out for dismissal as an exercise of reasonable prosecutorial discretion, this is it. Two individuals engaged in apparent mutual combat and inflicted minor injuries upon each other. The event took place with only one other person present, and that person has absolutely no recall of what transpired. Each of the combatants admits striking the other, but each claims it was done defensively. Other than their conflicting stories, there is no evidence of any kind sufficient to prove that a crime was committed with the requisite guilty mind. But somehow, this case proceeded to an improbable point where, after the trial had ended, the judge negated the defendant's self-defense testimony because she could not cite the federal law (ICRA) which would recognize self-defense. That decision of the court was prejudicial error.

The due process rights of criminal defendants on the Burns Paiute Indian Reservation include a presumption of innocence and a right to offer exculpatory evidence. The rights derive from the demand for basic fairness. They were denied to Teeman in this case when the court placed upon her the burden of proving a right to claim self-defense. When all of the resources, training and background knowledge in law repose within the government, it is basically unfair to shift to the presumptively innocent defendant the burden of proving the law.

Id. at 6199.

There are limits to a tribal court's capacity to comply with traditional notions of justice. For example, in Champagne v. People, 35 Indian L. Rep. 6004 (Little River Band of Ottawa Indians Tribal Ct.App.2007), the defendant, who was charged with attempted embezzlement (and was a sitting appellate justice), insisted that Anishinaabe tribal law did not recognize the crime of "attempt," at least in part because there is no word in *Anishinabemowin* (the language of the Anishinaabe people) for "attempt"; demanded to be tried before "traditional judges"; and argued that the tribe's borrowing of Michigan criminal law was inconsistent with Anishinaabe traditional law. Id. at 6005, 6007. The court rejected the argument, holding that the defendant's admitted effort to procure money from the tribe was still a crime:

> Among the many legal arguments made before this Court at oral argument * * *, Justice Champagne argues that the tribal customs and traditions of the Ottawa people do not recognize the crime of "attempt." Justice Champagne further appears to argue more generally that the Little River Band statute adopting relevant Michigan state criminal is inconsistent with Anishinaabek traditional tribal law and therefore this Court should not apply it to him. Cf. LaPorte v. Fletcher, [ ] 2006 WL 6351711, **4–5 (Little River Band Tribal Court of Appeals 2006) (Champagne, J.) ("It is the custom of the Little River Band of Ottawa Indians to believe that society must be mended to make whole again."). These are laudable and compelling

arguments relating to the seeming contradiction between tribal goals to develop a modern and sophisticated legal system based on Anglo-American legal models while attempting to preserve the cultural distinctiveness of Ottawa culture through the development of tribal law and the preservation of tribal customs and traditions. See generally Michael D. Petoskey, Tribal Courts, 67 Michigan Bar Journal, May 1988, at 366, 366–69; Frank Pommersheim, Braid of Feathers: American Indian Law and Contemporary Tribal Life 66–67 (1995). As such, we take these arguments seriously. In other factual and legal circumstances, we might be compelled to consider such an argument as dispositive, but this matter does not oblige us to question current tribal law. As Justice Champagne all but admitted at trial and at oral argument, he attempted to procure money that was not owed him by the Little River Band for his own purposes. It is not obvious to this Court that Justice Champagne's failure in his attempt should excuse him from liability. More importantly, Justice Champagne does not and cannot identify an Ottawa custom or tradition that would excuse him for his actions. In fact, it would be a sad day for this community to acknowledge that an action reflecting an intention of an individual to fraudulently procure money from the Band is excused because the word "attempt" does not exist in Anishinaabemowin, as Justice Champagne alleged at oral argument.

Id. at 6005 (citation omitted).

Similarly, in Smith v. Colville Confederated Tribes, 25 Indian L.Rep. 6156 (Colville Ct.App.1998), the court declined to apply the defendant's defense rooted in custom and tradition for failure to develop or prove the defense at trial in a sentence modification matter after the defendant's blood tested positive for marijuana. The defendant claimed the marijuana entered his bloodstream during a sweat:

> In the instant case, the record shows the trial judge was willing to address custom and tradition at a show cause hearing on the issue of use of marijuana. The record also shows the appellant alleged facts that could have supported such a finding. That is, he alleged: (1) he participated in a traditional sweat with others; (2) the others brought a mixture of something to smoke in the sweat; (3) the appellant did not know what was in the mixture, which could have contained marijuana; and (4) it would not have been traditional to ask what was in the mixture.

Id. at 6157. In a footnote, the court strongly suggested that the defendant's defense was a sham: "[W]e believe the appellant would have been hard pressed finding any elder or tribal traditionalist who could support the use of marijuana in a traditional sweat." Id. at 6157 n.3.

Some tribes have provided for a panel of non-parties with expertise in tribal custom and tradition to suss out relevant legal principles applicable to tribal court matters. E.g., Colville Confederated Tribes v. Marchand, 33 Indian L.Rep. 6036, 6037 (Confederated Tribes of the Colville Reservation Tribal Ct.2006) ("The Court has requested that an elders panel be formed to explain to the Court any traditions or customs as they relate to a right to confront accusers. The Court intends to use this information to determine the proper standards to use for the admissibility of statements in the face of the right to confrontation."); Marchand v. Colville Confederated Tribes, 33 Indian L.Rep. 6065, 2006 WL 6557715, at *2 (Confederated Tribes of the Colville Reservation Ct.App.2006) ("Marchand asks us to allow him to ask an Elder's Panel to extend this tradition ['when we speak, we speak the truth and we honor Our word'] to include a finding that the Prosecutor is like a traditional 'chief,' and as such can never withdraw a plea proposal in that tribal 'chiefs' did not go back on their words. In Smith v. CCT, [25 Indian L.Rep. 6156, 1998 WL 35315070] (1998), we held a request for an Elder's Panel cannot be a 'fishing expedition.' "); Gardner v. Littlejohn, 9 Am. Tribal Law 431, 439 (Ho-Chunk Nation Trial Ct.) ("The Judicial Branch, acting through the Ho-Chunk Nation Traditional Court, may articulate binding law in the form of hocąk tradition and custom."), rev'd on other grounds, 11 Am. Tribal Law 400 (Ho-Chunk Nation S.Ct.2011); Ho-Chunk Nation v. Olsen, 2 Am. Tribal Law 299, 304 & n.1 (Ho-Chunk Nation Trial Ct.2000) ("[A]ccording to the Ho-Chunk Nation's traditions and customs, once an agreement for the performance of services or production of goods is made, the parties have a duty to fulfill their obligation(s). * * * The trial Court consulted the Ho-Chunk Nation Traditional Court as to the customs or traditions of the Nation. As the Traditional Court does not formalize its decisions with a writing, no written decision of the variety one would usually expect from a court is available.").

1. FEDERAL LAW INFLUENCE ON TRIBAL CRIMINAL PROCEDURE

Modern tribal criminal procedure is largely governed by the Indian Bill of Rights as amended by statutes such as the Tribal Law and Order Act of 2010, codified in the Indian Civil Rights Act (ICRA), 25 U.S.C. § 1302. Prior to ICRA's enactment in 1968, tribal criminal procedure was rooted in custom and tradition. Consider Ex parte Crow Dog, 109 U.S. 556 (1883), decided by the United States Supreme Court. That case arose from a federal prosecution for capital murder in Lakota Indian country where the tribal elders and families of the victim and perpetrator reached an agreement not to execute or banish the perpetrator, instead requiring the perpetrator's family to pay damages to the victim's family. Crow Dog, the perpetrator, was sanctioned by the community after a lengthy negotiation, not a formal trial. Spotted Tail, the deceased, and Crow Dog were important tribal leaders and the community was loathe to lose two leaders in one fell swoop. The federal government, dissatisfied with it perceived as leniency by the tribe, sought a federal conviction, which was dismissed by the Supreme Court. As a consequence, federal officials asked and received from Congress authority to prosecute felonies in Indian country, the Major Crimes Act. 18 U.S.C. § 1153.

As tribal nations progressed through the mid-20th century, the informalities of their justice systems became a political liability on the national stage. In a series of hearings held by the Senate Committee on Constitutional Rights, several persons summarily convicted of crimes and sentenced to jail time by traditional tribal judges testified about the lack of fundamental fairness in tribal courts. Some tribal courts had prohibited the participation of lawyers in tribal court proceedings, arguing that the presence of lawyers would disrupt and harm the informal, traditional processes. This testimony led to ICRA's enactment and the codification of the Indian Bill of Rights.

The Indian Bill of Rights is not an exact copy of the federal Bill of Rights. Instead, it probably should best be understood as what the United States Congress of 1968 thought the Bill of Rights actually meant. Tribal governments were obligated to guarantee due process and equal protection to all persons under their jurisdiction. 25 U.S.C. § 1302(a)(8). ICRA also incorporated language about warrantless searches without probable cause, § 1302(a)(2); double jeopardy, § 1302(a)(3); the right against self-incrimination, § 1302(a)(4); speedy trials, § 1302(a)(6); and the right to confront witnesses, id., all of which are similar to rights under federal and state law. However, one right, the right to counsel, was modified. ICRA guarantees the right to counsel but only at one's own expense. Because tribal criminal prosecutions may be reviewed through a federal writ of habeas corpus, tribal courts generally apply federal precedents in reviewing procedural issues. However, tribal courts frequently ensure greater procedural protection to criminal defendants than they would receive in federal or state courts.

The final key element of ICRA was the creation of a federal habeas right for persons detained by order of a tribal court order. 25 U.S.C. § 1303. Since tribal courts' sentencing authority was initially limited to six months (later expanded to one year) in jail, and federal courts required detainees to exhaust their tribal remedies, e.g., Valenzuela v. Silversmith, 669 F.3d 1199 (10th Cir.2012); Jeffredo v. Macarro, 590 F.3d 751 (9th Cir.2009); Necklace v. Tribal Court of Three Affiliated Tribes, 554 F.2d 845 (8th Cir.1977), there were few federal habeas claims arising under ICRA. See generally Carrie E. Garrow, Habeas Corpus Petitions in Federal and Tribal Courts: A Search for Individualized Justice, 24 Wm. & Mary Bill of Rts.J. 137 (2015). One open question involves which law applies in ICRA habeas cases, federal or tribal. The only federal cases addressing the issue involve habeas petitions arising from tribal banishments, which do not involve detentions by tribal court orders, rendering the jurisdiction of those courts dubious at best. Compare Poody v. Tonawanda Band of Seneca Indians, 85 F.3d 874 (2d Cir.1996) (insisting on applying federal law in permanent banishment matters), with Taveras v. Whitehouse, 851 F.3d 863 (9th Cir.2017) (rejecting jurisdiction over temporary banishment and disenrollment matters).

The enhanced sentencing provisions of the Tribal Law and Order Act of 2010, 25 U.S.C. §§ 1302(b)–(d), and the special tribal jurisdictional provisions of the Violence Against Women Reauthorization Acts of 2013 and 2022 (VAWA), 25 U.S.C. § 1304, allow tribal nations to opt-in to expanded authority so long as the tribal court meets greater procedural guidelines than required under the Indian Bill of Rights. For tribal courts to employ the enhanced sentencing authority of three years in jail (or nine years if the sentences are stacked), 25 U.S.C. § 1302(a)(7), the tribal court must ensure that the defendant is provided paid counsel and that the judge is "licensed to practice law." 25 U.S.C. §§ 1302(c)(1)–(3). The last requirement seemingly goes beyond that required under federal or state law, where some judges are not required to be licensed to practice law. Further, for tribes to prosecute non-Indians for the crimes enumerated in VAWA, the tribal jury must reflect a cross-section of the community and must not bar non-Indians from participation. 25 U.S.C. § 1304(d)(3). Coupled with the requirement that the judge be licensed to practice law, this provision grants non-Indians greater criminal procedure protections than those provided under federal law.

2. RIGHT AGAINST SELF-INCRIMINATION

The right against self-incrimination is clear from the text of the United States Constitution and the Indian Bill of Rights, but the implementation and enforcement of the right is judge-made law. As such, tribal courts have flexibility in enforcing the right.

Consider Navajo Nation v. Rodriguez, 5 Am. Tribal Law 473 (Navajo Nation S.Ct.2004). There, the Navajo Nation Supreme Court declined to adopt the reasoning of the famed Miranda v. Arizona, 384 US 436 (1966), holding that the Diné people did not carry the Anglo-American tradition of using violent coercion to elicit confessions from criminal defendants. For the court, any degree of coercion was constitutionally unacceptable: "Though the Navajo Nation referred to a 'degree of coercion' without defining 'degree,' we do not see how coercion can be measured by degrees. Either the police coerced Rodriguez or it did not. [W]e find that any degree of coercion is in violation of the Navajo Bill of Rights." *Rodriguez*, 5 Am. Tribal Law at 477. The court, noting that "modern Navajo government * * * includes institutions such as police, jails, and courts that track state and federal government structures not present in traditional Navajo society," id. at 478, adopted a modified and more stringent version of the *Miranda* warnings:

> We hereby interpret the right against self-incrimination to require, at a minimum, clear notice by the police in a custodial situation that the person in custody (1) has the right to remain silent and may request the presence of legal counsel during questioning, (2) that any statements can be used against him or her, (3) the right to an attorney, and (4) the right to have

an attorney appointed if he or she cannot afford an attorney. * * *

However, we add the following. The mere giving of a standardized "advice of rights" form to a person in custody is not enough. The relationship between the Navajo Nation government and its individual citizens requires the same level of respect as the relationship between one person to another. In our Navajo way of thinking we must communicate clearly and concisely to each other so that we may understand the meaning of our words and the effect of our actions based on those words. The responsibility of the government is even stronger when a fundamental right, such as the right against self-incrimination, is involved.

Id. at 478–79. The court further noted that the requirements in *Miranda* arise from a much different cultural and legal background from which Navajos understand their laws to derive:

We are not guided in our own criminal jurisprudence by a legacy of internal oppression. Nevertheless, the U.S. Supreme Court's discussion reminds us of our Navajo principle of *hazhó'ógo*. *Hazhó'ógo* is not a man-made law, but rather a fundamental tenet informing us how we must approach each other as individuals. When discussions become heated, whether in a family setting, in a community meeting or between any people, it's not uncommon for an elderly person to stand and say *"hazhó'ógo, hazhó'ógo sha'álchíní*

> [*hazhó'ógo, hazhó'ógo* my children]." The intent is to remind those involved that they are *Nohookáá Diné'é* [Earth-surface-people (human beings)] dealing with another *Nohookáá Diné'é*, and that therefore patience and respect are due. When faced with important matters, it is inappropriate to rush to conclusion or to push a decision without explanation and consideration to those involved. *Áádóó na'níle'dii éí dooda.* [Delicate matters and things of importance must not be approached recklessly, carelessly, or with indifference to consequences.] This is *hazhó'ógo*, and we see that this is an underlying principle in everyday dealings with relatives and other individuals, as well as an underlying principle in our governmental institutions. Modern court procedures and our other adopted ways are all intended to be conducted with *hazhó'ógo* in mind.

Id. at 479–80 (footnotes omitted, text in brackets added). See also Southern Ute Tribe v. Henry, 2017 Southern Ute App. LEXIS 1, at *8–10 (Southern Ute Ct.App.2017) (requiring tribal police to advise suspects of the tribal right to "consult" counsel before a custodial interrogation, not merely to "obtain" counsel).

Other tribal courts tend to follow federal precedents allowing for waiver of the right against self-incrimination. E.g., Fort Peck Tribes v. Bighorn, 1 Am. Tribal Law 121, 122–23 (Fort Peck Ct.App. 1997) ("Voluntary statements made by an individual to a police officer outside of a custody interrogation, are admissible and do not violate the suspects right to protection from self-incrimination given by the 5th Amendment and the Indian Civil Rights Act of 1968."); Gaddy v. Hopi Tribe, 5 Am. Tribal Law 214, 217–18 (Hopi App.Ct.2004) (following *Miranda* and its progeny to find waiver of the right against self-incrimination during a traffic stop); People of the Pokagon Band of Potawatomi Indians v. Edelberg, 2019 Pokagon Band Tribal LEXIS 2, at *9 (Pokagon Band of Potawatomi Indians Tribal Ct.2019) (finding no right to counsel during police interview because defendant had not been charged); Swinomish Indian Tribal Community v. George, 2006 WL 7128881, at *2 (Swinomish Tribal Ct.2006) (same as *Gaddy*).

3. RIGHT TO COUNSEL

The right to counsel for indigent defendants remains a critical issue in modern tribal criminal procedure. Congress did not mandate that right for one stated reason and likely a second unstated reason. The stated reason was that most tribal nations at that time did not have resources to guarantee appointed counsel for indigent defendants. The Department of the Interior and the Department of Justice represented to Congress that the United States would be forced to pay for appointed counsel in tribal court. That might or might not have been the case. The unstated reason (and perhaps most likely) was that the Department of Justice still took the position that the right to counsel for indigent criminal defendants in federal and state prosecutions remained an open question, even after the groundbreaking decision in Gideon v. Wainwright,

372 U.S. 335 (1963). The last thing federal and state prosecutors wanted at that time was Congress codifying that right anywhere, even in a statute applicable only to tribal governments.

Gideon, of course, survived, but tribal criminal defendants remain governed by a federal law that does not mandate paid counsel for indigent defendants. Cf. United States v. Bryant, 579 U.S. 140 (2016) (allowing federal courts to apply uncounseled tribal court domestic violence convictions in sentencing recidivist federal court convictions under 18 U.S.C. § 117). See also Clancy v. Fort Peck Tribes, 1 Am. Tribal Law 107, 109 (Fort Peck Ct.App.1997) ("Appellant asserts that he had inadequate counsel. The Indian Civil Rights Act of 1968 does not afford the defendant the right to court appointed counsel."); Hoh Indian Tribe v. Penn, 15 Indian L.Rep. 6029, 6030 (Hoh Tribal Ct.App.1988) (recognizing the "tribal right to be represented by a lawyer or spokesperson at the defendant's expense"); Romero v. Pueblo of Nambé, 2007 SW Intertribal App. LEXIS 2, at *2 (Southwest Intertribal Ct.App. 2007) ("There are some tribes that have the funds to provide indigent legal counsel in criminal cases in tribal court, but apparently the Pueblo of Nambé does not provide that service."). One tribal court lamented:

> * * * [I]n his book, *Broken Landscape*[*: Indians, Indian Tribes, and the Constitution* (2012)], Professor [Frank] Pommersheim underscores the fact that the failure of Congress to include a right to counsel in the ICRA creates a structural weakness in the Tribal Court

> systems of this country that impedes perceptions of their legitimacy and can, in the absence of Congressional action, only be cured, as has been done in this jurisdiction, by a Tribal guarantee of the right to counsel or by a Constitutional amendment.

Eastern Band of Cherokee Indians v. Crowe, 9 Am. Tribal Law 27, 35 (Cherokee Ct. of the Eastern Band of Cherokee Indians 2010).

Tribal nations often do provide indigent criminal defendants access to paid counsel anyway. E.g., *Crowe*, 9 Am. Tribal Law at 35; Swinomish Indian Tribal Community v. Stone, 2007 WL 8080062, at *1 (Swinomish Tribal Ct.2007) ("Swinomish Tribal Code 3–03.215 provides: 'In all criminal prosecutions, the accused shall enjoy the right to have the assistance of counsel for his or her defense.' "). Typically, the right to paid counsel kicks in when the tribal prosecutor seeks jail time. E.g., Rangel v. People of the Pokagon Band of Potawatomi Indians, 2014 Pokagon Band App. LEXIS 1, at * 2 (Pokagon Band of Potawatomi Indians Ct.App.2014) ("[I]f a criminal defendant faces the possibility of jail time, an indigent defendant is entitled to paid counsel under tribal statute."). Tribes that wish to prosecute non-Indians for the enumerated crimes contained in 25 U.S.C. § 1304 or to sentence convicted criminals to more than one year in jail must provide paid counsel under 25 U.S.C. § 1302(c)(2). E.g., Bisonnette v. Fort Peck Tribes, 17 Am. Tribal Law 367, 369 (Fort Peck Ct.App.2024). Other tribal courts have concluded that the right to counsel is akin to a fundamental right. E.g., Haugooah v. Greyeyes, 11 Am. Tribal Law 171, 177 (Navajo Nation S.Ct.2018) ("The right to an attorney is one of the most important protections guaranteed by the Navajo Bill of Rights.").

In one extraordinary instance when criminal defense counsel repeatedly attempted to withdraw from representation due to the inability or refusal of the defendant to compensate them, the tribe acted to ensure their payment. See Navajo Nation v. MacDonald, 19 Indian L.Rep. 6053, 6055 (Navajo Nation S.Ct.1991). After the defendant was convicted, the defendant's appellate counsel argued that the fee dispute created a conflict of interest between the defendant and trial counsel, the court held that the defendant suffered "any impairment of the free exercise of professional judgment or the attorney-client privilege." Id.

Waivers of the right to counsel by criminal defendants must be knowing and voluntary. E.g., Poleahla v. Hopi Tribe, 1 Am. Tribal Law 265, 267 (Hopi App.Ct.1997) (citing Hopi Tribe v. Consolidated Cases of Ami, Gishey, & Pavatea, 1996 Hopi App. LEXIS 1 (Hopi App.Ct.1996)). Denial of the right to counsel by the omission of the court or by the failure of a defendant to ask for counsel violates the rights of criminal defendants. E.g., Savior v. Fort Peck Tribes, 15 Am. Tribal Law 197, 198 (Fort Peck Ct.App.2017) (finding denial of the right to counsel by not advising the defendant of the right violated tribal and federal due process and equal protection rights); In re Bell, 3 Am. Tribal Law 305, 309 (Fort Peck Ct.App.2001) (under tribal statute, oral notice from judge not sufficient to inform juvenile defendant of right to paid counsel").

Tribal courts may also require paid counsel in probation or parole revocation hearings or on appeal. One tribal court chose to make such a determination on a case-by-case, procedure-by-procedure basis rooted in the non-adversarial character of probation review and the worry that appointed counsel would create disruptive conflict:

> * * * Unlike the busier courts in the State or Federal systems, the Swinomish Tribal Court conducts regular probation review hearings. These are not adversarial proceedings, but afford the court an opportunity to meet with probationers and review their progress in meeting conditions of probation. This often means reviewing the probationer's progress in treatment and/or counseling programs. This increased level of contact between the court and the probationer is intended to promote the therapeutic goals of the Swinomish Tribal Court. It would burden the resources of the tribe to convert these regular review hearings into adversarial proceedings, requiring appointment of counsel in all cases, and more importantly, it would likely prove counterproductive to the therapeutic mission. In some instances, such as the instant case, it is clear during the review hearing that further proceedings, and possibly revocation of probation, may be necessary. In cases, the peculiarities of the case, or the necessity for sentencing, will make the

> appointment of counsel will become necessary to protect the probationers' due process rights. The court will make this decision on a case-by-case basis.

Swinomish Indian Tribal Community v. Stone, 2007 WL 8080062, at *2 (Swinomish Tribal Ct.2007).

4. RIGHT TO JURY TRIAL

The Indian Civil Rights Act preserves the right to a jury trial in a criminal proceeding in tribal court but not in civil cases. 25 U.S.C. § 1302(10). A right to a jury trial in criminal cases usually only vests where the criminal punishment includes jail time. E.g., Hoh Indian Tribe v. Penn, 15 Indian L.Rep. 6029 (Hoh Tribal Ct.App.1988). A defendant may waive the right to a jury trial so long as the waiver is knowing and intelligent. E.g., Confederated Salish & Kootenai Tribes v. Peone, 16 Indian L.Rep. 6136 (Confederated Salish & Kootenai Tribal Ct.1989).

Jury trials are often difficult to empanel in Indian country. The reservation populations of many tribal nations are very small and are, by definition, closely interrelated. Tribal nations that do not, for example, pay out gaming funds on a per capita basis may have trouble maintaining accurate and updated enrollment lists. At times, nonmembers of tribal nations have complained that a jury consisting of tribal members (and employees of the tribe) may be inherently biased toward the tribe because of their dependence on the tribe for services and jobs, but these claims have been rejected for the same reasons they are rejected in suits involving state and federal governments. E.g., Sanders v. Royal Associates Management, Inc., 24 Indian L.Rep. 6068, 6069 (Chitimacha Tribal Ct.App.1997).

Jury trials are costly burdens on already underfunded courts. E.g., Eriacho v. Ramah District Court, 6 Am. Tribal Law 624, 628 (Navajo Nation S.Ct.2005) ("The process to select a jury within the Navajo Nation is lengthy and costly for under-funded courts."). Occasionally, tribes provide for a jury trial only when the prosecutor informs the court that the government will seek jail time. E.g., Champagne v. People, 35 Indian L. Rep. 6004, 6006 (Little River Band of Ottawa Indians Tribal Ct.App.2007) (finding no right to a jury where the government merely sought fines of several hundred dollars); Pueblo of Pojoaque v. Jagles, 24 Indian L.Rep. 6137 (Pueblo of Pojoaque Tribal Ct.1997) (holding no right to jury trial attaches in criminal case where jail time is not sought by the government). Jury selection may require tribal courts to seek both members and nonmembers from the reservation community. E.g., Navajo Nation v. MacDonald, 19 Indian L.Rep. 6053, 6054 (Navajo Nation S.Ct.1991) (noting that "the court used voter lists of the Navajo Nation and Arizona's Apache and Navajo counties to select prospective jurors" in order to empanel "jury composed of both Navajos and non-Navajos").

Some tribal courts protect a criminal defendant's right to a jury trial beyond that required by federal law. In Eriacho v. Ramah District Court, 6 Am. Tribal Law 624 (Navajo Nation S.Ct.2005), the court noted that federal and tribal law required defendants to affirmatively ask for a jury trial or that right would be procedurally waived. The court declared that the right to a jury trial is a fundamental right under Navajo common law and further required the court to inform the defendant that inaction may mean waiver of the right:

> As *Hozho'go* requires meaningful notice and explanation of a right before a waiver of that right is effective, it requires, at a bare minimum, that the Nation give notice that the right to a jury trial may be waived by inaction. For notice to be meaningful, and therefore a waiver to be effective, the Navajo government must explain to the defendant that the jury trial right is not absolute, as it may be waived by doing nothing within a certain time. Absent this explanation, the information received by a defendant is incomplete, as it appears the right is automatic and perpetual, like the federal constitutional right. Without this information, the waiver by inaction is not truly knowing and intelligent, and would violate the defendant's right to due process. As the description of the right to jury trial in the waiver of arraignment form does not include a statement that the right must be exercised within fifteen days, Eriacho's failure to request it within that time was not a knowing and intelligent waiver.

Id. at 630 (footnote omitted). See also Confederated Salish & Kootenai Tribes v. Bigcrane, 2025 Mont. Salish & Kootenai Tribes LEXIS 2, at *18–19 (Confederated Salish & Kootenai Ct.App.2025) (failure to maintain contact with defense attorney is not a waiver of the right to a jury trial).

Governments often try to impose the costs of a jury trial on the defendant, but not necessarily tribal governments. In Fort Peck Tribes v. DeCoteau, 2 Am. Trial Law 143, 146 (Fort Peck Ct.App.1999), the court refused to allow enforcement of the tribal court's unwritten interpretation of tribal statutory provisions that supposedly justified the recoupment of jury trial costs from criminal defendants once they were convicted. "[T]he Tribal Court's unwritten policy of exacting recoupment of jury costs from convicted criminal defendants places an impermissible burden on those defendants' right to a trial by jury." Id. at 146. See also Johnson v. Tuba City District Court, 7 Am. Tribal Law 566, 573 (Navajo Nation S.Ct.2007) (vacating $1500 jury trial fee for failure of tribal court to justify the costs).

Under federal law, non-Indians are entitled to a jury that constitutes a "fair cross section of the community" and does not exclude non-Indians. 25 U.S.C. § 1304(d)(3). This right extends beyond the jury rights provided in federal and state courts.

5. SEARCHES AND SEIZURES

Tribal court decisions enforcing the prohibition on unreasonable searches and seizures tend to follow federal law closely. The vast majority of tribal police practices are in line with state and federal practices, a requirement for tribes under their 638 contracts and for entering into cross-deputization agreements with federal, state, and local jurisdictions. On occasion, tribal legislatures adopt their own criminal procedure code. The Winnebago Tribe of Nebraska's code reads:

> A police or law enforcement officer may make an arrest in obedience to an arrest warrant, or s/he may, without a warrant, arrest a person:
>
> A. For an offense committed in his/her presence.
>
> B. When s/he has reasonable cause for believing the person to have committed an offense, although not in his/her presence, and there is reasonable cause for believing that such person before a warrant can be obtained may:
>
> i. Flee the jurisdiction or conceal him/herself to avoid arrest, or
>
> ii. Destroy or conceal evidence of the commission of an offense, or
>
> iii. Injure or annoy another person or damage property belonging to another person.

Winnebago Criminal Procedure Code, Title 1B, Article 3, Rule 1B–304(2). The code largely replicates federal and state criminal procedure.

However, tribal courts occasionally face cases involving police incompetence. For example, in Eastern Band of Cherokee Indians v. Rattler, 5 Cher.Rep. 17, 2006 WL 6499919 (Cherokee Ct. of the Eastern Band of Cherokee Indians 2006), the court followed federal law in declining to suppress a search warrant even though the tribal officer had no training in drafting a warrant application. In Confederated Salish & Kootenai Tribes v. Mahkuk, 2025 Mont. Salish & Kootenai Tribe LEXIS 3 (Confederated Salish & Kootenai Tribes Ct.App. 2025), the court followed federal in affirmed the suppression of evidence collected by tribal police during a traffic stop. The court concluded that there was no particularized suspicion justifying the stop where the officer's stated reason for stopping the car was not backed by dashcam footage. In James v. Washoe Tribe of Nev. and Cal., 1998 WL 35297258, at *1, *2 (Nev. Inter-Tribal Ct.App.1998), the court invalidated a telephonic search warrant where the tape recording of hearing only played police officer's voice and there was no evidence that the officer's affidavit had been sworn. Additionally, the court noted that the tribal court did not conduct an initial probable cause hearing until 48 hours had passed, beyond that which was allowed under tribal codes. In Coeur d'Alene Tribe v. Goddard, 38 Indian L.Rep. 6019 (Coeur d'Alene Tribal Ct.2010) (suppressing evidence seized by tribal police where police department had no formal policies and procedures governing warrantless searches and seizures).

One tribal court sought briefing on the traditional tribal law on searches and seizures. In Winnebago Tribe of Nebraska v. Pretends Eagle, 24 Indian L.Rep. 6240 (Winnebago Tribal Ct.1997), the court identified the bear clan as the traditional clan identified with policing. Noting that the tribal court would interpret the Indian Bill of Rights in line with tribal custom and tradition, the court concluded:

> The clan of the Winnebago Tribe which is entrusted with the duty to protect the people of the Tribe is the Bear Clan. Particularly in any search and seizure case, this Court finds it hard to believe that there were no established customs when a Bear Clan member entered, searched, or detained an individual when investigating a complaint. Indeed, the Court finds it hard to believe that there were not highly developed customs in this particular area.

Id. at 6244. See also Winnebago Tribe of Nebraska v. Bird, 28 Indian L.Rep. 6132, 6134 (Winnebago S.Ct.2001) (applying *Pretends Eagle* and concluding: "A reasonable person would not feel free to leave when a police car pulls up behind a vehicle with its full array of pursuit lights flashing and an armed, uniformed officer approaches the car. Respect for law enforcement would compel the average person to stay and act compliantly; in other words to feel 'stopped.' Concomitantly, the officer cannot turn that respect and compliance into an opportunity for unjustified intrusiveness into constitutionally protected areas.").

6. RIGHT TO SPEEDY TRIAL

Tribal courts generally follow federal law in guaranteeing the right to speedy trial, provided for in 25 U.S.C. § 1302(a)(6). "The right to a speedy trial is designed to ensure that a criminal matter be heard in an expeditious manner to ensure that a criminal defendant is not subject to the infamy of a criminal prosecution against him for an inordinate amount of time." Eagle v. Fort Peck Tribes, 16 Am. Tribal Law 353, 355 (Fort Peck Ct.App.2022). Tribal courts tend to follow federal precedents in determining whether a trial delay violates the speedy trial requirement. In Casey v. Muscogee (Creek) Nation, 2022 Muscogee Creek Nation Supreme LEXIS 3 (Muscogee (Creek) Nation S.Ct.2023), the court adopted the following four part test from Barker v. Wingo, 407 U.S. 514 (1972): "(1) the length of the delay, (2) the reason for the delay, (3) whether the defendant had asserted his/her right to speedy trial, and (4) whether there was prejudice to the defendant due to the delay." Id. at *11–12. E.g., Seaton v. Greyeyes, 6 Am. Tribal Law 737, 743 (Navajo Nation S.Ct.2006) ("A defendant's right to a speedy trial cannot be compromised for the convenience of others.").

Speedy trial analyses require intensive fact finding by the court and diligence from the defense. In Tulalip Tribes v. Flores, 23 NICS App. 1 (Tulalip Tribal Ct.App.2025), the court reversed the dismissal of a criminal complaint for violation of the tribe's speedy trial statute caused, in part, by the failure of a sufficient number of jurors to appear for voir dire. The trial court had not made findings of fact regarding the final three factors. In Navajo Nation v. Bedonie, 6 Am. Tribal Law 725 (Navajo Nation S.Ct. 2006), the court vacated a conviction where the trial court had taken a year to comply with an earlier appellate court remand requiring that findings of fact and conclusions of law regarding the defendant's speedy trial claims.

Denial of a motion to dismiss on speedy trial grounds may be immediately appealable in some circumstances, especially where the prosecution has concurred with the motion to dismiss. E.g., *Eagle*, 16 Am. Tribal Law 353; Henderson v. Fort Peck Tribes, 16 Am. Tribal Law 346 (Fort Peck Ct.App.2022); Shields v. Fort Peck Tribes, 16 Am. Tribal Law 348 (Fort Peck Ct.App.2022).

7. JUVENILE JUSTICE

Tribal juvenile justice in Indian Country involves culturally-appropriate systems and approaches that tribal nations use to address, prevent, and respond to delinquency and victimization among Indigenous youth. These systems prioritize rehabilitation, skill development, and successful community reintegration, utilizing traditional healing methods and indigenous practices rather than solely punitive measures. They also aim to strengthen state-tribal partnerships and ensure culturally sensitive, effective services for Indigenous youth within a complex jurisdictional landscape that can involve tribal, state, and federal systems.

In many tribal communities, it is rare for tribal courts to order the detention of tribal citizens for juvenile delinquency or other offenses, unless there is clear evidence that the child is an immediate danger to themselves or others. E.g., In re M.G. v. Greyeyes, 7 Am. Tribal Law 514, 515 (Navajo Nation S.Ct.2007) ("The Navajo Nation Children's Code prohibits a family court from placing a child in need of supervision 'in a jail or other facility intended or used for . . . the detention of children alleged to be delinquent.' ") (quoting 9 Navajo Nation Code § 1111(B)).

Tribal customs and traditions are often crucial to the implementation and interpretation of a tribal juvenile justice code. The Nottawaseppi Huron Band of the Potawatomi code explicitly states a tribal intent not to incarcerate children:

> Children are the Tribe's most vital and cherished resource. The Tribe's future depends on the health and well-being of its children. Children have a sacred right to receive the care and guidance necessary for their spiritual, emotional, mental, and physical development. Feeling pride from their identity as Potawatomi will help them grow into strong, healthy, responsible adult tribal citizens. *The focus shall be on healing the parties rather than punishing the juvenile for his or her behavior*, to provide appropriate options at all levels of the juvenile matter regarding treatment, healing and rehabilitation of the minor, their families, and the victim.

Nottawaseppi Huron Band of the Potawatomi Code § 7.3–5 (emphasis added). The Nottawaseppi tribal nation also chose to interpret its juvenile justice code in light of the *Noeg Meshomsenanek Kenomagewenen*, or Seven Grandfather Teachings:

> In carrying out the powers of self-government in a manner that promotes and preserves our Bode'wadmi values and traditions, the Tribe

strives to be guided by the Seven Grandfather Teachings in its deliberations and decisions. The rights and limitations contained in this chapter are intended to reflect the values in the Seven Grandfather Teachings to ensure that tribal youth and community and other persons participating in youth development within the jurisdiction of the Tribe will be guided by the Seven Grandfather Teachings:

Bwakawen—Wisdom

Debanawen—Love

Kejitwawenindowen—Respect

Wedasewen—Bravery

Gwekwadzewen—Honesty

Edbesendowen—Humility

Debwewin—Truth

Nottawaseppi Huron Band of the Potawatomi Code § 7.3–6.

Many tribal nations tread carefully in juvenile justice, justifiably worried that Indigenous children are vulnerable to the ravages of the criminal justice system. For example, see In re J.P., 10 Am. Tribal Law 331 (Hopi Tribe App.Ct.2010), where the court reversed a conviction of child for negligent homicide. The child had been playing with a gun and shot another child. The prosecution relied on statements made by the child to tribal police that tended to be incriminating. The court adopted a theory of the "prudent juvenile":

> The statutory standard for negligence, by adopting "a prudent man" standard, immediately poses a difficult problem when applied to a juvenile in a Children's Court proceeding. Juveniles are adjudicated by separate proceedings not applied to adults precisely because their level of maturity differs from that of adults. In particular, due to their level of development, juveniles often lack the full appreciation of adults regarding questions of causation and risks leading to injury—one of the reasons teenagers often dangerously regard themselves invulnerable. To apply "a prudent man" standard to a juvenile therefore risks imposing an adult standard on the juvenile that his or her level of development and maturity renders inappropriate and unattainable. For that reason, this Court understands and interprets the "prudent man" standard of [Ordinance 21 §] 3.1.1(b), when applied to a juvenile in a Children's Court proceeding, to refer to a prudent juvenile, not a prudent adult.

Id. at 335–36. The court concluded that the evidence presented by the prosecution was a toss-up between showing a "tragic accident or [a] homicide," id. at 338, not proof beyond a reasonable doubt.

Procedural protections are also often enhanced. In Randall v. Children & Family Services, 11 Am. Tribal Law 72 (Colville Tribal Ct.App.2012), the court chastised the trial court's practice of "deny[ing] parents a right to present their cases when they are even just a little late for the hearing, that [minor in need of care] hearings are being treated like the adversarial proceedings in criminal cases." Id. at 76. The court pointed to the tribal code, which "must be interpreted liberally in order to preserve and strengthen a child's family ties as well as his cultural ties to the Tribes." Id. at 77. The court reversed the trial court's refusal to allow the child's parents to present evidence:

> The record does not reflect any reason the Court could not have heard from the parents and their spokesmen before entering its final adjudicatory order * * *. To treat the adjudicatory hearing as a pure adversarial hearing flies in the face of the purposes of the juvenile laws. [The denial of participation in the hearing can also be considered acultural. It is settled tradition that everyone who has an interest in a matter, and who wishes to have input is allowed to have his say. Judges, as tribal leaders, must be ever-vigilant in promoting our traditions whenever the opportunity arises in the court-context. In this way we can help preserve what makes tribal courts unique and necessary for resolution of tribal issues.] The parents have a due process right to present evidence; each case must be assessed individually on whether their late attendance is so egregious as to forego this right. This is the only way to ensure a child is given the full benefit of the law and of maintaining his ties to his family and culture.

Id. (footnote omitted).

The complexities and cost of exercising criminal jurisdiction often are too much for many tribal nations. Many tribes simply make a political decision not to enforce criminal laws or significantly limit their jurisdiction by choice. Moreover, only a few dozen tribal nations have chosen to exercise the enhanced sentencing authority and jurisdiction over non-Indians. All tribal nations depend on the federal and state governments to fill in the jurisdictional gaps rampant throughout Indian country jurisdiction. Collectively and tragically, the gaps remain substantial, leading to unnecessary pain and suffering in Indian country. On the other hand, studies show that Indigenous Peoples of the United States are still somehow overpoliced and disproportionately represented in the Nation's jails and prisons.

C. FEDERAL CRIMINAL JURISDICTION

Indian country criminal jurisdiction has been federalized to a large extent since 1790, when Congress passed the first Trade and Intercourse Act. Later in the 19th century, Congress asserted vast authority over Indian country crime. In the mid-20th century, Congress delegated criminal jurisdiction over about 70 percent of Indian reservations (which still only constituted a minority of the population of Indian country) to states. The federalization and checkerboard pattern of Indian country criminal jurisdiction is unnecessarily complicated and inefficient—and horribly tragic—but the overlapping federal, state, and tribal regimes are here to stay. For additional historical information, see Eastern Band of Cherokee Indians v. Johnson, 18 Am. Tribal Law 62, 66–68 (Cherokee Ct. of the Eastern Band of Cherokee Indians 2024).

Tracking the text of the United States Constitution, the first Congress enacted the Trade and Intercourse Act of 1790, the first Indian country criminal jurisdictional law. 1 Stat. 137. Sections 1 and 3 of the 1790 Act barred anyone from engaging in trade or intercourse with Indian tribes without federal permission. Section 5 made trespass into Indian country a federal offense. The 1790 Act expired and was replaced in 1793 with a new Trade and Intercourse Act, which granted federal courts criminal jurisdiction over any violations of the new act. 1 Stat. 330. In 1817, Congress enacted the Indian Country Crimes Act, which extended federal authority to prosecute any crimes committed by non-Indians against Indians in Indian country, now codified at 18 U.S.C. § 1152. In 1885, Congress asserted exclusive jurisdiction over an enumerated list of felonies committed inside Indian country, now codified as amended at 18 U.S.C. § 1153. Rounding out the general Indian country federal crimes statutes, Congress authorized federal prosecutors to assimilate state law to fill in subject matter gaps in Indian country criminal jurisdiction. 18 U.S.C. § 13. Over the years, Congress has also enacted certain specific categories of crimes, such as theft from a tribal organization. 18 U.S.C. § 1163.

The beginning of intensive federal control over Indian country crime began in the 1880s. In 1883, the United States Supreme Court held in Ex parte Crow Dog, 109 U.S. 556 (1883), that federal criminal jurisdiction over Indian-on-Indian crime in Indian country could not be implied from the duty of protection or ambiguous treaty terms like the so-called Bad Men clauses. The Court noted that federal authority could only derive from a federal statute that shows "a clear expression of the intention of Congress" or consent of the tribal nation. Id. at 572.

At the behest of the federal government, Congress passed the Major Crimes Act in 1885. The Act originally enumerated seven "major crimes" over which the United States would possess exclusive jurisdiction in Indian country over "any Indian." Over time, Congress expanded the number of enumerated crimes to encompass all the common law felonies.

Since the very beginning, Congress has determined that the criminal jurisdiction territorial hook has been "Indian country." Restatement of the Law of American Indians § 68. Indian country as a term of art began as a codified description of all lands located to the west of the original thirteen states to much more narrow description of types of land. Land is Indian country if the federal government set aside the land at any time for Indian or tribal purposes *and* it remains under federal superintendency. Indian country status is important for determining Indian country criminal jurisdiction because state law has no force in Indian country absent federal authorization.

At the beginning of the United States, Congress established that the key jurisdictional predicate for personal jurisdiction in Indian country is Indian status. Restatement of the Law of American Indians § 69. Early federal laws divided those persons subject to Indian affairs laws by race, sometimes stating that a law applied only to "Indians" or "non-Indians." For example, the First Congress in the Trade and Intercourse Act of 1790 established that no person may trade with "Indians" or "Indian tribes" without federal approval subject to criminal penalty. This choice tracked the text of the United States Constitution, which referenced "Indians not taxed" in the apportionment provision. Const. art. I, § 2, cl. 3 (repealed); Const. amend. XIV, § 2. Over the course of the 19th century, especially in tribes that "adopted" non-Indians into tribal citizenship, "Indian" status began to be determined by tribal citizenship or membership status. A classic example is Talton v. Mayes, 163 U.S. 376 (1896), where the tribal criminal defendant was a Cherokee citizen adopted into membership who likely was non-Indian.

The lower courts have concluded that for purpose of Indian country criminal jurisdiction, a person is an Indian if that person has any Indian ancestry and there is evidence that a tribal, state, or federal government has acknowledged that person is an Indian. This is the same test that many tribal courts have adopted. For example, the Hopi Appellate Court held that an Indian is, under tribal statute, "any person who is an enrolled member of any Federally recognized tribe or who has Indian Blood and is regarded as an Indian by the society of Indians among whom he lives." In re Certified Question, 2001 Hopi App. LEXIS 7, at *13 (Hopi App.Ct.2001). As cases in the previous section show, e.g., Taypayosatum v. Fort Peck Tribes, 16 Am. Tribal Law 224, at *3 (Fort Peck Tribes Ct.App.2020), the test is fraught, however, given the inherent ambiguities in determining what constitutes evidence of Indian status sufficient to confer jurisdiction on a prosecuting court. What is known is that the prosecution likely must prove beyond a reasonable doubt to a jury that in federal or state court is unlikely to include any Indian jurors.

The Indian status test is a mess, to be sure, but it is also criticized by many who mistakenly root the test in the white supremacy jurisprudence of the Antebellum era of the United States Supreme Court. Then, the Taney Court decided United States v. Rogers, 45 U.S. 567 (1846), where the Court confirmed federal criminal jurisdiction over a white man who had been adopted into tribal citizenship by the Cherokee Nation. The Court concluded that mere adopted into citizenship by a tribal nation was not sufficient to immunize Rogers from federal prosecution in a pre-Major Crimes Act era where the federal government did not possess jurisdiction to prosecute Indian-on-Indian crime in Indian country. The Court's analysis was certainly rooted in the bigotry of Chief Justice Taney, who falsely asserted that European nations never "acknowledged or treated . . . native tribes . . . as independent nations."

Id. at 572. That statement was incorrect the moment it was made, belied by the Supreme Court's earlier precedents holding tribes were nations, E.g., Cherokee Nation v. Georgia, 30 U.S. 1 (1831); Worcester v. Georgia, 31 U.S. 515 (1832), not to forget the long tradition of colonial nations and the United States of entering into treaty relationships with hundreds of tribal nations, including the Cherokee Nation. The Supreme Court a mere four years after *Rogers* would refer to the Cherokee Nation as "in many respects a foreign and independent nation[,] governed by their own laws. . . ." Parks v. Ross, 52 U.S. 362, 374 (1850). Despite the embarrassment that *Rogers* represents and the perception that *Rogers'* reasoning influenced the development of the modern day Indian status rule, *Rogers* is not to wholly to blame for the current "mess." The Cherokee Nation of that time regularly asserted criminal jurisdiction over non-Indians who were Cherokee citizens, e.g., Alberty v. United States, 162 U.S. 499 (1989) (affirming tribal criminal jurisdiction over tribal citizens who were not Indian); Lucas v. United States, 163 U.S. 612 (1896) (same); Talton v. Mayes, 163 U.S. 376 (1896) (likely the same, in that there was evidence that the defendant was a white man), belying the notion that Indian country criminal jurisdiction was divided on racial grounds in the 19th century. It says a lot that the original *Handbook of Federal Indian Law*, published in the early 1940s, mentioned *Rogers* as standing merely for the proposition that "Congress is not bound by the tribal rule regarding membership and may determine for itself whether a person is an Indian from the standpoint of a federal criminal statute." Felix S. Cohen, Handbook of Federal Indian Law 99 (1942 ed). Cohen does not mention a mandate from *Rogers* that Indian status requires Indian blood. Even so, the racialization of Indian Country criminal jurisdiction became complete in 1978 when the Supreme Court decided Oliphant v. Suquamish Indian Tribe, 435 U.S. 191 (1978), when the Court prohibited tribal courts from prosecuting *non-Indian* criminals (an issue Congress repeated in the *Duro* fix by reaffirming tribal powers over all *Indians*). Courts were then required to determine the race of victims and defendants.

Equal protection challenges to federal prosecutions rooted in Indian status are legion, but the United States Supreme Court conclusively held in United States v. Antelope, 430 U.S. 641 (1977), that the Major Crimes Act and similar statutes do not implicate the equal protection component of the Fifth Amendment's Due Process Clause. Challenges arise, typically, with differences in federal and state criminal sentences and substantive elements of crimes. Since the United States Constitution utilizes the term "Indian" without defining it, it would be normatively illogical to treat Indian criminal jurisdiction laws that use the same term as racial classifications subject to strict scrutiny.

Federal capital sentences are governed by tribal prerogatives, except in certain cases. E.g., Mitchell v. United States, 958 F.3d 775, 791 (9th Cir.2020) (Christen, J., concurring) (noting that Navajo Nation citizen was "the first person to be executed by the federal government for an intra-Indian crime, committed in Indian country, by virtue of a conviction for carjacking resulting in death").

D. STATE CRIMINAL JURISDICTION

State laws have no force in Indian country absent Congressional consent. Worcester v. Georgia, 31 U.S. 515, 561 (1832). As a consequence of that foundational rule, federal statutes dictate state criminal jurisdiction in Indian country. Congress has indeed authorized several states to assume criminal jurisdiction in Indian country to the exclusion of federal authority. These states include something like 70 percent of all reservations (though a considerable minority of Indian people). United States Supreme Court precedents have also granted states jurisdiction over non-Indian on non-Indian crimes, as well as non-Indian on Indian crime, even in the absence of explicit Congressional authorization.

The federalization of Indian country criminal jurisdiction was haphazard, but from the first Trade and Intercourse Act, state criminal jurisdiction was completely preempted by federal law. The first state criminal jurisdiction cases of note were State of Georgia v. Tassels, 1 Dud. 229 (Ga. 1830), a state conviction of a Cherokee citizen that the United States Supreme Court agreed to review and that was mooted by Georgia's execution of the defendant, and Worcester v. Georgia, 31 U.S. 515 (1832). In *Worcester*, Georgia asserted criminal jurisdiction over a non-Indian missionary, charging him with the crime of entering Indian country without the consent of the state. The Supreme Court held that the state's effort to assert criminal jurisdiction in Indian country were preempted by federal law, primarily the Cherokee treaties ensuring tribal self-government and the Indian Trade and Intercourse Acts.

Congress rarely, if ever, authorized states to exercise criminal jurisdiction until the 1940s and 1950s, but the United States Supreme Court granted states jurisdiction over non-Indian on non-Indians crime in Indian country by judicial fiat in a series of cases starting in the late 19th century. The first case, United States v. McBratney, 104 U.S. 621 (1881), recognized the State of Colorado's jurisdiction by virtue of the equal footing doctrine. Importantly, Colorado's admission act did not include a provision in which the new state would disclaim jurisdiction over Indian country, unlike many other states. The next case, Draper v. United States, 164 U.S. 240 (1896), recognized the State of Montana's jurisdiction even though Montana's admission act disclaimed jurisdiction over Indian lands forever. Decades later, the Court recognized jurisdiction in the State of New York, one of the original thirteen states, in New York ex rel. Ray v. Martin, 326 U.S. 496 (1946).

Beginning in the 1940s, Congress began to grant specific states criminal jurisdiction over Indian country within their borders. First, Congress granted New York and Kansas jurisdiction, then scattered reservations in North Dakota and Iowa. Then in 1953, Congress enacted Public Law 280, granting several states (California, Minnesota, Nebraska,

Oregon, and Wisconsin, later adding Alaska in 1959) criminal jurisdiction in Indian country. 18 U.S.C. § 1162. These states would become known as "mandatory" Public Law 280 states. Other states could opt in to jurisdiction. These states, notably Florida, Montana, Idaho, and Washington, became known as "permissive" Public Law 280 states, assuming all or portions of Indian country criminal jurisdiction. Some tribal nations in Maine, Rhode Island, Virginia, and elsewhere agreed to state jurisdiction as a condition of federal statutory acknowledgment of their sovereign status years later. Even so, Public Law 280 is an unfunded mandate, which requires states to foot their own costs of enforcing laws in Indian country. As a real consequence, state and local governments usually struggle greatly to deliver this service to Indian country. Cf. Eastern Band of Cherokee Indians v. Johnson, 18 Am. Tribal Law 62, 68 (Cherokee Ct. of the Eastern Band of Cherokee Indians 2024) (detailing the history of the State of North Carolina's repudiation of criminal jurisdiction over Indian country).

Congress amended Public Law 280 a decade later to bar states from assuming jurisdiction absent the consent of affected tribes. Congress also allowed for the retrocession of state jurisdiction back to federal jurisdiction. Importantly, Public Law 280 had no impact on tribal criminal jurisdiction, through states and federal agencies often attempted to impede tribal court development in Public Law 280 states. Occasionally, so did tribal court litigants.

In Hoopa Valley Tribal Council v. Jones, 11 NICS App. 100 (Hoopa Valley Tribal Ct.App.2013), the tribal council invoked the tribe's banishment ordinance, which allowed for the summary banishment of persons from the reservation for repeat violations of the tribe's anti-drug laws. The banishee argued that the tribal council's banishment order was a criminal penalty. Then, the banishee claimed that Public Law 280 stripped the tribe (which is located within California, a mandatory Public Law 280 state) of its criminal jurisdiction authority. The court disagreed on both fronts. First, the court concluded that the ordinance was not designed to punish or deter, but only to enhance public safety. Second, even if banishments were inherently criminal, the court concluded that Public Law 280 had no impact on tribal criminal jurisdiction. The Hoopa constitution also authorized the tribe to prosecute criminals if it so chose.

Once again resurrecting its power of judicial fiat, the United States Supreme Court in Oklahoma v. Castro-Huerta, 597 U.S. 629 (2022), held that, even absent Congressional authorization such as Public Law 280, states may prosecute non-Indians who commit crimes against Indians in Indian country. The Court first disposed of the presumption that state laws have no force in Indian country, originally established in *Worcester,* by pointing to the Court's general statements over decades that state law *do* extend into Indian country. For example, the Court pointed to the three cases mentioned earlier (*McBratney*, *Draper*, and *Martin*) in which the Court held that states have the power to assert jurisdiction over crimes committed by non-Indians against other non-Indians. The Court also pointed to Nevada v. Hicks, 533 U.S. 353 (2001) which made the bald assertion, "State sovereignty does not end at a reservation's border." Id. at 361. Then, the Court concluded that the General Crimes Act, 18 U.S.C. § 1152, did not preempt state criminal jurisdiction. That Act provides, "Except as otherwise expressly provided by law, the general laws of the United States as to the punishment of offenses committed in any place within the sole and exclusive jurisdiction of the United States, except the District of Columbia, shall extend to the Indian country." The Court was unpersuaded that the federalization of Indian country crime had an impact on the presumption of state sovereignty.

The practical impact of *Castro-Huerta* remains to be seen, but the initial response from states outside of Oklahoma was that they did not intend to assert this jurisdiction granted to them by the Supreme Court. The large majority of jurisdictions, even in Oklahoma, have already reached agreement on public safety jurisdictional matters. For states, Indian country criminal jurisdiction remains an unfunded mandate.

American Indians experience violent crime at rates higher than any other racial group in the U.S., with Native women and children facing particularly alarming levels of violence, including homicide and sexual assault. A significant part of the crisis involves the high number of missing and murdered Indigenous women and girls, a problem that has gained significant media attention and led to calls for increased federal action. Crimes against Indigenous Peoples in the United States are often committed by non-Native offenders, but federal law prohibits tribes from prosecuting non-Native individuals. This leaves jurisdiction solely to the federal or state governments, which face systemic reasons for being less engaged in reservation crimes, often resulting in non-Indian perpetrators escaping prosecution.

CHAPTER 6

INDIAN LANDS AND NATURAL RESOURCES

The clash of cultures between Indigenous peoples and the United States is intensely evident in the competing political and legal disputes over land and natural resources. As should be understood, all of the United States was once occupied by Indigenous peoples, the natural creatures and supernatural forces that Indigenous peoples call relatives, and the land, water, air, and sky that Indigenous peoples also call relatives. Unlike the western political philosophy that favors humanity, Indigenous peoples of the Americas did not seek dominion over the natural world, but instead worked toward harmony with it. Any Indigenous elder might point out that if humans are exercising dominion over the world, then the world is out of balance. After all, as Anishinaabe elders long have taught, trees do not need humans, humans need trees. Similarly, the Navajo Supreme Court once recognized, "*Hózhǫ́ǫ́go iiná*, literally meaning doing the harmonious plan, that the Diné shall live together as a viable community on our sacred lands in order to continue our way of life, *iina doo ninit'í*, which is an immutable principle of *Diné bi beenahaz'áanii*." Iina Ba, Inc. v. Navajo Business Regulatory Dept., 11 Am. Tribal Law 447, 457 (Navajo Nation S.Ct.2014).

After the United States and the colonizers that came before it dispossessed Indigenous peoples of bulk of their property and resources by the 1930s (and for some tribes, all of their lands), tribal nations' landholdings have largely remained stable. Tribal nations and their citizens either own or are the beneficial owners of significant acreage and, in some contexts, valuable natural resources. Tribal courts are aware of the history of land dispossession and the current tribal efforts to retain and regain control over Indigenous lands and resources. In Lopez v. Benecke, 28 Indian L.Rep. 6178 (Pueblo of Pojoaque Tribal Ct.2001), the court noted the Pueblo's recent history of interactions with nonmembers in light of its efforts to preserve its lands and culture:

> The Pueblo's land, its laws, and its people are inextricably enmeshed—this fact is reflected in its recent history.
>
> For instance, the Pueblo of Pojoaque insists that all neighbors requesting right-of-ways, or easements, crossing Pueblo land either appear before the Tribal Council or undergo an interview by the Realty Department. With few exceptions, all right-of-ways and easements do not "run with the land," the legal imperative favored by courts across America. The reason is simple—the Pueblo wishes to reserve the right to determine whether their neighbors are friends deserving of rights-of-way or persons who are unacceptable to the Pueblo way of life.

Id. at 6180.

Because the colonizer has been unusually creative in dispossessing tribal nations of lands and resources, Indian country property interests are similarly unusual.

A. INDIAN COUNTRY PROPERTY INTERESTS

Property interests in and around Indian country are often atypical compared to Anglo-American common law. As a matter of law (and for the purposes of this Nutshell), lands owned or controlled by tribal nations and/or the tribal citizens of that reservation are known as "Indian lands" or "tribal lands." E.g., Restatement of the Law of American Indians § 11 ("Indian lands"); Nelson v. Pfizer, Inc., 4 Am. Tribal Law 680, 682 n.1 (Navajo Nation S.Ct.2003) ("Tribal land includes both land held in trust by the United States, whether for the Navajo Nation or individual members, and land held in fee by the Navajo Nation or individual members."). This section summarizes various kinds of Indian country property interests, some of which are unique to Indian law.

1. ABORIGINAL TITLE

Aboriginal title, or Indian title or original Indian title, is a property interest invented by the United States Supreme Court in Johnson v. McIntosh, 21 U.S. 543 (1823). E.g., In the Matter of the Lawful Successors in Interest to the Rights of Peck, 24 Indian L.Rep. 6197, 6200 (Sitka Tribal Ct.1997) (describing aboriginal title rights of Alaska Natives prior to an allotment act or similar vesting of rights). There, the Court theorized that Indigenous Peoples were subhumans without the capacity to "own" land, there merely possessed a right of occupancy that could be extinguished by purchase or conquest by a "discovering" sovereign such as Spain or France. Restatement of the Law of American Indians § 77. Though virtually all land in the United States has been, at one time, purchased or acquired by the federal government or its predecessor colonizing nations (very little was actually conquered), so aboriginal title is largely a dead letter. Contra Pueblo of Jemez v. United States, 63 F.4th 881 (10th Cir.2023) (holding that Pueblo's aboriginal property interests to the Valles Caldera National Preserve remained extant).

However, there may be aboriginal property rights retained by Indigenous Peoples or tribal nations, such as the right to hunt, fish, or gather, because those rights have never been extinguished by the federal government, or to submerged lands. E.g., Restatement of the Law of American Indians § 80, *cmt.* d (submerged lands). On occasion, tribal citizens or other Indians claim aboriginal property interests in Indian or tribal lands. In Barber v. Simpson, 2006 WL 6358357 (Nev. Inter-Tribal Ct.App.2006), the court rejected an aboriginal property rights claim where the petitioner could not show in the historical record that his family had ever occupied the land at issue.

2. RESERVATION LANDS

Lands reserved through an Indian treaty, Act of Congress, or Executive Order for the use and benefit of Indian tribes are reservation lands. Lands reserved after the cession or extinguishment of original Indian title (and the resources upon them) are owned by the tribal nation and tribal citizens in common. Restatement of the Law of American Indians §§ 78, 80. In general, reservation lands owned by tribal nations are governed by the Non-Intercourse Act, meaning that they cannot be alienated without the consent of the federal government. 25 U.S.C. § 177. However, Congress has frequently confiscated reservation lands, often for allotment purposes, providing little in the way of due process and just compensation as required by the Fifth Amendment.

Today, reservation lands that have been alienated to individual Indians or to non-Indians retain their reservation status, so long as the reservation boundary remains extant. These lands are considered Indian country for criminal jurisdiction and other purposes. 18 U.S.C. § 1151(a). In general, tribal nations exercise plenary jurisdiction over Indian lands and the people upon them. E.g., Plains Commerce Bank v. Long Family Land & Cattle Co., 554 U.S. 316, 328 (2008) (noting that tribal "plenary jurisdiction" over "tribal land" is presumed unless the land is alienated to nonmembers).

The phrase "reservation lands" is confusing. Reservation lands may be land that is owned collectively by a tribe and its citizens, but reservation lands may also be lands located within the boundaries of a reservation regardless of ownership status. On occasion, tribal courts have held that the court possesses jurisdiction over property disputes arising on lands within a reservation that are owned by a political subdivision of a state. E.g., Flynn v. Smith, 16 Am. Tribal Law 139, 141 (Fort Peck Ct. App.2020) (assuming jurisdiction over a property dispute between two tribal citizens over lands owned by the city of Wolf Point, citing Williams v. Lee, 358 U.S. 217 (1959)).

3. ALLOTMENTS

Allotments are parcels of land that once were either reservation lands or federal public lands that the federal government "allotted" to individual tribal members and others. Allotments typically were held by the United States in trust for a 25 year period. At the expiration of the trust period, the federal government would issue a fee patent to the allotment owner. The allotment would then be held as a fee allotment. On some occasions, the federal government extended the trust period indefinitely, so there are also trust allotments. E.g., Vintage Petroleum, Inc. v. Tax Commission of the Kickapoo Tribe of Oklahoma, 6 Okla. Trib. 327, 1997 WL 33477674, at *3 (Kickapoo Tribe Dist.Ct.1997).

For examples of histories of allotment on a given Indian reservation, see, e.g., Allen v. Cherokee Nation Tribal Council, 6 Am. Tribal Law 18, 22–25 (Cherokee Nation Jud.App.Trib.2006); Mustang Fuel Corp. v. Cheyenne-Arapaho Tax Commission, 2 Okla. Trib. 158, 1991 WL 733406, at *2 (Cheyenne-Arapaho Dist.Ct.1991); Hoover v. Colville Confederated Tribes, 2002 WL 34540595, at *1–2 (Colville Tribal Ct.App.2002); Citizenship Board of the Muscogee (Creek) Nation v. Grayson, 2025 Muscogee Creek Nation Supreme LEXIS 3, at *6–8 (Muscogee (Creek) Nation S.Ct.2025); Sisseton-Wahpeton Sioux Tribe v. Max, 11 Indian L.Rep. 6038, 6039–40 (Sisseton-Wahpeton Tribal Ct.1984).

On occasion, the United States holds allotment land in trust for individual Indians outside of reservation boundaries. E.g., Gishie v. Morris, 7 Am. Tribal Law 624, 626 (Navajo Nation S.Ct.2008) ("However, as part of the allotment program authorized by the General Allotment Act, also known as the Dawes Act, Act of February 8, 1887, 24 Stat. 388, the United States set aside lands both within and outside the current Navajo Reservation in trust for individual Navajos, and not for the Nation itself."). While many allotments were located on reservations, some were made to individuals living off-reservation, establishing a trust relationship with the federal government over land not within a formal reservation.

Many Indian-owned allotments are held by many dozens of individuals who were the beneficiaries of an intestate descendent, a problem known as fractionated heirships. E.g., In the Matter of the Estate of Wauneka, 13 Indian L.Rep. 6049, 6050 (Navajo Nation S.Ct.1986) ("We adhere to the land policy of the Navajo Nation. We disfavor dividing up of small parcels of land. The practical effect of progressive fragmentation of land results in possession of even smaller parcels by an astronomical number of heirs. The probation of allotments is a prime example of problems with fragmentation we can do without on the Navajo Reservation."). Because either of the fractionation problem or because the allotment land is not suitable for anything else, the federal government administers many of these allotments, leasing them out to agricultural and extractive resources interests.

Allotments, whether owned by Indians or non-Indians, are considered Indian country. 18 U.S.C. § 1151. E.g., Simpson v. Barber, 2004 WL 5748396, at *6 (Nev. Inter-Tribal Ct.App.2004) ("We hold that the Washoe Tribal Court did not err in determining that the SAC–6 Allotment is Indian Country based on 18 U.S.C. § 1151(c)."). Tribal courts typically possess jurisdiction in boundary disputes between allotments. E.g., Smith v. Eckhart, 2000 Mont. Crow Tribe LEXIS 11, at ¶ 30 (Crow Ct.App.2000) ("[T]his court affirms that the Tribal Court had jurisdiction to issue the permanent injunction in the present case to resolve a dispute between Tribal heirs over the construction of a boundary fence between their two trust allotments."). However, tribal courts likely will not assert jurisdiction over a claim to partition a trust allotment, which is technically owned by the United States, making the federal government an indispensable party. E.g., Colorado River Indian Tribes v. Anderson, 12 Indian L.Rep. 6001 (Colorado River Tribal Ct.1984).

4. TRUST LANDS

Many millions of the acres of land are held by the United States in trust for individual Indians or tribal nations. The government acquired some of this land through the allotment process long ago. Most trust land acquisitions now are conducted through Section 5 of the Indian Reorganization Act or special Acts of Congress authorizing trust land acquisitions for tribes or Indians. 25 U.S.C. § 5108; Restatement of the Law of American Indians § 81. For the most part, tribal nations have governmental control over trust lands. However, because trust land is technically owned by the federal government, some activities require federal approval under statutes such as 25 U.S.C. § 81.

Indians and tribes are the beneficial owners of trust land. E.g., Medel v. Granados, 2006 WL 6358377, at *7 (Nev. Inter-Tribal Ct.App.2006) ("[T]he legal title to the [trust] allotments . . . is held by the United States, with the entire beneficial interest being in the individual allottees."). Tribal nations "make decisions in trust on the use of [tribal] lands for the community welfare." Neptune Leasing, Inc. v. Mountain States Petroleum Corp., 11 Am. Tribal Law 162, 169 (Navajo Nation S.Ct.2013). See also Throssell v. Throssell, 1992 Tohono O'Odham App. LEXIS 1, at *7–8 (Tohono O'Odham Ct.App. 1992) ("[T]he express will of the people of the Tohono O'Odham Nation in enacting their Constitution [was] to maintain all unallotted lands within the Nation as a valuable resource for public use, to be managed by the Nation's Legislative Council for the benefit and use of the Nation and its members.").

Trust land is considered Indian country because it is set aside by the federal government for the benefit of Indians or tribal nations and remains under federal superintendency. Restatement of the Law of American Indians § 3, *cmt.* f. In some cases, tribal courts will void a transaction involving the sale of a trust asset for failure to seek approval of the Secretary of the Interior. E.g., Pitts v. Earling, 1994 Mont. Salish & Kootenai Tribe LEXIS 6, at *19 (Confederated Salish & Kootenai Tribes Ct.App. 1994) ("[W]e hold that failure to secure secretarial approval prior to the attempted sale rendered the contract at issue null and void and unenforceable."); First Western Bank of Minot v. Bird Bear, 14 Indian L.Rep. 6019, 6020 (Three Affiliated Tribes of the Fort Berthold Reservation Tribal Ct.1987) (nullifying promissory notes issued by bank to tribal farmers operating on trust land for failure to secure federal approval). See also Warren v. Gardner, 1997 Mont. Crow Tribe LEXIS 1, ¶ 17 (Crow Ct.App.1997) (noting that under federal law, "any contract 'touching' trust allotments which has not been approved by the Secretary of the Interior is 'absolutely null and void' ") (citing 25 U.S.C. § 348).

For tribal nations, especially those that lost much of their lands to allotment or illegalities, acquiring land and placing that land in trust with the federal government is excellent public policy. Because the land is owned by the federal government but controlled by the tribal nation, trust land is the equivalent of reservation land (and/or the replacement for lost reservation land). In large respects, trust land is the gold standard for tribal sovereignty. Tribal nations possess considerable authority over activities on trust lands. Many federally-funded programs, most notably housing, must be administered on trust land.

Some tribal citizens residing or doing business on trust lands (and some tribal leaders) justifiably complain that continued federal superintendency over trust land is a serious problem that devalues the land by making it extremely difficult to collateralize the land, necessary for development. Economic studies tend to disagree on the valuation issue, but it is true that trust land cannot be collateralized, if at all, without complying with strict and unwieldy federal guidelines. Tribal nations also complain that unwanted federal regulation, largely environmental regulation, places an unnecessary burden on tribal activities.

5. RESTRICTED FEE

Some lands, usually known as restricted fee lands, are owned by individual Indians or tribal nations in fee but under a federal restriction on alienation such as the Non-Intercourse Act, 25 U.S.C. § 177. Restatement of the Law of American Indians § 79. The lands of the Pueblos of the southwest are typically restricted fee lands, as well as much of the land of the Haudenosaunee (Iroquois) nations. Restricted fee lands cannot be sold without the permission of the United States, but because these lands are not owned by the United States, many of the restrictions placed on federal trust land are not present.

6. FEE LANDS

Fee land, also known as fee simple land, refers to the most complete and traditional form of property ownership where the owner has full and absolute rights to both the land and any structures on it. This means the owner can use, sell, lease, or transfer the property as they see fit. Tribal nations and individual Indians can own land in fee. If fee land is located within the exterior boundaries of Indian reservation, regardless of the status of the owner, the land is considered Indian country. If lands are considered "dependent Indian community" lands, then they are also considered Indian country. 18 U.S.C. § 1151(b). E.g., In the Matter of the Lawful Successors in Interest to the Rights of Peck, 24 Indian L.Rep. 6197, 6199–03 (Sitka Tribal Ct.1997) (describing how the Sitka tribal community is a dependent Indian community).

Disputes arising on the fee lands of tribal citizens in Indian country are under the jurisdiction of tribal courts. E.g., Atkinson v. Beveridge, 2 Am. Tribal Law 197, 202 (Fort Peck Ct.App.2000) ("[T]o suggest . . . that the Fort Peck Tribal Court lacks jurisdiction to adjudicate a dispute, brought on by a tribal member against another tribal member involving fee patented property within the exterior boundaries of the Fort Peck Reservation, is wholly without merit.").

Tribal nations possess the power to sell fee land, absent a limitation of that power under tribal constitutional or statutory law. E.g., Tribal Members Advocacy Group v. Tribal Council of the Grand Traverse Band of Ottawa & Chippewa Indians, 1995

Grand Traverse Band App. LEXIS 1 (Grand Traverse Band of Ottawa and Chippewa Indians Ct.App.1995) (affirming the tribal council power to sell fee land after review of the tribal constitution). However, because the federal Non-Intercourse Act's language is nonspecific as to the type of lands over which the Act applies, occasionally tribal nations will seek a special Act of Congress authorizing the sale of fee lands.

7. TRIBAL LAND ASSIGNMENTS AND LEASES

Tribal nations generally possess the power to assign property interests to individual tribal citizens from reservation lands the tribe owns or trust lands over which the tribe possesses a beneficial interest. E.g., Gishie v. Morris, 7 Am. Tribal Law 624, 626 (Navajo Nation S.Ct.2008) ("Generally, lands within the Nation are held in trust by the United States for the Navajo Nation as a collective entity. Individual Navajos may possess interests in such lands, through customary use, or through modern interests such as homesite leases, business site leases, or land use permits.").

In general, tribal lands can be leased by the tribal government, but if there is continuing federal superintendency over the land (such as trust land), then the Secretary of the Interior likely must approve the lease before it can be enforced. 25 U.S.C. § 415. Tribal nations may enact leasing regulations (which must be approved by the Secretary) to take over the leasing function from the federal government. § 415(h). Typical kinds of lease holdings include agricultural, residential, commercial, educational (public schools), and natural resources extraction. E.g., Antoine v. Grand Traverse Band Housing Dept./ Authority, 2001 WL 36194123 (Grand Traverse Band of Ottawa and Chippewa Indians Tribal Ct.2001) (implied residential lease); Division of Land Management v. Ellis, 2010 Oneida Trial LEXIS 15 ([Wis.] Oneida Appeal Commission Trial Ct.2010) (agricultural lease); Cedar Unified School Dist. v. Navajo Nation Labor Commission, 7 Am. Tribal Law 579 (Navajo Nation S.Ct.2007) (school lease); Neptune Leasing, Inc. v. Mountain States Petroleum Corp., 11 Am. Tribal Law 162 (Navajo Nation S.Ct. 2013) (commercial lease for resource extraction).

Tribal courts possess jurisdiction over disputes arising on leased lands, whether in fee or in trust, beneficially owned by tribal nations or tribal citizens. E.g., Lande v. Schwend, 1999 Mont. Crow Tribe LEXIS 1, ¶ 42 (Crow Ct.App.1999) ("Against the backdrop of the strong federal policy promoting Tribal self-government, the Crow Tribe's inherent sovereign authority thus provides a sound basis for its assertion of jurisdiction to adjudicate disputes involving Reservation trust lands pursuant to Crow Tribal Code §§ 3–2–202, –204 and –205 (jurisdiction)."); Greywater v. Wallace, 1995 Northern Plains App. LEXIS 7, at *5 (Northern Plains Intertribal Ct.App.1995) ("[I]t is clear that [the nonmember's] actions of entering into commercial dealings with an enrolled Indian involving land within the reservation subject him to the civil jurisdiction of the tribal court for any dispute arising from said commercial dealings."). Tribal courts also possess jurisdiction over claims against nonmembers arising from a lease of allotted lands. E.g., Lande v. Schwend, 26 Indian L.Rep. 6049 (Crow Ct.App.1999).

Under federal and state common law of property, improvements made upon land owned by others (in this case, the tribal nation) become the property of the owner. However, some tribal nations acknowledge that improvements made still be owned by the person who made the improvements. In Hood v. Bordy, 18 Indian L.Rep. 6061, 6063 (Navajo Nation S.Ct.1991) (acknowledging "the Navajo Nation's implicit recognition that Navajos may acquire a private ownership right to improvements on land which belongs to the nation").

8. EASEMENTS AND RIGHTS-OF-WAY

Indian country easements, often called rights-of-way, are legal rights granted to pass over or under tribal land for specific purposes like building roads, railroads, and utilities, which are managed under a complex federal framework that balances tribal sovereignty with infrastructure needs. These easements involve a legal agreement with the tribe or individual tribal landowners, and require approval from the Bureau of Indian Affairs (BIA) to ensure they serve the landowners' best interests and comply with federal law. 25 U.S.C. §§ 323–328; 25 C.F.R. Part 169.

The United States Supreme Court has held that a federally approved easement granted to a state in order to erect and maintain a highway abrogates a tribe's inherent power to regulate activities on that land, as well as adjudicate disputes that arise on that land. Strate v. A-1 Contractors, Inc., 520 U.S. 438 (1997). Notwithstanding *Strate*, however, tribal nations often continue to regulate nonmember activities on easements.

Consider Hazelton v. Leech Lake Band of Ojibwe, No. AP-24-04 (Leech Lake Band of Ojibwe Tribal Ct.App.2025), the court affirmed the power of the tribal court to order nonmembers to allow tribal citizens to travel the Prince of Peace Lane, a road on the reservation with deep cultural significance to the tribal nation and its citizens. The court described the significance of the road as follows:

> Countless Leech Lake members and others have used the route now known as Prince of Peace Lane for two centuries. The route provided access to Prince of Peace Cemetery, in which Band members were buried even as early as 1820. Everyone connected to the Lane—land owners and possessors, the federal government, other governments, and the Band—has treated the Lane as a route open to the public. They have traveled on the Lane, mapped it, maintained it, and permitted others to travel on it. Even Appellants Hazelton—over whose property the Lane passed for the duration of their ownership—permitted the public to use the route for nearly 15 years. The first time anyone interfered with passage on the route was in July 2020, when Appellants Hazelton blocked the Lane.

Id. at 2. The court agreed with the claims asserted by the tribe:

> The Band contends that the Tribal Court correctly asserted subject matter jurisdiction because (1) the Aleksandrovich Appellants, the real parties in interest, agreed to Tribal Court jurisdiction, (2) the Hazeltons (to whose interests the Aleksandrovich Appellants succeeded) engaged in consensual relations with a Band member when they purchased the Lot 5 parcels, and (3) the transfer and use of Lot 5 implicates the Band's sovereign interests. The Band argues that Appellants' consensual relations give the Tribal Court jurisdiction under the first exception in Montana and the status and use of a right-of-way over Lot 5 affects the sovereign interests of the Band under *Montana*'s second exception.

Id. at 19. See also id. at 20–22 (finding consent to tribal jurisdiction); id. at 22–23 (finding serious negative impacts on the tribe and its citizens by the closing of the road).

B. PROPERTY RIGHTS MATTERS

Contrary to many stereotypes about Indigenous Peoples, tribal nations recognize robust property rights and always have. The cultural background of Indigenous Peoples that tends to elevate the interests of non-human creatures, plants, land, water, air, and even supernatural entities above that of humans. Federal and state law rooted in western political traditions does not recognize the special status of anyone or anything except humans. Because modern tribal nations are modeled on these legal and political structures, tribal laws on property usually (but not always) do not recognize or protect non-human property interests.

Tribal nations possess the inherent power to regulate land use and other property matters involving their citizens and their lands. Restatement of the Law of American Indians § 11 (defining "tribal lands"); id. § 23 (explaining scope of tribal powers over property). Tribal nations may also regulate land use by nonmembers, so long as federal law does not prohibit it. Id. § 27.

1. PROPERTY DISPUTES

Tribal courts regularly decide property disputes arising from tribal land assignments and probate, to name two examples. Because much of the real property within tribal jurisdiction is owned by the federal government in trust for a tribal nation or individual Indians, or because it is owned legally or culturally by a tribe, village, or clan, tribal governments have a particular interest in disputes over those lands. E.g., In re Estate of McKee, 2005 WL 6349846 (Nev. Inter-Tribal Ct.App.2005) ("Tribal lands of the Fort McDermitt Reservation are held as tribal lands and do not belong to individual Indians. * * * Only the Tribal Council has the right to assign lands. Lands may be assigned to members of the tribe. * * * Assignments known as standard assignments are made primarily to establish homes for landless members of the tribe.") (citing

Constitution and Bylaws of the Fort McDermitt Paiute and Shoshone Tribe). Cf. Chavez v. Sells Community Land Commission, 2022 Tohono O'Odham App. LEXIS 1, at *6–7 (Tohono O'Odham Ct.App.2022) ("While the Constitution vests in the Tohono O'odham Council this broadest authority over the use, assignment, and other disposition of unallotted lands, and interests in those lands, the Constitution also vests some authority in the districts. The districts may assign homesites to individual members 'under the customary procedures of their respective communities[.]' * * * The Constitution also limits districts' power to make assignments. The district must make the assignment to a member of the nation. * * * The assignment must be for 'beneficial use and occupancy[.]' Finally, the district cannot grant an unending perpetual property interest in unallotted lands.") (citing Tohono O'odham Constitution).

The application of tribal custom and tradition is accepted in tribal communities to decide property matters. Riggs v. Estate of Attakai, 7 Am. Tribal Law 534 (Navajo Nation S.Ct.2007), a decision of the Navajo Nation Supreme Court, is a leading tribal property case. There, a Navajo Nation woman named Mary Lou Riggs owned a grazing permit that was used by her sister, Sista Riggs, and her husband, Tom Attakai. After she walked on intestate, her widower and sister litigated over the ownership of the grazing permit going forward. The Navajo family court awarded the permit to Tom because he was the primary user of the permit, but the appellate court reversed. The court relied on Navajo custom and tradition:

> * * * Traditionally, women are central to the home and land base. They are the vein of the clan line. The clan line typically maintains a land base upon which the clan lives, uses the land for grazing and agricultural purposes and maintains the land for medicinal and ceremonial purposes. The crucial role of women is expressed in the principles established by White Shell Woman and are commonly referred to as *Yoolgaii Asdzáán Bi Beehazáanii*. These principles include *Iiná Yésdáhí* (a position generally encompassing life; heading the household and providing home care, food, clothing, as well as childbearing, raising, and teaching), *Yódí Yésdáhí* (a position encompassing and being a provider of, a caretaker of, and receiver of materials things such as jewelry and rugs), *Nitl'iz Yésdáhí* (a position encompassing and being a provider of and a caretaker of mineral goodness for protection), *Tsodizin Yésdáhí* (a position encompassing spirituality and prayer). This is why the women are attached to both the land base and the grazing permits.

Id. at 536.

Hopi property rights issues are complicated by the fact that the Hopi tribal courts are national courts, not traditional village forums. As a result, the Hopi courts have concluded that its jurisdiction can be limited by custom and tradition. For example, in Ross

v. Sulu, No. CIV-023-88 (Hopi App.Ct.1991), the court concluded that a property dispute arising between two clans (in that case, Tewa and Hopi clans) must be adjudicated in a traditional forum, the village: "The village procedures should be conducted through the leadership of the Kikmongwi, as explicitly recognized by the Hopi Constitution." In a later case, Honie v. Hopi Tribal Housing Authority, 1 Am. Tribal Law 346, 353 (Hopi App.Ct.1998), the court established procedures for the certification of a village decision.

In Sipaulovi Village Board v. Sunrise Quoyavema, 6 Am. Tribal Law 410 (Hopi App.Ct.2005), the court addressed a trespass action seeking the removal of human remains from traditional clan land holdings of the Village of Sipaulovi. The respondents argued that they had rights to use the land arising from a land assignment from the respondent's father, who they claimed was the village Kikmongwi with the power to make the land assignment. The village board argued that the village land assignment, if one existed, was void. Since the dispute was between the village board and a nonresident of the village, the court assumed jurisdiction. The court remanded the case for further factual development of the record. In dicta, the court noted that the village board should have initiated a traditional proceeding:

> We do not find that a western-style trespass action adjudicates Hopi title to the land pursuant to Hopi customary law. An action for trespass merely vindicates one's right to possession without affecting the underlying

> title. If the Village sought to adjudicate the underlying Hopi customary title, then proper jurisdiction to determine this would lie in the village forum unless that exclusive jurisdiction is waived. Such a process would have to comport with fundamental fairness concepts of Hopi justice. See Johnson v. Belgard, No. AP-003-94 (March 29, 1996). The village could then enforce its decision in Tribal Court pursuant to *Honie.*

Sipaulovi, 6 Am. Tribal Law at 415.

The Hopi courts were confronted with intra-village jurisdictional complexities in a case involving the probate of an estate where a Bacavi village citizen left property in the Hotevilla village to their relatives. In re Estate of Komaquaptewa, 4 Am. Tribal Law 432 (Hopi App.Ct.2002). Normally, one village would assume jurisdiction, but in this case, two villages could potentially assume jurisdiction. Ultimately, Bacavi disclaimed jurisdiction and Hotevilla had not yet responded. The court remanded the case to the trial court to make determinations in the absence of a factual record and a lack of village custom and tradition. See id. at 443 ("[W]here Hopi written laws or rules are not on point, the Court will first consider Hopi custom and tradition.").

In Smith v. James, 2 Am. Tribal Law 319 (Hopi App.Ct.1999), the court ordered the trial court to assess Hotevilla village customary law in a quiet title action between granddaughters and a maternal aunt. The court concluded that the law of the village was unique as to all the other villages due to the unique history of that village:

> It was necessary for the trial court to inquire into and apply village customary law and practice in the instant case because of the unique history of the Village of Hotevilla. Hotevilla came to be as a result of the split at Old Oraibi in 1906. The establishment of Hotevilla and other communities on Third Mesa, affected the traditional "clan lands" system in operation at Old Oraibi because the split did not necessarily fall along clan lines. Mischa Titiev, Old Orabi: A study of the Hopi Indians of Third Mesa (1944): 88–89. Under the clan lands system, inheritance of land was traditionally matrilineal, but after the split at Oraibi, inheritance could sometimes be patriline. See Peter M. Whiteley, Rethinking Hopi Ethnography (1998): 62. Furthermore, with clan lands the fields were always the woman's but with the establishment of these new villages, men came to have different rights in land. See id. at 62, 65. Because traditional systems of clan lands probably do not govern this dispute, it was necessary for the court to apply Village custom.

Id. at 323–24.

Some tribal nations' laws allow for review of disputes over tribal lands assignments, e.g., McDade v. Garcia, 1997 WL 34704353 (Nev. Inter-Tribal Ct.App.1997) (South Fork Band of the Te-Moak Tribe of the Western Shoshone Indians), and some do not, e.g., In re Estate of McKee, 2005 WL 6349846 (Nev. Inter-Tribal Ct.App.2005) (Fort McDermitt Paiute and Shoshone Tribe). In Beck v. Eastern Band of

Cherokee Indians, 18 Am. Tribal Law 234 (Eastern Band of Cherokee Indians S.Ct.2025), the tribal constitution granted exclusive authority to the tribal council to manage all tribal property, precluding the tribal court's jurisdiction over a claim arising from the tribe's management of law: "Plaintiff's complaint is nonjusticiable under the political question doctrine because the case or controversy between the parties involves decisions regarding interests in Tribal lands, a matter over which the Tribal Council has exclusive power and authority." Id. at 240.

Disputes in tribal court over land assignments and other land rights are often complex factual matters, complicated further by the historic intervention of the federal government in land assignments as well as the reality that the parties are often not represented by counsel. In Raphael v. Grand Traverse Band of Ottawa and Chippewa Indians, 1996 Grand Traverse Band App. LEXIS 4 (Grand Traverse Band of Ottawa and Chippewa Indians App.Ct.1996), the court initially noted that the colonizer's dispossession of the tribe's reservation lands was so complete as to make tribal lands scarce:

> It is well known that Michigan Indians were very effectively dispossessed from their land by non-Indians. The impact on the Grand Traverse Band and the relevance to this matter is that almost all of the historic tribal lands were taken from the Tribe and that the modern-day land base of the Tribe is very limited. In fact, tribal lands at Peshawbestown had all but completely disappeared. It was only because Leelanau

> County Department of Social Services was convinced by the local county prosecutor to take the little remaining Indian land into trust for residential purposes for the most needy Indian families that kept Indian people from being completely dispossessed of all their land. This little remaining Indian land is the beginnings of the modern-day land base for the Tribe. Adding to this very modest land holding, the Tribe has been able to buy back land from non-Indians for tribal purposes. It should be fairly evident, given the price for land in Leelanau County and the numerous demands for tribal land usage, that the Tribe has neither sufficient financial resources to purchase back a sufficient land base to meet all current land needs or demands.

Id. at *3–4. The court then explained that the lack of available land made tribal land assignments difficult:

> These realities mean that no individual member has an absolute right to tribal land. Rather, land use decisions are made based upon all the various governmental, economic development and residential needs. This is an important point to be made because in the beginning of court proceedings in this matter Plaintiff's Counsel was under the mistaken impression that every tribal member was entitled to a tribal lot. Certain tribal lands are designated for residential purposes and are "assigned" for residential purposes only based upon particular criteria, with need at the

> forefront. Land lots so assigned are not "owned" by the member who receives the assignment. The lot is actually leased to them for residential purposes only and for a specified number of years. Thus, the assignment holder has a legal possessory interest only. The legal title to land held in trust for the Tribe is held by the United States. The tribal government is the beneficiary under the trust.

Id. at *4–5. At Grand Traverse Band, a treaty tribe that was federally acknowledged in 1980 after being administratively terminated for more than a century, the tribal entity that petitioned for federal acknowledgement in 1978 was called Leelanau Indians, Inc. (LII). Upon the acknowledgment of the Band itself in 1980, LII officials continued to act in the stead of the Band, leading to legal conflict in federal court. Grand Traverse Band of Ottawa and Chippewa Indians v. Leelanau Indians, Inc. and Leelanau County, No. G 83-834 (W.D.Mich.). In *Raphael*, LII had granted a land assignment to a citizen without authority to do so, forcing the court to invalidate the assignment. The tribal council did grant Raphael a land assignment for residential purposes, but the court did not require the tribe to do so.

Trespass actions in tribal courts are fairly common. In O'Campo v. Twyman, No. CV-AP-2022-0002 (Colorado River Indian Tribes App.Ct.2023), the court affirmed the eviction of a nonmember resident of a Mutual Help and Occupancy home (MHO) who claimed a lease had granted them an interest in the home. The resident's property interest in the home expired when the tribal citizen's lease of their land assignment to the resident expired. See also Blakely v. Morgan, 2007 WL 7561597, at *6 (Leech Lake Band of Ojibwe Tribal Ct.2007) (unlawful detainer action); Seneca Nation of Indians v. Williams, 23 Indian L.Rep. 6254 (Seneca Nation Peacemakers Ct.1996) (trespass action on lands on Seneca common lands owned by the tribe).

Parties may attempt to invoke tribal custom and tradition in trespass matters. In Navajo Nation v. Arviso, 6 Am. Tribal Law 675 (Navajo Nation S.Ct.2011), the court reversed a trial court decision favoring a trespasser, invoking Navajo common law:

> The Crownpoint District Court declined to evict Alonzo because it concluded the Nation waited too long (over twenty-seven years) to demand rent and demand that Alonzo quit the premises. The court also determined that pursuant to the Navajo principle of *k'é* (which the court characterized, in application, as a covenant of good faith and fair dealing), the Nation should have not been so "aggressive" in its demands and should have been flexible enough to seek a solution ("The Way Out, or *ch'ìhónit'i'*"), including attempts to negotiate a new lease.

Id. at 678. The court disagreed, holding that "under *Diné bi beenahaz'áanii* that Alonzo does not have the right to occupy the property. . . ." Id. See also Kayenta Township Comm'n v. Ward, 9 Am. Tribal Law 484, 491 (Navajo Nation S.Ct.2011) ("*Diné bi* *beenahaz'áanii* has application to all facets of life, including an eviction from a business site. * * * A land use decision by the people through their governments is the balance struck between the individual land user and the needs and desires of the community. * * * However, * * * *k'é* does not mandate the Navajo Nation to engage in negotiations with the trespasser.") (following *Arviso*); Southern Puget Sound Intertribal Housing Authority v. Johnson, 16 Indian L.Rep. 6076, 6077 (Shoalwater Bay Tribal Ct.1989) (applying "Indian custom" to hold that a mutual help and occupancy tenant who was a "Indian fisher[man] who follow[ed] the fish from one location to another" did not breach their agreement with the housing authority by subleasing home while away).

Conversely, in Campos v. Eastern Band of Cherokee Indians, 18 Am. Tribal Law 137 (Eastern Band of Cherokee Indians S.Ct.2024), the court rejected an effort by the plaintiff in a wrongful death claim to invoke Cherokee custom and tradition to show liability against a property owner. The court noted first that it had an obligation to assess claims of Cherokee custom and tradition, which would include:

> hearing testimony regarding pertinent custom and tradition from witnesses learned in EBCI culture and tradition who are recognized in the EBCI community as Cherokee knowledge keepers, and making determinations on the record as to whether specific customs or traditions put forth to the trial court should establish a Cherokee common law claim or

> defense as alleged, or whether the court should establish an alleged legal standard informed by a purported Cherokee custom and tradition to be recognized in this jurisdiction as an established duty to be utilized in deciding issues brought before the court

Id. at 159. The court articulated a standard that parties must show before the court can assess the custom and tradition-based claim:

> A plaintiff cannot, however, expect to avoid dismissal of an alleged EBCI custom and traditions claim pursuant to Rule 12(b)(6) by merely reciting the words "Cherokee common law" or "custom and traditions" in the complaint. At a minimum, a plaintiff must articulate a colorable Cherokee common law claim or identifiable Cherokee custom and traditions in the complaint (along with any supporting documentation attached thereto and incorporated therein) and sufficiently allege how the purported Cherokee common law or the specific custom and traditions apply to, materially bear on, and potentially control the issue(s) at hand while also providing a forecast of evidence to support the existence of the asserted Cherokee common law, or a roadmap to show how alleged Cherokee custom and traditions can be utilized to inform the establishment of legal duties or standards owed by the Tribe or another party.

Id. at 159–60 (footnote omitted). The court concluded that the Plaintiff's tribal common law-based claims would too indeterminate, too broadly favored visitors to others' property, and were never shown to actually be the custom and tradition of Cherokee people:

> * * * The trial court then found that "[t]here [was] no credible record presented to the [c]ourt" that Plaintiff's interpretation and theory of liability "has been or is the public policy or culture of the [EBCI]," which implicitly indicates that the trial court's review included the purported breach of the Cherokee common law claim and the alleged premises liability-based negligence claim(s) based on non-specific Cherokee custom and traditions, and concluded that Plaintiff had failed to state a claim on which relief could be granted.

Id. at 162. The court held that merely stating the words "customs and traditions" is insufficient:

> * * * The complaint primarily relies on the mere recitation of the words "custom and traditions" to support his alleged claim, and merely includes conclusory statements of how unspecified Cherokee common law should be interpreted and applied, thus neglecting to provide foundational support for his alleged breach of Cherokee common law claim or the custom and traditions that he asserts are mandatory for the trial court to apply.

Id.

2. LAND USE

Tribal nations possess the power to exercise police powers to govern land use on tribally owned and controlled lands, as well as lands owned by tribal citizens, Restatement of the Law of American Indians § 46 & *cmt.* e, and possess some limited authority over nonmember owned and controlled lands as well, id. § 48. Land use decisions by tribal nations are often driven by cultural interest, customary law, and local traditions. As the Navajo Nation Supreme Court put it, the interests of the tribal citizenry figure "prominently":

> * * * There is no more desirable a proceeding in our culture than where disputes are confronted and a solution reached that is often a balance of hardships. The goal is *Hózhó*—harmony, beauty and balance. As this case concerns land use, the interests of the people as a collective whole must also figure prominently. Part and parcel of the responsibilities of a Navajo court sitting in equity *are yiní dilyingo nábináhaazláago t'áá'a ltso aheelt'éego baantsá hákeesgo bá hasht'éédoolnííl*—rendering a decision with fundamental fairness to all.

Navajo Nation v. RJN Construction Mgmt., Inc., 10 Am. Tribal Law 265, 272 (Navajo Nation S.Ct.2012).

Land use disputes between tribal citizens and tribal nations are unusual but complex when they do occur. In Gobin v. Board of Directors, 6 NICS App. 101 (Tulalip Tribes Ct.App.2001), a tribal citizen owned a real estate development company that purchased fee land from nonmembers within the reservation, developed residential properties on part of the land and allowed the tribe to assume authority over the remainder. At the beginning of one such transaction, where the tribal citizen was planning to purchase 70 acres, the tribe put a moratorium on further development. The court declined to assume jurisdiction over the tribal citizen's claim on two grounds, the lack of standing of the tribal citizen (who had not yet purchased the property) and the land use ordinance, which stripped the court of jurisdiction. See also Gobin v. Tulalip Tribes, 6 NICS App. 120 (Tulalip Tribes Ct.App.2001) (companion case). In another case involving a tribal moratorium on all development on tribal lands, the court concluded that any business activities occurring prior to the moratorium were not barred. See San Xavier Dist. Council of the Tohono O'Odham Nation v. Francisco, 1988 Tohono O'Odham Jud. LEXIS 3, at *12 (Tohono O'Odham Judicial Ct.1988).

Tribal nations have the power to impose civil and criminal penalties for violations of tribal environmental codes as well. E.g., Doka v. Fort McDowell Yavapai Apache Nation, 5 Am. Tribal Law 132 (Fort McDowell Yavapai Nation S.Ct.2004) (affirming criminal conviction for violations of tribal environmental code). In one leading case, Sherman v. Enbridge Energy LLC, 10 Am. Tribal Law 66 (Leech Lake Band of Ojibwe Tribal Ct.2009), the Leech Lake Band of Ojibwe tribal court asserted jurisdiction over a claim brought by tribal citizens to enjoin the construction of a petroleum pipeline within the boundaries of the reservation. The tribe had reached an agreement with the pipeline company to allow construction. The pipeline company had consented to tribal court jurisdiction by entering into a written agreement with the tribe, but the court declined to enjoin construction. The court pointed out that the tribal agreement did not guarantee that any pipeline would be constructed at all, that several federal and state agencies and legal authorities needed to be satisfied before the pipeline construction could proceed.

Nonmember land use issues figure prominently in many reservations that had been subject to allotment, which allowed many nonmembers to purchase land in fee within reservation boundaries. Because the lands at issue are often outside state or local authority, these nonmembers frequently can claim complete immunity from tribal and state land use or zoning regulations. E.g., Donius v. Rincon Band of Luiseño Indians, 2020 Rincon Band Luiseno App. LEXIS 1, at *33 (Rincon Band of Luiseño Indians Ct.App. 2020) (recognizing that "local government shows no interest in zoning, regulating, or exercising any form of regulation dealing with any control over non-Indian owned fee land located on Indian reservations in San Diego County"). Cf. Gobin v. Snohomish County, 304 F.3d 909, 917 (9th Cir. 2002) ("[T]he County's land use regulations have no force."). Absent nonmember consent to tribal jurisdiction over nonmember-owned lands, however, tribal jurisdiction is fraught, even unpredictable, especially with the potential for federal court review. E.g., Brendale v. Confederated Tribes and Bands of Yakima Indian Reservation, 492 U.S. 408 (1989) (finding tribal jurisdiction over nonmembers in "closed" portion in reservation but not in "open" portion). At bottom, tribal courts act to ensure that nonmembers receive procedural fairness when subject to tribal authority. E.g., Rowland v. Hoopa Valley Tribe, 2 NICS App. 185 (Hoopa Valley Tribal Ct.App.1992) (holding nonmember gravel extraction business' contractual relationships would be injured by tribal prohibition on removal of materials from job site).

In land use disputes involving routine conflict between nonmember developers or residents against tribal prerogatives, tribal courts point to settled principles of federal Indian law to justify tribal jurisdiction. E.g., Cavenham Forest Industries, Inc. v. Colville Confederated Tribes, 18 Indian L.Rep. 6037, 6038 (Colville Tribal Ct.App.1991) (relying upon United States Supreme Court statements and Interior Solicitors' opinions confirming that tribal nations retain their inherent sovereignty absent divesture by agreement or by Congress); Grand Portage Band of Chippewa v. Melby, 28 Indian L.Rep. 6156, 6157–58 (Grand Portage Band of Chippewa Indians Tribal Ct.App.2000) (applying United States Supreme Court statements).

The occasions in which tribes successfully assert jurisdiction and later prevail in federal court involve devastating environmental contamination or cultural protection. In FMC Corp. v. Shoshone-Bannock Tribes Land Use Department and Fort Hall Business Council, Nos. C-06-0069, C-07-0017, and C-07-0035 (Shoshone-Bannock Tribal Ct.App.2012), the tribal government asserted jurisdiction over the nonmember company's hazardous waste storage facility where the company had stored 22 million tons of hazardous and non-hazardous waste for many decades. The Environmental Protection Agency had forced the company to pay a permit fee to the tribe of $1.5 million a year. After four years, the company gave notice to the tribe that it would cease payment, leading to a tribal court action involving the scope of tribal regulatory authority over the company. The tribal court, applying the *Montana* analysis, concluded that the nonmember company had consented through the agreement to pay the permit fee. The court also concluded that the company's storage of hazardous waste on the reservation substantially impacted the political integrity, economic security, and health and welfare of the tribe and its members, again invoking *Montana*. After a federal court challenge to tribal jurisdiction, the Ninth Circuit agreed with the tribal court. FMC Corp. v. Shoshone-Bannock Tribes, 942 F.3d 916 (9th Cir.2019), cert. denied, 141 S.Ct. 1046 (2021).

Tribal courts have also found jurisdiction to regulate nonmember land use, for example, in cases where nonmember residential housing development proposals. In Hoover v. Colville Confederated Tribes, 2002 WL 34540595 (Colville Tribal Ct.App.2002), the Environmental Protection Agency had recognized the authority of the tribe to enact water quality standards for the reservation, which supplemented the tribe's inherent authority to regulate nonmember land use. The court held that the nonmember development proposal would greatly impact the reservation's "ecology and environment," potentially harming tribal citizens:

> Hoover's planned development would have an impact on the ecology and environment because any increase in the number of homes within the Reserve would directly affect the deer and elk population. Were he granted permission to construct his development, the Tribes would have no ground to prevent other non-member fee owners from developing their properties within the Reserve. It is clear from the evidence adduced at trial that the Tribes had little choice in preventing Hoover from proceeding. They either had to allow him and others to build in the Reserve, and thus destroy or greatly diminish an important, necessary food and culture source, or prevent him from building and thus preserve a valuable source of subsistence hunting and cultural participation.

Id. at *9. The court also noted that the nonmember's development project would impact Colville spiritual and cultural preservation:

> * * * It is well known in Indian Country that spirituality is a constant presence within Indian tribes. Meetings and gatherings all begin with prayers of gratitude to the Creator. The culture, the religion, the ceremonies-all contribute to the spiritual health of a tribe. To approve a planned development detrimental to any of these things is to diminish the spiritual health of the Tribes and its members. * * * It is the "harmony of man with his surroundings" that the Tribes seek in

> maintaining the Reserve in a state compatible with nature.* * * The evidence is highly persuasive that the encroachment of human habitation would have a detrimental effect on the animals, plants, and herbs used for sustenance, medicinal, and ceremonial purposes-the continued existence of which is vital to the spiritual health of the Tribes and their members.

Id. at *10.

Similarly, in Donius v. Rincon Band of Luiseño Indians, 2020 Rincon Band Luiseno App. LEXIS 1 (Rincon Band of Luiseño Indians Ct.App. 2020), the tribe attempted to enforce its land use ordinance against a nonmember business operating on fee land within the reservation. The tribe adopted land use and zoning laws that assume federal Indian law principles governed the scope of the tribe's jurisdiction over nonmembers. The nonmember business refused to allow the tribe to enforce the law by denying entrance to tribal regulators to inspect the land. In past years, there had been a series of fires and other events at the property that had threatened the tribe's gaming operations and its water supply. The tribe's land use ordinance tracked United States Supreme Court decisions, barring tribal civil regulatory authority over nonmembers on fee land absent consent of the nonmember or "catastrophic consequences" to the tribe and its citizens. *Donius*, 2020 Rincon Band Luiseno App. LEXIS 1, at *15. See also Rincon Tribal Code § 8.301(b). The tribal appellate court concluded that the nonmember's activities had the real potential of causing catastrophic impacts on the tribe, justifying tribal authority to regulate the nonmember business:

> The trigger point for tribal jurisdiction under § 8.301(b)(4)(B) in this case is the potential for the defendants' activities to create catastrophic consequences that can spread to tribal lands. To review, the trial court found conclusively (1) that the Appellants failed to maintain their property; (2) that the Appellants' land constitutes a fire hazard in an area that is unusually threatened by fire; (3) that the Appellants' actions and inactions have contributed to a significant threat to the pristine character of the tribe's water supply; and (4) that the Appellants' assertion of immunity from tribal jurisdiction, together with local government's demurrer, creates a lawless enclave within the reservation.
>
> We conclude that the Appellants' land use choices on its own property have the potential to create catastrophic impacts on the Rincon Band's lands. We hold that the RMCA [Rincon Mushroom Corp. of America]/Donius' conduct has long created the potential for catastrophic consequences on the tribe. There are two critical facts that undergird our holding. First, the Tribe is dependent on a single water source, the groundwater underneath both the Tribe's lands and the RMCA/Donius' lands. Second, the Tribe is dependent on a major source of revenue from its gaming operations, which are located across the street from the defendants' property. If

> either of those resources are threatened with catastrophic harm, then tribal law authorizes the Tribe to assert jurisdiction over the defendants.

Donius, 2020 Rincon Band Luiseno App. LEXIS 1, at *31–32. The Ninth Circuit later confirmed tribal jurisdiction over the nonmember business. Rincon Mushroom Corp. v. Mazzetti, 490 Fed.Appx. 11 (9th Cir.2022).

Tribal powers over nonmember activities may also be employed to protect tribal cultural and religious interests. In Hoopa v. Valley Tribe v. Bugenig, 25 Indian L.Rep. 6137 (Hoopa Valley Tribal Ct.1996), aff'd in part, 5 NICS App. 37 (Hoopa Valley Tribal Ct.App.1998), the court affirmed the authority of the tribe to prohibit logging in an area the tribal council labeled a "buffer zone" around a tribal sacred site. The tribe had sought and received significant public comment on its land use and permitting process, leading federal, state, and local governments to defer to the tribe's choices. The tribal appellate court agreed with the tribe, writing, "[A] timber harvest regulation, neutrally applied, the purpose and effect of which is to preserve the sanctity of the Hoopa Tribe's most sacred spiritual location for the present and future use of tribal members would be a right retained by the Hupa people to ensure that their reservation remained livable." Id. at 49. The nonmember challenged tribal jurisdiction in federal court and initially prevailed before a Ninth Circuit panel, which held that the nonmember's interference with the tribe's sacred site did not rise to the level demanded by the *Montana* decision. However, an en banc panel of the Ninth Circuit confirmed tribal jurisdiction on a different theory, that the federal government delegated authority to the tribe to regulate all reservation residents by ratifying the tribe's constitution, which asserted that power, in the Hoopa Yurok Settlement Act. Bugenig v. Hoopa Valley Tribe, 266 F.3d 1201 (9th Cir.2001) (en banc).

3. DOMESTIC PROPERTY MATTERS

Tribal nations possess plenary power to regulate domestic relations, prescribe rules of inheritance, and regulate the use and disposition of property. Restatement of the Law of American Indians §§ 19–20, 23.

Tribal jurisdiction over the internal domestic matters of tribal nations can be presumed, but some tribal nations may limit tribal court jurisdiction. For example, in Sanchez v. Garcia, 2 Am. Tribal Law 334 (Hopi App.Ct.1999), the court noted some tribal villages delegate authority to handle inheritance matters to a "village member":

> A village member is a traditional legal authority in the area of inheritance law where there is a longstanding custom within the village recognizing his or her power to resolve inheritance disputes. This acknowledged power to resolve inheritance disputes may stem from the village member's status within the community, or his or her relationship to the parties. For instance, it is a common practice at Hopi for the heirs of a decedent to take any

> inheritance dispute that may arise among them to the appropriate clan relative, who determines how the decedent's estate should be distributed. In recognition of this practice, this Court hereby takes judicial notice that there is a "generally known and accepted" custom at Hopi recognizing the appropriate clan relatives as traditional legal authorities with the power to resolve inheritance disputes.
>
> Clan relative settlement is an effective means to resolve intra-village inheritance disputes in a traditional Hopi manner and in a traditional Hopi legal forum. For the Tribal Courts to disregard this method of dispute resolution would be to show disrespect for traditional Hopi law and traditional legal authorities within the villages. Perhaps more to the point, the Hopi Constitution mandates that the Tribal Court give deference to the villages in inheritance matters. Because the villages have exclusive jurisdiction over intra-village inheritance disputes under Article III, Section 2(c), the Hopi courts cannot overrule a village decision in this area.

Id. at 339 (citation omitted). Because the village made a determination in this matter, the Hopi court had no jurisdiction to upset that decision. However, where a village declines to make its own determination, Hopi courts may assume jurisdiction. See In re Estate of Komaquaptewa, 4 Am. Tribal Law 432 (Hopi App.Ct.2002), where the court reasoned:

> If the Tribal Court did not exercise jurisdiction after a village declined its right to decide a member's probate claim, village members would be left without a tribal forum in which to assert their property rights. Hopi tribal members would be unable to raise factual and legal matters affecting their cultural and legal interests in property, leading to a violation of substantial rights and leaving aggrieved parties to contest probate matters in non-tribal judicial forums. Moreover, Hopi tribal and village customs and traditions would not receive the same consideration in a non-tribal forum and the results could be devastating to Hopi parties, the Tribe and the Villages. Therefore, this Court finds as a matter of law and public policy that the tribal court has jurisdiction to decide inheritance matters when a village declines to or avoids its responsibility to do so.

Id. at 442–43 (footnotes omitted).

Tribal courts also possess jurisdiction over the disposition of the property of decedents. E.g., Rios v. Lilley, 13 Am. Tribal Law 420, 429–31 (Fort Peck Ct.App.2016) (reversing trial court's decision to revoke will and determine heirs); In re Estate of Summers, 2002 WL 34534293 ([Wis.] Oneida Tribal Judicial System Trial Ct.2002) (adjudicating real property inheritance rights of tribal citizen child and nonmember surviving spouse); In re Estate of Hughes-Juan, 2023 Tohono O'Odham Jud. LEXIS 4 (Tohono O'Odham Judicial Ct.2023) (enforcing will of decedent expressing wish to exclude estranged spouse). The Navajo Supreme Court articulated the interests at play in such matters:

> It is not proper to talk about death or dying. In re Estate of Tsosie, 4 Nav. R. 198, 200 ([Window Rock] Dist.Ct.1983). Moreover, burials and property distribution are to be accomplished without undue delay out of respect for the deceased and without dispute in order to protect surviving family members. Watson v. Watson, 8 Am. Tribal Law 135, 140 (Nav.Sup. Ct.2009). "Out of respect for the deceased," *kwá'ásiní báhozhdísin*, means that prompt attention should be given to the disposition of property so as to allow the deceased to complete Life's journey and so that the survivors can complete the transitional (cleansing) process to resume Life. Thereupon, one can treat and utilize the property as one's own personal property.

In re Estate of Benally, 8 Am. Tribal Law 246, 250–51 (Navajo Nation S.Ct.2009).

Tribal courts regularly exercise jurisdiction over marriage dissolutions, which often lead to determinations of how to split marital property. For example, in Rodarte v. Rodarte, 1997 WL 34704390 (Nev. Inter-Tribal Ct.App.1997), the court affirmed a decision of the trial court that funds from an inheritance were not considered marital property where they were not commingled with marital property. A Navajo trial court applied a Navajo common law principle (of sorts) to reach the conclusion that a divorced spouse is not entitled to the life insurance proceeds of a former spouse: "To permit a former spouse to keep such ties that she or he may be said to be lurking behind the hogan waiting to take a portion of the corn harvest is unthinkable, since each spouse returns to his or her own family after the divorce." Apache v. Republic National Life Ins. Co., 11 Indian L.Rep. 6005, 6006 (Navajo Nation Window Rock Dist.Ct.1982). Trust assets are sometimes at issue in marriage dissolutions, creating jurisdictional complexities. E.g., Rickman v. Junaluska, 3 Cher.Rep. 39, 2002 WL 34536628, at *2 (Cherokee Ct. of the Eastern Band of Cherokee Indians 2002) (disclaiming jurisdiction over trust assets in divorce action pending resolution of tribal council, which was required under tribal statute).

Mixed marriages may create jurisdictional complexity where the marriage is dissolved. In too many cases, there is a race to file, where one married partner seeks a divorce in tribal court and the other in state court. In Turpen v. Turpen, 20 NICS App. 1 (Muckleshoot Tribal Ct.App.2022), the court affirmed tribal court jurisdiction over a dissolution where the enrolled tribal member filed in tribal court. The tribal member and nonmember former spouse shared a home off the reservation that was financed by a tribal home finance program. The court held that the nonmember had consented to tribal jurisdiction under the *Montana* test.

> It is undisputed that, in addition to entering into marriage with Appellee, a Tribal Member, he also entered into a contract to receive

> financial support for the purchase of the marital home through the Elder's Pay Back Program. Respondent does not and cannot dispute this fact. By entering into that contract, he entered into a consensual relationship with the Tribe which allows the Muckleshoot Tribal Court to exercise jurisdiction over him for purposes of this dissolution.

Id. at 4. A year later, a federal court agreed. See Turpen v. Muckleshoot Tribal Court, 2023 WL 4492250 (W.D.Wash. July 12, 2023).

Child support orders from state and tribal courts must be given full faith and credit under federal law. 28 U.S.C. § 1738B. Tribal courts, however, do not have to follow state law on child support matters. In Attikai v. Thompson, 21 Indian L.Rep. 6001 (Northern Plains Intertribal Ct.App.1993), the court refused to follow South Dakota law that privileged children of a first marriage over those from subsequent marriages. The court remanded the matter to the trial court to "to determine whether the Crow Creek Sioux Tribe accepts as part of its cultural standard that the firstborn child has the paramount right of support over later born children, whether born within a marriage or outside of a marriage. . . ." Id. at 6002.

At Navajo, tribal common law determines domestic relations law. The Navajo Supreme Court described the contours of that regime:

> The Navajo People's segmentary lineage system (clanship system) is the foundation of

Navajo Nation domestic relations law. The system itself is law. Traditional Navajo society is matrilineal and matrilocal, which obligates a man upon marriage to move to his wife's residence. The property the couple bring to the marriage mingle and through their joint labors create a stable and permanent home for themselves and their children. The wife's immediate and extended family benefit directly and indirectly, in numerous ways, from the marriage.

If the marriage does not survive, customary law directs the man to leave with his personal possessions (including his horse and riding gear, clothes, and religious items) and the rest of the marital property stays with the wife and children at their residence for their support and maintenance. Whatever gains the marital property generates goes to support the wife and children and to a lesser extent the wife's close relatives. This longstanding customary law is akin to modern spousal maintenance. Therefore, we conclude that Navajo common law gives the Navajo Nation courts' authority to award spousal maintenance in appropriate cases even in the absence of statutory law on the subject. Our laws require our courts to apply Navajo common law equally to both spouses when addressing spousal maintenance issues.

Naize v. Naize, 1 Am. Tribal Law 445, 449 (Navajo Nation S.Ct.1997). Cf. In re Validation of the Marriage of Francisco, 16 Indian L.Rep. 6113, 6113

(Navajo Nation S.Ct.1989) ("The lack of a coherent Navajo domestic relations code has caused Navajo courts to mingle common-law marriage with traditional Navajo marriage.").

Occasionally, plaintiffs bring domestic claims they argue are rooted in tribal custom and tradition. For example, in Rosario v. Arneach, 5 Cher.Rep. 10, 2006 WL 6500567 (Cherokee Ct. of the Eastern Band of Cherokee Indians 2006), the court rejected a claim for alienation of affections and criminal conversation, torts originating in English common law. The court initially noted that such torts "originated in the English common law concept that the wife was the 'property of her husband. * * * The common law considered the wife the chattel of the husband." Id. at *2. Conversely, Cherokee law did not recognize women as property:

> The parties agree that in Cherokee culture and tradition the roles of females and males were very different than in European society. The parties stipulate that, in Cherokee culture and tradition, Cherokee wives were never considered the property of their husbands. Rather, Cherokee women held an amount of societal power that was stunning to Europeans.
>
> When Cherokees met Europeans, the Europeans assumed that one of the reasons that the Cherokees were uncivilized was because the women had so much power. Their power was tied to their role as producers and mothers. The Cherokee and Euro-American worldviews differed dramatically regarding

> appropriate gender roles, marriage, sexuality and spiritual beliefs. As we have seen, Cherokee women were farmers, and Cherokee men were hunters. Their society was matrilineal and matrilocal, which meant that the women owned their residence and the fields they worked. Cherokee women were healers, producers, warriors, traders, wives, and mothers. They taught their daughters to cook, prepare game, do beadwork, and make baskets, pottery, and clothing. They enjoyed sexual freedom and easy divorce, but the clans maintained strict incest taboos, and in all their actions tribe members had to take the welfare of the community into account. Cherokees believed in a sexual division of labor, but the difference was associated with complementarity and equality, not hierarchy or domination. Their religious beliefs differed greatly from Christian theology. Because the public and private spheres were not highly differentiated, Cherokee women enjoyed a higher status than in those societies where there is little permeability.

Johnston, Cherokee Women in Crisis: Trail of Tears, Civil War, and Allotment, 1838–1907 (2003), pp. 146–7; see also, Perdue, Our Indian Heritage, Our Mountain Heritage (Lovin, ed.) (1979), p. 39.

If the power that Cherokee women held was alien to Europeans, so too to the Cherokee was the European concept of marriage, consisting of a man and his chattel.

> The members of a Cherokee household were usually a mother, her daughters, her daughters' children, and her unmarried sons. The husbands of the women of the household also lived with the family and contributed to its support; but since Cherokee marriages were frequently of a short duration, their continued presence was not assured. In the event of a marital separation, the husband returned to the household of his mother and sisters, while his children remained with his wife and her family.

Perdue, p. 44. The husband "spent much of his time with his own lineage because these were his kinsman, while his wife's people, including his wife and children, were not." Id. at 46.

Id. at *4–5. Needless to say, the Cherokee tribal court refused to acknowledge the plaintiff's claims.

Tribal nations may create property interests in Indian gaming proceeds, leading to disputes over the vesting of those property rights in numerous contexts. In Squirrell v. Queen, 9 Am. Tribal Law 421 (Eastern Band of Cherokee Indians S.Ct.2010), the court concluded that personal property purchased with tribal gaming per capita funds is not marital property if a spouse had no intention of converting those funds into marital property. See also State ex rel. Maney v. Maney, 4 Cher.Rep. 23, 2005 WL 6438072, at *4 (Cherokee Ct. of the Eastern Band of

Cherokee Indians 2005) (holding that a tribal citizen's entire per capita gaming payment may be allocated to child support, adding, "This decision is in accord with the culture and traditions of the Eastern Band of Cherokee Indians in securing support for the Tribe's children, especially where a responsible parent by a deliberate criminal act has impaired or destroyed support for a child.").

C. RIGHTS OF NATURE

Several tribal nations recognized the inherent personhood of nature or things within nature. Most tribal rights of nature statutes only date back as far as 2018, but the Navajo Nation codified their laws decades ago. Diné Natural Law provides:

A. The four sacred elements of life, air, light/fire, water and earth/pollen in all their forms must be respected, honored and protected for they sustain life; and

B. The six sacred mountains, *Sisnajini, Tsoodzil, Dook'o'oosłííd, Dibé Nitsaa, Dził Na'oodilii, Dził Ch'ool'í'í*, and all the attendant mountains must be respected, honored and protected for they, as leaders, are the foundation of the Navajo Nation; and

C. All creation, from Mother Earth and Father Sky to the animals, those who live in water, those who fly and plant life have their own laws, and have rights and freedom to exist; and

D. The Diné have a sacred obligation and duty to respect, preserve and protect all that was provided for we were designated as the steward of these relatives through our use of the sacred gifts of language and thinking; and

E. Mother Earth and Father Sky is part of us as the Diné and the Diné is part of Mother Earth and Father Sky; The Diné must treat this sacred bond with love and respect without exerting dominance for we do not own our mother or father.

F. The rights and freedoms of the people to the use of the sacred elements of life as mentioned above and to the use of the land, natural resources, sacred sites and other living beings must be accomplished through the proper protocol of respect and offering and these practices must be protected and preserved for they are the foundation of our spiritual ceremonies and the Diné life way; and

G. It is the duty and responsibility of the Diné to protect and preserve the beauty of the natural world for future generations.

1 Navajo Nation Code § 205.

The Yurok Tribe recognized the "rights of the Klamath River to exist, flourish, and naturally evolve; to have a clean and healthy environment free from pollutants; to have a stable climate free from human-caused climate change impacts; and to be free from contamination by genetically engineered organisms." Yurok Tribal Council, Res. No. 19-40 (May 9, 2019).

Some litigation over the rights of nature has begun in tribal courts, but not much jurisprudence has come of it so far. Recently, the White Earth Nation of Ojibwe adopted a statute designed to grant personhood to *manoomin*, or wild rice. That statute provides in part:

> *Manoomin*, or wild rice, within all the Chippewa ceded territories possess inherent rights to exist, flourish, regenerate, and evolve, as well as inherent rights to restoration, recovery, and preservation. These rights include, but are not limited to, the right to pure water and freshwater habitat; the right to a healthy climate system and a natural environment free from human caused global warming impacts and emissions.

1855 Treaty Authority, Resolution Establishing Rights of Manoomin, Res. No. 2018-05 (Dec. 5, 2018). *Manoomin* advocates brought suit in White Earth Tribal Court seeking to bar the State of Minnesota from enabling the continuation of the Enbridge Line 3 petroleum pipeline, which threatened *manoomin* habitat. The tribal court confirmed *manoomin*'s standing to sue and confirmed its jurisdiction over the state, but the tribal appellate court dismissed the suit on federal law grounds. Minnesota Dept. of Natural Resources v. Manoomin, No. AP21-0516 (White Earth Band of Ojibwe Ct.App. 2022).

The Sauk-Suiattle Indian Tribe brought suit against the City of Seattle to fight for the rights of salmon, or *Tsuladx*^{w}, which the tribe claimed was threatened by Seattle's hydroelectric dams. Complaint, Sauk-Suiattle Indian Tribe v. City of Seattle, No. SAU-CIV-01/22/001 (Sauk-Suiattle Tribal Ct.2022). As background for the suit, the tribe explained the importance of *Tsuladx*^{w}:

> *Tsuladx*^{w}, our relatives under on water [sic], are the most important cultural and sacred food of the Sahkuméhu and have been a part of our traditional stories, teachings, lifeways and spirituality since the earliest times to the present day. For the Sahkuméhu, *Tsuladx*^{w} is sentient like all living creatures and they are our relations. We Sahkuméhu have a sacred covenant with *Tsuladx*^{w}, the water and all living creatures, without which we cannot live.
>
> For us *Tsuladx*^{w} is a gift from the Creator and because of this spiritual connection and relationship with them the Sahkuméhu expressly reserved the right maintain a relationship with them. They are central to our cultural identity, spiritual traditions, and physical wellbeing. It is an important species to the ecology and provides critical food and habitat to both endemic and migratory species.

Id. at 3. The Sauk-Suiattle suit was later settled to the benefit of the tribe and *Tsuladx*^{w}.

D. TRIBES' AND TRIBAL CITIZENS' RIGHTS TO RESERVATION NATURAL RESOURCES

Tribal nations and their citizens possess rights to water, land, and other natural resources under tribal law and, to a lesser extent, federal law. The United States Supreme Court has repeatedly confirmed that tribal nations own the resources on their reservations. Restatement of the Law of American Indians §§ 82, 85. Tribal nations also possess rights to resources and the power to enforce tribal laws regulating those resources. Id. § 85, cmt. c.

In general, tribes can regulate and adjudicate claims involving on-reservation resources. In Estate of Jorgenson v. DHS Drilling Co., 11 Am. Tribal Law 123 (Shoshone and Arapaho Tribal Ct.2011), the Shoshone and Arapaho Tribal Court for the Wind River Indian Reservation confirmed tribal court jurisdiction over acts by a nonmember owned drilling company on the reservation. The tribe and tribal member plaintiffs had alleged various tort and contract claims against the company.

Hunting, fishing, and gathering rights are critical to tribal citizens because they are essential for cultural identity, economic well-being, food security, and environmental stewardship. These rights, often reserved in treaties, are more than legal entitlements; they are foundational to Indigenous existence and sovereignty. Federal Indian law recognizes that these rights are owned by the tribal nation, similar to English and American common law, granting tribal nations the power to regulate hunting, fishing, and gathering. "Tribal members may exercise the treaty right to hunt on the reservation in accordance with tribal customs and laws." Williams v. Cheyenne River Sioux Tribe, 18 Indian L.Rep. 6091, 6092 (Cheyenne River Sioux Tribe Ct.App.1991).

Occasionally, tribal courts are forced to apply default federal hunting and fishing regulations where the tribal government has not yet done so. In Yurok Tribe v. Oliver, 1996 WL 34573149 (Yurok Ct. of Indian Offenses 1996), the court ordered that federal fishing regulations applied to fishing activities within the exterior boundaries of the reservation on a temporary basis. The defendants were charged with eel hooking salmon and dip-net fishing, traditional Yurok fishing methods, in violation of in-seasons adjustment orders issued by federal officials. The court dismissed the charges against the defendants because the federal official had not published the adjustment rules in the Federal Register.

Once the tribe does enact its own fishing ordinance, the tribal court will apply those rules. In Nelson v. Yurok Tribe, 1999 WL 35015757 (Yurok Tribal Ct.App.1999), the tribe had adopted the Yurok Tribal Fishing Rights Ordinance. The ordinance restricted traditional tribal fishing methods, limiting the times at which tribal fishers could get in the water. The Yurok Tribal Court of Appeals (note: no longer the Court of Indian Offenses or Court of Indian Appeals) rejected a constitutional challenge to the fishing limits. The tribal constitution protected "traditional practices." Yurok Const. art. IX. The tribe responded with a bevy of arguments supporting its limits, mostly rooted in the tribe's conservation interests. The court agreed: "The Tribe's exercise of its governmental powers was based upon a legitimate, rational constitutionally provided mechanism to protect its tribal resources. There was no constitutional violation when the Yurok Tribe exercised its governmental authority to protect its resources by limiting a tribal member's right to fish in accordance with its ordinance and Harvest Management Plan." *Nelson*, 1999 WL 35015757 at *9. See also Leech Lake Band of Ojibwe v. Rock, 2008 WL 8565701 (Leech Lake Band of Ojibwe Tribal Ct., Trial Div. 2008) (convicting tribal member of violating tribal conservation code's ban on shooting from a road); Leech Lake Band of Ojibwe v. Littlewolf, 2007 WL 7561596 (Leech Lake Band of Ojibwe Tribal Ct., Trial Div.2007) (affirming issuance of citation for violation of tribal ricing code); Mitchell v. Natural Resources Commission, 2002 WL 34504819 (Little River Band of Ottawa and Chippewa Indians Tribal Ct.) (affirming decision of commission to revoke tribal member's fishing permits), aff'd, 2002 WL 34504828 (Little River Band of Ottawa and Chippewa Indians Ct.App.2002); People v. Searles, 2012 MI Odawa Tribal LEXIS 21 (Little Traverse Bay Bands of Odawa Indians Tribal Ct.2012) (assuming jurisdiction over a citation issued by the Michigan State Police to a tribal citizen for fishing without a license).

Tribal nations and individual Indians often possess water rights deriving from the cession of lands to the United States and the subsequent creation of reservations. Restatement of the Law of American Indians § 86. Since western law is based in the doctrine of prior appropriation (i.e., first in time users receive priority access), tribal nations usually possess priority rights to water over all others. Id. § 87. Once priority is established, tribes and tribal members must demonstrate their uses to state or federal courts to determine the quantity of water to which they are entitled. Id. § 90.

E. OFF-RESERVATION HUNTING, FISHING AND GATHERING RIGHTS

Tribal nations often possess off-reservation hunting, fishing, and gathering rights. These rights tend to be governed by tribal-state-federal agreements arising from litigation over the scope of tribal treaty rights such as United States v. Washington, 384 F.Supp. 312 (W.D.Wash.1974), aff'd, 520 F.2d 676 (9th Cir.1975); and United States v. Michigan, 471 F.Supp. 192 (W.D.Mich.1979). Those agreements generally allow tribes to enforce their own regulations against their own citizens for both on- and off-reservation conduct.

There are plenty of examples of tribal nations regulating tribal citizen exercise of these off-reservation treaty rights. Consider People v. Krull, 2017 Sault Ste. Marie Chippewa App. LEXIS 4 (Sault Ste. Marie Chippewa App.Div.2017). There, a citizen of the Sault Ste. Marie Tribe of Chippewa Indians poached a deer within the tribe's off-reservation treaty territory. He was caught by state police officers, who located the deer at the residence on a neighboring tribe's reservation. The tribal appellate court affirmed Sault Tribe jurisdiction over the crime. The tribe's constitution provided:

> The jurisdiction of the tribe shall extend to all of the lands of the tribe to the extent not inconsistent with Federal law and, further, for the purpose of exercising and regulating the rights to fish, hunt, trap and other usual rights of occupancy, such *jurisdiction shall extend to all lands and waters described in the Treaty of March 28, 1836 (7 Stat. 491)*, and to all lands and waters described in any other treaties which provide for such rights to the extent such jurisdiction is not inconsistent with Federal law.

Sault Tribe Const. art. II, § 2 (emphasis added).

Tribal courts are called upon to adjudicate the regulation of off-reservation tribal treaty fishers. In People v. Duhamel, No. 96-10-038-CCV, 1997 WL 34703661 (Grand Traverse Band of Ottawa and Chippewa Indians Tribal Ct.1997), the court found a treaty fisher liable for failing to properly attend their nets, allowing the fish caught within to rot and causing the tribal conservation department to dispose of the decayed fish. Tribal courts also moderate conflicts between treaty fishers arising from the exercise of off-reservation treaty rights. In People v. Raphael, No. 00-03-131-CR, 2000 WL 35749808 (Grand Traverse Band of Ottawa and Chippewa Indians Tribal Ct.2000), the Grand Traverse Band of Ottawa and Chippewa Indians convicted a tribal citizen of illegally cutting the nets of another tribal treaty fisher.

F. CULTURAL PROPERTY

Tribal nations exercise jurisdiction to protect, define, and regulate cultural property. Hundreds of tribal nations have now enacted statutes to govern cultural property issues. See Angela R. Riley, The Ascension of Indigenous Cultural Property Law, 121 Mich.L.Rev. 75 (2022), for a survey of tribal cultural property laws.

Matters involving items of cultural property in tribal communities are often complicated by the adversarial court process. Occasionally, tribal courts simply disclaim jurisdiction over these items as non-justiciable matters of culture. In some cases, such as In the Matter of the Sacred Arrows, 3 Okla. Trib. 332 (Cheyenne-Arapaho Tribes Dist.Ct.1990), the court declined to adjudicate the ownership of sacred ceremonial objects, instead deferring to traditional persons and practices. In a later decision following the reasoning of *Sacred Arrows*, Redman v. Birdshead, 10 Okla. Trib. 110, 2007 WL 9193014 (Cheyenne-Arapaho S.Ct.2007), the court dismissed another dispute over possession of sacred items:

> We are confident that the bonds of history, blood, language, shared experiences, friendship, and much more—which trace back aeons, perhaps to the "beginning of time as we know it"—are far more powerful than any decision by the Judicial Branch of an elected tribal government (however such a court might decide things) could strain. Unlike Mr. Birdshead, Mr. Spottedwolf, and the * * * Appellants, we are not traditional Arapaho Chiefs, ceremonial Elders,

> Counselors, and/or Ceremonial Men, and we can only decide (consistent with the Cheyenne and Arapaho Constitution) that the religious/ cultural issues placed before us are not for us to resolve. We leave those matters to the aforementioned traditional leaders, and to the Arapaho People themselves.

Id. at *17. Cf. Cook v. Cook, 32 Indian L.Rep. 6138 (Cheyenne River Sioux Tribal Ct.App.2005) (affirming power of tribal court to change legal name of tribal citizen, but not to bestow Lakota traditional name on tribal citizen, which requires an appropriate ceremony).

Occasionally, tribal courts are forced to address these questions in more detail than the court may be comfortable in doing. In Clark v. Diné College, 9 Am. Tribal Law 359 (Navajo Nation S.Ct.2010) (*Clark II*), the President of the college claimed to be the ceremonial protector of sacred items possessed by the college. The Navajo Nation Supreme Court had previously held that the President was properly removed from office. Clark v. Diné College, 9 Am. Tribal Law 348 (Navajo Nation S.Ct.2010) (*Clark I*). Petitioning for reconsideration, the President claimed that their status as ceremonial protector [the author's characterization] immunized them from removal from office until another ceremony transferring those duties to another person was performed. The court rejected that argument. The court worried that the parties in the adversarial process were not properly or respectfully discussing the sacred items: "Matters of sacred ceremonies ought to be discussed with a heightened measure of *k'é*—a sense of balance, restoration among the parties, and coming from the heart. *K'é* is naturally diminished in an adversarial forum where one party is accusing the other and there is no consensus that an ongoing relationship is even desired." *Clark II*, 9 Am. Tribal Law at 361. The court concluded that the President's assertions of immunity from removal by virtue of their status as a ceremonial protector conflicted with the non-hierarchical purposes of those objects:

> Unlike mere job duties, sacred items confer duties of the heart and spirit. We note that traditionally, a *jish* is entrusted to a medicine man who may then perform ceremonies, songs and prayers. The association of other sacred ceremonial items (which also may constitute part of a *jish*) with an institution such as Diné College is a modern-day development where the holder, here the President of the College, appears to be relieved of the actual ceremonial duties and instead, is given intangible duties of heart and spirit to uphold Diné philosophy in the education of our children. The establishment of hierarchical institutions is also a modern-day development, and perhaps it is inevitable that there will be confusion regarding the symbolism of sacred objects when associated with such institutions. We note that such sacred items are not mere symbols, but are medicine as traditionally used by the Diné. This is another reason why this Court would prefer making no further comment.

> We take judicial notice that sacred items have never been taken as conferring hierarchical authority and power over institutions or people, only duties and responsibilities of the heart and spirit to protect and heal. The Diné, being an egalitarian people, have traditionally not conferred authority on those not deserving, and in no event on the basis of heredity or the holding of sacred or other objects. The sacred items are not like a *bilagaana* scepter or crown or a great seal of office.
>
> If such sacred items are to be viewed as symbolizing an authority of office, this would be the first time such items are used in such a manner. Therefore, it must be clearly stated by the government or program in which such items are intended to be used as conferring power and authority. No presentation has been made that the Board's Bylaws and Manual dictate ceremonial passage of the sacred items before its holder may begin performing job functions and draw a salary, or be terminated and the salary ended. Therefore, we affirm our holding.

Id. at 362. The court added that to even be forced to discuss and analyze claims over the sacred items in an adversarial proceeding was unacceptable, but the President forced the court to do so:

> We note in closing that it is beyond the jurisdiction of any adversarial proceeding to dictate the proper handling of sacred ceremonial items, to make findings on the story of their creation, or to settle the guidelines for their use.

> This Court will not engage in adversarial sparring concerning these matters, and such matters are not to be discussed in the environment of gamesmanship and obfuscation that often takes place in adversarial forums.
>
> Appellee was entrusted with sacred items for which he and the College know the purpose and instructions by which they were bestowed upon him. He is to approach this entrustment honorably in the proper passage of the College's sacred items for the sake of the mental, psychological and emotional well-being of the students of Diné College. We cannot otherwise mandate the disposition of such sacred items.

Id. See also Percy v. Swan, 24 Indian L.Rep. 6173, 6173 (Ho-Chunk Nation Trial Ct.1996) ("Many aspects of this tradition are closely intertwined with the Ho-Chunk religion which forbids written accounts of these oral customs and traditions.").

Other tribal nations are more comfortable in authorizing their judiciaries to adjudicate such matters. These tribes tend to adopt complex and detailed cultural property ordinances that provide guidance to courts on how to assess these claims. In Chilkat Indian Village, I.R.A. v. Johnson, 20 Indian L. Rep. 6127 (Chilkat Indian Village Tribal Ct. 1993), the tribal court enforced a 1976 tribal ordinance that prohibited keepers of cultural property from removing historic artifacts and selling them on the public market. See also Chilkat Indian Village, I.R.A. v. Johnson, 19 Indian L.Rep. 6010 (Chilkat Indian Village Tribal Ct.1991) (addressing the power of the court to enforce the tribe's artifacts ordinance and personal jurisdiction over the defendant).

The ordinance provided:

> No person shall enter onto the property of the Chilkat Indian Village for the purpose of buying, trading for, soliciting the purchase of, or otherwise seeking to arrange a removal of artifacts, clan crests, or other traditional Indian art work owned or held by members of the Chilkat Indian Village or kept within the boundaries of the real property owned by the Chilkat Indian Village, without first requesting and obtaining permission to do so from the Chilkat Indian Village Council.
>
> No traditional Indian artifacts, clan crests, or other Indian art works of any kind may be removed from the Chilkat Indian Village without the prior notification of and approval by, the Chilkat Indian Village Council.

The artifacts, called the Whale House artifacts, were created in 1830 by artisans as part of a ceremony to unify house groups within a clan. The artifacts were declared clan cultural property at that time. Tlingit persons took the artifacts and delivered them to a dealer in Seattle who intended to sell them for enormous sums of money. The Tlingit defendants claimed that their uncle ordered them to take the artifacts and deliver them to the dealer as part of a defense that they had no choice under customary law but to honor their uncle's wishes. They also claimed as a defense, paradoxically, that Tlingit culture is dead. The court rejected both defenses.

Witnesses explained the significance of the Whale House artifacts:

> The primary significance is knowing who you are. . . . The primary significance is knowing who you are . . . with us, these particular artifacts tell a story. . . . When you're selling an artifact. . . you're not only getting rid of a piece of wood . . . you're getting rid of the music, the song, the dance, and the good, the bad, and the ugly.
>
> The worm dish story of a young woman nursing a worm as a pet which became a threat to the entire community . . . is right up there in the 21st century. If the problem was not resolved it would have ended in the destruction of not just the clan that was involved, but the entire community. . . . A similar thing 2,000 years later is happening. Is that of the mind? Is that just happening within the intellect? It doesn't involve the soul and the spirit? A script could be written: "Wormdish Revisited, the Community of Chilkat, 2,000 years later." This is why we need to keep these things here; this is why we sing the song, and this is why we need them for our ceremonial parties. That's the significance of the artifacts.

20 Indian L.Rep. at 6135.

The court asserted jurisdiction over the artifacts even though they were temporarily housed in a storage facility in Seattle in accordance with a federal court order. See Chilkat Indian Village v. Johnson, 870 F.2d 1469 (9th Cir.1989).

Similarly, see In the Matter of the Guardianship and Conservatorship of Bell, 24 Indian L.Rep. 6105 (Three Affiliated Tribes of the Fort Berthold Reservation Trial Ct.1997), the court adjudicated the "ownership" of a document known as the "Fort Laramie Treaty Document of 1851." The "keeper" of this document through much of the 20th century was William Bell, Sr., a tribal citizen who had served in World War II and Korea, served on the tribal council after his military service concluded, and was the fourth generation grandson of Hidatsa Chief Four Bears. When he became afflicted with Alzheimer's disease, he entered a nursing home and could no longer "keep" the document. His daughter unfortunately attempted to sell the document to non-Indian collectors.

The court held that direct male descendants of Four Bears became "Keepers" of the document. The court noted that to "keep" the document was not to own the document: "It was the testimony of the tribes' expert that the term 'Keepers,' pursuant to this traditional custom, is not defined as possessing ownership rights, but more as a trustee to safeguard the document on behalf of the entire tribe." Id. at 6106. The court concluded that the document could not be sold by anyone, even the tribe itself:

> The ownership of this treaty document is not with the "Keepers"; its possession is vested with the Three Affiliated Tribes as a "Holder."

> According to the tradition and custom, it belongs to the entire tribe, not to any individual tribal member, nor to any individual of the Bell family, and probably not even to the governing body of the tribe, who are to become "Holders" of this treaty document with the continuing responsibility with the Bell family, in accordance with tradition, to keep the tribe from selling or otherwise disposing of the treaty document and depriving the members of the tribe from their possessory right to this treaty document.
>
> It is the decision of this court that the original copy of this historic agreement given to Chief Four Bears 150 years ago cannot be sold by Wilma Nelson [Bell's daughter]. It cannot be sold by the Tribal Council. It cannot be sold by anyone. It is not a part of the conservatorship of William Bell, Sr. It is as sacred to the Hidatsa Nation as is the original copy of the Declaration of Independence is to the United States of America.

Id.

However, the efforts of Indigenous People to enforce name and likeness rights of their ancestors under federal intellectual property have been less successful (at least in court). See In the Matter of the Estate of Tasunke Witko v. G. Heilman Brewing Co., 23 Indian L.Rep. 6104 (Rosebud Sioux S.Ct.1996), the court asserted jurisdiction over a nonmember brewing company that used the name, image, and likeness of Tasunke Witko, also known as Crazy

Horse, to market and sell malt liquor products (and non-alcoholic beverages to reservation Indians on the reservation). Concluding its jurisdictional analysis, the court stated that a tribal court forum was consistent with fair play and justice:

> Finally, the exercise of a forum's jurisdiction must be reasonable and comport with fair play and justice. The burden on the defendants to litigate in the tribal forum is minimal. They are all national corporations engaged in extensive interstate commerce. The scope of defendants' resources and the nature of modern transportation and communication make any ensuing burdens in defending this lawsuit slight. The reservation forum is likely to be the most convenient for all parties, while it would be correspondingly difficult both economically and geographically for the plaintiff to file his lawsuit in another forum far away from the reservation.

Id. at 6110–11. The court added that the plaintiffs had asserted a tribal common law cause of action, which would best be resolved by the tribal court:

> The local forum is also best situated to provide convenient and effective relief for the plaintiff estate should it prevail at a trial on the merits. This is particularly significant in light of the fact that some of the causes of action asserted by the plaintiff involve questions of tribal custom and tribal common law that, as questions of first impression, will not be readily discerned or easily answered in a state or federal forum at a substantial cultural and geographical remove

> from the reservation forum. The reservation forum is also the most efficient forum for this lawsuit because it has already dealt with the issue of jurisdiction (which is likely to arise in any forum) and because of its expertise in evaluating claims grounded in whole or in part in tradition, custom and/or tribal common law.

Id. at 6111. Although the federal courts excused the brewing company from tribal jurisdiction, see Hornell Brewing Co. v. Rosebud Sioux Tribal Court, 133 F.3d 1087 (8th Cir.1998), the company ultimately settled with the estate, agreeing to no longer sell the undeniably racist beverage. One tribal court later opined in dicta that if the Rosebud reservation had not been a dry reservation and the brewing sold Crazy Horse there, the tribal government would have had jurisdiction under federal liquor laws. Delorme v. Stearns, 2002 Turtle Mt. App. LEXIS 2, at *8–9 (Turtle Mountain Tribal Ct.App.2002).

CHAPTER 7

TRIBAL ECONOMIES

The United States as colonizer effectively destroyed tribal economic strength throughout most of the 19th and 20th centuries. The federal government coerced tribal nations into giving up the large majority of their natural resources and lands. Even tribes able to retain a significant asset base were forced to deal with the federal government's ongoing colonizing activities, including the government asserting the power of guardianship over tribal nations and individual Indians as a means of controlling reservation assets. The government's policies enabling an influx of nonmembers into Indian country as landowners also gutted the ability of tribal nations to establish stable economies. In the 1950s, the government even attempted to force Indian people to leave their homelands, relocating them to urban areas to search for work, resulting in miserable failure and the rise of urban Indian ghettoes.

By the time Congress turned to tribal self-determination in the 1970s, tribal economic activity was virtually nonexistent. Few tribal nations that did have economic activity rarely benefitted from it. Indian reservations were the poorest locations in America. Indian people were the poorest and least healthy demographic. Self-determination contracting under Public Law 638 allowed many tribes for the first time to generate economic activity, even if only though the expenditure of federal appropriations to provide basic services.

Beginning in the 1970s and 1980s, many tribal nations and individual Indians began to establish business operations. Some started retail businesses selling low-tax or tax-free tobacco products and motor fuels, undercutting off-reservation retailers forced to collect high state taxes. Some tribes opened high-stakes bingo halls, again outcompeting non-tribal bingo halls that were heavily regulated by state and local governments. While reduced tax retail sales were gutted by judicial fiat in a series of United States Supreme Court cases, tribal gaming grew dramatically under the Indian Gaming Regulatory Act of 1988, 25 U.S.C. § 2701 et seq. Meanwhile, tribal nations with access to extractive natural resources began to exercise greater control over those activities.

In the 21st century, tribal nations are often important regional economic engines, especially in rural areas. Many tribal nations and their citizens have exploited their natural resources to great gain, though income through extractive industries often depend on highly volatile international markets and whether poorly negotiated legacy contracts remain in place. Many tribal nations also benefit from federal government military and homeland security contracting set-asides under the Section 8(a) Business Development Program.

Even so, many tribal nations do not benefit much from economic activity. Some tribal economies are enormous and many tribal economies are terrific failures. This century, tribal nations are both economic actors and economic regulators.

A. TRIBES AS ECONOMIC ACTORS

Tribal nations generate economic activity both by operating businesses on and off the reservation, but also by virtue of their governmental activities. The role of tribal nations as economic engines is an important one. Due to the impacts of colonization, most tribal nations have little or no tax base. Most tribal lands are either owned by the tribe or the federal government, meaning the ability of tribal governments to raise revenue through property taxes is nominal. Similarly, tribal income taxes raise minimal revenue, given that many tribal citizens often do not make enough taxable income. Sales and use taxes are viable, but again reservation retail transactions are often limited by a lack of tribal economic activity. As a consequence of the federal government's duty of protection to tribal nations, the United States as a matter of policy chooses not to tax tribal governmental income or other tribal business activities.

In the absence of a viable tax base, tribal nations seeking to enhance the meager federal appropriations coming their way each year must engage in economic activity designed to raise revenue for government services. The reality that tribal nations can act simultaneously as governments and businesses at the same time is exemplified in cases like LaBoy v. Pokagon Band Gaming Commission, 2019 Pokagon Band Tribal LEXIS 4 (Pokagon Band

Tribal Ct.2019). There, the Pokagon Band of Potawatomi Indians tribal court rejected a claim that the tribal gaming enterprise was obligated to follow the tribal open meetings act on the ground that the gaming commission was immune from suit. Typically, tribal enterprises operate outside of the political sphere on the theory that business decisions should not be politicized. It bears noting that tribal enterprise profits are usually taxed by the tribal government for revenue to fund governmental services.

Indian reservations, especially those far from population centers, contain some of the bleakest economic outlooks of any regions in the United States. Poverty and unemployment rates are often extraordinarily high. Tribal leaders are constantly seeking ways to generate governmental revenue. Prior to the rise of the internet economy, tribal nations with no gaming market or natural resources depended on federal governmental programs and funding alone for their economic activity. Some tribes have been able, temporarily, to exploit economic opportunities generated in selling goods that are heavily taxed or regulated by states, such as tobacco and motor fuel products, though the United States Supreme Court in the 1970s through the 1990s and (later) Congress largely put an end to that market. With the rise of the internet, some tribes have attempted to enter the internet gaming market and yet others have attempted to engage in sovereign lending (usually known as internet payday lending).

Federal law allows set-asides for minority owned businesses for federal contracting (with stark limits on the size of the contracts), most notably defense and homeland security contracting. Congress recently uncapped the size of federal contracting for tribally owned or controlled business entities. Moreover, tribal entities benefit from no-bid contracts, awarded in times of defense or immigration "emergencies." Some tribal business entities have profited greatly from this contracting. Defense and homeland security logistics contractors often build military bases, border walls, and immigration detention facilities, as well as provide security for these facilities.

Even with great success for some tribal nations, that success is uneven across Indian country. Tribal nations often remain desperate for economic opportunity, sometimes rendering tribal leadership susceptible to valueless or fraudulent business proposals. The most successful tribal economies are home-grown.

Indian country economic infrastructure is often lacking. Many critics of tribal economic plans assail the very idea of tribal government serving as both an economic actor and as a regulator. It is fair to say that tribal governmental economic success is more difficult, but most commentators agree that tribal governmental and economic infrastructure is the key to growth. Infrastructure includes the development of laws and regulations, notably including judicial systems.

1. TRIBAL CORPORATE STRUCTURES

Tribal business activities often involve corporate structures unique to Indian law and policy. See Restatement of the Law of American Indians § 50. There are many benefits to tribes in chartering their own corporations. State law does not apply. Core governmental assets can be protected, siloed away from business assets that may be at risk from business losses or liability. Tribal nations, if they wish, can staff a corporate board of directors with apolitical individuals, helping to separate tribal business from tribal politics. Enterprise entity employment can be treated differently from tribal governmental employment that may be governed by civil service-type protections. Profits generated from tribal enterprises can be used to reinvest in the businesses or to supplement tribal governmental program funds. See, e.g., Kakwitch v. Menominee Tribal Enterprises, 21 Indian L.Rep. 6112 (Menominee Tribal S.Ct.1994) (detailing the creation of Menominee Tribal Enterprises and its purposes).

Impliedly recognizing that reality as early as the 1934 Indian Reorganization Act, Congress authorized the Secretary of the Interior to charter economic development corporations for tribal nations. These corporations are called Section 17 corporations, named after the provision in the 1934 Act authorizing their creation. 25 U.S.C. § 5124. The 1934 Act was not the first federal statute to regulate tribal economic activity, but it was likely the first to place some control in the hands of tribal actors. For many decades, the Secretary of the Interior utilized form language to charter the corporations. But starting in the self-determination era, tribal nations would draft bespoke charter language that incorporated tribal codes, assuming more control over the structure of their federally chartered corporations. Federally chartered corporations (as opposed to those chartered under state law) are a bit of an anomaly. Obviously because state law has no force in Indian country, state law reporting requirements, for example, are not applicable. But there is not a lot of law on whether Section 17 corporations can declare bankruptcy, for example.

Tribal nations also enact their own business organizations codes. Under these codes, tribes and others can charter corporate entities just as state governments do. These entities are often called tribally chartered corporations. Tribal nations possess plenary jurisdiction to regulate these corporations in light of the corporation codes' provisions. E.g., Sac and Fox Nation v. Native Tobacco Direct Co., 7 Okla. Trib. 512, 2002 WL 32099966 (Sac and Fox Nation Dist.Ct.2002) (restricting the authority of a tribally-chartered corporation to do business until the corporation files its annual reports as required under tribal law). It is fair to say that most corporate entities charted under tribal codes are owned by the tribal nations themselves.

Tribes have also purchased corporate entities chartered under state law. These entities are governed by state law, just as the articles of incorporation likely require. They are therefore subject to state taxation and regulation, as well as state court jurisdiction.

Because tribes are both governments and business entities, tribal business and politics occasionally mix. Tribal nations may place restrictions on the power of elected officials to participate in tribal enterprise governance. For example, in Cantrell v. Cherokee Nation, 1 Am. Tribal Law 2 (Cherokee Nation Judicial Appeals Trib.1997), the court held that under tribal law tribal council members were prohibited from serving on the board of Cherokee Nation Enterprises, a wholly owned corporation of the Nation. The court pointed to the separation of powers provision in the tribal constitution that barred council members from serving on any tribal corporate boards. The decision wiped out a board action that would have terminated the corporate chief executive. Other tribal councils may appoint themselves the directors of tribal corporate entities. It is not entirely clear that one method is superior to another.

In a sort of worst-case scenario, two factions of a Navajo Nation's Section 17 corporation's board of directors litigated over control of the corporation, each claiming to act on behalf of the corporation. In Navajo Nation Oil and Gas Co. v. Window Rock District Court, 12 Am. Tribal Law 22 (Navajo Nation S.Ct.2014), shareholder representatives purported to suspend or remove the directors of the corporation. The CEO of the corporation attempted to sue in the corporation's name in tribal court to prevent the board (that had just purportedly been removed by shareholders) from removing him as CEO. The directors countersued against the CEO, also invoking the corporate name. The Navajo Nation Supreme Court issued a writ of prohibition against the Window Rock District Court on sovereign immunity grounds, but insisted that

> the individuals who make up the various corporate organs in this case are in positions of a *naat'áanii* as caretakers of assets of immense value to the Navajo People and, therefore, understand their duty of trust and responsibility to engage in reasonable collaborative settlement in the best interest of the corporation. This responsibility is not fully performed if the *naat'áanii* immediately resort to lawyers, who due simply to the nature of that adversarial profession, frequently find barriers to resolutions that require compromise.

Id. at 25. After the parties could not reach agreement, they returned to the court for clarification. The court reminded the parties that a Section 17 corporation is designed to allow tribal nations to operate businesses in the arena of American corporate law, which should prevent the kind of catastrophic infighting presented by the parties:

> * * * The Navajo Nation chose NNOGC to operate within the establishment of American corporations, beholden to the same general corporate principles, and its corporate organs must therefore be obedient to the spirit and letter of those principles. No general principle of corporate law would allow a governing Board to

> be so diminished below quorum so that an officer/CEO becomes the sole decision-maker without any Board oversight for his or her transactions. Had all parties faithfully observed the Charter and Bylaws, intended as complete documents providing for procedures for internal resolution for every business-related eventuality, this matter should never have needed the equitable remedy of injunctive relief through our courts. The courts are not a forum for validating noncompliance with legal constraints calculated to protect all stakeholders, nor are they to be resorted to by individuals to forestall internal inquiries into their performance or actions by other corporate organs. Where corporate matters are governed by statutes, corporate charters, and bylaws, our courts shall apply their mandatory language.

Id. at 30. The court reminded the parties that political disputes have no place in tribal corporate activities and that the parties owe significant fiduciary duties to the Nation:

> * * * Businesses—even Navajo enterprises or instrumentalities covered by governmental protections—must be able to conduct their business transactions and internal affairs free of influence or pressure by the government. A corporation, under established fiduciary principles, must be run autonomously as a business. If politicians participate in a business, it cannot be in their governmental capacities. This is true for NNOGC. See Charter, Art.

> § X(C) (providing that "shareholder representatives shall sit in their capacity as representatives of the sole shareholder and not as members of the Navajo Nation Council."). The Navajo Nation is sole shareholder of NNOGC "for the benefit of the Nation and its enrolled members." Charter, Art. V(B), and as stated above, 100% of NNOGC revenues go toward governmental services for the people. Navajos think in communal ownership. Its shareholder representatives are, essentially, trustees of a public trust asset for the Navajo people and must exercise their fiduciary responsibility.

Id. at 31 (footnote omitted). The court ultimately clarified that the shareholder efforts to remove the board were therefore invalid.

Corporations doing business in Indian country likely must seek permission or a license to do so from the tribal government. In Graven v. Morgan, 11 Am. Tribal Law 59 (Navajo Nation S.Ct.2012), the court barred a foreign corporation from bringing suit in the tribe's courts because the corporation had not sought and received permission to act on tribal lands. In the absence of that permission, the corporation had no standing to bring suit.

Tribal courts have assumed jurisdiction over nonmember corporations doing business on tribally owned or controlled lands or doing business with tribal entities. For example, in United States ex rel. Auginash v. Medure, 8 Am. Tribal Law 304 (White Earth Band of Chippewa Indians Trial Ct.2009), the court assumed jurisdiction over a nonmember corporation doing business on tribal lands with a tribal business. The court held that the contracts between the tribe and the corporation established nonmember consent to tribal court jurisdiction for assessing the validity of those contracts and for an action seeking to pierce the corporate veil. Id. at 328 (noting that "the provision of services like the restroom facilities at the temporary casino site in exchange for net revenue distributions is a prime example of a consensual, commercial relationship"). Moreover, the nonmember's actions, according to the court, negatively impacted the "economic improvement and stability of the Tribe." Id. at 329. See also Colorado River Indian Tribes v. Water Wheel Camp Recreation Area, Inc., No. 08-0003 (Colorado River Indian Tribes Ct.App.2009) (affirming the trial court's orders piercing the corporate veil of the nonmember owned company).

In a years long and wide ranging series of disputes between the Hualapai Nation and its nonmember business partner, Grand Canyon Skywalk Company, the tribe attempted to resolve their contract dispute by exercising the power of eminent domain over the contract, seeking to force the business into tribal court to adjudicate just compensation over the contract. The contract involved the construction and development of the famed Grand Canyon Skywalk, a glass walkway that runs out in a semi-circle over the Grand Canyon, allowing patrons to look straight down from about a mile high. The developer constructed the Skywalk, which opened to much fanfare, but the contract also required the developer to construct additional tourist facilities and to share revenue with the tribe. Disputes arose over the contract, leading to the developer seeking arbitration under the terms of the contract. The tribe responded by condemning the contract with its power of eminent domain. The nonmember business sought to be excused from tribal court jurisdiction, claiming the tribe's actions were in bad faith. The developer also sought a federal injunction against the tribe's condemnation action. Both claims failed. Grand Canyon Skywalk Dev., LLC v. 'SA' Nyu Wa Inc., 715 F.3d 1196 (9th Cir.2013). In a related proceeding, however, the developer prevailed in the arbitration against the tribe and persuaded a federal court to enforce the award, more than $28 million. Grand Canyon Skywalk Dev., LLC v. 'Sa' Nyu Wa, Inc., 923 F.Supp.2d 1186 (D.Ariz.2013). Eventually, the parties reached a confidential settlement in 2014.

2. INDIAN GAMING

Indian gaming arose in the 1960s and 1970s (though the first Indian gaming facility of note came about in the late 1940s) around the same time that tribes and individual Indians attempted to sell tobacco and gas tax-free under the federal Indian law principle that holds state law has no force in Indian country. Outside of Nevada and New Jersey, states banned all forms of gambling, leaving open an opportunity for tribes to allow it. For example, in the 1970s, the Keweenaw Bay Indian Community granted a license to one of its tribal citizens, Fred Dakota, to open up a small casino in his garage. The main problem at the time (in addition to fervent opposition from virtually all surrounding jurisdictions) was that the federal Johnson Act, 15 U.S.C. § 1175, prohibited the possession and transportation of "gambling device[s]" into Indian country. As a consequence, early tribal and Indian gaming facilities focused on bingo. States often allowed highly-regulated, low-stakes bingo, say, for charitable purposes at schools and churches. By the mid-1980s, numerous tribal nations had opened up high-stakes bingo halls, leading to legal and political conflict that came to a head in the late 1980s.

Tribal nations now operate gaming enterprises subject the Indian Gaming Regulatory Act of 1988 (IGRA). 25 U.S.C. § 2701 et seq. Congress enacted IGRA in the wake of the United States Supreme Court's decision in California v. Cabazon Band of Mission Indians, 480 U.S. 202 (1987). *Cabazon Band* held that state and local governments did not possess the power to regulate Indian bingo operations, even in Public Law 280 states. IGRA codified aspects of that decision by creating classes of Indian gaming. Class I gaming includes traditional tribal games that federal and state governments have no power to regulate. 25 U.S.C. § 2703. Class II gaming is bingo, §§ 2703(7), 2710(c), like in *Cabazon*, that states cannot regulate (though federal approvals are still required). In recent decades, Class II bingo has become more popular and profitable due to the rise of technological aids that render bingo digitally. E.g., Captain v. Ross, 22 Indian L.Rep. 6123 (Miami Agency, Ct. of Indian Offenses 1995). Class III is all other gaming, including casino-style gambling. §§ 2703(8); 2710(d). Tribal nations must negotiate a Class III gaming compact with the governors of the states in which they are located in order to operate a Class III facility. § 2710(d). At present, tribal gaming operations exceed $43.9 Billion in revenue nationally, continuing a rising trend going back decades. However, like most tribal economic activity, this revenue is unevenly distributed across Indian country, with a few tribes earning vast sums while the majority of tribal nations earning little or nothing from gaming.

Regulation of tribal gaming is largely conducted by tribal regulatory entities, though states may negotiate for a larger role in a Class III compact. Congress created the National Indian Gaming Commission to regulate aspects of tribal gaming, notably management contracts. 25 U.S.C. §§ 2704–2706, 2711. See also New Gaming Systems, Inc. v. Sac & Fox Nation, 11 Okla. Trib. 216, 2007 WL 9193007 (Sac & Fox Nation Dist.Ct.2008) (deferring to some extent to a determination by the National Indian Gaming Commission in a similar matter that a contract was a management contract). But most regulation is done by tribes. As agencies of the tribal government, tribal gaming commissions are entitled to deference in the interpretation of tribal gaming ordinances. E.g., Cholka v. Ho-Chunk Gaming Commission, 23 Indian L.Rep. 6075 (Ho-Chunk Nation Trial Ct.1996) (affirming gaming commission decision to suspend gaming employee for gambling during working hours); Creapeau v. Ho-Chunk Gaming Commission, 23 Indian L.Rep. 6078 (Ho-Chunk Nation Trial Ct.1996) (affirming gaming commission decision to suspend gaming employee repeated no-shows to work).

Every person employed and every entity doing business with tribal gaming enterprises must obtain a gaming license from tribal gaming regulators. For example, in Dodge v. Hoopa Valley Gaming Commission, 7 NICS App. 51 (Hoopa Valley Tribal Ct.App.2005), the court assessed a decision by the tribal gaming commission to summarily suspend the gaming license of a tribal gaming employee. Gaming licenses are sometimes difficult to obtain, especially for persons who have had contacts with the criminal justice system. See also In re Dewar, 2007 Grand Ronde Trib. LEXIS 1 (Confederated Tribes of the Grand Ronde Community of Oregon Tribal Ct.2007) (reversing a gaming commission decision to deny a petitioner a gaming license because of a past arrest that led to criminal charges that were later dropped); Reimer v. Ho-Chink Nation Gaming Commission, 24 Indian L.Rep. 6126 (Ho-Chunk Nation Trial Ct.1996) (vacating adverse employment action against gaming license holder for violations of due process); Mandel v. Miccosukee Tribal Gaming Agency, 22 Indian L.Rep. 6148 (Miccosukee Tribal Ct.1994) (affirming denial of gaming license to individuals who admitted to selling illegally untaxed cigarettes at the casino, made inconsistent factual representations on their gaming license applications, and had connections to organized crime). Once an individual obtains a gaming license, they possess a vested property interest in that license and must be offered due process before revocation. E.g., Parks v. Tulalip Gaming Commission, 22 Indian L.Rep. 6080 (Tulalip Ct.App.1994) (requiring due process protections before tribal gaming regulator revokes tribal gaming license).

Tribal nations often rely on management companies with experience in gaming to operate their gaming facilities. Under IGRA, a gaming management company is a third-party entity contracted by a tribe to manage their gaming operation or facility, requiring approval from the National Indian Gaming Commission and subjecting the company and its personnel to background checks and suitability standards to protect the integrity of tribal gaming. These contracts ensure that the management contractor is suitable and does not pose a threat to the public interest or the effective regulation of gaming. See 25 U.S.C. § 2711. Legal conflicts with gaming management companies can involve high stakes, especially where a tribal nation decides it no longer needs to depend on a management company.

In GNS, Inc. v. Blackhawk, 24 Indian L.Rep. 6260 (Winnebago S.Ct.1997), the court reversed a trial court order and ordered the dismissal of a suit by the tribe's former gaming management company on sovereign immunity grounds. GNS and the tribe became disenchanted with each other's performance. In the court's words, "[I]t appears that an atmosphere of mistrust and miscommunication led to the acrimonious end of mutual business relations." Id. The management company alleged that the tribe as gaming regulator improperly changed its licensing requirements in an effort to force the company out. The court noted that that tribe

> has broader interests and responsibilities than does the casino management company. Both have a bottom-line mutual interest in the business profitability of their dealings. But the Tribe also has a responsibility to be responsive to IGRA requirements and to otherwise function as a government, promulgating laws and regulations governing its own jurisdictional world as well as its relations with the outside world.

Id. at 6260 n.1. The tribe's actions in modifying the regulatory requirements for the renewal of the management company's gaming license was valid governmental action, but the management company argued that the tribe's actions worked a taking of the company's vested property interest in remaining the tribe's management company. The court concluded that the company's vested property interest dissipated when it did not seek or receive renewal of its gaming license, which put the company in default of the management contract.

Tribal regulators also oversee non-tribal gaming on Indian lands which, when it occurs, is likely illegal. In Helgeson v. Lac du Flambeau Band of Lake Superior Chippewa Indians, 25 Indian L.Rep. 6045 (Lac du Flambeau Tribal App.Ct.1998), the court affirmed the power to confiscate illegal gaming devices located at a nonmember-owned convenience store on nonmember-owned fee land and issue a civil citation against the owners. The court relied on federal court precedents supportive of tribal authority to regulate nonmember activity that violates tribal law, but also federal policy favoring tribal regulation of gaming activities on reservation lands. The court stated that IGRA "recognized the *inherent sovereign right* of tribes to operate *and their exclusive right to regulate on Indian lands gaming* . . . ." Id. at 6050 (emphasis in original).

Tribal gaming must be conducted on "Indian lands" as defined by IGRA, 25 U.S.C. § 2703(4), and by federally acknowledged tribal nations, § 2703(5). It is rare for tribal subgovernmental entities to engage in gaming operations, but it does happen in some tribal communities. In Ellis v. Bristow Muscogee Indian Community, 11 Okla. Trib. 403, 2009 WL 10270097 (Muscogee (Creek) Nation Dist.Ct.2009), the court held that a tribally chartered political subdivision was without authority to unilaterally distribute gaming proceeds to community members on a per capita basis absent tribal and federal authorization through a revenue allocation ordinance compliant with IGRA.

State governments have attempted to interfere with tribal gaming, notwithstanding IGRA, with limited success. For example, in Coeur d'Alene Tribe v. AT&T Corp., 23 Indian L.Rep. 6060 (Coeur d'Alene Tribal Ct.1996), the court assumed jurisdiction over a telephone utility that provided services to the reservation. The tribal gaming enterprise had sought an 800 toll-free number to use for gaming purposes. Ten states had sent notices to the telephone company asserting that AT&T would be in violation of the federal Wire Act that prohibited the transmission of betting and wagering information. 18 U.S.C. § 1804.

The tribal court concluded that Congress intended § 1804 to prohibit sports betting by telephone, not the proposed tribal lottery. A Ninth Circuit panel would later hold that federal law stripped the tribal court of jurisdiction over the case, citing the Federal Communications Act, but effectively ratified the tribal court's analysis on the lottery issue, holding that the states had no authority to threaten AT&T and interfere with the tribe's gaming operations. AT&T Corp. v. Coeur d'Alene Tribe, 295 F.3d 899 (9th Cir.2002).

3. NATURAL RESOURCE EXTRACTION

Indian reservations comprise nearly 56 million acres. Several Indian reservations contain enormous exploitable natural resources. These resources include without limitation coal, copper, lithium, natural gas, oil, sand and gravel, timber, uranium, and water. For much of the history of the United States, the federal government dominated most of the natural resource extraction operations in Indian country, usually to the severe detriment of tribal nations.

The tragic story of the Osage murders of the early 20th century is just the most notorious example of governmental paternalism meeting non-Indian greed and ruthlessness. There, the federal government had severed the mineral estate from the surface estate. While much of the Osage reservation land had been allotted (and much of it already lost to non-Indians), the federal government continued to collect revenue from oil and gas extraction activities on behalf of individual Osages. Many Osage citizens became wealthy from their headrights, but the federal government declared full-blood Osages legally incompetent and allowed local political and business leaders as well as non-Indian spouses of Osages to serve as their guardians. These "guardians" frequently exploited and all-too-often murdered their wards in order to secure the headrights. There are many Osage people alive today whose grandparents were murdered by other grandparents. This scenario was not unique to Osage, but the Osage experience became nationally known.

In recent decades, many tribes have asserted more control over their resources. Even so, tribal nations must deal with the legacy of greed and corruption that the federal government and its reservation business partners often perpetrated for decades prior to the rise of tribal self-determination. Tribal regulatory structures are often nascent to non-existent, sometimes leaving tribes at the mercy of the federal government and resource extractors, especially where harmful legacy agreements have not yet expired. Unless the tribe or tribal citizens themselves own the businesses that extract the resources, tribal nations must deal with nonmember business activities on tribal lands. Tribal nations must also weigh competing interests in generating sustainable economic activity while attempting to preserve cultural sites and ecological values. All the while, federal regulatory overlays often impede tribal prerogatives.

In recent years, advocates have identified the negative impacts that introducing resource extraction activities into Indian country can have. For example, during the fracking boom on the Bakken formation on the northern Great Plains of the 2000s, vast wealth came to tribal nations and some Indian allotment holders, but so too came environmental devastation and violent crime that contributed greatly to the rise in missing and murdered Indigenous Peoples.

One of the most interesting cases involves the famed Osage mineral estate, now administered by the Osage Minerals Council (OMC). In Boone v. Osage Nation of Oklahoma, 2016 Osage Sup. LEXIS 1 (Osage Nation S.Ct.2016), the court held that the council was subject to the Osage Nation Ethics Law. The council had argued that the Osage mineral estate and the council that administered it were the creatures of federal law through the Osage Allotment Act and related federal actions. The tribal constitution conferred independent status on the council, subject to the laws of the Osage Nation. Osage Const. art. XV, § 4, ¶ 3. The court concluded:

> The Osage Minerals Council occupies an important position within the Nation and it has been granted as a matter of Constitutional law considerable authority and autonomy in relation to the administration and development of the Mineral Estate. Unlike its federal counterparts, the members of the OMC are elected by the shareholders, rather than appointed by a chief executive, subject to legislative confirmation.

> This alone affords significant protection of the OMC's independence in the exercise of its constitutionally delegated authority. Agency independence, however, does not mean that the OMC is separate and apart from the Nation nor free of accountability. Neither is it outside the reach of the Nation's laws. No government official of the Osage Nation whether elected, appointed, or simply employed by the Nation is above the law or outside its reach.

2016 Osage Sup. LEXIS 1, at *43.

Tribal courts also assert jurisdiction over natural resource extraction companies alleged to have committed torts or contract breaches. In Estate of Jorgenson v. DHS Drilling Co., 11 Am. Tribal Law 123 (Shoshone and Arapaho Tribal Ct.2011), appeal dismissed sub nom., Encana Oil and Gas (USA), Inc. v. Estate of Jorgenson (Wind River Indian Reservation Ct.App.2011), the Shoshone and Arapaho Tribal Court of the Wind River Indian Reservation found, over the objections of the nonmember company, that the reservation boundaries remained extant. The court further found that the nonmember business entered into an oil and gas lease with the tribe, tribal employment rights agreements, business license agreements, and paid tribal severance taxes, fulfilling the *Montana* test of the United States Supreme Court. Prior decisions of the Wind River court have reached similar conclusions involving injuries suffered on the job. E.g., Marathon Oil Co. v. Johnston, 2006 WL

6926419 (Shoshone and Arapaho Tribal App.Ct. 2006).

4. FEDERAL CONTRACTING

Tribal nations benefit from federal contracting preferences such as the Section 8(a) Business Development Program. The program allows for sole source contracting with the federal government. Some tribal corporations have enjoyed enormous success in winning sole source military and homeland security contracts, subcontracting with massive defense and logistics contractors to great profit.

The program is designed to promote economic development and combat poverty within tribal communities by providing tools for them to participate in government contracting. Businesses must be at least 51% owned by a federally recognized Native American tribe or Alaska Native Corporation and meet the general 8(a) program requirements for being socially and economically disadvantaged. Tribal 8(a) firms enjoy advantages not available to other 8(a) participants, such as higher sole-source contract limits and the ability to have multiple 8(a) entities. Federal agencies can award contracts directly to eligible 8(a) firms without a competitive process, up to specific dollar thresholds. Awards made to Tribal 8(a) firms cannot be challenged through the normal protest processes.

Some observers express the view that the Section 8(a) program is vulnerable to challenge as violative of the equal protection component of the Due Process

Clause of the Fifth Amendment, similar to challenges to other "affirmative action"-type set asides in federal contracting. However, for reasons that may have to do with judiciary's deference to the defense and homeland security interests of the federal government (and the value that tribal 8(a) entities offer), those challenges have not taken hold.

5. SOVEREIGN LENDING

Tribal sovereign lending involves lending businesses owned and operated by tribal nations, functioning under tribal laws, regulated by tribal regulators, and often protected by tribal sovereign immunity. These enterprises, usually online lenders, are a key source of economic development, revenue, and jobs for tribes, particularly in remote areas. The practice is controversial, raising legal questions about the scope of tribal immunity and whether such lenders must adhere to state interest rate caps and consumer protection laws.

As state laws have no force in Indian country and federal consumer protection regulators are hamstrung by the lack of explicit authority to regulate tribal nations, tribal sovereign lending entities operate exclusively under tribal laws. However, the business models that tribal sovereign lending companies employ often leave their business partners open to lawsuits or state regulation. Nonmember payday lenders often set up a nominal affiliation with a tribal nation, where the tribe typically receives a small portion of the revenue in exchange for lending its name and legal status. If sued, the payday lender claims it is an "arm of the tribe" and is therefore entitled to sovereign immunity, making it difficult for consumers or state authorities to sue and enforce applicable state laws. Frequently, however, that legal defense fails for the nonmember. Compare Ransom v. GreatPlains Financing, LLC, 148 F.4th 141 (3rd Cir.2025) (finding nonmember was not immune); People v. Miami Nation Enterprises, 386 P.3d 357 (Cal.2016) (same), with Williams v. Big Picture Loans, LLC, 929 F.3d 170 (4th Cir.2019) (finding nonmember lending immune); Great Plains Lending, LLC v. Department of Banking, 259 A.3d 1128 (Conn.2021) (same).

6. OUTSIDE EXPLOITATION OF TRIBAL ECONOMIC VENTURES

Tribal leaders are often highly motivated to seek out economic opportunities to develop or diversify tribal economies. This motivation often places them in the sights of unethical and even criminal elements that hope to exploit those motivations. According to the Internal Revenue Service, examples of abuses and schemes include without limitation, improper sheltering of taxable gains by passing third party transactions through Indian tribes; disguising of enterprises to appear as tribally-owned so as to evade federal taxes and oversight by state regulators; embezzlement from tribal enterprises; use of casino comps for purposes unrelated to gaming play; and illegal activities (i.e., bribes and kickbacks) in enterprises where tribes lack adequate internal control.

In 2020, three Mandan Hidatsa Arikara Nation government officials were charged with conspiracy and federal programs bribery for accepting bribes and kickbacks from a contractor. In 2023, a former official from the same nation was sentenced to prison for soliciting and accepting bribes and kickbacks from a construction contractor. An FBI investigation led to the conviction of a corrupt Choctaw Nation official, Jason Merida, who ran a "pay to play" system. Merida extorted contractors for money, trips, and other items, submitted false invoices, and stole over $500,000 from the Choctaw Nation.

The Peter MacDonald scandal involved widespread corruption, including fraud, bribery, and racketeering, committed by the former chairman of the Navajo Nation during the 1980s. The most notorious element of the scandal was a fraudulent land deal in which MacDonald and his associates profited from the inflated sale of a ranch to the Navajo people. The crisis culminated in his removal from office, multiple convictions in both tribal and federal courts, and a deadly riot involving his supporters. See generally Navajo Nation v. MacDonald, 17 Indian L.Rep. 6014 (Navajo Nation Window Rock. Dist.Ct.1989) (affirming tribal council decision to place tribal chair and vice-chair on administrative leave based on credible reports of financial misconduct and self-dealing). See also In re Certified Questions I (Navajo Nation v. MacDonald), 16 Indian L.Rep. 6098 (Navajo Nation S.Ct.1989) (holding that the Navajo chairman, who had been criminally indicted, had no independent authority to appoint tribal judges).

Perhaps the worst scandal (one that likely involved the most money) involved a political subdivision of the Oglala Sioux Tribe, the Wakpamni Lake Community and the Wakpamni Lake Community Corporation (WLCC). A convicted fraudster, Jason Galanis, and his co-conspirators engineered a $60 million fraud scheme involving the WLCC. The scheme, which ran from 2014 to 2016, fraudulently convinced the tribe to issue municipal bonds under false pretenses, sold these worthless bonds to unsuspecting investors, and then misappropriated the proceeds.

Tribal tax-exempt bond financing involves a federally-recognized tribe issuing bonds to fund projects, such as infrastructure or housing, where bondholders receive interest that is exempt from federal (and often state) income tax. This tax exemption lowers the interest rate the tribe pays, providing significant cost savings compared to taxable debt. The interest rate savings for the bondholders allow the tribe to borrow money at a more favorable rate, making the financing more affordable for projects that serve a public purpose.

Galanis and his father, John Galanis, convinced the WLCC to issue approximately $60 million in bonds. They falsely promised that the bond proceeds would be used for tribal economic development and invested safely in an annuity. Instead of investing the money in an annuity for the tribe, the conspirators siphoned the bond proceeds into a bank account they controlled. Jason Galanis personally misappropriated over $8.5 million of the stolen money for luxury purchases, travel, and his home. WLCC never received the promised investments, and the pension fund clients were left holding worthless, unsellable securities.

B. TRIBES AS ECONOMIC REGULATORS

Tribal nations also exercise governmental regulatory and adjudicatory power over economic actors within reservation boundaries. Economic regulation includes adjudication, employment, taxation, environmental regulation, and the judicial development of tort and contract common law. E.g., Davis v. Superpumper, 17 Indian L.Rep. 6063 (Turtle Mountain Tribal Ct.1990) (issuing order setting gas prices on the reservation). Most tribal nations require any person or entity doing business on tribal lands to acquire a business license. E.g., Cheyenne River Sioux Tribe v. Isabel City Package Liquor, 18 Indian L.Rep. 6079 (Northern Plains Intertribal Ct.App.1990); Rosebud Sioux Tribe v. Walsh, 19 Indian L.Rep. 6030 (Rosebud Sioux Tribal Ct.1991). Cf. United States ex rel. The [Tulalip] Tribes v. First Choice Business Machines, 28 Indian L.Rep. 6038 (Tulalip Tribal Ct.2000) (federal Indian trader license).

1. ADJUDICATORY JURISDICTION

Tribal justice systems possess authority to adjudicate commercial matters arising in Indian country, even involving nonmembers. For example, in Neptune Leasing, Inc. v. Mountain States Petroleum Corp., 11 Am. Tribal Law 162 (Navajo

Nation S.Ct.2013), the court held that it possessed personal jurisdiction over two nonmember businesses in a dispute about the ownership of a business located on trust land. Similarly, in Dale Nicholson Trust v. Chavez, 5 Am. Tribal Law 365 (Navajo Nation S.Ct.2004), the court asserted jurisdiction over a dispute between a nonmember trust (with a tribal member beneficial interest) located on Indian lands and subject to the State of New Mexico's taxation authority.

Tribal nations may also possess authority to regulate off-reservation, nonmember businesses that conduct business on trust lands. In Ford Motor Co. v. Kayenta District Court, 7 Am. Tribal Law 652 (Navajo Nation S.Ct.2008), the court held that a car manufacturer that supplied tribal police cars could be sued for product defects. In that case, the court relied on the 1868 Treaty of Fort Sumner, the "old law":

> The Navajo Nation retains civil jurisdiction over claims arising within the Nation by inherent sovereignty under Article II of the Treaty. To the Navajo, the Treaty is the organic law. It is the old law made at Fort Sumner by our ancestors following years of captivity to secure the Nation's prosperity. *Hwéeldidi Beehaz'áanii Sáni Nihizázíni' nee'niji' bee hoot'ih dooleel yiniyé nihá áyiilaaígíí*. This is why the Treaty is considered a sacred document. This Court cannot ignore this law which embodies *'Naayéé' yee ak' ehdeesdlíį́'go Hózhǫ́ǫ́jíí yee ak'ïdiyaa silįį'* (they overcome adversity

> through Protective Way to restore peace and harmony) between our ancestors and the United States. This Court's precedents have emphasized the Treaty as the primary source of the Nation's authority over non-Indians within the Nation.

Id. at 656. The court noted that Ford had negotiated sales with tribal officials with the understanding that the vehicles would be utilized by tribal police. Ford would not be surprised that the vehicles could be used on trust lands within the Nation.

Similarly, in Muscogee (Creek) Nation ex rel. Beaver v. American Tobacco Co., 5 Okla. Trib. 401, 1998 WL 1119774 (Muscogee (Creek) Nation Dist.Ct.1998), appeal dismissed sub nom., Brown & Williamson Tobacco Co. v. District Court, 5 Okla. Trib. 447, 1998 WL 1119774 (Muscogee (Creek) Nation S.Ct.1998), the Muscogee (Creek) Nation District Court asserted jurisdiction over a claim against national tobacco companies seeking money damages caused by the marketing, sale, and consumption of tobacco products in Creek Indian country. The court concluded that it possessed personal jurisdiction over the nonmember business under the person contacts test borrowed from federal law: "The Muscogee (Creek) Nation does not exceed its powers, as a matter of tribal law or under notions of federal due process, if it asserts personal jurisdiction over a corporation that delivers its products into the stream of commerce with the foreseeability and expectation that the product will be purchased by consumers in the Muscogee (Creek)

Nation." 1998 WL 1119774, at *4. The court also rejected the tobacco companies' claims that the termination of the tribal government by the United States:

> The twentieth century brought changes to the government of the Muscogee (Creek) Nation, including Oklahoma statehood and allotment of tribal lands. However, even the shifting federal policy that called for the abolition of Muscogee (Creek) Nation's government did not have a lasting effect. . . . Congress enacted the [Oklahoma Indian Welfare Act], which restored the Muscogee (Creek) Nation's governmental powers and lead to the re-establishment of this Court.
>
> In 1979, the Muscogee (Creek) Nation reorganized their tribal government under the OIWA and adopted a new Constitution, which was approved by the United States Department of the Interior. The present Constitution, like the 1867 Constitution it replaced, organizes the tribal government into executive, legislative, and judicial branches, with no divestiture of authority over non-Indians or corporations.

Id. at *11. The tribal court relied extensively on tribal constitutional and statutory provisions to reach its conclusion that the court had personal jurisdiction over nonmembers reaching from afar into Indian country to do business.

Tribal nations may also possess authority delegated to them by federal statute and/or executive branch action. Examples include treatment-as-state status conferred on tribal nations by the Environmental Protection Agency. Another example is Indian country liquor regulation. E.g., Cheyenne River Indian Tribe v. American Legion Club, 19 Indian L.Rep. 6097 (Cheyenne River Tribal Ct.App. 1992).

2. TRIBAL ENTERPRISE AND COMMERCIAL EMPLOYMENT

Tribal nations enact laws governing employment on Indian lands that apply to tribal businesses, tribal member businesses, and nonmember businesses. Tribal laws also apply to employees of tribal enterprises. Typically, tribal enterprise employees have fewer remedies available to them than tribal government employees, though tribal citizens enjoy Indian preference in employment and contracting.

As sovereigns, tribes adopt tribal employment rights ordinances, ofttimes called TEROs. TEROs are enforced by tribal employment rights offices, also called TEROs. These offices are creatures of tribal government but tend to possess significant independence from the political branches of tribal government. The purpose of the creation of a TERO is to remedy "a high rate of unemployment among Indian persons on the reservation" and "to assist Indian persons in training for or securing employment would be of great value in securing future employment with public and private employers operating on or near the reservation."

Pendleton Ready Mix, Inc. v. Jackson, 16 Indian L.Rep. 6014, 6016 (Umatilla Tribal Ct.App.1988).

Employment regulation cases are legion, especially in large, landed reservations like Navajo. The Navajo Nation enacted the Navajo Preference in Employment Act, 15 Navajo Nation Code § 604, which is enforced by the Navajo Nation Labor Commission and frequently adjudicated in Navajo courts. For example, in Cabinets Southwest, Inc. v. Navajo Nation Labor Commission, 5 Am. Tribal Law 378 (Navajo Nation S.Ct.2004), the court enforced the preference act against a business vendor of a governmental subdivision of the tribal government, the Navajo Housing Authority. The vendor was nonmember-owned and located off-reservation, but the court pointed out that the entity was a subsidiary of the Navajo Housing Authority and had consented to tribal jurisdiction. But see Tsosie v. Arizona Public Service, 16 Am. Tribal Law 146 (Navajo Nation S.Ct.2020) (affirming the dismissal of a Four Corners Power Plant employee's complaint before the Navajo Nation Labor Commission after the tribal council stripped the Commission of authority to hear complaints from that power plant, invoking the Diné Fundamental Law principle that "the opening of the sacred wedding basket imparts that leadership must find a solution, for it is always available") (citing Thinn v. Navajo Generating Station, 7 Am. Tribal Law 558 (Navajo Nation S.Ct.2007)).

Other tribal courts have reached similar outcomes, such as the Shoshone-Bannock Tribes of the Fort Hall Reservation. E.g., Shoshone Bannock Tribes v.

FMC Corp., 14 Indian L.Rep. 6046 (Shoshone Bannock Tribal Ct.1987) (ordering nonmember company to comply with tribe TERO laws), aff'd, 15 Indian L.Rep. 6023 (Shoshone-Bannock Tribal Ct., App.Div.1988). See also FMC Corp. v. Shoshone-Bannock Tribes ex rel. TERO Corp., 16 Indian L.Rep. 6026 (Shoshone-Bannock Tribes Tribal Ct., App.Div. 1988) (issuing compliance plan order). Ultimately, the Ninth Circuit excused FMC from tribal jurisdiction. FMC v. Shoshone-Bannock Tribes, 905 F.2d 1311 (9th Cir.1990).

Tribal businesses establish laws designed to protect and recruit employees for tribal business enterprises, but with protections for the tribal employer as well. Consider Shananaquet v. Grand Traverse Band of Ottawa and Chippewa Indians Economic Development Corp., 8 Am. Tribal Law 160 (Grand Traverse Band of Ottawa and Chippewa Indians App.Ct.2009). There, the tribe terminated the employment of a tribal citizen employed by the tribe's Section 17 corporation, referred to as the EDC. The citizen administratively challenged the termination under the rules governing the EDC, which prohibited an appeal to the tribal court (unlike tribal government employment, which allowed such appeals). The tribal citizen sued in tribal court anyway under a provision in the tribe's constitution waiving tribal immunity for suits brought by tribal citizens against tribal officials for prospective, injunctive relief. The Grand Traverse Band appellate court rejected the claim, largely because the tribal citizen sought money damages. The tribal citizen also alleged that the EDC's charter, which included a "sue-and-be-sued" clause, itself waived immunity. The court rejected that claim because the clause could only operate as a waiver of sovereign immunity if the tribal council enacted positive legislation doing so.

Tribal judicial review of tribal enterprise employment matters may be severely limited or barred altogether. In Nigrelli v. Mashantucket Pequot Gaming Enterprise, 1 Mash. Rep. 183, 1996 WL 34402644 (Mashantucket Pequot Tribal Ct. 1996), a tribal gaming enterprise employee was banished from the reservation by the tribal gaming regulatory body, effectively ending the employee's employment. The employee tried to sue the gaming commission, but the tribal government had not waived tribal immunity to allow tribal judicial review of gaming commission decisions. See also McGee v. Spirit Mountain Gaming, Inc., 5 Am. Tribal Law 75 (Confederated Tribes of the Grand Ronde Community Tribal Ct.2004) (holding that a terminated tribal enterprise employee could not sue the tribe absent a waiver of immunity and also because the tribal enterprise, not the tribe, took the action).

Some tribes allow tribal judicial review of appeals of adverse enterprise employment actions, but require the judiciary to defer to the tribal managers' decision. For an example, see In re Dombrosky, 2006 WL 6545562 (Confederated Tribes of the Coos, Lower Umpqua, and Siuslaw Indians Tribal Ct.2006), where the tribal court of the Confederated Tribes of the Coos, Lower Umpqua, and Siuslaw Indians applied a tribal statute imposing an abuse of discretion or arbitrary and capricious standard of review of the termination of an at-will employee (which is more review than an actual at-will employee would normally receive). See Coos, Lower Umpqua, and Siuslaw Indians Code § 9–4–4(h)(3). In Gwin v. Four Bears Casino, 32 Indian L.Rep. 6066 (Northern Plains Intertribal Ct.App.2005), the appellate court reversed the trial court where the trial court had second-guessed a factual determination of the administrative board related to the explanations for an employee's absences.

Many tribal nations attempt to label enterprise employees as at-will employees, or employees whose employment can be terminated at will, for no cause or any cause at all. Cf., e.g., Bullcreek v. Goshute Housing Authority, 36 Indian L.Rep. 6093 (Confederated Tribes of the Goshute Reservation Tribal Ct.2009) (affirming termination of at will employee in the absence of valid discrimination claim). Tribal courts regularly find that even a plainly stated at-will employment relationship can be converted to a protected employment status. For example, in Johnson v. Mashantucket Pequot Gaming Enterprise, 1 Mash. App. 21, 1996 WL 34403257 (Mashantucket Pequot Ct.App.1996), the Mashantucket Pequot appellate court found that provisions in the employee manual establishing a policy that employee rights would be protected was enough to convert a purported at-will employment relationship into a protected status employment. Once any employment rights are created, they become vested property rights to continued employment. Any tribal governmental action that adversely impacts those rights is subject to a takings analysis, in which the government must ensure due process before taking the property interest and then paying just compensation for any takings. See 25 U.S.C. §§ 1302(a)(5), (8).

Other tribes provide procedural protections to enterprise employees akin to those afforded governmental employees. E.g., Frogg v. Ho-Chunk Casino, 23 Indian L.Rep. 6197 (Ho-Chunk Nation Trial Ct.1996) (awarding retroactive pay increase to enterprise employee); Anderson v. Sisseton-Wahpeton Oyate, No. 15-988-688 (Sisseton-Wahpeton Oyate S.Ct.2016) (holding that an employer drug test is a search under ICRA that requires reasonable suspicion); Gourd v. Robertson, 28 Indian L.Rep. 6047 (Spirit Lake Tribal Ct.2001) (finding employer violated enterprise employee's ICRA rights by subjecting to mandatory drug testing in violation of employer's policy); Strickland v. DeCoteau, 31 Indian L.Rep. 6021 (Turtle Mountain Tribal Ct.2003) (same).

3. INDIAN PREFERENCE IN EMPLOYMENT AND CONTRACTING

Tribal nations typically allow for Indian preference in enterprise employment (and in contracting). Title VII of the federal Civil Rights Act of 1964 excludes tribal employers from the federal law barring race discrimination. 42 U.S.C. § 2000e(b). Indian preference policies were established to combat the historical underemployment, poverty, and discrimination faced by Indigenous Peoples. By guaranteeing preferences for jobs, training, and contracts on reservations, tribes can ensure that tribal members are the primary beneficiaries of economic opportunities within their own territories.

Indian preference in employment means that employers can freely recruit qualifying Indians to apply for tribal jobs. When Indians do apply and are qualified to perform the job, the tribal employer may then grant them the preference over similarly situated candidates. Tribal employers do not grant preference to unqualified Indian candidates, nor do they usually hire qualifying Indians with significantly lesser qualifications than their non-Indian competitors. At times, tribal nations grant tribal preference, a preference for their own citizens over those of other tribal nations.

Indian preference in contracting requires that when awarding contracts and subcontracts, priority is given to Indian-owned and controlled businesses and that Indian individuals are given preference in employment and training opportunities connected to the contract, especially near or on reservations. Contractors must provide opportunities for employment and training to Indians who can perform the required work.

Many tribes employ a TERO office to enforce the Indian preference rules, though many tribes simply rely on the enterprise human resources/personnel or procurement departments to comply with the rule. Some tribes exclude the government from TERO enforcement. E.g., In re Sanders, 4 Am. Tribal Law

24, 36 (Cherokee Nation Judicial App.Trib.2002) (holding tribal immunity bars enforcement by TERO against tribe); Gabriel v. Cox, 14 Am. Tribal Law 171, 174 (Colville Tribal Ct.App.2017) (same).

Many tribal nations limit the scope or the enforceability of Indian preference requirements in the context of enterprise employment. For example, in DeSouza v. Mashantucket Pequot Tribe, 4 Mash.Rep. 167, 2003 WL 25586069 (Mashantucket Pequot Tribal Ct.2003), the court dismissed a claim brought by nonmember Indians challenging adverse employment actions by the tribal gaming enterprise as violative of the tribe's Indian Preference Policy (IPP). The court dismissed equal protection and statutory tort claims because they were not allowed by the tribe's IPP, but did allow a negligence claim (provided for under the IPP) to go forward. Similarly in Lowe-Innes v. Cash Systems, Inc., 7 Am. Tribal Law 133, 143 (Ho-Chunk Nation Trial Ct.2007), the court rejected a claim by an at-will employee of a private enterprise.

4. FEDERAL EMPLOYMENT STATUTES OF GENERAL APPLICABILITY

Numerous lower federal courts have held that certain federal statutes of general applicability apply to tribal enterprise employment and other enterprise activities. Many of these federal statutes are silent as to their applicability to tribal enterprise employment, meaning that enforcing them against tribal nations would run afoul of the clear statement rule that protects tribes from federal laws limiting or regulating tribal sovereignty in the absence of a clear expression of intent to do so from Congress. E.g., Ex parte Crow Dog, 109 U.S. 556, 572 (1883) (requiring a "clear expression of the intention of Congress" to limit tribal inherent powers). Most federal courts have coalesced around a theory called the *Tuscarora-Coeur d'Alene* approach. Wenona T. Singel, Labor Relations and Tribal Self-Governance, 80 N.D.L.Rev. 691, 691 (2004) (citing Federal Power Commission v. Tuscarora Indian Nation, 362 U.S. 99 (1960), and Donovan v. Coeur d'Alene Tribal Farm, 751 F.2d 1113 (9th Cir. 1985)). This approach presumes that the federal statute applies to tribal employment, but that presumption can be overcome if the statute touches upon the exclusive right of tribal self-government or tribal treaty rights.

Tribal courts have held that federal employment statutes do interfere with tribal self-government, even with casino employment. In DeLorge v. Mashantucket Pequot Gaming Enterprise, 2 Mash. Rep. 78, 1997 WL 34641750 (Mashantucket Pequot Tribal Ct.1997), the Mashantucket Pequot Tribal Court held that the federal Age Discrimination in Employment Act was inapplicable to tribal gaming enterprise employment. Under the Indian Gaming Regulatory Act, gaming profits must go to the tribal government to fund governmental programs. 25 U.S.C. §§ 2710(b)(2)(A), 2710(d)(1)(A)(ii). Most tribal nations with successful gaming operations depend heavily on gaming revenues to fund government programs. Any impact on gaming revenues directly impacts tribal self-government.

Outside of the gaming context, tribal courts have reached similar conclusions. E.g., Coffin v. Clifford, 10 Indian L.Rep. 6057 (Colorado River Tribal Ct.1983) (holding that federal law requiring tribe to comply with state worker's compensation laws was inapplicable to privately employed bricklayer).

Similarly, the National Labor Relations Board declined to exercise jurisdiction over the Chickasaw Nation's casino on the ground that the 1830 Treaty of Dancing Rabbit Creek expressly prohibited the application of federal laws absent the consent of the tribe. Chickasaw Nation d/b/a Winstar World Casino and International Brotherhood of Teamsters Local 886, 362 N.L.R.B. 942 (2015).

5. TAXATION

Tribal authority to tax on-reservation commercial activity long has been recognized as an inherent power possessed by all tribal nations. Restatement of the Law of American Indians § 21. The tribal power to tax tribal citizens is a given, perhaps due to the reality that tribal citizenship is rooted in literal tribal consent. However, most tribes do not collect income or property taxes from tribal citizens. Virtually all disputes that arise from the imposition of tribal commercial taxes on nonmembers. Most of these cases depend on whether the nonmember business has consented in writing to the enforcement of tribal laws. In general, nonmembers do consent and the cases so reflect. E.g., Navajo Communications Co. v. Navajo Tax Commission, 1991 Navajo Sup. LEXIS 1, at *7 (Navajo Nation S.Ct.1991) ("The Navajo Nation has the inherent sovereign power to tax both members and non-members engaged in economic activities within its territorial borders. The Navajo Nation's taxing power is a necessary instrument of self-government and territorial management. . . . This power to tax is not one granted to the Navajo Nation by the federal government. Rather, it is a fundamental attribute of tribal sovereignty which the Indian tribes retain unless divested of it by Congress or by necessary implication as a result of their dependent status.") (citation omitted).

Tribal nations possess authority to tax tribal member business activities on allotted lands belonging to individual tribal members. In Mustang Fuel Corp. v. Cheyenne-Arapaho Tax Commission, 4 Okla. Trib. 1, 1994 WL 1047927 (Cheyenne-Arapaho Tribes S.Ct.1994), the court held that allotments owned by individual Indians were considered Indian country over which tribal nations possessed the power to tax. In that case, the tax protesters were nonmember oil companies that were the lessees of tribal member allotment owners. In the federal court proceedings that followed where the nonmember challenged tribal tax authority, the Tenth Circuit concluded that the tribe did possess the power to tax in that situation. Mustang Fuel Corp. v. Harrison, 94 F.3d 1382 (10th Cir.1996). The *Mustang* precedents have been followed by other tribal courts as well. E.g., Vintage Petroleum, Inc. v. Tax Commission, 6 Okla. Trib. 125, 1999 WL 33589140 (Kickapoo Tribe S.Ct. 1999).

On nonmember owned or controlled lands, tribal taxing authority is limited by federal Indian law. Consider In the Matter of Atkinson Trading Co., Inc., 1 Am. Tribal Law 451 (Navajo Nation S.Ct.1997). There, the court affirmed the authority of the Nation to tax a nonmember owned business that was located on nonmember fee land surrounded by Nation trust lands. The trading company was the beneficiary of federal laws allowing nonmembers to open Indian trading posts within Indian reservations. The company benefitted from tribal governmental services, like police, ambulance, and other public safety services. The company appealed to federal courts, leading to a United States Supreme Court decision excusing the company from paying tribal taxes. Atkinson Trading Co., Inc. v. Shirley, 532 U.S. 645 (2001). That result can easily by remedied by tribal nations that can negotiate with the nonmember to pay taxes in exchange for the continued duty to provide governmental services, sometimes known derisively as "pay-to-pay."

Most tribal nations have reached agreement with state and local governments to collect and remit state taxes. These agreements tend to involve compromises by both tribal and state parties that can, in certain circumstances, prejudice the interests of individual Indian businesses. In Lanphere v. Wright, 10 NICS App. 20 (Puyallup Tribal Ct.App. 2011), the Puyallup Tribal Court of Appeals rejected challenge to a tribal-state tax agreement brought by a tribal member retailer and a nonmember customer. The court largely relied on tribal sovereign immunity to dismiss the suit, but reaffirmed the inherent power of tribal nations to tax Indian and non-Indian business activities on tribal lands. To hold otherwise, ironically, would be to reject the United States Supreme Court's repeated holdings that tribal and Indian retailers must collect and remit state taxes on nonmembers.

6. TORT CLAIMS

Accidents happen. Tribal courts are developing their own tort law, taking into account the unique needs and expectations of their communities. This is particularly important because tribal nations and members face unique challenges, such as environmental harms and personal injuries. Tort law provides a mechanism for individuals to seek compensation for injuries suffered due to the actions of others.

By establishing rules of conduct and consequences for violations, tort law helps to deter harmful behavior within the community. For example, the Mescalero Apache Tribal Code includes provisions for additional penalties in cases of deliberate harm (such as cyberstalking, unlawful distributions of intimate images), which aims to deter such actions. Mescalero Apache Tribe, Ordinance 22–11. The law of torts in general aims to keep society in balance and harmony, important to many tribal communities. E.g., Mahler v. Hinshaw, 17 Indian L.Rep. 6044, 6046 (Confederated Salish & Kootenai Tribes App.Ct. 1990) ("Tribal governments, like state governments, have an interest in developing and enforcing safety standards designed to encourage attentiveness and caution on the part of all persons operating vehicles on roads open to the public within the reservation.").

Importantly, because state law has no force in Indian country (absent Congressional authorization) and because federal courts do not possess subject matter jurisdiction over tort claims absent a federal hook, tribal courts are often the only available forum to resolve tort claims in Indian country. See generally Restatement of the Law of American Indians §§ 55–58. E.g., Benoist v. Hunt, 25 Indian L.Rep. 6065 (Cheyenne River Sioux Tribal Ct.1998) (allowing tort claim brought by nonmember against member, in part, because state courts would not jurisdiction over the tribal member defendant for an on-reservation claim). Usually, tribal courts rely on the state common law of torts, often citing directly to the restatements on torts or other secondary authorities elucidating blackletter law. E.g., Gesinger v. Gesinger, 22 Indian L.Rep. 6025 (Cheyenne River Sioux Tribal Ct.App.1995) (state precedents in conversion action); Larive v. Royal Associates Mgmt., Inc., 25 Indian L.Rep. 6128 (Chitimacha Indian Tribal Ct.App.1998) (allowing dram shop action to proceed, invoking Louisiana law); Sherman v. Scottsdale Ins. Co., 23 Indian L.Rep. 6232 (Chitimacha Indian Tribal Ct.App.1996) (applying Louisiana law in a personal injury action); Bartell v. Kerr, 23 Indian L.Rep. 6209 (Confederated Salish & Kootenai Tribal Ct.1996) (applying Montana law in a jury instruction on survival in a wrongful death action); Bighorse v. Confederated Salish & Kootenai Tribes, 15 Indian L.Rep. 6048 (Confederated Salish & Kootenai Tribal Ct.1988) (applying law of respondeat superior), rev'd in part, Estate of Bighorse v. Confederated Salish & Kootenai Tribes, 17 Indian L.Rep. 6003 (Confederated Salish & Kootenai App.Ct.1989); Governing Board of Education of the Hotevilla Bacavi Community School v. Shingoitewa, 26 Indian L.Rep. 6056 (Hopi Tribe App.Ct.1998) (applying state law on unjust enrichment); Mahan v. Mashantucket Pequot Gaming Enterprise, 4 Mash.Rep. 499, 2007 WL 2851074 (Mashantucket Pequot Tribal Ct.2007) (citing Restatement (Second) of Torts § 314); Chavez v. Tome, 14 Indian L.Rep. 6029 (Navajo Nation S.Ct.1987) (adjudicating libel claim and relying on federal precedents); General Motors Acceptance Corp. v. Bitah, 16 Indian L.Rep. 6002 (Navajo Nation S.Ct.1988) (applying state law on fraudulent misrepresentation); Sheffield v. Grand Casinos of La., Inc., 25 Indian L.Rep. 6242 (Tunica-Biloxi Tribal Ct.App.1998) (applying state tort law in affirming negligence decision); Davis v. LaFountain, 16 Indian L.Rep. 6047 (Turtle Mountain Tribal Ct.1989) (adjudicating libel claim and relying on *Corpus Juris Secundum*).

Other tribal courts have declined to apply state common law tort defenses, for example, contributory negligence. In Howard v. Sharp, 10 Indian L.Rep. 6027 (Colorado River Indian Tribes Tribal Ct.1983), the court noted that state policy behind allowing the contributory negligence defense was to encourage "rapid industrial growth." Id. at 6027. The court held that tribal citizens owe themselves a higher standard of care to each other:

> The common law of the four tribes in residence is as far removed from "rugged individualism" as is possible to be. As befits people who choose to live in tribal and clan units the standard of care owed to others is higher than that owed to oneself and is not easily excused. Consequently, the use of contributory negligence as an affirmative defense is as out of place in this court as a suit of armor in a swimming pool.

Id. at 6028.

However, because the Indian Civil Rights Act does not guarantee a right to a jury for civil claims, many tribal courts do not provide that option in civil cases. However, in one important Navajo Nation decision, Downey v. Bigman, 22 Indian L.Rep. 6145 (Navajo Nation S.Ct.1995), the court reversed a trial court decision ordering a new trial and reinstated a jury verdict favoring the defendant in a personal injury action. The court invoked Diné common law in supporting the verdict where the jury forwarded questions to the judge to ask the witnesses.

> A modern Navajo jury continues the fundamental tradition of community participation in the resolution of disputes through deliberation and consensus. A jury consists of members of the parties' community who bring their "experience, culture and community standards into the jury box." Bryant v. Bryant, 3 Nav. R. 194 (Shiprock Dist. Ct. 1981). The jury engages in deliberations, relying upon persuasion to reach consensus, to reach its verdict. These essential characteristics of a

> Navajo jury make it a modern expression of our longstanding legacy of participatory democracy.
>
> A reformulation of the jury's duties to permit it to ask questions of the witnesses during trial is more reflective of Navajo participatory democracy. To maintain impartiality, all the questions will be channeled through the judge, whose authority to permit or forbid the question is discretionary. This modification of jury trials in the Navajo Nation courts is a natural step back to traditional ways and a means to secure the future.

Id. at 6146 (citing Raymond Austin, ADR and the Navajo Peacemaker Court, 32 Judges' J. 8 (1993)).

Culturally, not all tort claims are adversarial in character. In Allstate Indemnity Co. v. Blackgoat, 6 Am. Tribal Law 631 (Navajo Nation S.Ct.2005), the court explained the Diné common law concept of *nályééh*:

> The Navajo Common Law doctrine relevant to our analysis is *nályééh*. * * * *Nályééh* is the Navajo Common Law method by which parties come to an agreement on compensation for an injury. * * * *Nályééh* is a unique Navajo doctrine based on the effects of the injury. * * * As the means by which Navajos customarily compensate injuries, Navajo Nation courts use *nályééh* to assess the adequacy of damages in tort claims. * * * [*N*]*ályééh* includes the responsibility to respectfully talk out disputes. * * * While a "flexible concept of distributive

> justice" depending on the circumstances of the injury and the positions of the parties, * * * a central purpose of *nályééh* is to restore harmony between the parties by adequately compensating the injured person or persons. * * * Therefore, the amount of compensation arising out of that process "should be enough so that there are no hard feelings." * * * Based on these principles, *nályééh* incorporates what might be expressed in Anglo terms as a procedural requirement and a substantive result.

Id. at 635–36 (citations omitted). The court employed *nályééh* to conclude that Navajo common law recognized prejudgment interest.

Similarly, in Kalk v. Mille Lacs Band of Ojibwe Corporation Commission, 2004 WL 5746060 (Mille Lacs Band of Chippewa Indians Ct.App.2004), the court affirmed the dismissal of a slip-and-fall tort claims against the tribal corporate commission. The plaintiff first attempted to sue the tribe in state court. After the plaintiff filed suit later in tribal court, the tribal defendant did not file a brief within the time frame allowed by the court rules. The court ultimately dismissed the suit for failure to file within the tribe's three year limitations period, excused any procedural irregularities, and rejected the plaintiff's claim that the tribe should be equitably estopped from asserting sovereign defenses. The court concluded:

> The traditional theory of law of the Mille Lacs Band as explained in the written statute states:

> "The purpose of *sha wa ni ma* is to keep the people together as one. This purpose is good for all people. It serves to balance the forces of life and brings stability to the people. To achieve this way of life, the laws of the Band shall be construed to balance the rights of the individual with the need to continue to co-exist in peace and harmony with one another. In this way, order will be preserved and justice shall be accorded to each person who has cause to appear before the Court of Central Jurisdiction."

24 MLBSA [Mille Lacs Band Stat.Ann.] § 2003.

Additionally, the written statute states that the judicial philosophy of the Court of Central Jurisdiction is to promote the traditional teachings of the elders in order to restore the circle of life "in a manner that permits the integrity of the individual to be maintained so that the community will continue to grow and prosper." Id. at § 2002.

The statute of limitations included in the written statutes of the Band serves the purposes outlined above. It balances the rights of the individual with the needs of the community for peace and harmony. It does this by allowing a reasonable time period to bring actions before the Court while also ensuring that the community will be able to move forward in achieving peace and harmony by preventing perpetual disruptions in the circle of peace and harmony. Hence, Band Assembly has balanced

> these issues in enacting the three year statute of limitations.

Id. at 65–66.

Tribal courts routinely assume jurisdiction over tort claims where nonmembers have intentionally engaged in commercial relations on Indian or tribal lands. In Garfield v. Sherman Motor Inn, 2006 WL 7137863 (Fort Peck Ct.App.2006), the court assumed jurisdiction over a tribal member's premises liability suit against a nonmember business where the incident was alleged to have occurred on nonmember-owned fee land within the boundaries of the reservation. Rejecting the defendant's federal Indian law defenses, the court applied blackletter tort principles in finding jurisdiction:

> * * * [W]e find that a consensual relationship begins as a member of the Tribes enters the Sherman Inn for purposes of purchase of the goods and services offered therein. Although the Sherman Inn argues that a consensual relationship would not have arisen until Mr. Garfield actually ordered some service or goods, we conclude otherwise. In order to be in a position to order services or goods, one must first enter the premises. The consensual relationship commences when one enters the property legitimately for the purposes of transacting business offered therein. The Sherman Inn's argument that any duty owed to Mr. Garfield would not come into being until he had entered the restaurant and ordered his food would lead to the illogical conclusion that the hotel

> restaurant owes a duty to patrons leaving the premises but not to those entering the premises. By contrast, as Amicus Fort Peck Tribes points out, our reasoning also fits within the traditional tort principles set forth in the Restatement 2nd of Torts § 332(3) (1965). As a patron of the Sherman Inn, Mr. Garfield was subject to the implied representation that reasonable care has been taken to make the premises safe for the purpose for which they are open to him.

Id. at *3. See also Hitchcock v. Shaver Mfg. Co., 23 Indian L.Rep. 6137 (Confederated Salish & Kootenai Tribes Ct.App.1996) (finding personal jurisdiction over off-reservation farm products company in products liability claim).

Most tribes borrow aspects of state law consistent with the tribal nation's cultural and economic interests. For example, the Mohegan Tribe borrows Connecticut's tort claims limitations period. Lubrano v. Brennan Beer Gorman Architects, LLP, 7 Am. Tribal Law 369, 378 (Mohegan Gaming Disputes Ct.App.2008). See also HKS, Inc. v. Mashantucket Pequot Tribal Nation, 5 Mash.Rep. 377, 389–90 (Mashantucket Pequot Tribal Ct.2010) ("The discovery doctrine applies to Mashantucket tort claims. Mashantucket law requires that causes of action arising in tort be brought within one year of the 'act or omission complained of' and states that claims will begin to accrue on the date of injury. 12 M.P.T.L. [Mashantucket Pequot Tribal Laws] ch. 1, § 4(a)(2). A party must be made aware of the injury before the statute of limitations will begin to run.").

But only rarely do tribes adopt state law entirely. For example, the Mohegan tribal court held that the tribe had not recognized incorporation of the Connecticut Product Liability Act. Dell v. Mohegan Tribal Gaming Authority, 17 Am. Tribal Law 135, 137–38 (Mohegan Gaming Disputes Tribal Ct.2020).

Some tribal legislatures limit the power of tribal courts to recognize common law torts in the absence of a tribal statute explicitly enumerating types of tort claims recognized by the tribal nation. E.g., Kimsey v. Reibach, 6 Am. Tribal Law 119, 124–25 (Confederated Tribes of the Grand Ronde Community Tribal Ct.2005) (declining jurisdiction over defamation action where the parties "radically disagree as to whether the alleged statements of Mr. Reibach violate Tribal law, whether Tribal law allows for actions of slander per se, and whether such torts may be brought against a 'marital community' underscore the necessity of having a specific tribal enactment setting out the standards for adjudicating such actions"). Other tribal courts insist on requiring a jurisdictional statute authorizing the court to hear tort claims at all. E.g., Nissen v. Coquille Economic Development Corp., 37 Indian L.Rep. 6091 (Coquille Indian Tribal Ct.2010).

7. CONTRACT CLAIMS

Tribes assert jurisdiction over contract claims to secure a neutral and appropriate forum for resolving disputes involving tribal interests, as federal and state courts often lack the authority and tribal courts are better suited to resolving claims. Asserting jurisdiction protects the tribe's economic interests, preserves its self governance, and provides certainty for business partners by establishing clear rules for resolving disputes rather than being subject to external legal systems that may be biased or ill-equipped to handle tribal-specific issues. Honoring contracts is also important public policy in insular Indigenous communities. and non-members within the tribe's jurisdiction have a means of recourse when they are harmed. E.g., Ben v. Burbank, 24 Indian L.Rep. 6001, 6002 (Navajo Nation S.Ct.1996) ("[W]hen people make promises between one another, oral or written, they should honor those promises."); Benalli v. First National Ins. Co. of America, 1 Am. Tribal Law 498, 508 (Navajo Nation S.Ct.1998) ("We take this opportunity to clarify the Navajo common law concept of *nalyeeh* as a separate ground for finding that Benalli was [covered by] the policy. * * * Here, the Board can be likened to a clan group. While there were no corporations or other fictitious entities under Navajo common law, clans have always been recognized as an identifiable group. The Board assumed Benalli into its 'clan' membership. It expected that Benalli would be one of its 'relatives' if she got hurt.").

As sovereign nations, tribes possess inherent governmental authority to govern their land and people, including businesses operating on their territory. Asserting jurisdiction over contract claims is a way to exercise this authority, ensure the enforcement of tribal law, and protect the economic and cultural interests of the tribe and its members. Many commercial contracts involving reservation business activities or involving tribal nations are governed by complex federal Indian law. Tribes may assert jurisdiction to ensure that these contracts are adjudicated in their own courts, which are better equipped to understand and apply tribal laws, regulations, and cultural contexts than federal or state courts. Cf. Coin v. Mowa, 25 Indian L.Rep. 6208 (Hopi Tribe App.Ct.1997) (asserting jurisdiction over a contract claim arising on the village of Shungopavi after the Kikmongwi was unable to resolve the dispute). Tribes and their business partners need a fair and reliable forum to resolve disputes arising from commercial activities in Indian Country. E.g., Parisien v. Twin City Construction Co., 16 Indian L.Rep. 6012, 6014 (Turtle Mountain Ct.App.1986) ("Viewed as a single incident, such an occurrence, never will give rise to a governmental interest sufficient to justify tribal jurisdiction. Viewed as a part of a class of such occurrence, however, contractual injury to a tribal member clearly affects the welfare of the tribe and the tribe may bring its power to bear to redress the injury and govern the conduct causing it. Tribal courts offer a forum where the specific legal landscape of Indian country can be properly addressed, leading to more equitable and efficient outcomes.").

Under federal Indian law, state courts have no jurisdiction over claims brought against tribal nations and tribal members in Indian country. E.g., Williams v. Lee, 358 U.S. 217 (1959) (contract claim against tribal citizens). Federal courts are courts of limited jurisdiction and do not have subject matter jurisdiction over contract claims absent federal subject matter jurisdiction (which does not include contract claims). Moreover, tribal nations are not citizens of any state for diversity jurisdiction, so unless a federal entity is a party to a contract claim, federal courts cannot assume jurisdiction. E.g., Sandoval v. Tinian, Inc., 13 Indian L.Rep. 6041 (Navajo Nation Crownpoint Dist.Ct.1986) ("If this court declined to accept jurisdiction, then, plaintiffs could be left without a forum."). See generally Restatement of the Law of American Indians §§ 55–58.

Tribal courts usually rely on the state common law of contracts, often citing directly to the restatement or other authorities that elucidate blackletter law. E.g., Lulow v. Peterson, 22 Indian L.Rep. 6069 (Confederated Salish & Kootenai Tribes Trial Ct.1995) (following state law of contract breach and unjust enrichment); Basu v. Colebut, 5 Mash.Rep. 365, 2010 WL 4872978, at *2 (Mash. Pequot Tribal Ct.2010) (citing Restatement (Second) of Contracts §§ 17–19, *cmt.* c (1981)); Tomahawk Enterprises, Inc. v. Fort Totten Housing Authority, 24 Indian L.Rep. 6088 (Northern Plains Intertribal Ct.App.1996) (equitable tolling of limitations period); United States ex rel. Auginaush v. Medure, 8 Am. Tribal Law 304, 323 (White Earth Band of Chippewa Tribal Ct.2009) (quoting Restatement (Second) of Contracts § 175 (1981)). Cf. First National Bank of Browning v. Kittson, 10 Indian L.Rep. 6021 (Blackfeet Tribal Ct.1982) (assuming jurisdiction over a claim for equity in replevin).

Dispute resolution provisions in contracts between tribal nations or tribal citizens and private parties depend heavily on bargaining power. If tribal interests have superior bargaining power, contracts typically will make tribal courts the forum for dispute resolution, with the governing law the law of the tribal nation. If private parties have the edge, state courts and state law will be the preferred forum and governing law. For example, in Lake of the Torches Economic Development Corp. v. Saybrook Tax Exempt Investors LLC, No. 13 CV 115 (Lac du Flambeau Band of Lake Superior Chippewa Indians Ct.2013), the parties had reached an agreement for a proposed off-reservation gaming venture. The tribe agreed in a series of contracts to forum selection clauses that named state and/or federal courts in Wisconsin as the forum of choice for any disputes between the parties, with Wisconsin law as the controlling law. After a contract dispute arose, the tribe brought a claim in tribal court. The nonmember parties adverse to the tribe moved to dismiss on the pleadings, pointing to the forum selection clauses. The tribal court denied the motion to dismiss, holding that under Wisconsin law, the courts of which had adopted a liberal construction doctrine of interpreting forum selection clauses. The tribal court held that the forum selection clauses potentially allowed for tribal court jurisdiction by not explicitly precluding tribal court jurisdiction. The nonmembers sought to be excused from tribal court jurisdiction in federal court, which ultimately applied Seventh Circuit law, rejecting the tribal court's theory. Stifel, Nicolaus & Co., Inc. v. Lac du Flambeau Band of

Lake Superior Chippewa Indians, 807 F.3d 184 (7th Cir.2015). Ultimately, the tribe and their former business partners reached a confidential settlement.

Contracting parties might also agree to arbitrate contract disputes. Where a tribe or tribal entity has agreed to arbitrate disputes with a business partner, an employee, or any other person or entity, the parties must determine in the contract which court or courts can enforce the award. Arbitration can be conducted under the laws of the tribal nation, through the American Arbitration Association, or some other forum. The Federal Arbitration Act declares strong support for the validity and enforcement of arbitration awards. 9 U.S.C. § 1 et seq.

Tribal arbitration laws largely track state and federal arbitration laws. E.g., Stopp v. Cherokee Nation Entertainment, 15 Am. Tribal Law 18 (Cherokee Nation S.Ct.2017) (enforcing tribal arbitrator's award in worker's compensation dispute); Saginaw Chippewa Indian Tribe of Michigan v. Cunningham, 27 Indian L.Rep. 6052 (Saginaw Chippewa Indian Tribe of Mich.App.Ct. 1999) (assuming jurisdiction over nonmember defendant in breach of contract action related to construction of tribal casino and ordering stay pending completion of arbitration); Taylor v. Eastern Shoshone Housing Authority, 2015 WL 13767949 (Shoshone and Arapaho Tribal Ct.2015) (rejecting challenge to arbitration award by tribal nation). Arbitration awards must still be supported by the evidence, e.g., Ward v. Cherokee Nation, 12 Am.

Tribal Law 333 (Cherokee Nation S.Ct.2015) (refusing to enforce tribal arbitration award); and they must comply with applicable law, e.g., First Specialty Insurance Corporation v. Confederated Tribes of Grand Ronde Community of Oregon, 16 Am. Tribal Law 390 (Confederated Tribes of the Grand Ronde Community Ct.App.2006) (rejecting arbitrator's imposition of attorney fees on tribal nation). Tribal courts, like state and federal courts, will dismiss or stay a contract breach action where the parties have agreed to resolve disputes by arbitration. E.g., Grand Traverse Band of Ottawa and Chippewa Indians v. C.H. Smith Co., Inc., 2002 WL 34487861 (Grand Traverse Band of Ottawa and Chippewa Indians Tribal Ct.2002) (ordering dismissal); Oglala Sioux Tribe v. Alltell Communications, 38 Indian L.Rep. 6033 (Oglala Sioux Nation S.Ct.2010) (ordering stay pending arbitration). But cf. Mashantucket Pequot Tribal Nation v. Paul Steelman, Ltd., 5 Mash.Rep. 31, 2008 WL 961024 (Mashantucket Pequot Tribal Ct.2008) (declining to dismiss suit where the contract term required mediation, not arbitration).

In one wide-ranging case involving tribal and federal courts, the Colville Confederated Tribes entered into contracts for the construction and management of a tribal sawmill on tribal lands, with any disputes to be arbitrated, with Stock West, Inc., a nonmember-owned company. The contracts included a provision stating that the contract required federal approval under 25 U.S.C. § 81. However, the Bureau of Indian Affairs, relying on an opinion from the Office of the Solicitor of the Interior, declined to approve or disapprove the contract, asserting that no such authorization was necessary. The parties proceeded with the performance of the contract, but eventually the tribe sued for breach. The tribal court first held that it possessed jurisdiction over the nonmember defendant. Confederated Tribes of the Colville Reservation v. Stock West, Inc., 14 Indian L.Rep. 6025, 6027–28 (Colville Confederated Tribes Tribal Ct.1987). The court then held, disagreeing with the Interior Solicitor's opinion, that the contract was void ab initio for failure to secure federal approval. Confederated Tribes of the Colville Reservation v. Stock West, Inc., 15 Indian L.Rep. 6019 (Colville Confederated Tribes Tribal Ct.1988). Stock West had sought to enforce the arbitration provision in federal court and enjoin the tribal court action, but the Ninth Circuit held the case in abeyance pending the outcome of the tribal court case. Stock West, Inc. v. Confederated Tribes of the Colville Reservation, 873 F.2d 1221 (9th Cir.1989). Stock West also sued Colville's attorney, Michael Taylor, a nonmember Indian, in federal court for malpractice and misrepresentation for issuing a letter to his client (the tribe) opining that federal approval was required after all, and that Stock West was the intended beneficiary of the opinion. The Ninth Circuit allowed the federal courts to assume jurisdiction over that claim. Stock West Corp. v. Taylor, 942 F.2d 655 (9th Cir.1991). After the federal court again dismissed the action on remand, the Ninth Circuit affirmed the dismissal pending exhaustion of Stock West's remedies against Taylor in tribal court. Stock West

Corp. v. Taylor, 964 F.2d 912 (9th Cir.1992). Stock West also sued the Secretary of the Interior for failure to approve the contracts, but the Ninth Circuit affirmed the dismissal of that action. Stock West Corp. v. Lujan, 982 F.2d 1389 (9th Cir.1993).

Arbitration awards must also comply with tribal public policy. In Green Tree Servicing, LLC v. Duncan, 7 Am. Tribal Law 633 (Navajo Nation S.Ct. 2008), the court refused to enforce an arbitration agreement in a mobile home contract due to the coercive character of the arbitration requirement. First, the court identified applicable tribal common law principles:

> * * * Fundamental Law principles * * * inform Navajo public policy on arbitration agreements in mobile home contracts. The Navajo maxim of *házhó'ógó* mandates "more than the mere provision of an English form stating certain rights . . . and requires a patient, respectful discussion . . . before a waiver is effective." * * * *Házhó'ógó* requires a meaningful notice and explanation of a right before a waiver of that right is effective. * * * *Házhó'ógó* is not man-made law, but rather a fundamental tenet informing us how we must approach each other as individuals. * * *
>
> Several other principles are relevant. In a recent case, the Court discussed the Navajo concept of *nábináheezlágo be t'áá lahjį algha' deet'ą*, which is, finality is established when all participants agree that all of the concerns or issues have been comprehensively resolved in

> the agreement. * * * It is also said that in the process of "talking things out," or meeting the Navajo common law procedural requirement that everything must be talked over, * * * there is a requirement of *íishjání ádooniíl*, that is, making something clear or obvious. * * * Navajo decision-making is practical and pragmatic, and the result of "talking things out" is a clear plan. * * * When faced with important matters, it is inappropriate to rush to conclusion or to push a decision without explanation and consideration to those involved. *Áádóó na'nile'dii éi dooda*, that is, delicate matters and things of importance must not be approached recklessly, carelessly, or with indifference to consequences. * * * This is *házhó'ógó*. * * * If things are not done *házhó'ógó*, it is said that it is done *t'aa bizaka*.

Id. at 641–42. Applying those principles, the court concluded that the arbitration clause must be interpreted in light with the Diné respect for the home and family:

> An arbitration clause must be set in the manner of *házhó'ógó* (standard of care), so as to make a clause *íishjání ádooniíl* (clear and obvious), therefore it will not be made *t'aa na'nile'dii* (not recklessly, carelessly or with indifference to consequences) resulting in making the arbitration clause *nábináheezlágo be t'áá lahjį algha' deet'ą* (comprehensive agreement). * * *

> Finally, these principles must be applied in the context of the importance of a home in Navajo thought. This Court has noted that a home is not just a dwelling, but a place at the center of Navajo life. * * * Based on this principle, the Court scrutinizes procedures to make sure they protect a home owner's ability to maintain a healthy home and family.

Id. at 642. The court invalidated a clause requiring arbitration to the exclusion of access to the courts where the tribal housing authority could bring suit but the tribe's tenants could not.

Similarly, in Morigeau v. Confederated Salish & Kootenai Tribes, 32 Indian L.Rep. 6071 (Confederated Salish & Kootenai Tribes Ct.App. 2005), the court addressed conflicts in tribal employment law in a suit for wrongful discharge of a tribal government employee. The oldest tribal code required aggrieved employees to utilize an administrative process, followed by limited judicial review. The second ordinance waived immunity for a specific remedy, assuming the employee exhausted all administrative remedies. The final ordinance provided for "binding arbitration" at the conclusion of the administrative process. The tribe insisted that tribal law required such suits to be arbitrated rather than adjudicated in tribal court. The court noted initially several public policy concerns relating to arbitration:

> Arbitration developed as a supposed speedy, low cost alternative to litigation. Originally disfavored by the courts, its acceptance and

> indeed encouragement by the judiciary grew as the courts became increasingly backlogged. However, inevitable abuses developed. Parties of superior bargaining power, such as employers and financial institutions, imposed onerous provisions; including inconvenient locations, arbitrators preselected by the superior party and excessive charges. These provisions could be "agreed to" by accepting employment or making a credit card purchase after receipt of a printed notice with a monthly statement. These schemes are inconsistent with the original idea of arbitration as a voluntary, low cost dispute resolution alternative. Any arbitration scheme other than one entered into by fully informed parties after the particular dispute has arisen should be examined very closely for fairness and compliance with fundamental due-process rights. On the other hand, a governmental body enjoying sovereign immunity might grant an exception to that protection subject to conditions which, in any other context, could be considered unconscionable.

Id. at 6072. The court concluded that employees completing the administrative process who wish to appeal the tribe's decision must first pursue arbitration (with the tribe covering administrative costs, save attorney fees, for the petitioner), and then may seek tribal court review.

Tribal courts routinely assume jurisdiction over contract breach claims where nonmembers have intentionally engaged in commercial relations within

Indian or tribal lands. In Ho-Chunk Nation v. Olsen, 2 Am. Tribal Law 299 (Ho-Chunk Nation Trial Ct.2000), the court assumed jurisdiction over a contract dispute between the tribe and a nonmember. Applying the United States Supreme Court's personal jurisdiction reasoning of International Shoe Co. v. Washington, 326 U.S. 310 (1945) and its progeny, the court noted that the nonmember had fairly and substantially availed themselves of tribal jurisdiction:

> * * * Negotiations for the "Purchase Agreement" took place on tribal trust land, the down payment was received on tribal trust land, and the products were to be delivered to a business located on either tribal trust land or land owned by the tribe in fee. The defendant purposefully engaged in contact with the Ho-Chunk Nation for the purpose of doing business, and it is reasonable and fair for him to be haled into the Ho-Chunk Nation's courts to answer the plaintiff's claims.

Id. at 307 (footnote omitted). See also Fort Peck Housing Authority v. Home Savings & Loan Assn., 16 Indian L.Rep. 6083 (Fort Peck Tribal Ct.1989) (asserting jurisdiction over nonmember lending institution that had contracted to secure the construction of 27 tribal houses); Warren v. Gardner, 1997 Mont. Crow Tribe LEXIS 1, ¶ 19 (Crow Ct.App. 1997) (asserting jurisdiction over an allotment appraisal contract where "performance of the contract necessarily involved physically inspecting the land on the Reservation, and that one of the parties was a Tribal member residing on the Reservation"); Wolf Point Organization v. Investment Centers of America, Inc., 3 Am. Tribal Law 290, 300–01 (Fort Peck Ct.App.2001) (asserting jurisdiction over contract dispute where plaintiff alleged that nonmember defendant had engaged in commercial activity at tribe's casino); Tulalip Tribes of Washington v. Seven Arrows LLC, 24 Indian L.Rep. 6092, 6093 (Tulalip Tribal Ct.1997) (following *International Shoe* in finding personal jurisdiction over tribal contracting partner), appeal dismissed, 25 Indian L.Rep. 6217 (Tulalip Tribal Ct.App.1997). But see Crow Tribal Housing Authority v. Little Horn State Bank, 13 Indian L.Rep. 6029 (Crow Tribal Ct.1986) (rejecting personal jurisdiction over nonmember bank under *International Shoe* and *Montana* where business transactions occurred off-reservation).

Nonmembers may invoke tribal jurisdiction to enforce contracts. In Ducheneaux v. First Federal Savings & Loan Assn. of Rapid City, S.D., 16 Indian L.Rep. 6147 (Cheyenne River Sioux Tribal Ct.App.1989), tribal citizens agreed to allow their nonmember mortgage holder foreclose on their personal property. The court held that the tribal citizens did not possess the authority to grant state law remedies to the nonmember bank, but the bank could invoke tribal laws in a tribal forum to remedy its injury.

As tribal nations develop their economic and governmental capacities, tribal economies likely will develop as well. The probable future of tribal economies includes continued diversification beyond gaming, accelerated growth through technological adoption, and increased leveraging of sovereignty for economic advantage. Despite historical and ongoing challenges, strong tribal governance and renewed self-determination are driving economic growth and creating more resilient communities.

CHAPTER 8

TRIBAL ADMINISTRATION

For the past half century or so of federal support for tribal self-determination, tribal governments have focused or begun to focus on governing. Typically, tribal nations receive Congressional appropriations through negotiated Public Law 638 contracts or self-governance contracts, supplement those funds with tribally generated revenues, and use those funds to administer tribal government programs. Because tribal governments are federal government contractors, they must develop a bureaucratic infrastructure to administer those programs.

The political branches of tribal governments tend to be led by elected officials, but the real governance on the ground is conducted by tribal bureaucrats. Tribal governments have adopted a corporate structure, in many respects similar the very same structures originally theorized by Felix Cohen, John Collier, and others during the New Deal era. At the top of these hierarchical structures are the political leaders of the tribal nations, usually elected officials. Organizationally below the political leadership are the various tribal governmental programs organized like how federal and state agencies operate beneath political leaders. Tribal programs include without limitation housing, health care, law enforcement and public safety, membership and enrollment, social services, family and child welfare, judiciary, prosecutors and public defenders, conservation and environmental services, land use and planning, and so on.

The tribal bureaucracies make discretionary choices and take actions that are occasionally controversial, leading to conflicts. Tribal employment matters arise again and again within virtually every tribal government, for example. Tribes and their officials are occasionally accused of negligence and other tort claims. Lawyers work for and against tribal interests within tribal jurisdictions.

A. TRIBAL SELF-GOVERNMENT UNDER FEDERAL SELF-DETERMINATION LAWS

Tribal nations typically govern under a legal infrastructure established in the Indian Self-Determination and Education Assistance Act of 1975, usually referred to as Public Law 638. 25 U.S.C. § 5301 et seq. Prior to Public Law 638, the Bureau of Indian Affairs (BIA), the Indian Health Service (IHS), and the Department of Housing and Urban Development provided services to reservation communities, with the tribal nation offering limited services by comparison, with tribal prerogatives often overridden by federal officials. Federal officials often had little accountability to tribal nations in the services provided. Congress attempted to change that all with Public Law 638 by allowing and enabling tribes to contract with the federal agencies to manage those programs themselves, though the effort took many years to reach fruition.

Under a self-determination contract or compact, often called a 638 contract, tribal nations can select from the list of federal services provided to a reservation community by a federal agency and offer to take over those functions. The federal agency must accept the tribe's offer, except in limited circumstances. The feds and the tribes will negotiate about aspects of this contract, but Congress intended tribes to have the upper hand in those negotiations. Relatedly, Congress also authorized qualifying tribes to manage all the programs provided to the tribe by an agency. These tribes are often called self-governance tribes. The agencies that do the most contracting with tribal nations are the Bureau of Indian Affairs and the Indian Health Service, but Congress can authorize other agencies to do the same as well. Tribes can choose to contract for a portion of a service or an entire federal program. Once contracted, the tribal nation has the autonomy to manage the program, make decisions, and implement services in a way that best serves their community.

In addition to chronically underfunding tribal programs, Congress and the Department of the Interior have played games with contract support costs. In most funding situations, a funded entity, like a tribal nation, must spend the appropriated funds on the actual provision of services. Tribal nations taking over from the BIA and the IHS had little in the way of infrastructure—buildings, supplies, employees, and so on—meaning that the contract funds could not be spent until the tribe had developed that infrastructure. Normally, the funding entity would supply contract support costs on top of the program funds. For decades, the federal government underfunded or denied outright contract support to tribes. In a series of United States Supreme Court cases, tribes and the federal government have fought over contract support costs. For the most part, tribal nations have prevailed. In Cherokee Nation v. Oklahoma v. Leavitt, 543 U.S. 631 (2005), the United States Supreme Court rejected the IHS's claims that support costs could not be paid because Congress did not appropriate enough funds. In Salazar v. Ramah Navajo Chapter, 567 U.S. 182 (2012), the Supreme Court again rejected the federal government's efforts to avoid paying contract support by allowing tribes to win money damages under the Contract Disputes Act. 41 U.S.C. § 601 et seq.

1. PUBLIC DOCUMENTS LAWS

Tribal nations are not subject to state or federal public documents laws such as the federal Freedom of Information Act. However, tribal nations may adopt their own laws. In Shananaquet v. Gasco-Bentley, 2022 MI Odawa Tribal LEXIS 1 (Little Traverse Bay Bands of Odawa Indians Tribal Ct.2022), the Little Traverse Bay Bands of Odawa Indians tribal court rejected a request by a tribal citizen to release the names of persons who received tribal funding from the COVID-19 Emergency Homeowner Assistance Program. Under the tribe's Public Documents Act, all tribal government documents are available to tribal citizens unless specifically exempted by the statute. The relevant exemptions from the tribe's code provide, "Documents that contain specific personal information affecting an individual's privacy are exempt from disclosure. This exemption would include employment personnel files, social security numbers, medical records and similar records that constitute a clearly unwarranted invasion of an individual's privacy." Waganakising Code § 6.1906(A). The court first concluded that the release of the names "meets the threshold of a substantial privacy interest." *Shananaquet*, 2022 MI Odawa Tribal LEXIS 1, at *19. The court concluded that the petitioner could not show an interest in disclosure that overrode the interest in personal privacy that the tribal statute protected.

2. FEDERAL TORT CLAIMS ACT

Tribal employees acting in accordance with a tribal self-determination or tribal self-governance contract are covered by the Federal Tort Claims Act. Stago v. Wide Ruins Community School, Inc., 4 Am. Tribal Law 614, 617 (Navajo Nation S.Ct.2002); 25 C.F.R. § 900.180 et seq. (addressing Federal Tort Claims Act coverage of tribal self-determination contracts); cf. 25 U.S.C. § 5321(c)(1) ("Beginning in 1990, the Secretary shall be responsible for obtaining or providing liability insurance or equivalent coverage, on the most cost-effective basis, for Indian tribes, tribal organizations, and tribal contractors carrying out contracts, grant agreements and cooperative agreements pursuant to this chapter. In obtaining or providing such coverage, the Secretary shall take into consideration the extent to which liability under such contracts or agreements are covered by the Federal Tort Claims Act."). FTCA's coverage includes permanent employees, temporary employees, and individuals providing services without compensation, provided they are acting within the scope of their employment and the scope of the agreement. Federal employees assigned to the tribe and certain contractors are also covered under these agreements. In the event tribal officials are sued under the FTCA, the United States Department of Justice will defend them if these conditions are met. There is occasionally litigation between tribal nations and the federal government over whether the FTCA covers the tribal officials. Most federal courts have concluded that, under the FTCA, the law of the state in which claim arose governs, not the law of the tribal nation where the claim actually occurred.

The FTCA does not necessarily preempt suits against the tribe or tribal officials in tribal court, however. In Welch v. Eastern Band of Cherokee Indians, 6 Cher.Rep. 20, 2007 WL 7079613 (Cherokee Court of the Eastern Band of Cherokee Indians July 16, 2007), the Cherokee Court for the Eastern Band of Cherokee Indians held that a former police officer could sue the tribe under a waiver of tribal immunity under the Indian Civil Rights Act. The tribe had argued that the FTCA was the exclusive forum in which to sue. See also Rusk v. Fallon Paiute-Shoshone Tribes, 1998 WL 35297248 (Nev. Inter-Tribal Ct.App.1998) (holding FTCA did not abrogate tribal subject matter jurisdiction over suit against tribal police). Similarly, in Stago v. Wide Ruins Community School, Inc., 4 Am. Tribal Law 614 (Navajo Nation S.Ct.2002), the Navajo Nation Supreme Court held that FTCA also does not preempt employment applicants from suing under the Navajo Preference in Employment Act. 15 Navajo Nation Code § 604. Other tribal courts, however, have reached the conclusion that employees covered by the FTCA cannot be sued in tribal court. E.g., Palmer v. Millard, 23 Indian L.Rep. 6094 (Colville Tribal Ct.App.1996); Green v. Oneida Health Center, 1999 WL 35009251 ([Wis.] Oneida Trial Ct.1999). Still other tribal courts have concluded that any tribal court tort action should be stayed pending resolution of an FTCA claim in federal court on the same issues. E.g., Carmona v. Acoma Pueblo Tribal Court, 25 Indian L.Rep. 6123 (Acoma Pueblo App.Ct. 1998).

3. TRIBAL ETHICS RULES

Tribal governments, like all sovereign governments, rely on the faith and confidence of their members and the broader community. Ethics codes help to promote high moral and ethical standards among officials, ensuring they act in the best interests of the tribe and not for personal gain. Ethics rules are an exercise of a tribe's right to govern itself and its people, demonstrating a commitment to self-determination. By establishing their own standards, tribes can assert their authority and protect themselves from external interference. Rules define standards of conduct to prevent officials from using their positions for private financial or other benefit, safeguarding the government process from nepotism and abuse. They require officials to avoid business activities or offers that could appear unethical or illegal. E.g., Navajo Nation v. MacDonald, 17 Indian

L.Rep. 6014 (Navajo Nation Window Rock. Dist.Ct. 1989) (affirming tribal council decision to place tribal chair and vice-chair on administrative leave based on credible reports of financial misconduct and self-dealing). Cf. Brandon v. Tribal Council, 18 Indian L.Rep. 6139 (Confederated Tribes of the Grand Ronde Community Tribal Ct.1991) (affirming tribal council decision to place tribal official on leave based on vulgar statements made by petitioner).

Not all tribal governments enact ethics rules, however. Michigan tribal judge Michael Petoskey called upon the tribal council to enact formal ethics rules after a tribal councilor was removed in the absence of such rules. E.g., In re McSauby, 1997 WL 34691849, at *5 (Grand Traverse Band of Ottawa and Chippewa Indians Tribal Judiciary 1997) ("The tribal community has every right to expect that tribal officials and employees will avoid conflicts-of-interest. Tribal members have a right to loyal service and fulfillment of confidence placed in officials and employees. Tribal officials have a fiduciary responsibility to tribal membership. Good government will require that even the appearance of a conflict-of-interest be avoided. In that regard, the Tribal Council is urged to seriously consider the adoption of a code of ethics for tribal official and employee conduct to provide additional guidance beyond that offered in this Opinion."). Another court simply ordered tribal council members to return bonus or merit pay funds they awarded themselves from federal indirect costs. Bordeaux v. Wilkinson, 21 Indian L.Rep. 6133 (Three Affiliated Tribes of the Fort Berthold Reservation Tribal Ct.1994).

Tribal council members, elected officials, are subject to tribal ethics rules. Because elected officials occupy a special space in tribal government, tribal nations must choose which persons or entities can enforce those rules. Tribal constitutional or statutory law should make this clear. For example, see In re Leno, 2 Am. Tribal Law 89 (Confederated Tribes of the Grand Ronde Community Tribal Ct.2000), where the tribal council served as the enforcement tribunal. There, a tribal citizen filed a complaint with the council about one of its members, alleging that the council member had attempted to intimidate or coerce the tribe's finance officers into making favorable decisions for his spouse. The council sanctioned the council member, suspending him for two months. The ethics statute stated that once the council issued a sanction, the tribal court possessed jurisdiction to hear appeals, but under the deferential abuse of discretion standard. The court affirmed the standard. The sanctioned council member argued that the structure violated his due process rights, given that the tribunal consisted of other elected officials with whom he would compete against in election campaigns. The court rejected that claim, pointing to the unique status of tribal governments and the limited role to be played by the judiciary:

> The Grand Ronde Community has a nine member Tribal Council with a bloc of seats open in each election cycle, whereby candidates compete with each other for a number of available seats but not directly one-on-one for any particular seat. * * * It is conceivable that

> conflicts could exist which would command the recusal of a Council Member from considering the sanctioning of a co-Council Member. Based on the record, however, this is not such a case. In this case, there is an insufficient showing of a due process violation. To hold that a due process violation results simply because two Council members are standing for reelection—where one candidate is the subject of an ethics complaint and the other candidate is one of the Council members reviewing that complaint—would interfere unnecessarily with the Tribe's ability to govern itself and to structure the form of its own government. The Court is not convinced that such an intrusion on the Tribe's self-governance is either wise or warranted.

Id. at 99–100. See also Kinslow v. Business Committee, 15 Indian L.Rep. 6007, 6009 (Citizen Band Potawatomi S.Ct.1988) ("It is difficult to imagine that the framers did not anticipate a circumstance where a member of an elective body is accused of misconduct wherein another member or members of that body is a victim or witness to that misconduct. In effect, appellant urges that we adopt a constitutional rule which would silence members of the business committee who may be aware of misconduct in office by other members of that committee.").

Conversely, some tribes place the role of ethics enforcement with the tribal judiciary. See In re McSauby, 1997 WL 34691849 (Grand Traverse Band of Ottawa and Chippewa Indians Tribal Judiciary

1997), where the tribal constitution required the council to refer any council member removal proceedings to the tribal court, which would then sit en banc. There, a council member had attempted to use his influence to push the tribe into purchasing land he owned. Initially upon referral, it became clear to the judiciary that the council member had no real awareness of the ethics rules or understanding of the court rules, so the court ordered the appointment of counsel at the tribe's expense. After the referred council member was represented and the case was heard on the merits, the court removed the councilor.

Some tribes do not allow for judicial review of ethics violations decisions involving council members. For example, in Vandever v. Navajo Nation Ethics and Rules Office, 1 Am. Tribal Law 524 (Navajo Nation S.Ct.1998), the court interpreted the Navajo ethics code, which provided, "No sanctions or penalty provided herein shall limit any other powers of the Navajo Nation Council, Navajo Nation Courts, Judicial, Executive or Legislative Branches of the Navajo Nation, nor of any other entity or administrative officials or employees under other applicable law, rules, regulations or procedures." 2 Navajo Nation Code § 3780(c). Because the Navajo courts are courts of limited jurisdiction, the court could not find "explicit" authority to review the decision. *Vandever*, 2 Am. Tribal Law at 526. See also Lewis-Williams v. Colville Confederated Tribes, 15 Am. Tribal Law 253 (Colville Tribal Ct.App.2019) (confirming the council had exclusive jurisdiction over removal of council member).

Tribal employees are also subject to tribal ethics rules. In Barton v. Navajo Nation Ethics and Rules Office, 4 Am. Tribal Law 676 (Navajo Nation S.Ct.2003), the court affirmed the sanction imposed on a tribal employee who had attempted to use "flex-time" to be paid while attending a council meeting, which was barred by the ethics code. Similarly, in Oneida Personnel Commission v. Danforth, 1999 WL 35010342 (Oneida Tribal Judicial System, Trial Ct.1999), the court confirmed the removal from the commission a member of the commission who had spoken out of order at a general council meeting and revealed inside knowledge and information about the commission to the public.

Many tribal nations bar certain officials from serving in more than one branch of government. For example, see In re Oneida Appeals Commission Judicial Code/Judicial Ethics, 2004 WL 5799799 ([Wis.] Oneida Tribal Judicial System, Trial Ct. 2004), where the court held that a tribe judge may not serve as a legislative analyst for the council at the same time.

Tribal judges also must comply with ethics codes, though judicial codes are usually separate from the ethics codes that apply to executive and legislative branch officials. In Anwash v. Enrollment Committee, 12 Am. Tribal Law 113 (Ho-Chunk Nation S.Ct.2014), the court held that a judge need not be recused from an enrollment appeal due to their sixth degree of kindred and shared experience with the National Native American Law Students Association where they only interacted briefly.

B. TRIBAL REGULATORY ENTITIES

Traditionally, tribal public policy decisions were made by consensus. "Tribes generally were guided by consensus oriented leaders who achieved control over members by persuasion and inspiration, rather than preemptory commands." Middlemist v. Member of the Tribal Council, 23 Indian L.Rep. 6141, 6143 (Confederated Salish & Kootenai Tribes Ct.App. 1996) (quoting Cohen's Handbook on Federal Indian Law 230 (1982 ed.)).

Now tribal nations govern through bureaucracy, depending heavily on regulatory entities. Tribal regulatory entities are the various organizations, both tribal and governmental, that create, implement, and enforce regulations concerning tribal governments, businesses, lands, and their populations. These entities, organized under tribal law, also play a regulatory role by establishing internal rules and policies that govern their operations and employees.

Examples of tribal regulatory bodies that are the sources of much litigation include tribal housing authorities or tribal housing departments. A tribal housing authority is an entity established by an Indian tribe to provide housing and related services for its members, often using federal funding from the United States Department of Housing and Urban Development under programs like the Indian Housing Block Grant. See generally In the Matter of the Lawful Successors in Interest to the Rights of Peck, 24 Indian L.Rep. 6197, 6198 (Sitka Tribal Ct.1997) (describing formation of Indian housing authority). These authorities can be departments within the tribe, separate entities with their own boards, or even nonprofit organizations. Their primary goal is to address housing needs such as home repair, new construction, and rental assistance, adapting programs like the Native American Housing Assistance and Self-Determination Act, 25 U.S.C. § 4101, et seq. to their specific communities.

A tribal health clinic is a healthcare facility, often a Federally Qualified Health Center, that is owned and operated by a federally recognized American Indian tribe or tribal organization. These clinics provide comprehensive, culturally sensitive healthcare services to Native American and Alaska Native communities as part of the Indian Health System. The goal of these clinics is to improve the physical, mental, social, and spiritual well-being of their communities, often integrating traditional knowledge and practices into their care models.

Other tribal regulatory bodies administer tribal elections, enrollment, social services, Indian child welfare matters, finance and procurement, land use and zoning, and virtually any other area of government. Cf., e.g., In re Mary Ellis Joe Customary Use Area, 17 Indian L.Rep. 6053, 6055 (Navajo Nation S.Ct.1990) ("[W]e suggest to the lawmaking body a need for an administrative body composed of non-elected officials which can efficiently and quickly decide these types of cases.").

Tribal regulatory bodies often make discretionary decisions involving tribal citizens, nonmembers, and business operations. These decisions often put tribal nations in adversity to their own citizens and other persons or entities under tribal jurisdiction. As such, tribal individual rights protections and the Indian Bill of Rights, 25 U.S.C. § 1302(a), apply to these governmental decisions.

Additionally, tribal courts usually require tribal citizens to exhaust tribal administrative remedies before seeking tribal court relief. Tribal courts have pointed to administrative and judicial efficiency as justifications:

> There are sound policy reasons for this requirement, namely the availability of an inexpensive and more speedy resolution of disputes for the parties, and the preservation of judicial resources where forums already exist to decide the case. The costs of litigation today have risen to the point where other remedies which provide similar relief are more beneficial for all concerned. Therefore, a party should first seek relief in any available tribal administrative or quasi-judicial forum before seeking to invoke the jurisdiction of the tribal court.

Ponca Tribal Election Board v. Snake, 17 Indian L.Rep. 6085, 6091 (Ponca Tribe Ct. of Indian Offenses Ct.App.1988). See also Blaze Construction, Inc. v. Navajo Tax Commission, 1 Am. Tribal Law 463, 467 (Navajo Nation S.Ct.1997). They also pointed to the expertise of subject matter experts in tribal entities to resolve matters of administrative law in the first. *Snake*, 17 Indian L.Rep. at 6092 ("We believe that the tribal forum [election board] clearly has the expertise and authority to resolve these questions, even though complex issues are involved.") "[T]he exhaustion doctrine helps prevent confusion between the courts and the administrative bodies which would arise if a party were able to seek relief in two different forums." *Blaze*, 1 Am. Tribal Law at 467.

Tribal public housing disputes are a leading source of litigation in tribal courts. Tribal housing authorities or departments may act to evict or otherwise punish housing tenants. Procedural protections for individuals are critical. For example, Lawrence v. Southern Puget Sound Housing Authority, 14 Indian L.Rep. 6011 (Suquamish Tribal Ct.1987), the court vacated an intertribal housing authority's termination of a mutual help and occupancy agreement for failure to follow its own grievance procedures. Housing officials declined to inform her of her rights, provide documentation of the housing policy, and failed to grant her a hearing before an impartial tribunal. See also Colville Indian Housing Authority v. Swan, 15 Indian L.Rep. 6031 (Colville Confederated Tribes Tribal Ct.1988) (dismissing housing authority complaint for failure to effectuate service on tenant); Southern Puget Sound Inter-Tribal Housing Authority v. Whittington, 22 Indian L.Rep. 6077 (Nisqually Ct.App.1994) (vacating eviction order for lack of notice to change in tenant agreement prejudicial to tenant); Puyallup Nation Housing Authority v. Miles, 21 Indian L.Rep. 6049 (Puyallup Tribal Ct.App.1991) (overturning eviction order for lack of compliance with housing authority procedures); Rosebud Housing Authority v. Young, 15 Indian L.Rep. 6001

(Rosebud Sioux Tribe Ct.App.1987) (invalidating housing authority complaints to collect unpaid rent exceeding the limitations period for filing and, in the alternative, holding that laches applied to invalidate claims); Tulalip Housing Authority v. Alcombrack, 22 Indian L.Rep. 6119 (Tulalip Ct.App.1994) (noting that housing authority had grounds to terminate tenancy, but did not comply with terms of mutual help and occupancy agreement); Monette v. Schlenvogt, 32 Indian L.Rep. 6074 (Turtle Mountain Band of Chippewa Indians Ct.App.2005) (vacating eviction order for lack of notice, ordering remand, and ordering that a law-trained judge handle the matter going forward).

In Sharp v. Sault Tribe Housing Authority, 2024 Sault Ste. Marie Chippewa App. LEXIS 11 (Sault Ste. Marie Tribe of Chippewa Indians Ct.App.2024), the court affirmed an eviction order where the tenant had time to comply with the lease terms, missed every deadline, but claimed to be in compliance at the time of the appeal. The court concluded:

> The Anishinaabe teachings of *nibwaakaawin* (wisdom-use of good sense), *minadendmowin* (respect—act without harm), as well as *ayaangwaamizi* (careful and cautious consideration) guide this Courts decision-making. Applying such teachings, this Court notes that current compliance is not a mitigating factor to remedy past violations. There is no indication in the record that the Appellee acted outside of the mandates of Tribal law or that the Tribal Court erred in its finding of fact or

> application of Tribal law. While this Court is compassionate to the Appellant's housing situation, this Court cannot modify the requirements in the Appellee's agreement, enlarge timelines for compliance, or excuse the Appellee's failure to act in a timely manner.

Id. at *16–17.

C. TRIBAL GOVERNMENT EMPLOYMENT

Tribal government employment is important because it provides structure, services, and economic opportunities essential for Tribal sovereignty and self-determination. These jobs create opportunities for community members, enable the provision of vital services like healthcare and education, and foster the management of cultural and natural resources, contributing to community well-being and economic stability. Tribal self-determination contracts provide funding that allows tribes to hire their own employees. Tribal nations also utilize enterprise revenue to supplement federal money.

Tribal nations have adopted Indian preference in employment statutes, in line with the federal Indian preference statutes. Some tribes, like the Navajo Nation, have adopted tribal preference in employment statutes, granting enhanced preference to tribal citizens over nonmember Indians. Complicating matters, some lower federal courts have held that federal employment statutes of general applicability apply to tribal employment unless they interfere with tribal treaty rights or self-government.

1. INDIAN PREFERENCE

Since the Indian Reorganization Act of 1934, it has been federal policy to grant preference in employment decisions involving the BIA and (later) the IHS to tribal citizens. 25 U.S.C. §§ 5116, 5117. Tribal nations (who are stepping in the shoes of the federal government) must also do the same under laws they enact. Tribal citizens qualify for the preference, as do nonmember Indians, depending on the tribal statute or policy. Title VII of the federal Civil Rights Act of 1964 excludes tribal employers from the federal law barring race discrimination. 42 U.S.C. § 2000e(b). Indian preference policies were established to combat the historical underemployment, poverty, and discrimination faced by Indigenous Peoples. By guaranteeing preferences for jobs and training on reservations, tribes can ensure that tribal members are the primary beneficiaries of economic opportunities within their own territories.

Indian preference means that employers can freely recruit qualifying Indians to apply for tribal jobs. When Indians do apply and are qualified to perform the job, the tribal employer may then grant them the preference over similarly situated candidates. Tribal employers do not grant preference to unqualified Indian candidates, nor do they usually hire qualifying Indians with significantly lesser qualifications than their non-Indian competitors. At times, tribal nations grant tribal preference, a preference for their own citizens over those of other tribal nations.

Many tribes employ a Tribal Employment Rights Office (TERO) to enforce the Indian preference rules, though many tribes simply rely on the tribal human resources or personnel department to comply with the rule. On one occasion, a tribal court ordered the tribal government's compliance department to investigate an alleged Indian preference violation. Harms v. Oneida MIS Dept., 2005 WL 6409000 ([Wis.] Oneida Tribal Judicial System Ct.App.2005).

Nonmember entities may be required to comply with tribal Indian preference rules as well, usually as a condition of entry into tribal lands. E.g., Office of Navajo Labor Relations ex rel. Jones v. Central Consolidated School District No. 22, 4 Am. Tribal Law 599 (Navajo Nation S.Ct.2002).

2. ADVERSE TRIBAL GOVERNMENTAL EMPLOYMENT ACTIONS

Tribal government employees are civil servants with enhanced protection of their tenure as employees, though these protections are often not as formal as state or federal civil service. Tribal government employment is a vested property interest protected by tribal and federal governmental due process and takings clauses, excepting employees in their initial probationary periods and, typically, non-salaried employees. Tribal governments usually establish procedures for employment separation and discipline in tribal employment ordinances and personnel manuals. Many tribes rely on an administrative board to adjudicate government employee grievances.

Tribal laws usually dictate tribal court deference to the administrative board's decisions akin to how federal courts defer to federal agency determinations under the Administrative Procedures Act. First, tribal courts typically require grieving employees to exhaust any tribal administrative remedies. In Simplot v. Ho-Chunk Nation Dept. of Health, 23 Indian L.Rep. 6235 (Ho-Chunk Nation Trial Ct. 1996), the court explained the reasons for the exhaustion of remedies in a governmental employment context:

> The purpose and policies which underlie the doctrine include permitting the agency to correct its own errors thereby obviating the need for judicial review, taking advantage of the agency's expertise in its area of specialty, permitting the agency to develop a full factual record, and discouraging parties from deliberately bypassing the administrative process and thus undermine the agency's independence. * * * The purpose of the exhaustion rule in the employment context is to force potential litigants to present their case first to an administrative review so that employers/ managers can review disciplinary actions to see if they were properly made. This process also narrows and focuses the issues so that the court is not confronted with trivial or petty issues better left to the employee and employer to resolve. The exhaustion rule serves to protect the prerogatives and rights of the executive branch by letting it settle most disputes in-house, so that the courts are not routinely asked

> to second-guess managerial employment decisions.

Id. at 6239 (citations omitted). Failure to exhaust administrative remedies is grounds for dismissal of a tribal court action. E.g., Kendall v. Brown, 24 Indian L.Rep. 6025 (Mashantucket Pequot Tribal Ct.1995) ("It is well settled that a jurisdictional prerequisite to seeking relief in a court of law is that all available administrative remedies must have been exhausted.") (citation omitted). However, in one unusual case, the court excused full exhaustion of administrative processes where the grieving party was terminated by a supervisor two levels above her, but prevailed before her immediate supervisor. Tree Top v. Lebeau, 38 Indian L.Rep. 6007, 6009 (Cheyenne River Sioux Tribal Ct.App.2011).

A key foundational case articulating the broad scope of procedural protections available to tribal government employees is Hoopa Valley Indian Housing Authority v. Gerstner, 3 NICS App. 250 (Hoopa Valley Tribal Ct.App.1993). There, the Indian housing authority first suspended, then terminated, an employee for violations of the housing authority's procedures. The housing authority set a hearing to allow the terminated employee to challenge the decision, but with few procedural protections and almost no notice. Of note, the housing authority denied the right to counsel for the employee. Also, the same group of people that decided to take the action would serve as the hearing tribunal. The court held that the housing authority's actions violated the procedural rights of the terminated employee. The court held that tribal governmental employees possess a protected property interest (unless they are at-will employees) under the Indian Civil Rights Act, 25 U.S.C. §§ 1302(a)(5), (8). The court concluded that the terminated employee was entitled to adequate notice, an independent tribunal, a favorable burden of proof, the right to confront witnesses and present evidence, subpoena power, the right to counsel, and post-hearing appeal rights. Other courts have reached similar conclusions. E.g., Schwab v. CTEC Construction, 21 Indian L.Rep. 6027 (Confederated Tribes of Colville Reservation Tribal Administrative Ct.1994) (ordering reinstatement of employee with full back pay after employee terminated in violation of notice provisions of employee handbook); Regan v. Finkbonner, 21 Indian L.Rep. 6026 (Nooksack Ct.App.1990) (ordering new administrative hearing in employee grievance due to lack of notice given to employee). Cf. Ames v. Hoopa Valley Tribal Council, 21 Indian L.Rep. 6039 (Hoopa Valley Tribal Ct.App. 1991) (reversing termination of tribal police officer on grounds that he should have known his brother had illegally poached an elk); id. at 6040 (Irvin, J., concurring) ("This jurist would take judicial notice of the fact that news travels fast on the reservation. It is highly likely David Ames knew something about the incident, but exactly what and when is unclear. Even if he had heard a rumor, there was no policy for treatment of rumors in the department.").

Administrative procedures allowing for tribal government employees to challenge adverse actions against them are fraught and complicated. One difficulty involves power disparities in the process.

Tribal employers are usually represented by tribal counsel, whereas employees often are uncounseled. Some tribal governments have attempted to assist grieving employees by barring tribal counsel from these proceedings, but additional complications can arise. In Synowski v. Confederated Tribes of the Grand Ronde Community, 3 Am. Tribal Law 276 (Confederated Tribes of the Grand Ronde Community Tribal Ct.2001), the Confederated Tribes of the Grand Ronde Community trial court found serious due process violations where a tribe barred attorneys from a grievance hearing. The court found that the lack of legal counsel, even just for one party, led to a chaotic grievance hearing:

> * * * The Court has carefully reviewed the record of each of these proceedings, including the transcripts of the three IRB hearings, and the Court finds that, in each instance, the Petitioner was unfairly blind sided by one or more issues that arose at the hearing and of which the Petitioner had no advance notice. The hearings were relatively lengthy, unstructured, and undisciplined. In each hearing, the case against the Petitioner was presented almost in a stream-of-consciousness fashion, with one accusation and criticism followed more-or-less randomly by another. By the conclusion of each hearing, any sense of orderly presentation of the issues was lost amid the myriad of additional claims that had been raised. The Petitioners were not given adequate notice of the plethora of claims that they would have to face at these hearings, and even the IRB panel members

> sometimes appear to have been confused about which issues were before them.

Id. at 281. The appellate court affirmed. Synowski v. Confederated Tribes of the Grand Ronde Community, 4 Am. Tribal Law 122 (Confederated Tribes of the Grand Ronde Community Ct.App.2003). Other tribal courts have also lamented the inequity that can occur when a tribal entity is represented by counsel but the opposing party is not. E.g., Cheyenne River Housing Authority v. Howard, 32 Indian L.Rep. 6165, 6166 n.3 (Cheyenne River Sioux Tribal Ct.App.2005) ("The case unfortunately demonstrates the legal imbalances created by the lack of any statutory right to appointed defense counsel in civil proceedings.").

Occasionally, tribal governments impose mandatory arbitration on employees who wish to grieve an adverse employment decision. E.g., Morigeau v. Confederated Salish & Kootenai Tribes, 32 Indian L.Rep. 6071 (Confederated Salish & Kootenai Tribes of the Flathead Reservation Ct.App. 2005).

Some tribal government employees are considered political appointees under tribal law and their employment rights are limited. In Reising v. Mashantucket Pequot Tribal Nation, 5 Mash. App. 30, 2010 WL 276240 (Mashantucket Pequot Ct.App. 2010), the Mashantucket Pequot appellate court held that a person retained by the tribe as a political appointee could not sue in tribal court for wrongful termination of employment. There, the court actually held that the tribe had never executed a written contract with the purported employee, and thus never created employment rights for them. Many tribal nations also bar elected officials from serving as employees of the tribe in other capacities. In Harrington v. Tribal Council, 2001 WL 36217435 (Little Traverse Bay Bands of Odawa Indians Tribal Ct.2001), the Little Traverse Bay Bands of Odawa Indians tribal court rejected a claim from a sitting council member that the tribe's ban on tribal governmental employment for elected officials was unconstitutional. The court held that the ban was rationally related to the prevention of conflict of interest situations that may arise:

> * * * This policy is rationally directed toward ensuring good government. It seeks to minimize the number of conflict-of-interest situations that would otherwise arise. It is true that many tribal governments do not have such a prohibition, as plaintiff contends. He argues that conflict-of-interest situations are not a problem in those communities. However, the reality is that there are a number of conflict-of-interest situations that arise and work against fair, open government with a separation of functions and systems of "check and balance". One cannot be both employee and employer. The Tribal Council does have a fiduciary responsibility to develop reasonable and prudent employment criteria that best meets to needs and interests of the Tribe. The employment prohibition in question was adopted to meet that fiduciary responsibility. It is a rational condition of employment designed to avoid the conflict-of-

> interest situations that plague many tribal governments.

Id. at *2. The court also rejected the plaintiff's equal protection arguments for similar reasons, holding that an elected official and tribal citizens are not similarly situated for purposes of equal protection rights to employment.

Relatedly, tribal governments possess power to remove members of tribal boards and commissions. Some tribes reject judicial review of the removal of board or commission members. For example, in Blankenship v. Eastern Band of Cherokee Indians, 16 Am. Tribal Law 30 (Eastern Band of Cherokee Indians S.Ct.2019), the court held that the tribal council could remove gaming commissioners without due process. The court's reasoning involved the tribal constitution's establishment of a robust separation of powers between the political and judicial branches of tribal government:

> Under a system of government providing checks and balances between branches, it is a well-settled principle that the courts have no role in decisions about the impeachment or removal of public officers. These decisions are intentionally entrusted to one or both of the political branches, that is, a branch of government that is held directly accountable to the voters at the ballot box. . . . In fact, decisions about impeachment and removal of public officers are the "best example" of a political question because the grounds for

nonjusticiability in these matters are stronger than for any other area . . .

The governmental structure set out in the Charter and in the Cherokee Code reveals the separation of powers considerations that are involved in this case. The [Tribal Gaming Commission, or] TGC is an independent regulatory authority created for the benefit of the [Eastern Band of Cherokee Indians, or] EBCI and accountable to the EBCI. The TGC has the critical role of establishing the licensing requirements and controlling the licensing of persons, management entities and suppliers of gaming goods and services as well as facilities involved with the EBCI gaming business operations. Cher. Code § 16–4.09–§ 4.10. Tribal Council, as the legislative branch of government directly accountable to the tribe, retains the authority to remove TGC commissioners for cause by majority vote. Cher. Code § 16–2.01; see also Charter § 16. Therefore, the removal of a TGC commissioner from office implicates separation of powers issues and requires the judiciary to carefully adhere to the political question doctrine. Additionally, and pursuant to a separate provision in the Cherokee Code, Tribal Council solely holds the power to cancel, limit, revoke, suspend, terminate or modify the gaming licenses of TGC commissioners. Cher. Code § 16–2.03(b).

Id. at 37–38 (citations omitted). After reviewing the relevant tribal codes, the court concluded that the tribal council's authority to remove gaming commissioners was a nonjusticiable political question.

3. TRIBAL EMPLOYMENT REGULATORY BODIES

Tribal nations also regulate reservation employment through tribal regulatory bodies implementing and administering tribal employment laws. In Milligan v. Navajo Tribal Utility Authority, 6 Am. Tribal Law 731 (Navajo Nation S.Ct.2006), the Navajo Nation Supreme Court held that a reservation utility that laid off an employee was subject to the Navajo Nation Labor Commission's jurisdiction. In that case, the defendant claimed that a mere layoff was not an "adverse action" that would not be valid absent "just cause" under the Navajo Preference in Employment Act, 15 Navajo Nation Code § 604. The court concluded that a layoff was an adverse action, but that financial or operational constraints could be just cause for a layoff.

Tribal courts often hold that public school districts must also comply with tribal employment laws, but those holdings are frequently contested in federal court for lack of tribal jurisdiction. In Office of Navajo Labor Relations ex rel. Bailon v. Central Consolidated School District No. 22, 5 Am. Tribal Law 412 (Navajo Nation S.Ct.2004), for example, the Navajo Nation Supreme Court held that the school district must comply with Navajo employment preference laws. The school district had signed a lease in which it expressly agreed to comply with

Navajo employment preference laws. Other tribal courts have relied on inherent tribal sovereignty theory. E.g., Goodwin v. Turon, 21 Indian L.Rep. 6022 (Colville Tribal Ct.1994).

Non-tribal governmental entities are also regulated by tribal laws and regulatory agencies. In Thinn v. Navajo Generating Station, 7 Am. Tribal Law 558 (Navajo Nation S.Ct.2007), the Navajo Nation Supreme Court held that an employee at the utility company remained subject to the Navajo Preference in Employment Law. The original 1969 lease of the land to the utility contained a tribal waiver of authority to regulate the operation of the generating station. However, a separate writing required the utility to comply with Navajo preference in employment laws. The court began its analysis with a reference to the 1868 treaty (the "old law") that expressly provided for the Nation to assert jurisdiction over nonmembers. The court referenced the "Navajo principle that words are sacred and never frivolous, and therefore agreements must be fulfilled." Id. at 562. The court reasoned that Navajo fundamental laws compelled the conclusion that the lease and other writings must be construed to confirm tribal authority because the tribal leadership is not authorized to waive employment laws protective of tribal citizens:

> Just as there are fundamental rights and freedoms of individuals as acknowledged by the Council in the Navajo Bill of Rights, there are fundamental rights of the collective People, the tribal nation, as acknowledged and recognized in

the Fundamental Law statute. See 1 N.N.C. §§ 202(B) (recognizing the "collective rights and freedoms of the *Diyin Nihookáá Diné* as a distinct people"); 204 (identifying several rights of the People) (2005). It is central and foremost that the Council protects the rights of the tribe and its government. The duty to protect the government is essential, for it is through the government that the People exercise their inherent right of self-government, including conducting the business of government with other governments and regulating and approving the use or disposition of the People's communal property the land and its resources. The government in turn must protect all persons within the Nation, through, among other things, regulating the relationship between employers and employees. Through employment, the people, both employees and business owners, provide for themselves and their families, and such employment assists them in living a good life. Because employment is central to living a good life, in that it provides for the well being of the people, the duty and authority to legislate or regulate for the protection of employees and employers cannot be delegated to a non-Navajo entity. The trust placed with the Council to protect employment relationships through laws and regulations cannot be handed over wholesale to a non-Navajo entity; that would be a betrayal of the trust.

Under Fundamental Law, the leaders do not ever lay down this trust and the laws because a leader is taught that they must find the solution, for it is always available. *Naat'áanii ídlį́įgo éí t'áá nantł'a dóó t'áá nahontł'alá, háálá łahgóó t'áá nístł'a dahwiizt'i' ákondi, Diné Bibeehaz'áanii dóó hane' binahjį' baantsáhákeesgo éí choó'į́įł dóó hasih ntsáhákeesígíí beego éí t'áá bik'ee'aan hodeezt'i' dóó ch'ídahwiizt'i', dóó índa bikáá' háadahwiizt'i'. Diyin Dine'é Ts'aa' hadeiidiilaaígíí éí t'áá ákót'éigo yił hadadeiidiilaalá; yah'ahóót'i', ałhééhonit'i' dóó ch'ééhonít'i', doo éí t'óó dádeestł'ǫ́ǫ da. Binahjį' éí t'áá hat'éigi shį́į hanahat'a' bee nistl'ajiyáago, hanahat'a' bee hazhdinoodzíí' dóó ajisiihgoda éí dóó hanahat'a' dóó habeehaz'áanii doo t'óó ni' nizhdooléełda, hatsodizin dóó haáne' éí bee bikáá' haazhdoodááł dóó bee nistł'ahazt'i'ęę bee hózhǫ́ǫgo bik'idiyaa nízhdooleeł dóó bi'ąązh doo gááł.* As explained above, and as demonstrated in the design of the sacred wedding basket, a leader through adherence to the laws, the analysis of the stories of the Diné journey, and a positive approach will find a solution (*bi'ą'iídzá*) around, through, or over that which confronts the people.

Under the circumstances of this case, the Council could not have legally agreed to waive employment regulation, and, per Bailon, could not have legally delegated the power to waive such regulation to the Advisory Committee. . . . Therefore, the delegates could not have understood the waiver of "operation" regulation to surrender their responsibility to protect and

> regulate employment relationships on the Navajo Nation. Thus, there is no unmistakable waiver in the lease, as such waiver is inconsistent with Navajo principles of leadership responsibility to the people.

Id. at 563–64. The court noted a precedent of the Ninth Circuit, Arizona Public Service Co. v. Aspaas, 77 F.3d 1128 (9th Cir.1995), that had held the Navajo Tribal Council had waived its authority to regulate nonmember employment at the generating station. The Navajo court concluded that Navajo fundamental law governed the tribe's authority, not federal appellate precedents, which the court further held cannot override the Navajo court's interpretation of its own law of jurisdiction: "The federal courts may not override this Court's interpretation that under Navajo law there is no valid waiver of the Council's authority to regulate employment within the Nation." *Thinn*, 7 Am. Tribal Law at 566.

4. FEDERAL EMPLOYMENT LAWS OF GENERAL APPLICABILITY

Federal employment laws of general applicability do not apply to the tribal administration of self-government. E.g., Mitchell v. Pequette, 2008 WL 8567012 (Leech Lake Band of Ojibwe Tribal Ct., Trial Div.2008) (holding that federal Fair Labor Standards Act and Portal-to-Portal Act do not apply to tribal public employment). Cf. In re Estate of Jumbo, 17 Indian L.Rep. 6042, 6043 (Navajo Nation S.Ct.1990) (employing a clear statement rule to find the Federal

Employees' Group Life Insurance Act inapplicable to probate proceeds and stating that "the Navajo Tribal Council's policy of exercising full Navajo sovereignty makes us reluctant to apply general federal statutes to the derogation of Navajo sovereignty without clear evidence of Congress' intent").

Tribal courts have occasionally addressed the federal judiciary's *Tuscarora-Coeur d'Alene* line of reasoning. The tribal court for the Little Traverse Bay Bands of Odawa Indians stated that rule as follows:

> * * * A statute of general applicability does not apply to the Indians if: (1) the law touches exclusive rights of self-governance in purely intramural matters; (2) the application of the law to the tribe would abrogate rights guaranteed by Indian treaties; or (3) there is proof by legislative history or some other means that Congress intended [the law] not to apply to Indians on their reservation.

Harrington v. Little Traverse Bay Bands of Odawa Indians, 2007 WL 6930560, at *4 (Little Traverse Bay Bands of Odawa Indians Tribal Ct.2007) (quoting Reich v. Great Lakes Indian Fish and Wildlife Commission, 4 F.3d 490, 499 (7th Cir.1993)). There, the court rejected a claim by a tribal citizen that federal Fair Labor Standards Act should apply to tribal government employment. The court disagreed with the employee, noting that the actual law that applied was the laws adopted by the tribe, not by Congress:

> Plaintiff here appears to be arguing here that the Tribal Court, as a court of general jurisdiction, under its equity powers—that is its power to hear and decide cases where no applicable tribal council statute has been passed, may hear a claim under the Fair Labor Standards Act. This raises the question as to whether the Court should (or whether it has a practice of) hearing claims to generally remedy wrongs in employment matters. In the western system courts will issue non-monetary remedies such as an injunction or specific performance, especially when monetary damages cannot adequately redress the injury. Plaintiff is asking for overtime pay, which would satisfy his alleged wrong. Plaintiff's claim and requested relief are not of a nature typically handled in western courts of equity (courts of general jurisdiction). Plaintiff's claim and requested remedies derive from a statutory scheme—from law, and in this case, the law of a different sovereign. Until the LTBB Tribal Council adopts a similar law, Plaintiff lacks a cognizable quasi-FLSA claim in either law or equity in the LTBB Tribal Court.

Id. The court did not apply the *Tuscarora-Coeur d'Alene* rule, but even if it had, the court likely would have held that the federal statute implicated the tribe's exclusive right of self-governance, especially since the plaintiff was a tribal citizen. Regardless, tribal nations serving Indian country as federal government contractors typically do comply with federal laws as a matter of policy.

Similarly, in MacDonald ex rel. Benally v. Ellison, 2 Am. Tribal Law 180 (Navajo Nation S.Ct.1999), the court rejected a claim that the federal Employee Retirement Income Security Act preempts tribal court jurisdiction over life insurance policy of tribal citizen. The court noted that even if the *Tuscarora-Coeur d'Alene* test applied, the outcome would be the same:

> The present matter deals purely with issues of internal relations and intramural Navajo Nation affairs. The decedent was an enrolled member of the Navajo Nation, and she lived and worked within the Navajo Nation's borders at all relevant times. Further, she procured her life insurance policy while working for a company located within the Navajo Nation. Also, the minor child and Appellee Ellison are enrolled members of the Navajo Nation, and both live within its borders. For these reasons, the dispute over the proper distribution of the insurance proceeds is properly viewed as arising on the Navajo Nation. Moreover, the underlying, substantive aspects of this case deal with marital, family and social relations among Navajo people. Such domestic issues constitute areas where Navajo traditions and principles of self-governance are the strongest.

Id. at 484–85.

In other contexts, federal forums have held that federal statutes of general applicability that interfere with tribal treaty rights also do not apply. In Scalia v. Red Lake Nation Fisheries, Inc., 982 F.3d 533 (8th

Cir.2020), the Eighth Circuit held that the federal Occupational Safety and Health Act regulations did not apply to a tribal fishery business organized under tribal law to exercise fishing rights.

5. EMPLOYMENT DISCRIMINATION

Tribal governments prohibit employment discrimination to fulfill inherent sovereign responsibilities, address historical disenfranchisement, and promote self-governance and economic stability within their communities. They enact their own anti-discrimination laws, similar to the goals of the federal government's Equal Employment Opportunity Commission, to reduce turnover, improve morale, and ensure a fair marketplace for tribal members by providing remedies for discrimination not necessarily covered by federal law. Observers occasionally assert that since tribal employers are excluded from the definition of employer in Title VII of the Civil Rights Act of 1964, 42 U.S.C. § 2000e(b), tribal governments may freely engage in race and sex discrimination. In fact, tribal nations have enacted their own laws prohibiting race and sex discrimination, often enforced by Tribal Employment Rights Offices. Moreover, the Indian Civil Rights Act also guarantees equal protection of the laws. 25 U.S.C. § 1302(a)(8).

Examples of tribal court decisions finding employment discrimination or otherwise allowing suits to survive motions to dismiss include without limitation Brooks v. Cherokee Nation, 5 Okla.Trib.

178, 1996 WL 1132752, at *2–3 (Cherokee Nation Judicial Appeals Trib.1996) (affirming termination of employee for sexual harassment); Mashantucket Pequot Tribal Nation v. Couillard, 2025 WL 1407951, at *8 (Mashantucket Pequot Tribal Ct.2025) ("That it may have been the culture of the firehouse to handle issues of harassment internally does not change the fact that the policy Appellee, as fire captain, was bound to uphold made it mandatory that he report any conduct he was aware of that may constitute harassment. Based on Appellee's own testimony, he failed to report conduct he was aware of that certainly may be, and very likely amounted to, harassment. Such admitted failure to report is substantial evidence that Appellee was aware of conduct which may constitute harassment and failed to report the conduct to Human Resources/Employee Relations. Accordingly, the only conclusion that could be drawn from a reasonable basis considering the evidence credited here by the Board is that Couillard violated the Harassment Policy.") (quotation marks omitted); McKay v. Oneida Bingo and Casino Cage/ Vault Supervisor, 2002 WL 34527413, at *3 ([Wis.] Oneida Tribal Judicial System, App.Ct.2002) (finding tribal human resources department failed to investigate sexual harassment complaints, justifying reversal of the decision of the Oneida Personnel Commission's decision to terminate complaining employee).

In one unusual case, a tribal government employee was terminated for engaging in conduct "seriously prejudicial" to the best interests of the tribal government. In Moon v. Hoopa Valley Tribe, 18 NICS

1 (Hoopa Valley Tribal Ct.App.2020), the court held that the tribe was justified in terminating the employment of a male employee who had engaged in arguably threatening and sexist communications with his female supervisor.

Tribal courts may also assume jurisdiction over employment discrimination suits involving non-tribal businesses. In Burnett v. Pioneer Chevrolet, Inc., 27 Indian L.Rep. 6100 (Confederated Salish & Kootenai Tribes Ct.App.2000), the court assumed jurisdiction over an age discrimination suit against a private employer. The employee initially attempted to utilize the Montana Human Rights Commission to initiate a claim, which issued a right to sue letter. The state court previously dismissed the plaintiff's suit because the business was licensed by the tribe and located on the reservation.

Because tribal courts usually follow federal and state law in assessing employment discrimination cases, the burden on the employee to show discrimination or harassment is high. For example, in Hoopa Forest Industries v. Jordan, 25 Indian L.Rep. 6159, 6160 (Hoopa Valley Tribal Ct.1998), the court echoed non-tribal courts in rejecting a sexual harassment claim based on one incident: "[O]ne incident, no matter how distasteful, does not support the conclusion that harassment is pervasive or the workplace hostile. There must be substantial proof of ongoing sexual harassment directed toward the individual that unreasonably interferes with the individual's work."

Some tribal courts reject the theory of respondeat superior in sexual harassment cases. In Schock v. Mashantucket Pequot Gaming Enterprise, 3 Mash.Rep. 129, 1999 WL 34828705 (Mashantucket Pequot Tribal Ct.1999), the court followed Connecticut law and held that the tribal enterprise employer was not liable for an act of sexual harassment by one employee against another because sexual harassment, by definition, was an act outside the scope of the employee's duties equivalent to an abandonment of the employee's duties.

Tribal nations have only been the primary governance engines in Indian country for a few decades. They are seeking to enhance self-determination, driven by technological adoption and advancements in data sovereignty, even while facing challenges from shifting federal policies. Tribal nations are leveraging new technologies to enhance efficiency and governance, but must also contend with significant resource disparities and political uncertainty.

Recent rescissions of executive orders related to tribal sovereignty and self-governance have created uncertainty. These actions raise concerns about the erosion of tribal authority and self-determination. Tribes continue to face systemic barriers to federal assistance due to capacity limitations, financial requirements, and bureaucratic red tape. A lack of funding or delays in federal disbursements disproportionately affects smaller tribes and those in remote areas.

Overall, the trajectory for tribal governmental administration is towards greater self-reliance, leveraging technology to build stronger virtual and administrative infrastructures while navigating persistent funding barriers and a complex, and at times contradictory, federal policy landscape.

CHAPTER 9

SOVEREIGN IMMUNITY

Tribal sovereignty is the reason why Indigenous Peoples and federally acknowledged tribal nations exercise self-government, why they can protect their lands, resources, cultures, languages, and religions, and why they engage in economic activity. But sovereignty for some is a double-edged sword, sometimes cutting against the governmental accountability that Indigenous Peoples expect of their leaders. The culture-based governance of ages past was non-hierarchical, with every person possessing equal political power. Leadership was temporary and came only from necessity and skill rather than the monopoly on violence depended upon by governments modeled by western political theories. Sovereignty assumes an all-powerful governmental body at the top of the legal and political hierarchy that cannot be second-guessed.

A. PHILOSOPHICAL AND POLICY BASES OF TRIBAL SOVEREIGN IMMUNITY

Sovereign immunity is a European legal theory deriving from the absolute power of secular and religious political leaders, people like kings, emperors, and popes. As several tribal judges have pointed out, tribal sovereign immunity is related to the English maxim, "The king can do no wrong." Deckrow v. Little Traverse Bay Bands of Odawa Indians, 1999 WL 35000425, at *2 (Little Traverse Bay Bands of Odawa Indians Tribal Ct.1999);

Jenkins v. Mashantucket Pequot Gaming Enterprise, 1 Mash.Rep. 9, 1993 WL 13609561, at *2 (Mashantucket Pequot Tribal Ct.1993); Bear Don't Walk v. Confederated Salish and Kootenai Tribal Council, 5 Am. Tribal Law 44, 46 (Confederated Salish and Kootenai Tribes Ct.App.2004). Under English legal theory, every leader is the nation and every act by the leader is law, hence no nation or leader can be sued because they cannot be in violation of the law, by definition.

Tribal nations have internalized this theory and asserted the doctrine of sovereign immunity. As the Navajo Nation Supreme Court explained, sovereign immunity is an unassailable inherent power of tribal nations:

> The right of the Navajo Nation to assert a defense of sovereign immunity whenever it is sued is beyond question. The Navajo Nation retains all those attributes of sovereignty which has not been taken away by Congress or ceded by treaties between the Navajo Nation and the United States. The power to raise a defense of sovereign immunity, and to waive the doctrine of sovereign immunity, is still within the inherent sovereign powers of the Navajo Nation. The Navajo Tribal Council exercised this power in 1966, when in the course of enacting laws pertaining to housing projects, it expressed the Navajo Nation's right "to assert the defense of sovereign immunity in any lawsuit against the Navajo Tribe." 6 [Navajo Nation Code] § 616(b)(1) (1978).

Johnson v. Navajo Nation, 14 Indian L.Rep. 6037, 6038 (Navajo Nation S.Ct.1987). Key reasons for tribal courts to respect tribal political decisions on sovereign immunity is to prevent tribal judiciaries from asserting their own policy preferences on whether and how to expose the tribal treasury to tort, contract, and property claims:

> The Navajo people are entitled to a representative and accountable Navajo tribal government. For this reason, important decisions having direct consequences on the Navajo tribal treasury should be made by the elected representatives of the Navajo people. If we hold that the [Indian Civil Rights Act] has waived the sovereign immunity of the Navajo Nation in Navajo courts, we will be sanctioning an attack on the tribal treasury. Such decisions are best made by elected Navajo representatives after consultation with their constituents.

Johnson, 14 Indian L.Rep. at 6040. See also Jones v. Chitimacha Tribal of Louisiana, 23 Indian L.Rep. 6225, 6226 (Chitimacha Indian Tribal Ct.App.1996) ("It is axiomatic to say that governments have to function for the benefit of the people, and hence there would be a disruption in government if people could indiscriminately file suits over any actions taken by government and/or related enterprises."); WD at the Canyon, LLC v. Hwal'Bay Ba: J Enterprises, Inc., No. 2015-AP-004, slip op. at 5 (Hualapai Nation Ct.App. 2016) ("If anything, tribal governments have greater need for sovereign immunity than federal, state, or local governments, because tribal governments have less capacity to raise tax revenues and are at an earlier stage of economic development. Large monetary judgments and even the costs of litigation could overwhelm tribal treasuries. Further, to the extent sovereign immunity promotes governmental dignity interests and respect for sovereign status, tribes need it to combat the many threats to that status, historic and contemporary, from federal and state courts and legislatures.").

Even so, legions of tribal judges have criticized the consequences of the imposition of the doctrine of tribal sovereign immunity, especially in domestic and political disputes. It is well established that tribal sovereign immunity protects tribal coffers that are far from running over, but in many cases it appears that sovereign immunity simply prevents tribal citizens from seeking accountability from their leaders in tribal justice systems. See O'Brien v. Fort Mohave Tribal Court, 11 Indian L.Rep. 6001, 6002 (Fort Mohave Tribal Ct.1983) (rejecting absolute immunity for tribe and tribal officials, labeling the doctrine of sovereign immunity as a "dinosaur of injustice"). Cf. Clement v. LeCompte, 22 Indian L.Rep. 6111, 6117 (Cheyenne River Sioux Tribal Ct. App.1994) (asserting that "cultural fidelity to Lakota principles of equity and fairness" demand waivers of tribal immunity to allow for individuals to seek relief in tribal court); Dick v. Colville Confederated Tribes, 17 Am. Tribal Law 9, 12 (Colville Tribal Ct.App.2022) ("This court is not blind to the unfortunate position to which the Appellants are left by our decision. As Judge Aycock identified in his first ruling in this matter, the Appellants were wronged by the Tribes' actions, and they deserve a remedy."); WD at the Canyon, LLC v. Hwal'Bay Ba: J Enterprises, Inc., No. 2015-AP-004, slip op. at 31 (Hualapai Nation Ct.App. 2016) (Clinton, J., concurring and dissenting) ("The fatal flaw in [tribal immunity] can be demonstrated by applying * * * a truly, and admittedly, extreme hypothetical. Assuming a cash strapped Hualapai Tribe Council needed to replace an aging fleet of police cruisers for law enforcement personnel, under the view articulated by the majority in this decision, the Tribal Council could simply conscript all late model vehicles owned by Tribal members on the reservation or, even, perhaps all vehicles owned by one politically-disfavored extended family and use them for law enforcement, displacing at least the use by, and perhaps the ownership of, the tribal members."); Rave v. Reynolds, 23 Indian L.Rep. 6150, 6158 (Winnebago S.Ct.1996) ("In small, close-knit tribal communities, like the Winnebago Tribe of Nebraska, denying an opportunity to air and heal grievances in a neutral forum otherwise possessed of jurisdiction, such as the tribal courts, could have disruptive effects by sowing dissension, hostility and distrust that otherwise could be ameliorated by airing and resolving the dispute."). Skeptical of immunity, some tribal courts are more likely to interpret silence in a tribal constitution on the question of sovereign immunity in favor of tribal citizens suing the tribal government. E.g., Butler v. Siletz Tribal Council, 16 Indian L.Rep. 6044, 6045 (Confederated Tribes of Siletz Indians Tribal Ct. 1989) ("A careful analysis of the Siletz Constitution and ratification indicates that the power of this court under art. IV is sufficiently broad to raise considerable question of whether tribal members, when they ratified this constitution, ever intended to grant such immunity to the tribe from suits brought by tribal members in tribal court.").

In Hoffman v. Board of Directors, 2022 Sault Ste. Marie Chippewa App. LEXIS 5 (Sault Ste. Marie Tribe of Chippewa Indians Ct.App.2022), the court held that, although the tribal citizen suing the government claimed that tribal government actions created "unfairness under certain western principles of justice," id. at *18, tribal immunity controlled the day. Still, the court reviewed traditional Anishinaabe notions of tribal justice and found them inconsistent with tribal immunity:

> In the Anishinaabe's traditional governance structure, tribal customs and usages, both past and evolving, a healing approach was used to resolve tribal disputes. We are advised by our Elders that our Sault Tribe traditions encouraged participatory and consensual resolution of disputes, maximizing the opportunity for airing grievances (i.e., hearing), participation, and resolution in the interests of healing the participants and preventing friction within the tribal community. This Court is further advised that ceremonies provided context to *Anishinaabe-inaakonigewin* (Anishinaabe law) pursuant to the principle of *mno-bimaadiziwin*, as achieved through the implementation of the seven grandfather teachings, by infusing the governance process

> with life energy and spirit. This principle is evident in the concept *zagaswe'idiwin*—defined by our Anishinaabemoen as council or a council meeting. Through ceremony, participants were establishing a reciprocal spiritual relationship, as this relationship transcended the physical realm and became recognized within the spiritual realm. Thus, the reason many tribal councils start their meetings with smudging, prayer and the drum. To that end, traditional practices advise that all governance decisions that were made during ceremony are considered sacred and binding.

Id. at *19–20 (footnotes omitted). Despite its misgivings, the court noted that tribal common law still favored deference to tribal leadership:

> Here, it seems current elected tribal leadership made a decision they believed to be correct for the Tribe creating a new path for the future—one in which the tribal membership choose their chairperson without question. Just as our Anishinaabe teachings of *nibwaakaawin* (wisdom-use of good sense), *zaagi'idiwin* (practice absolute kindness), *minadendmowin* (respect—act without harm) as well as *ayaangwaamizi* (careful and cautious consideration) must guide this Court's decisionmaking, this Court posits that these teachings guide all decision-making. When that happens, this Court must trust that the right decision will be made for the community as a whole. In accordance, with traditional practices

> of governance (described above), and the current structure of the Tribe's government, in this instance, the decision of the Board of Directors is final.

Id. at 20–21. See also Rave v. Reynolds, 23 Indian L.Rep. 6150, 6161 (Winnebago S.Ct.1996) (asserting that tribal sovereign immunity has "no parallels in traditional Indian life where most positions of leadership were the result of earned respect or lineage and leaders ruled by example, wisdom, and respect, rather than coercion.").

Modern tribal governments and tribal laws are heavily influenced by and modeled after federal and state governments and laws. Federal and state sovereign immunity is an incredibly robust body of judge-made law that has little or no basis in the United States Constitution (the Eleventh Amendment includes the only reference to sovereign immunity). And because the judiciary accepts that every sovereign entity has a claim to sovereign immunity, including foreign nations, tribal nations do as well. The United States Supreme Court acknowledged the lack of federal court jurisdiction over money damages claims against tribal nations and tribal leaders as early as 1850. Parks v. Ross, 52 U.S. 362 (1850). Congress likely could do away with tribal sovereign immunity, at least in federal and state courts, if it so wished to exercise its Indian affairs powers, but it has not done so on a wide basis.

In Santa Clara Pueblo v. Martinez, 436 U.S. 49 (1978), the United States Supreme Court roundly confirmed tribal sovereign immunity in federal courts in its interpretation of the Indian Civil Rights Act of 1968. The Court concluded that Congress did not abrogate tribal immunity in federal courts (and presumably state courts) to allow suits to enforce the Indian Bill of Rights, 25 U.S.C. § 1302(a). In the same case, the Court concluded that individual tribal leaders and officials are not immune from suit, meaning they can be sued in their individual capacity for ongoing violations of federal law for prospective, injunctive relief. However, the Court further concluded that Congress did not intend to open up the federal courthouses to suits to enforce the Indian Bill of Rights. While there are many other federal court cases assessing tribal immunity from suit, *Martinez* and its interpretation of the Indian Civil Rights Act is by far the most important, given its relationship to individual rights in tribal communities.

As a matter of positive law (written law enacted by tribal legislators or the People in statutes and constitutions), tribal sovereign immunity appears in print more than it does under federal constitutional law, but still only intermittently. Even in the absence of positive tribal law on immunity, most tribal courts will find that it exists as a matter of tribal common law. E.g., McLean v. Office of Director of Regulation, 5 Am. Tribal Law 273, 275 (Mohegan Gaming Disputes Ct.App.2004) (recognizing "common-law immunity from suit traditionally enjoyed by sovereign powers") (quoting Santa Clara Pueblo v. Martinez, 436 U.S. 49, 58 (1978)).

B. TRIBAL GOVERNMENTAL IMMUNITY

Tribal courts interpret tribal sovereign immunity based on each tribe's specific laws, ordinances, and governing documents, as tribal courts are empowered to adopt, reject, or waive the doctrine. While federal law prohibits tribes from being sued without congressional authorization or tribal consent in state or federal court, tribal courts apply their own common law and statutes to determine the scope of immunity, including its extension to tribal governmental officials, tribal business entities, and subordinate entities. Tribal immunity bars all suits, including those for money damages and those for injunctive relief.

Generally speaking, tribal courts rely on federal precedents (in the absence of tribal precedents) to determine the scope of tribal immunity. E.g., Argyle v. Gaming Commission, 8 Am. Tribal Law 167, 169 (Grand Traverse Band of Ottawa and Chippewa Indians Tribal Ct.2009) ("It is federal law which provides the parameters for tribal sovereign immunity.").

The United States Supreme Court has acknowledged that tribal nations are immune from suit absent a tribal or Congressional waiver of immunity in commercial activities. In Kiowa Tribe v. Manufacturing Technologies, Inc., 523 U.S. 751 (1998), the United States Supreme Court reluctantly affirmed that tribal immunity extends to commercial activities, even those occurring off-reservation. The Court insisted that tribal immunity in such circumstances was bad public policy, but Congress took no action to regulate tribal immunity. In Michigan v. Bay Mills Indian Community, 572 U.S. 782 (2014), the Court again reaffirmed tribal immunity, but narrowly, with a 5–4 decision. The narrowness of that decision and the fact that sovereign immunity is judge-made law was underscored by Justice Scalia's dissent. Scalia had voted in favor of tribal immunity in *Kiowa* but changed his mind for policy reasons. Id. at 814 (Scalia, J., dissenting).

Tribal nations have largely responded to the Supreme Court's policy concerns by enacting limited waivers of tribal immunity addressed below. Other concerns, such as the potential unwillingness of business partners to engage in business activities with tribal nations or the perceived unfairness of engaging in business with an enterprise that can claim immunity from suit are addressed in the open market. No one is forced to do business with tribes. Smart business owners can retain their own counsel for advice on how and whether to proceed with tribal businesses. Cf. Board of Trustees of the Sisseton-Wahpeton Community College v. Wynde, 18 Indian L.Rep. 6033, 6036 (Northern Plains Intertribal Ct.App.1990) (recommending that parties to contracts with tribal entities secure counsel first).

Tribal court decisions dismissing suits against tribal nations on sovereign immunity grounds are legion. Tribal immunity extends to counterclaims as well. E.g., St. Regis Mohawk Tribe v. Basil Cook Enterprises, 23 Indian L.Rep. 6172 (St. Regis Mohawk Tribal Ct.1996).

C. TRIBAL ABSOLUTE IMMUNITY

Tribal courts generally recognize absolute immunity for certain tribal leaders, primarily elected officials, political appointees, tribal judges, and other legal officials, shielding them from the threat of personal liability to ensure they can perform their essential governmental functions without fear of being sued. Absolute immunity provides complete protection from civil lawsuits for government officials when they are acting within their official duties, regardless of bad faith or malicious intent. E.g., Smith d/b/a Frosty's v. Confederated Salish & Kootenai Tribes, 23 Indian L.Rep. 6256, 6257 (Confederated Salish & Kootenai Tribes Ct.App.1996) ("The members of the tribal council enjoy legislative immunity for all actions taken within the scope of their legislative duties. * * * We view the scope of legislative duties with great breadth.") (citations omitted); Gonzales v. Allen, 16 Indian L.Rep. 6048, 6049 (Shoshone-Bannock Tribal Ct.1989) ("Absolute immunity has been provided for legislators while conducting legislative functions, for judges in their judicial functions, for prosecutors, etc."). One tribal court noted that to allow suits against tribal lawmakers or policymakers simply for making law or policy would "very soon lead to the courts substituting for the legislatures." Means v. Oglala Sioux Tribal Council, 11 Indian L.Rep. 6013, 6013 (Oglala Sioux Tribal Ct.1984). This immunity protects officials from liability for actions taken within the scope of their official duties. E.g., Quileute Nation v. Jamie, 15 NICS App. 13 (Quileute Tribal Ct.App.2017) (dismissing criminal charges assessed against tribal council members for actions taken in legislative capacity).

At least one tribal court has noted that the federal doctrine of absolute immunity appears in the Speech and Debate Clause of the United States Constitution, Art. I, § 6, necessitating a separate review for the source of absolute immunity under tribal law. See Cleveland v. Garvin, 8 Am. Tribal Law 21, 32 (Ho-Chunk Nation Trial Ct.2009). The court did not reach the question of whether absolute immunity exists under that tribe's law. In similar case, a tribal court held that the absence of a Speech and Debate Clause in the tribal constitution meant that tribal legislators did not enjoy absolute immunity. See Stone v. Swan, 19 Indian L.Rep. 6093, 6094 (Colville Tribal Ct.1992).

Tribal courts may still consider federal law as persuasive authority in finding absolute immunity. In Mazzetti v. Kolb, No. AP-0001-23 (Rincon Band of Luiseño Indians Ct.App.2024), the court followed the federal court articulation of the absolute immunity doctrine, noting the following factors the court would consider:

(a) [T]he need to assure that the individual can perform his functions without harassment or intimidation;

(b) the presence of safeguards that reduce the need for private damages actions as a means of controlling unconstitutional conduct;

(c) insulation from political influence;

(d) the importance of precedent;

(e) the adversary nature of the process; and

(f) the correctability of error on appeal.

Id., slip op. at 10–11 (citing Cleavinger v. Saxner, 474 U.S. 193, 202 (1985)).

Tribal courts, usually applying some or all of these factors, have recognized absolute immunity for tribal judges, e.g., Martin v. Little River Band of Ottawa Indians, 2010 MI Ottawa Trib. LEXIS 14, at *15–17 (Little River Band of Ottawa Indians Tribal Ct.2010); Sampson v. Bryan, 2003 WL 25856845, at *2 (Nev. Inter-Tribal Ct.App.2003), and tribal council members, e.g., The Legislature v. Flyingman, 11 Okla. Trib. 837, 2009 WL 10271467, at *4 (Cheyenne-Arapaho Tribes S.Ct.2009); Quileute Nation v. Jamie, 2017 Quileute App. LEXIS 2, at 12 (Quileute Tribal Ct.App.2017). Tribal courts have also recognized absolute immunity for other tribal officials, including, for example, tribal historic preservation officers, Drabik v. Mohegan Tribe of Indians of Connecticut, 15 Am. Tribal Law 121, 129 (Mohegan Tribal Trial Ct.2018), tribal enrollment commission officers, *Mazzetti*, slip op. at 11–12; and veterans, Gardner v. Littlejohn, 9 Am. Tribal Law 431, 440–41 (Ho-Chunk Nation Trial Ct.), rev'd, 11 Am. Tribal Law 400, 405 (Ho-Chink Nation S.Ct.2011). Cf. Ho-Chunk Nation v. Bank of America, N.A., 6 Am. Tribal Law 275, 299 (Ho-Chunk Nation Trial Ct.2006) (attorney-client privileged documents).

Federal courts also have recognized absolute immunity for a variety of tribal officials. E.g., Penn v.

United States, 335 F.3d 786, 788–89 (8th Cir.2003) (tribal judge immune, even if exercising judicial power in excess of the court's jurisdiction); Runs After v. United States, 766 F.2d 347, 354–55 (8th Cir.1985) (tribal legislators); Acres v. Marston, 72 Cal.App.5th 417, 441 (2021) (tribal judges, law clerks, and other court staff immune, even where tribal judge acted with a conflict of interest).

Tribal officials found to be acting outside of the scope of their duties, or illegally under tribal law, likely will not enjoy absolute immunity. E.g., Tribal Council Members v. Harrington, 13 Am. Tribal Law 287, 290, 292 (Little Traverse Bay Bands of Odawa Indians Tribal App.Ct.2015). Tribal officials engaged in administrative activities, such as managing employee issues, are not afforded absolute immunity. E.g., Gonzales v. Allen, 16 Indian L.Rep. 6048, 6049 (Shoshone-Bannock Tribal Ct.1989) ("Council members are not, however, entitled to as broad an immunity when conducting non-legislative business or performing administrative functions. * * * Administrative activities by governmental officials, where discretion is appropriately limited, have been accorded a lesser type of immunity.").

D. SUITS AGAINST TRIBAL OFFICIALS FOR PROSPECTIVE, INJUNCTIVE RELIEF

Suits against tribal officials designed to perform an end-around tribal immunity are disfavored by tribal courts. In general, tribal officials are cloaked with tribal immunity as well. In Satiacum v. Sterud,

10 Indian L.Rep. 6013 (Puyallup Tribal Ct.1982), the court explained the interests at stake:

> Tribal officers, who perform all of the acts of the tribal government, must be able to exercise their duties free from intimidation, harassment and the threat of lawsuits resulting from acts performed in the course of their official duties. Against these policy considerations the court weighs the interests of the community, which expects and deserves protection against malicious and unlawful acts.

Id. at 6016. The court then formulated a standard that mirrors official immunity jurisprudence in state and federal courts:

> Accordingly, the following standard is to be applied in this and future litigation against tribal officials. First, the tribe's immunity from suit shall extend only to persons acting in their official capacity at the time the act complained of occurred. Second, the officer must have acted in good faith to enjoy the immunity. Third, an official shall be liable for acts that a reasonable person would know were in excess of his or her lawful authority.

Id. See also Hicks v. Harold, 20 Indian L.Rep. 6091 (Fallon Paiute-Shoshone Tribal Ct.1993) (holding that tribal judge and tribal police were acting in their official capacities and without bad faith).

Under federal law, governmental officials engaged in ongoing unlawful actions may be sued to prevent the continuation of that illegal activity, though they may not be sued for money damages. That theory, often called a legal fiction, derives from Ex parte Young, 209 U.S. 123 (1908), and applies to state officials violating federal law. In Santa Clara Pueblo v. Martinez, 436 U.S. 49 (1978), the United States Supreme Court seemed to extend the *Ex parte Young* theory to tribal officials as well. However, in *Martinez*, the Court added that federal courts may not assume such jurisdiction unless Congress has enacted legislation explicitly authorizing courts to enforce a given federal law, which it had not done in ICRA.

Many tribal nations have enacted laws barring most suits for money damages, but allowing for suits tribal officials (or the tribe itself) for prospective, injunctive relief. E.g., Judy v. White, 5 Am. Tribal Law 418, 433 (Navajo Nation S.Ct.2004) (citing 1 Navajo Nation Code. § 554(G)). Tribal courts also allow suits for prospective, injunctive relief against tribal officials. E.g., Committee for a Clean Government v. Cheyenne River Sioux Tribal Council, 11 Indian L.Rep. 6043, 6043 (Cheyenne River Sioux Tribal Ct.App. 1984); Laban v. Yu Weh Loo Pah Ki Community, 4 Am. Tribal Law 449, 453 (Hopi App.Ct.2003); LaRose v. Wilson, 2003 WL 26066795, at *3 (Leech Lake Band of Ojibwe Tribal Ct., Trial Div.2003) (citing Francis v. Wilkinson, 20 Indian L.Rep. 6015 (Northern Plains Inter-Tribal Ct.App. 1993); and *Martinez*), but pleading such cases is difficult.

If a plaintiff seeks retrospective relief or money damages, tribal courts will dismiss those actions absent a waiver of immunity. E.g., Kirkwood v. Decorah, 6 Am. Tribal Law 188, 202 (Ho-Chunk Nation Trial Ct.2005) (dismissing suit seeking retrospective injunctive relief). In Fox v. Brown, 6 Am. Tribal Law 446 (Mohegan Tribal Trial Ct.2005), the court recognized that tribal immunity protects officials "acting within their representative capacity and within the scope of their official authority." Id. at 448 (quotation omitted). The plaintiff alleged that tribal elected officials had violated tribal law, but sought money damages, forcing dismissal of the suit. In Gallegos v. French, 18 Indian L.Rep. 6151, 6157 (Delaware Tribe of Western Okla. Ct. of Indian Appeals 1991), where the court found that the election board officials had acted beyond the scope of their authority by acting illegally, but where the plaintiffs only sought prospective, injunctive relief, the court allowed the case to proceed.

If a plaintiff seeks an order directing the tribe to hire a job applicant, tribal courts are likely to find that type of remedy beyond the scope of prospective, injunctive relief. In Thomas v. Coquille Indian Tribe, 31 Indian L.Rep. 6083 (Colquille Indian Tribal Ct.2004), the court dismissed a claim demanding that the court order the tribe to hire him as a tribal police officer. The court invoked separation of powers principles in justifying the limits on its judicial powers:

> It is worthwhile to reflect upon the policy interests that are at stake. If upheld, plaintiff's claims would shift ultimate authority for filling positions open to tribal members from

> administrative officials to the court; the court would have the power to subsequently replace a hired employee with a tribal member applicant; and the discretion granted to administrative officials in the Coquille Indian Tribe Personnel Manual would be rendered meaningless. Since "entitlement" is the value underpinning all of plaintiff's claims, it is easy to imagine the court being called upon to adjudicate future claims of multiple tribal members seeking the same or similar relief. The absence of legal authority supporting the court's power to effect change of such major proportions is commensurate with the chaos that would ensue if the court were to follow that path.

Id. at 6087.

One example of viable claim against tribal officials is Tribal Council Members v. Harrington, 13 Am. Tribal Law 287 (Little Traverse Bay Bands of Odawa Indians Tribal App.Ct.2015). There, the tribal chairperson sued the council, asserting that the council had violated the tribal constitution by enacting a budget by motion rather than formal resolution. The appellate court held that if the tribal court determines that the individual council members acted illegally under the constitution, then they acted outside of the scope of their authority. Conversely, in a similar case, the court concluded that a council decision to enact a budget by continuing resolution during the COVID-19 pandemic was valid. Thundercloud v. Ho-Chunk

Nation Executive Branch, 16 Am. Tribal Law 357 (Ho-Chunk Nation S.Ct.2021).

Tribal officials sued for failure to perform mandatory duties may also be sued, typically for a writ of mandamus to compel the official to action. E.g., High Elk v. Iron Hawk, 6 Am. Tribal Law 80 (Cheyenne River Sioux Tribe Ct.App.2006) (ordering tribal secretary to issue a certificate of incorporation as mandated by tribal statute); Combrink v. Allen, 20 Indian L.Rep. 6029 (Tonkawa Tribe Ct. of Indian Appeals 1993) (ordering president of tribe to call a special meeting of the tribal council).

In cases involving a challenge to the constitutionality of a tribal law, some tribal courts have allowed suits to proceed even in what appears to be any absence of an immunity waiver. For example, in Fort Peck Sioux Council v. Fort Peck Tribes, 4 Am. Tribal Law 292 (Fort Peck Ct.App. 2003), the court refused to dismiss a constitutional challenge to the tribe's Comprehensive Code of Justice in the face of another code provision that provided, "The Tribes shall be immune from suit. Nothing in the Code shall be construed as consent of the Tribes to be sued." Fort Peck Tribes Comprehensive Code of Justice (2000) § 110. The court held that justice required that the case continue:

> [W]e come to the critical question before us: Does the defense of sovereign immunity advance its purposes and rationale when invoked against a claim that challenges the constitutionality of a provision in the Comprehensive Code of Justice

(2000)? We think not. We see no benefit flowing from sovereign immunity when it does nothing more than shield an inquiry into whether a provision of existing law passes constitutional muster. Such invocation does nothing more than take a doctrine intended for the people's protection and use it as a weapon of deprivation. Neither our Tribal Council nor this Court can condone such misuse. We are confident that our Tribal Council shares our belief that a government can only be as strong as its will to treat its people righteously.

Fort Peck Sioux Council, 4 Am. Tribal Law at 298–99.

Similarly, in Deckrow v. Little Traverse Bay Bands of Odawa Indians, 1999 WL 35000425 (Little Traverse Bay Bands of Odawa Indians Trial Ct.1999), the court pointed the interim tribal constitution's guarantee of the right to petition for the redress of grievances in finding jurisdiction to hear an election dispute:

ARTICLE VIII of the Tribe's Interim Constitution entitled "Bill of Rights" expressly provides that members have ". . . *the right to petition for action or the redress of grievances* . . ." This is the supreme law of Tribe because the Tribal Constitution is the supreme law. It is the peoples' expression of its delegation of power to the government. The right to petition for action or redress would be rendered meaningless if sovereign immunity is deemed to be a bar. If the provision is meaningless, why the expression of

> a right? Why bother? The expression must have a purpose, otherwise the language would not be included. Thus, the Court construes the cited constitutional provision to be an express waiver of sovereign immunity by the Tribe. Whether the "Bill of Rights" provision of the Interim Tribal Constitution is construed a reservation of the power in the people or a waiver of immunity by those who drafted its provisions is not significant for the purposes of deciding the instant matter. It is still an express waiver. **For all of the foregoing, sovereign immunity is not a bar to this action.**

Id. at *3 (emphases in original). See also Hudson v. Hoh Indian Tribe, 21 Indian L.Rep. 6045, 6046 (Hoh Tribal Ct.App.1992) (holding that "the right to petition for redress of grievances guaranteed to Hoh tribal members in the Constitution of the Hoh Tribe must be read as a limitation upon any sovereign immunity that the Hoh Tribe may possess"); Hockaday v. Karuk Tribal Housing Authority, 32 Indian L.Rep. 6169, 6170 (Karuk Tribal Ct., Civ.Div. 2005) (finding a waiver in the tribal constitution's guarantee of the right to petition for redress of grievances); Miller v. Adams, 10 Indian L.Rep. 6034, 6038 (Northern Plains Intertribal Ct.App.1982) (same, relying on provision in Sisseton-Wahpeton tribal constitution). Cf. Gray v. Hoopa Valley Tribal Election Board, 26 Indian L.Rep. 6138, 6139 (Hoopa Valley Tribal Ct.1999) (finding no sovereign immunity defense for the election board, relying on legal scholarship asserting that tribal immunity only extended to trust lands) (quoting Ralph Johnson,

Sovereign Immunity in Indian Tribal Law, 12 Am. Indian L.Rev. 153 (1987)).

One tribal court worried that the refusal of some tribes to provide an adequate forum to resolve important disputes within the tribal community would encourage tribal judges to seek any avenue for providing relief. See Rave v. Reynolds, 23 Indian L.Rep. 6150, 6162 (Winnebago S.Ct.1996) ("One unfortunate consequence of this approach [focusing on a government official's scope of authority] is that it frequently forces tribal courts to find waivers of sovereign immunity, which ultimately could adversely affect the tribe in unintended ways albeit not in the pending case, merely to adjudicate legitimate claims against misguided tribal officials who seriously harm persons while acting within the scope of their authority.").

E. LIMITED WAIVERS OF TRIBAL IMMUNITY

A limited waiver of tribal sovereign immunity is a specific agreement where a tribal nation voluntarily agrees to be sued in court, but only under strict conditions. These conditions often include restrictions on the type of claims, the amount of monetary damages, the duration of the waiver, or the specific jurisdiction where a lawsuit can be filed. Limited waivers are commonly used in contracts to enable business transactions and allow for dispute resolution while still protecting the tribe's inherent sovereign status. E.g., Jones v. Chitimacha Tribal of Louisiana, 23 Indian L.Rep. 6225, 6226 (Chitimacha

Indian Tribal Ct.App.1996) ("[W]ith the need for increased economic development on reservations, there has to be some remedy and relief to be given in order to encourage people to enter into contracts, agreements and business enterprises with Tribal governments and/or their business entities.").

Again following the colonizer's legal traditions, tribal courts usually interpret ambiguities in constitutional, statutory, and contractual text with an eye toward preserving sovereign immunity. For courts, sovereign immunity is jurisdictional, meaning that a court simply cannot act at all where an immune sovereign is the defendant. Sovereign immunity is a jurisdictional defense. Navajo Housing Authority v. Howard Dana and Associates, 5 Navajo Rep. 157, 160 (Navajo S.Ct.1987). Waivers of sovereign immunity are typically interpreted through the principle of strict construction, which means they are construed in favor of the sovereign, limiting their scope to the exact language of the waiver and not beyond. Courts must look for explicit, unambiguous language from the government to find a waiver of immunity. E.g., Bethel v. Mohegan Tribal Gaming Authority, 2 Am. Tribal Law 373, 379 (Mohegan Gaming Disputes Ct.App.200) ("Statutes in derogation of sovereign immunity must be strictly construed. In order for the sovereign to be sued without its consent, there must be a clear intention by the legislative body through the use of express terms."). Moreover, even when a trial court has denied a tribal sovereign's motion to dismiss on immunity grounds, tribal courts are likely to grant interlocutory review in order to address the immunity issue. But see, e.g., Kalantari v. Spirit Mountain Gaming, Inc., 6 Am. Tribal Law 94 (Confederated Tribes of the Grand Ronde Community Tribal Ct.App.2005) (rejecting interlocutory appeal in non-damages case over dissent).

One tribal court, however, interpreted a limited waiver of immunity broadly, invoking tribal common law. In Wright v. Nottawaseppi Huron Band of the Potawatomi, 2022 Nottawaseppi Huron Band Supreme LEXIS 1 (Nottawaseppi Huron Band of the Potawatomi S.Ct.2022), the tribal constitution allowed tribal court suits against the tribe for prospective injunctive relief under tribal law. Nonmembers brought suit in tribal court seeking enrollment in the tribe. The tribe argued that the limited waiver could only apply to tribal citizens. The court disagreed:

> [T]he concept of *Debwewin* (truth), one of the *Noeg Meshomsenanek Kenomagewenen* (Seven Grandfather Teachings), strongly compels the judiciary to reach the merits. *Debwewin* asks us to seek the truth of the matter, which can be "detected through the beat of the heart and through the voice of the person and how the person speaks." Mark F. Ruml, The Indigenous Knowledge Documentation Project—Morrison Sessions: *Gagige Inaakonige*, The Eternal Natural Laws, 30(2) Religious Studies and Theology 155, 164 (2011). The Tribal Council's invocation of sovereign immunity is a demand to silence the Wright petitioners before they can

> speak on the merits of their claims. Silencing the petitioners prevents us from knowing who they are and, ultimately, prevents us from discovering the truth of this matter. While this court could not and would not override the plain language of the Constitution's authorization to sue the tribe or tribal officials, the plain language does not explicitly forbid this suit.

Id. at *15–16.

1. TRIBAL CONSTITUTIONAL WAIVERS

Tribal constitutions regularly include provisions on sovereign immunity, often addressing its scope and outlining the process for waiving it. However, many tribal nations have either not ratified a constitution or their constitutions do not mention immunity. Many tribal constitutions enacted during the years following the enactment of the Indian Reorganization Act contain no mention of sovereign immunity, although many tribes have amended their constitutions to explicitly reserve immunity.

Tribal constitutional provisions can also allow for limited waivers. For example, the Constitution of the Grand Traverse Band of Ottawa and Chippewa Indians allows tribal citizens to bring suits for prospective, injunctive relief only against the tribe. E.g., Fall v. Grand Traverse Band of Ottawa and Chippewa Indians, 2003 WL 25836853 (Grand Traverse Band of Ottawa and Chippewa Indians Tribal Ct.2003) (dismissing suit brought by nonmember under Article XIII, § 1 of tribal constitution).

In Bordeaux v. Wilkinson, 21 Indian L.Rep. 6131 (Three Affiliated Tribes of the Fort Berthold Reservation Tribal Ct.1993), the court asserted jurisdiction over a claim involving tribal council officers awarding themselves a bonus or merit pay. The court noted that the tribe's constitution waived sovereign immunity for ICRA claims.

2. TRIBAL TORT AND CONTRACT CLAIMS ACTS

Tribal nations regularly enact generally applicable waivers of immunity to ensure accountability for tortious actions and contract breaches by tribal nations and their commercial entities. Tribal tort claims ordinances are largely modeled on similar federal or state government waivers. Tribal ordinances route tort claims into tribal courts, establish specific notice requirements, set limitations periods, and establish damages caps. The enactment of tort claims ordinances often follows pressure from tribal citizens and others impacted by tribal government action.

Tribal tort claims ordinances often set shorter limitations periods than under state law. And because these ordinances are limited waivers of governmental immunity, there usually is no equitable tolling of the limitations period. For example, in Dyer v. Pokagon Gaming Authority, 2015 Pokagon Band App. LEXIS 1 (Pokagon Band of Potawatomi Indians Ct.App.2015), the Pokagon Band of Potawatomi Indians appellate court affirmed the dismissal of a slip-and-fall tort claim against the tribal gaming enterprise. The tribal tort claims ordinance set a 180 day limitations period. The plaintiff sued after the expiration of the limitations period, but argued that the period should be extended via equitable tolling. The court held that the limitations period was jurisdictional in nature and therefore equitable tolling does not run against a tribal sovereign. Even under the laws of the State of Michigan, equitable tolling would not have been allowed in that case.

Tribal tort claims ordinances also govern the types of torts to which tribal governments are accountable. For example, in Sauter v. Spirit Mountain Gaming, Inc., 12 Am. Tribal Law 81 (Confederated Tribes of the Grand Ronde Community Tribal Ct.2013), the court dismissed a claim by a tribal employee who was physically assaulted by their supervisor. The tribal tort claims ordinance explicitly barred suits against the tribe rooted in intentional tort claims. See also Galardi v. Mashantucket Pequot Gaming Enterprise, 24 Indian L.Rep. 6191 (Mashantucket Pequot Tribal Ct., Gaming Enterprise Div.1996) (dismissing portion of complaint seeking loss of consortium, a tort not allowed under the tribal tort claims act); Pazienza v. Mashantucket Pequot Gaming Enterprise, 24 Indian L.Rep. 6129 (Mashantucket Pequot Tribal Court, Gaming Enterprise Div.1996) (allowing claim for loss of privacy but not strict liability under the tribal tort claims act).

Proper notice to the tribal defendant is also critical. In Lesperance v. Sault Ste. Marie Tribe of Chippewa Indians, 2015 Sault Ste. Marie Chippewa

LEXIS 2 (Sault Ste. Marie Tribe of Chippewa Indians Tribal Ct.2015), the tribal court for the Sault Ste. Marie Tribe of Chippewa Indians dismissed a tort claims suit against the tribe. The tribal tort claims ordinance limitations period was 120 days. The ordinance required claimants to describe the claim in detail and serve it on the tribal secretary, an elected position. The plaintiff worked with the tribe and its insurance company but ultimately did not file suit until after the 120 day limitations period. Though the tribe had actual notice of the claim, the notice requirements of the tort claims ordinance were jurisdictional. When they were not met by the plaintiff, the tribal court dismissed the action.

Tribal tort claims ordinances must be clear, lest confusion arise. In Northern Edge Casino v. Window Rock District Court, 14 Am. Tribal Law 157 (Navajo Nation S.Ct.2017), the court inspected the legislative history regarding 1993 amendments to the Navajo Sovereign Immunity Act. Finding that the tribal council expressed an intent to "avoid what was referred to in the legislative record as a 'notice of default' against the Nation with no complaint ever being filed," merely a notice of claim. Id. at 160. The tribal entity had complained that plaintiffs had often merely filed a notice of claim, not the actual complaint, and then, confused, moved for a default judgment against the tribal defendant after the tribal entity did not file a responsive pleading to the notice of claim.

Tort claims ordinances sometimes waive immunity for claims against the tribal government for tortious acts by tribal government employees. Tort claims against tribal governments tend to be rarer than tribal enterprises, but they do occur. For example, in Bradley v. Tulalip Tribes, 2012 Tulalip App. LEXIS 10 (Tulalip Tribal Ct.App.2012), the Tulalip Tribal Court of Appeals allowed a claim for malicious prosecution by a tribal member who was prosecuted by the tribe but then acquitted after trial. The trial court had dismissed the tort claim because the tribal tort claims ordinance did not waive claims against the tribe, but did authorize such claims against tribal officials, so long as the plaintiff showed the officials were acting outside the scope of their authority.

In Watts v. Sloan, 23 Indian L.Rep. 6033 (Navajo Nation S.Ct.1995), the court ordered the dismissal of a legal malpractice action against attorneys employed by the Navajo Nation Legal Aid and Defender Office. As such, the attorneys were covered by the tribe's limited waiver of sovereign immunity contained in the Navajo Nation Sovereign Immunity Act's provision governing legal malpractice. 2 Navajo Tribal Code § 354(h). Because the plaintiff failed to fulfill the requirement that they obtain authorization from the tribe's Governmental Services Committee, the court held that the claim must be dismissed.

3. CONTRACTUAL WAIVERS

Tribal nations also face pressure to enact waivers of tribal immunity to handle contract breaches by tribes and tribal entities. Tribal courts confronted with tribal immunity defenses have also expressed concern that tribes are undercutting their own economic potential by not agreeing to waive immunity. The Navajo Nation Supreme Court, in TBI Contractors, Inc. v. Navajo Tribe of Indians, 6 Nav. Rep. 57, 1988 Navajo Sup. LEXIS 3 (Navajo Nation S.Ct.1988), analyzing the 1980 Navajo Sovereign Immunity Act, recommended that the tribe allow for contractual waivers of immunity:

> We would like to conclude that the Navajo Tribal Council must look forward to the goal of economic development in future amendments to the Navajo Sovereign Immunity Act. One of the most severe problems facing the Navajo Nation is that of unemployment caused by the lack of economic development within the Navajo Nation. One path in which the Navajo Nation may strengthen its economic base is by drawing companies onto Navajo Indian Country. If the Navajo Nation is to compete with the states for industrial and business contracts, the Navajo Tribal Council must allow for contractual waivers of the tribe's immunity from suit. The Navajo Tribal Council may achieve this contractual waiver of immunity from suit through an amendment to the Navajo Sovereign Immunity Act, or through the inclusion of individual waivers written into each contract. The Navajo Nation must realize that private corporations will not choose Navajo Indian Country to do business on, unless they know that they will have a forum in which they will receive a fair hearing in the event of a contract dispute.

Id., 1988 Navajo Sup. LEXIS 3, at *12–13.

Navajo did not amend their code, but some tribes have adopted a tribal contract disputes waiver. The Grand Traverse Band of Ottawa and Chippewa Indians waived immunity as a general matter for certain types of contract claims:

> [T]he Tribe hereby waives its sovereign immunity, as well as the sovereign immunity of the Grand Traverse Band Economic Corporation, for any contract claim brought in accordance with this section, provided:
>
> (1) The claim arises from an express, written contract signed by all parties to the contract;
>
> (2) The claim is brought by a party to the contract or a party expressly made a third-party beneficiary under the terms of the contract;
>
> (3) The contract was entered into by the Grand Traverse Band Economic Development Corporation or a Tribal Business Enterprise, . . . subordinate to the Grand Traverse Band Economic Development Corporation; and
>
> (4) The contract was entered into in the performance of a proprietary function, which means any activity conducted primarily for the purpose of producing a pecuniary profit for the Tribe, the Grand Traverse Band Economic Development Corporation, or a Tribal Business Enterprise excluding, however, any

activity normally supported by a government unit by taxes or fees.

6 GTB Code § 207(a).

In Woodward v. Mohegan Tribal Gaming Authority, 2010 Mohegan Gaming Trial LEXIS 13 (Mohegan Gaming Disputes Trial Ct.2010), the court noted that the language in the code must be strictly followed or else no waiver can be found:

> The defendant, however, recognizes that the Mohegan Constitution, Article XIII, § 1, grants the MTGA the authority to waive its sovereign immunity in contractual matters: "The Tribal Gaming Authority shall have the power to grant a limited waiver of sovereign immunity as to its Gaming matters, to contracts relating to Gaming. . . ." But because the Mohegan Tribe has not enacted an ordinance that waives its sovereign immunity from claims of breach of contract, "[i]t is up to each contracting party to negotiate for a contractual waiver of sovereign immunity." . . . Further, the Tribe, in establishing the Mohegan Gaming Disputes Court, actually provides the format for such a waiver of sovereign immunity in a contract: "An express waiver of sovereign immunity in a contract must use the following format: 'The Mohegan Tribe (or the name of its entity or instrumentality) expressly waives its sovereign immunity for (name of specific even, time frame, maximum dollar amount and other limitations).' Without this specific language, no waiver of

> sovereign immunity shall exist." Mohegan Code of Laws, Mohegan Court System, Article I, § 1.6.

Id. at *5–6.

Tribes waive sovereign immunity in contractual relations to make business deals feasible and enforceable, as without a waiver, other parties cannot sue them to resolve disputes or enforce judgments, effectively barring tribes from large-scale commercial activities like major construction projects or financing agreements. By waiving immunity, tribes provide a degree of legal recourse to their business partners, which is crucial for building trust and facilitating complex financial and commercial interactions.

Like statutory waivers, contractual waivers are strictly construed. In Big Bubba's BBQ, LLC v. Mohegan Tribal Gaming Authority, 12 Am. Tribal Law 290 (Mohegan Gaming Disputes Trial Ct.2015), the Mohegan Gaming Disputes Trial Court rejected a contract claim arising from a lease that provided:

> * * * Landlord expressly waives its immunity from unconsented suit for the purpose of permitting a suit by Tenant in any court of competent jurisdiction for any claims by Tenant for the purpose of enforcing this Lease and any judgment arising out of this Lease. Landlord's waiver of immunity from suit is specifically limited to the following actions and judicial remedies: (a) the enforcement of Landlord's obligations under this Lease with an award of actual damages in connection with any breach of

> the provisions hereof provided, however, that the court shall have no authority or jurisdiction to order execution against any assets or revenues of Landlord except cash of Landlord (other than cash which Landlord can demonstrate was derived from a source other than the Retail Facilities); and (b) an action to prohibit Landlord from taking an action that would prevent the operation of the Lease pursuant to its terms, or that requires Landlord to specifically perform any obligation under this Lease. In no instance shall any enforcement of any kind whatsoever be allowed against any assets of Landlord other than the limited assets of Landlord specified in the foregoing clause (a).

Id. at 293–94. The plaintiff's suit claimed damages arising from an alleged violation of the Indian Civil Rights Act. The contractual waiver did not extend that far.

As noted, implied waivers of tribal immunity are disfavored by the courts. The federal and state court tradition is to interpret narrowly any statutory or contractual language that could be construed as an implied waiver of immunity, favoring the government if at all possible. However, guided by federal court decisions, some tribal courts are finding implied waivers of sovereign immunity. For example, since many tribal contracts provide for disputes to be resolved through arbitration, tribal courts are addressing whether and how an arbitration clause waives tribal immunity. Arbitration clauses are complicated by the United States Supreme Court decision in C&L Enterprises, Inc. v. Citizen Band Potawatomi Indian Tribe of Oklahoma, 532 U.S. 411 (2001). The Court held that a tribe that executed a contract in which there was (1) an arbitration clause, (2) governed by state law, (3) enforceable in state court, (4) excluding any reservations of tribal sovereign immunity was adequate to impliedly waive tribal immunity for the enforcement of the arbitration award, and (5) there are no issues involving the authority of the tribal party to execute valid waivers. See Ho-Chunk Nation v. B&K Builders, Inc., 3 Am. Tribal Law 381, 390 (Ho-Chunk Nation Trial Ct.2001).

Tribal business partners sometimes assume that all arbitration provisions automatically constituted a tribal waiver, post-*C&L Enterprises*. Not so. Consider First Specialty Insurance Corp. v. Confederated Tribes of the Grand Ronde Community of Oregon, 16 Am. Tribal Law 390 (Confederated Tribes of the Grand Ronde Community Ct.App.2006), aff'g, Confederated Tribes of Grand Ronde v. Strategic Wealth Management, 32 Indian L.Rep. 6148 (Confederated Tribes of the Grand Ronde Community Tribal Ct.2005). There, the Grand Ronde Community entered into a contract with a group called Strategic Wealth Management (SWM). The tribe cancelled the contract and sought an arbitration award. The arbitrator ruled against the tribe and, in accordance with the American Arbitration Association's rules in place at that time, ordered the tribe to pay attorney fees and costs to SWM. In assessing an action seeking a declaration that the tribe's immunity prevented the attorney fees award, the appellate court for the Grand Ronde Community agreed with the tribe:

> The Tribe did agree in the 1992 Agreement that "[a]ny arbitration shall be in accordance with the rules then applying of the American Arbitration Association, New York Stock Exchange or the National Association of Securities Dealers, at Client's election." ER 90. The Tribe's attorneys selected the AAA and its rules when they brought the arbitration against the Sizemores and SWM and Paradigm. The AAA rules in 1992 and in 2001 apparently allowed awards of fees and costs. But we must decide if those rules applied only to the issues that the Tribe agreed could be part of "any arbitration."
>
> Notwithstanding the broad reference to the AAA rules, we have already held that the 1992 Agreement did not clearly or expressly waive the Tribe's immunity to an award of fees and costs. Hence, those issues could not be raised in or be a part of "any arbitration" that was authorized by the 1992 Agreement. The Tribe simply did not waive its immunity for fees and costs and did not agree to allow those issues to be arbitrated. The issues of fees and costs, then, could not be and were not part of an arbitration that was subject to the AAA rules. The provision in the 1992 Agreement referencing the AAA rules does not stand for anything more remarkable than that the Tribe agreed to apply the AAA rules to the

> specific items it agreed to arbitrate, and had waived its immunity to, in the 1992 Agreement.
>
> The mistake in Appellants' argument is that they skip the vital first step of answering exactly what issues the Tribe agreed to arbitrate and to which issues the AAA rules applied. The Tribe did not agree in the 1992 Agreement to arbitrate the issue of fees and costs. Thus, those items could not be part of "any arbitration" that would be subject to the AAA rules.

Id. at 399. Attempting to avoid the tribal court order, SWM's insurance company sued in federal court seeking an order that the tribal court did not have jurisdiction over SWM, a nonmember-owned company. The federal court disagreed. First Specialty Ins. Co. v. Confederated Tribes of the Grand Ronde Community of Oregon, 2007 WL 3283699 (D.Or. 2007). For a similar example, see Lower Sioux Indian Community v. Prescott, 35 Indian L.Rep. 6050, 6052 (Lower Sioux Indian Community in Minn.Ct.App. 2008) (finding arbitration clause in contract does not waive sovereign immunity in light of tribal statutes).

Similarly, tribal courts are split on whether a tribal entity's purchase of insurance constitutes an implied waiver of sovereign immunity. In Campos v. Eastern Band of Cherokee Indians, 18 Am. Tribal Law 137 (Eastern Band of Cherokee Indians S.Ct. 2024), the court concluded that the tribe's purchase of an insurance policy did not abrogate tribal immunity. The plaintiff brought a slip-and-fall action against the tribal gaming operation. The court examined the insurance policy language and found no waiver.

Thus, the question that this Court must now answer is whether, as Plaintiff contends, the Gemini Policy speaks directly to Tribal Council's intent to provide for a waiver of sovereign immunity to allow for a plaintiff to bring a Tribal "tort claims" action against the Tribe in the Cherokee Court. Unfortunately, Plaintiff fails to point to any language in the Gemini Policy that speaks directly to the Tribe's intent to provide for a waiver of sovereign immunity for his purported Tribal "tort claims" action against the Tribe, let alone language that demonstrates that Tribal Council expressly and unequivocally waived sovereign immunity as to such Tribal "tort claims" action or any specific tort claims covered by the Gemini Policy. Here, the language in the Gemini Policy merely provides that "[a]ny use of the Sovereign Immunity defense will only apply to coverage and limits of this insurance policy" and that "[t]he Carrier is not authorized or empowered to waive . . . the 'Insured's' Sovereign Immunity outside or beyond the scope of coverage or limits of this insurance policy," which makes it clear to this Court that the intent behind said language was narrow in purpose and specifically designed to strictly address the scope of coverage or limits of the policy, and that the Gemini Policy itself had no material bearing on whether, as a fundamental matter of jurisdiction, Tribal Council waived the Tribe's sovereign immunity

> to allow Plaintiff to bring his purported Tribal "tort claims" action or specific tort claims against the Tribe seeking damages under [Cherokee Code] § 1–2(g)(3). Therefore, the Court concludes that the language in the Gemini Policy advanced by Plaintiff here does not constitute an express and unequivocal waiver of tribal sovereign immunity by Tribal Council in a Tribal contract in accordance with C.C. § 7–13. Accordingly, the Court holds that Plaintiff has failed to demonstrate that Tribal Council expressly and unequivocally waived tribal sovereign immunity in accordance with C.C. § 7–13 as to the purported Tribal "tort claims" action that Plaintiff desires to bring against the Tribe seeking the limited relief found under C.C. § 1–2(g)(3), and, consequently, that the trial court did not err in dismissing Plaintiff's complaint against the Tribe and its entities, including [Tribal Gaming Casino Enterprise], pursuant to Rule 12(b)(1) for lack of subject matter jurisdiction based on the defense of tribal sovereign immunity.

Id. at 191.

Similarly, in Teesateskie v. Eastern Band of Cherokee Indians Minors Trust Fund, 13 Am. Tribal Law 180, 185–87 (Eastern Band of Cherokee Indians S.Ct.2015), a class of minors sued the tribal trustees of a gaming per capital trust fund for failure to responsibly invest the trust funds. The court rejected the claim on sovereign immunity grounds. The plaintiffs argued that the Cherokee Code requiring the tribe to acquire insurance served to abrogate tribal immunity. Cherokee Code § 1–2(g)(3). The court pointed to other code provisions within the judicial ordinance, Cherokee Code § 7–13, and the gaming revenue allocation ordinance, Cherokee Code § 16C–5(*l*)(13), that explicitly stated that any provision in the code that could be construed as a waiver of immunity must not be construed as such by the tribal judiciary.

Other tribal courts agree that "[t]he mere purchasing of liability insurance is insufficient to constitute such a waiver." Mountain v. Fort Berthold Housing Authority, 31 Indian L.Rep. 6102, 6103 (Northern Plains Intertribal Ct.App.2003).

Conversely, in Kalantari v. Spirit Mountain Gaming, Inc., 5 Am. Tribal Law 94 (Confederated Tribes of the Grand Ronde Community Tribal Ct. 2004), the court held that the tribe's gaming compact requiring the tribal gaming enterprise to maintain public liability insurance and requiring the tribe to agree that it would not raise sovereign immunity "up to the limits of the policy" worked to abrogate tribal immunity. Id. at 100. See also Jones v. Chitimacha Tribal of Louisiana, 23 Indian L.Rep. 6225, 6227 (Chitimacha Indian Tribal Ct.App.1996) ("It is clear from a reading of the Tribal/State Compact Agreement, the Gaming Ordinance and the Tribal Constitution, that pursuant to the I.G.R.A. [Indian Gaming Regulatory Act] terms and conditions, that it was the intent of the Tribe to fashion a remedy for injured patrons pursuant to the extent of liability insurance coverages as mandated by the State of

Louisiana with the Chitimacha Tribe of Louisiana for gaming purposes, pursuant to the Compact Agreement.").

Some tribal nations have enacted legislation amounting to a limited waiver of immunity allowing suits where the tribe is covered by insurance. E.g., Johnson v. Navajo Nation, 14 Indian L.Rep. 6037, 6039 (Navajo Nation S.Ct.1987) ("The intent behind the insurance exception led us to conclude that sovereign immunity is waived and the court has jurisdiction * * * if there is evidence that the Navajo Nation was insured for plaintiff's claim when suit was filed.") (interpreting 7 Navajo Nation Code § 854(c)).

F. IMPACT OF THE INDIAN CIVIL RIGHTS ACT & *MARTINEZ*

In the wake of Santa Clara Pueblo v. Martinez, 436 U.S. 49 (1978), tribal courts were split on whether the *Martinez* decision served as an abrogation of tribal sovereign immunity for the enforcement of the Indian Civil Rights Act. Compare Pawnee Tribe of Oklahoma v. Franseen, 19 Indian L.Rep. 6006, 6008 (Pawnee Tribe Ct. of Indian Appeals 1991) ("[T]he Indian Civil Rights Act did not * * * explicitly waive a tribe's immunity in tribal court actions."); McCormick v. Election Committee of the Sac & Fox Tribe, 1 Okla. Trib. 8; 1980 WL 128844, at *5 (Sac & Fox Court of Indian Offenses 1980) ("It would be [a] contradiction of *Santa Clara* to hold on the one hand that the Indian Civil Rights Act is ineffective to waive tribal sovereign immunity by implication in the federal courts and on the other hand to hold that the same legislative enactment is effective to waive the sovereign immunity by implication in tribal courts."), with Dupree v. Cheyenne River Housing Authority, 16 Indian L.Rep. 6106, 6108 (Cheyenne River Sioux Ct.App.1988) (concluding that *Martinez*'s reasoning "means * * * that tribal courts must entertain causes of action based on the ICRA of 1968 and a claim of a bar to such actions based on the doctrine of sovereign immunity is inapposite"); Cudmore v. Cheyenne River Sioux Tribal Council, 10 Indian L.Rep. 6004, 6004 (Cheyenne River Sioux Tribal Ct.1981) ("When a federal law, such as the Indian Civil Rights Act of 1968, has declared that the tribe is required to act or prevented from acting in a prescribed manner, the tribal court is an available forum for redress in cases of noncompliance."); Kizer v. Walker River Housing Authority, 23 Indian L.Rep. 6214, 6215 (Nev. Inter-tribal Ct.App.1996) (holding ICRA waives immunity to avoid the problem of "a right, the breach or denial of which, is without a remedy"); Oglala Sioux Personnel Board v. Red Shirt, 16 Indian L.Rep. 6052, 6052–53 (Oglala Sioux Tribe Ct.App.1983) (tribal sovereign immunity cannot be relied upon in "internal controversies" between a tribal member and the tribe); Jackson v. Kahgegab, 33 Indian L.Rep. 6105, 6107 (Saginaw Chippewa Indian Tribe App.Ct.2006) (finding a waiver and noting, "the due process and equal protection guarantees of ICRA also vindicate important tribal cultural values that ought not to be jeopardized by unduly expansive notions of tribal sovereign immunity"); Davis v. Keplin, 18 Indian L.Rep. 6148, 6149 (Turtle Mountain Tribal Ct.

1991) (deferring to "plenary" federal power and holding ICRA abrogates tribal immunity). Cf. Stone v. Somday, 10 Indian L.Rep. 6039 (Colville Tribal Ct. 1983) (declining to apply *Martinez*'s holding that tribal officials can be sued over tribal statute extending immunity to tribal officials). However, the cases that have held *Martinez* worked to abrogate tribal immunity to enforce ICRA now appear to be outliers.

The great weight of tribal court authority now holds that *Martinez* did not abrogate tribal immunity. E.g., Bonacci v. Tribal Council, 2003 WL 25836561, at *1 (Grand Traverse Band of Ottawa and Chippewa Indians Tribal Ct.2003) ("It has been argued by some that this federal law provision, which granted persons certain rights vis-a-vis an overly-intrusive tribal government, is in effect a Congressional waiver of tribal sovereign immunity. * * * This Court is persuaded by the tribal Court's reasoning in *McCormick* that the ICRA does not waive tribal sovereign immunity."); Terry-Carpenter v. Las Vegas Paiute Tribal Council, 29 Indian L.Rep. 6041, 6046 (Las Vegas Paiute Ct.App.2002) (quoting portion of *Martinez* decision referencing "[n]onjudicial tribal institutions" as "competent law-applying bodies" to justify rejecting argument that *Martinez* held that tribal courts must be open to allow enforcement of ICRA), aff'd in relevant part, 30 Indian L.Rep. 6150 (Las Vegas Paiute S.Ct.2003); Lonchar v. Victories Casino, 2002 WL 34512648, at *1 (Little Traverse Bay Bands of Odawa Indians Tribal Ct.2002) (relying on *McCormick*); Schock v. Mashantucket Pequot Gaming Enterprise, 3

Mash.Rep. 129, 1999 WL 34828705 (Mashantucket Pequot Tribal Ct.1999) ("In accordance with *Santa Clara Pueblo*, several tribal courts have held that ICRA does not effectuate a general waiver of a tribe's sovereign immunity and that a waiver of tribal sovereign immunity cannot be implied but must be unequivocally expressed."); Boice v. Washoe Tribe of California and Nevada, 2001 WL 36209875, at *3 (Nev. Inter-Tribal Ct.App.2001) (noting "great majority of Tribal Courts agree" that *Martinez* did not abrogate tribal immunity). Some tribal courts that have found a waiver in the reasoning of *Martinez* have been reversed. E.g., Bethel v. Mohegan Tribal Gaming Authority, 1 Am. Tribal Law 420, 430 (Mohegan Gaming Disputes Trial Ct.1998) (relying on *Dupree*), rev'd, 2 Am. Tribal Law 373 (Mohegan Gaming Disputes Ct.App.2000).

Many tribal nations have simply waived tribal immunity to allow enforcement of ICRA in tribal court. E.g., Jacobson v. Eastern Band of Cherokee Indians, 33 Indian L.Rep. 6001, 2005 WL 6438040, at *1 (Cherokee Ct. of the Eastern Band of Cherokee Indians 2005) (quoting Cherokee Code § 1–2(g)(1)).

G. FEDERAL CIVIL RIGHTS ACTIONS UNDER 42 U.S.C. § 1983

Although now a historical footnote, for a time tribal courts asserted jurisdiction over civil rights actions brought against state law enforcement officials for violations of federal or tribal law. That statute, intended to enforce the Fourteenth Amendment of the United States Constitution, effectuates a waiver of state sovereign immunity protecting state officials. The statute allows for enforcement in courts of general jurisdiction. Many tribal courts are courts of general jurisdiction.

In Allen v. Myers, 20 Indian L.Rep. 6105 (Nez Perce Tribal Ct.App.1993), the court concluded that § 1983 vested tribal courts with jurisdiction over tribal citizens' claims against state law enforcement officials accused of false imprisonment. The tribal citizen claimed that state law enforcement had no jurisdiction to arrest them. The court relied on the inherent tribal sovereignty theory to find jurisdiction, locating no explicit federal law barring tribal courts from assuming jurisdiction over § 1983 claims. The court also noted that the tribe had a substantial interest in regulating foreign law enforcement activities on tribal lands and against tribal citizens:

> * * * These jurisdictional provisions reflect a legitimate concern of the Nez Perce Tribe to promote the safety and well-being of all persons within the reservation. It is logical to conclude that these provisions as general as they are encompass the authority to adjudicate civil rights cases based on negligence or intentional conduct. Protecting community residents, Indian or non-Indian, from the wrongful conduct of law enforcement officers who operate within the exterior boundaries of the Nez Perce Reservation is a legitimate safety concern.

Id. The court also added that since ICRA imposed federal constitutional principles on tribal nations enforceable only in tribal court, enforcement of § 1983 by tribal courts was further justified. The county took the case to federal court, which excused the county police from tribal jurisdiction. County of Lewis v. Allen, 163 F.3d 509 (9th Cir.1998).

In 2001, the United States Supreme Court held that § 1983 does not confer jurisdiction over state officers in tribal courts. Nevada v. Hicks, 533 U.S. 353 (2001).

H. TRIBAL SUBORDINATE AND CORPORATE ENTITIES

Tribal subordinate and corporate entities may also be cloaked with a tribe's sovereign immunity, though state and federal courts employ versions of the arm-of-the-tribe test to determine whether a given corporation is immune. Restatement of the Law of Americans § 51 & cmt. d.

In tribal courts, tribal statutes generally determine whether an entity is cloaked with immunity. For example, in Quarti v. Mashantucket Pequot Gaming Enterprise, 6 Mash. Rep. 15, 2012 WL 3126782, at *3 (Mashantucket Pequot Tribal Ct.2012), the court pointed to the tribal code to confirm that the tribal gaming enterprise is the tribe for purposes of sovereign immunity. 4 Mashantucket Pequot Tribal Law § 1(a). See also Carey v. Victories Casino, 2006 WL 6369537, at *2 (Little Traverse Bay Bands of Odawa Indians Tribal Ct.2006) (noting that the "Little Traverse Bay Bands of Odawa Indians, *including all subordinate entities*, shall be immune from suit except to the extent that the Tribal Council clearly and expressly waives its sovereign immunity") (quoting Little Traverse Bay Bands of Odawa Indians Const. art. XVIII) (emphasis added). Some tribes choose not to cloak subordinate entities with immunity. E.g., Blaze Construction, Inc. v. Crownpoint Institute of Technology, 1 Am. Tribal Law 470, 476 (Navajo Nation S.Ct.1997) (finding no statute extending sovereign immunity to tribal school at the time of contracting with construction company); Holy Rock v. Tribal Election Board, 10 Indian L.Rep. 6009 (Oglala Sioux Tribal Ct.1982) (finding no positive law immunizing tribal election board from suit); Murphy v. Standing Rock Sioux Election Commission, 17 Indian L.Rep. 6069, 6070 (Standing Rock Sioux Tribal Ct.1990) ("Since the tribal constitution provides that the judicial power extends to all cases arising under the constitution and Code of Justice of the tribe or ordinances of the tribe, there must be a forum available to hear the plaintiff's case."); Davis v. Turtle Mountain Housing Authority, 17 Indian L.Rep. 6035 (Turtle Mountain Tribal Ct.1990) (quoting tribal code § 14.0401, which waived the housing authority's immunity).

In decades past, courts focused on whether the corporate entity's charter contained a "sue and be sued" clause, standard language in charters for for-profit corporations under state law and were occasionally required by federal agencies working with tribal nations. Restatement of the Law of American Indians § 51, Reporters' Notes, *cmt.* c. E.g., Wells v. Fort Berthold Community College, 24 Indian L.Rep. 6157 (Three Affiliated Tribes of the Fort Berthold Reservation Tribal Ct.1997) (holding that a "sue and be sued" clause effectively waives immunity). Many Section 17 corporations also contained that language. See Naff v. Colville Confederated Tribes, 22 Indian L.Rep. 6032, 6035–36 (Colville Tribal Ct.App.1995) (noting that Section 17 corporations' "sue or be sued" clauses were typical) (quoting Cohen's Handbook of Federal Indian Law 326 (1982 ed.)).

However, tribal courts tend to look beyond the "sue and be sued" language to other aspects of tribal law to determine whether an entity might still be immune from suit. E.g., Sturgeon Electric Co., Inc. v. AHA MACAV Power Service, 26 Indian L.Rep. 6026 (Fort Mohave Indian Reservation App.Ct.1998) ("The Constitution of the Fort Mojave Tribe is very clear as to the sovereign status and the need for intentional and deliberate waiver of immunity by the governing body. This has been bestowed upon tribal enterprises and is evidenced in the language of the Fort Mojave Tribal Business Corporation Act."); McLean v. Rosebud Housing Authority, 26 Indian L.Rep. 6147, 6149 (Rosebud Sioux Tribal Ct.1999) (rejecting claim that housing authority charter's "sue and be sued" clause abrogates immunity); Gonzales v. Allen, 17 Indian L.Rep. 6121, 6122 (Shoshone-Bannock Tribal Ct.1999) ("The fact that a tribe may or not be sued is not determinative of whether the tribe possesses sovereign immunity. The fact that tribes may initiate lawsuits does not automatically make them susceptible to suits by others."); Laducer v. Fort Totten Housing Authority, 28 Indian L.Rep. 6101 (Spirit Lake Tribal Ct.2000) (holding that "a 'sue and be sued' clause creating a tribal entity does not ipso facto waive that entity's immunity from suit in a court of appropriate jurisdiction, but instead permits that entity to contractually waive its immunity from suit," relying on Dillon v. Yankton Sioux Tribe Housing Authority, 144 F.3d 581 (8th Cir.1998)). Modern tribal corporate entities usually include language reserving tribal immunity, leading tribal courts to read the "sue or be sued" clauses as dependent on the presence of other explicit waivers of immunity. E.g., Navajo Nation Oil and Gas Co. v. Window Rock District Court, 12 Am. Tribal Law 22, 26 (Navajo Nation S.Ct.2014) ("The Charter expressly provides that NNOGC 'is an instrumentality of the Navajo Nation and is entitled to all of the privileges and immunities of the Navajo Nation . . . including but not limited to the Navajo Sovereign Immunity Act at 1 N.N.C. § 551 et seq.' Charter, Art. XVI(A). The corporation has the power to waive immunity in order '[t]o sue or be sued in its corporate name to the extent provided in Article XVI of [the] Charter, and to that extent only.' Charter, Art. VIII(K)."); Laverdure v. Turtle Mountain Housing Authority Board, 35 Indian L.Rep. 6131, 6133 (Turtle Mountain Tribal Ct.App.2008) ("[T]he [sued and be sued] clause is an enabling clause and does not waive immunity by itself."); Mitchell v. Warm Springs Forest Products Industries, 16 Indian L.Rep. 6162, 6165 (Confederated Tribes of the Warm Springs Reservation Tribal Ct.1989) (holding tribal tort claims act controls over tribal corporate entity's "sue or be sued" clause). Cf. Board of Trustees of the Sisseton-Wahpeton Community College v. Wynde, 18 Indian L.Rep. 6033 (Northern Plains Intertribal Ct.

App.1990) (holding that contract term guaranteeing "due process" was insufficient to waive tribal entity immunity, also rejecting claim that "sue and be sued" clause of entity charter was sufficient to waive immunity).

In the absence of clear tribal statutory authority, tribal courts will borrow the state and federal law arm of the tribe test. In Pequot Pharmaceutical Network v. Connecticut Hospice, Inc., 6 Mash. Rep. 323, 2015 WL 9601099 (Mashantucket Pequot Tribal Ct.2015), the court articulated (without applying) several aspects of this test:

> The basic inquiry for an "arm of the tribe" analysis is whether the tribal entity is sufficiently related to its respective tribe to be protected by tribal sovereign immunity. Courts have applied different tests in determining whether a tribal entity or corporation is an arm of the tribe. For example, the Tenth Circuit weighs several factors in determining whether a tribal entity is entitled to immunity as an arm of the tribe including, (1) method of creation, (2) purpose, (3) structure, ownership, and management, (4) tribal intent to bestow immunity, (5) financial relationship between the tribe and the entity, and (6) whether purpose of tribal sovereign immunity is served by granting immunity to the entity.... Similarly, the Minnesota Supreme Court considers (1) whether the business entity is organized for a purpose that is governmental in nature, rather than commercial, (2) whether the tribe and the

> business entity are closely linked in government structure and other characteristics, and (3) whether federal policies intended to promote Indian tribal autonomy are furthered by the extension of immunity to the business entity.

Id. at *10 (citations omitted).

In general, Section 17 corporations and tribally-owned corporations chartered under tribal law are cloaked in tribal immunity. Tribal-owned corporations chartered under state law typically are not cloaked in immunity, as exemplified by the Tenth Circuit's decision in Somerlott v. Cherokee Nation Distributors. Inc., 686 F.3d 1144 (10th Cir.2012). However, in Redsleeve Golf, LLC v. Sequoyah National Golf Club, LLC, 13 Am. Tribal Law 203 (Cherokee Ct. of the Eastern Band of Cherokee Indians 2014), the court held that state incorporation does not automatically abrogate tribal immunity, following Haile v. Saunooke, 246 F.2d 293 (4th Cir.1957). Still, after application of the six-factor test articulated in Breakthrough Management Group, Inc. v. Chukchansi Economic Development Authority, 629 F.3d 1173 (10th Cir.2010), relied upon in *Pequot Pharmaceutical Network* and *Somerlott*, the court concluded that the tribal entity was not entitled to sovereign immunity. The court noted that the business was incorporated under state law and was designed to simply run a golf course for profit.

Tribal statutes typically extend immunity to tribal corporations. E.g., Hwal'Bay Ba:J Enters. v. Beattie, 2009 Hualapai App. LEXIS 1, at *12 (Hualapai Ct. App.2009) ("The Corporation shall be entitled to all the privileges and immunities of the Hualapai Indian Tribe. The Corporation and its directors, officers, employees, and agents while acting in the official capacities are immune from suit, and the assets and other property of the Corporation are exempt from any levy or execution as provided in this Article.") (quoting Hwal'Bay Ba:J Enterprises, Inc.'s Amended and Restated Plan of Operation § 11.1 and 'Sa' Nyu Wa, Inc.'s Plan of Operation § 11.1); 15 Grand Traverse Band Code § 204 ("This Corporation shall have the same immunity from taxation under federal and Tribal law as the Grand Traverse Band but shall be subject to Tribal taxes where applicable.").

Private parties that incorporate an entity under a tribal business organizations code do not enjoy sovereign immunity simply by virtue of doing so. E.g., Smith v. Port Susan Camping Club, 16 Indian L.Rep. 6169 (Tulalip Tribal Ct.App.1989).

I. AUTHORITY TO WAIVE IMMUNITY

Tribal enterprises regularly (and tribal governments perhaps less so) agree to limited waivers of immunity in contracts, but those waivers usually must comply with tribal constitutional or code provisions that detail the scope of the waivers, the process for approving those waivers, and the entities, officials, or employees actually authorized to approve those waivers.

Tribal constitutions often contain procedural requirements for waivers of immunity. For example, the Article XIII, § 1 of the Grand Traverse Band of Ottawa and Chippewa Indians provides, "The Tribal

Council shall not waive or limit the right of the Grand Traverse Band to be immune from suit, except as authorized by this Article or in furtherance of tribal business enterprises upon a resolution approved by an affirmative vote of five (5) of the seven (7) members of the Tribal Council." Contained in this language are restrictions on the purposes for which the council may waive immunity and a super-majority voting requirement.

In Martin v. Hopi Tribe, 1996 Hopi App. LEXIS 5 (Hopi Tribe App.Ct.1995), the court found no evidence that the defendant had validly waived its immunity, forcing the dismissal of the action. There, tribal employees who had been laid off brought a grievance to a tribal administrative review board. The tribe's personnel manual had reiterated to the employees that the tribe had agreed to be named as a party in appeals to the tribal court arising from the grievance process. The grievance board purported to waive tribal immunity, but the court held that only the tribal council could do so. See also Gabriel v. Cox, 2017 Colville App. LEXIS 6, at *3 (Colville Tribal Ct.App.2017) ("The doctrine of sovereign immunity requires the waiver to be explicit and unequivocally expressed, it must be in writing, *it must be authorized or provided by a party with the authority to waive immunity*, and any waiver must be strictly construed in favor of the tribal sovereign party.") (emphasis added).

Federal courts are split on the question of whether an unauthorized tribal official can operate to waive tribal immunity in contracts. Compare Memphis

Biofuels, LLC v. Chickasaw Nation Indus., Inc., 585 F.3d 917, 922 (6th Cir.2009) (no valid waiver in contract executed by tribal official without tribal board of directors authority to waive immunity), with StoreVisions, Inc. v. Omaha Tribe of Neb., 795 N.W.2d 271 (Neb. 2011) (valid waiver in contract executed by tribal official without tribal board of directors authority to waive immunity). See generally Restatement of the Law of American Indians § 25, *cmt.* c and Reporters' Notes.

J. INDIVIDUAL CAPACITY SUITS FOR MONEY DAMAGES

In state courts, tribal employees acting within the scope of their tribal authority can be sued for state law claims so long as they are sued in their individual capacities, according to the United States Supreme Court's decision in Lewis v. Clarke, 581 U.S. 155 (2017). Some plaintiffs have attempted to extend that holding to tribal jurisdictions, but so far unsuccessfully.

In Mazzetti v. Kolb, No. AP-0001-23 (Rincon Band of Luiseño Indians Ct.App.2024), the appellate court for the Rincon Band of Luiseño Indians rejected an effort to sue tribal enrollment commission members for money damages by suing them in tribal court in their individual capacities. There, persons seeking enrollment with the tribe and/or modification of their legal blood quantum sued members of the enrollment commission when the commission allegedly failed to act on their applications in a timely manner, invoking *Lewis v. Clarke*. They sought money damages from the commission members, but tribal law provided that all commission members were cloaked in the tribe's immunity for any actions (or inactions) made in the scope of the commission's authority, effectively preempting any application of *Lewis v. Clarke*. Moreover, the court added that even if the court applied federal law, the commission members would have been considered quasi-judicial officers cloaked with absolute immunity.

CHAPTER 10

HUMAN RIGHTS IN INDIAN COUNTRY

Human rights are fundamental rights inherent to all human beings, regardless of nationality, sex, national or ethnic origin, color, religion, language, or any other status. These rights are universal, inalienable, and equally applicable to everyone, and are essential for a life of dignity. They include basic rights like the right to life, liberty, and security of person, as well as social, economic, and cultural rights like the right to education, work, and health.

Tribal governments are dedicated to enhancing human rights. Indigenous cultures tend to emphasize the interests of individuals over governmental and commercial interests. Culturally, Indigenous Peoples retain a special connection to family, community, and environment. Tribal citizens emphasize individual well-being. Government is expected to guarantee good health care, public safety, housing, education, social welfare services, employment, environmental protection and natural resources conservation, and cultural and religious protections. Politically, tribal leaders are elected by their friends, neighbors, and relatives. Outside campaign money from special interests usually is limited-to-non-existent in tribal electoral campaigns.

Tribal justice systems often focus on justice for individuals in a way that is rare in state and federal justice systems, though the influence of the colonizer often suppresses that emphasis. It is likely that tribal nations given the opportunity to establish their own bill of rights would emphasize positive human rights like a right to education and health care. These types of positive human rights are not protected or enhanced by the United States Constitution and are often excluded from state constitutions as well. Most tribal nations have adopted a form of the federal Bill of Rights or the Indian Bill of Rights from the Indian Civil Rights Act. These laws focus on negative rights protecting individuals from certain types of government actions, such as property rights takings or viewpoint discrimination, but guarantee few if any positive human rights. Unfortunately, given the long history of the federal government's actions to limit Indian affairs policies and programs that continues to manifest as dramatic underfunding of Indian country programs, resources to ensure positive human rights are limited.

Even so, tribal human rights law often displays enormous respect for individual human rights. Areas of positive human rights regularly adjudicated in tribal justice systems include Indian child welfare, speech and religious freedom matters, criminal justice remedies, and discrimination and inequality matters. In many respects, tribal justice systems are far better forums than state or federal courts for those attempting to vindicate individual human rights. See generally Kristen A. Carpenter & Angela R. Riley, Indigenous Peoples and the Jurisgenerative Moment, 102 Calif.L.Rev. 173 (2014).

A. UNITED NATIONS DECLARATION ON THE RIGHTS OF INDIGENOUS PERSONS

The United Nations Declaration on the Rights of Indigenous Peoples (UNDRIP), a United Nations resolution adopted in 2007, sets global standards for the human rights of Indigenous peoples. It affirms rights such as self-determination, cultural preservation, access to resources, freedom from discrimination, and participation in decision-making processes that affect them, adopting a best practices standard applicable to colonizing nations known as "free, prior, and informed consent" or FPIC, before nations take action that affect Indigenous Peoples. UNDRIP serves as a framework for reconciliation and promotes harmonious relations between Indigenous peoples and states.

Many tribal nations and tribal organizations have embraced and are actively working to implement the UNDRIP, using it as a tool in their advocacy for rights such as self-determination, cultural protection, and economic well-being, even though the U.S. government only officially endorsed it in 2010 after initially voting against it in 2007. Tribes and their allies advocate for its principles to be incorporated into state laws, policies, and judicial decisions.

Organizations like the Native American Rights Fund (NARF) and the University of Colorado Law School work with tribal leaders to implement UNDRIP through education and advocacy, specifically through The Implementation Project, or TIP. TIP has published guides to assist tribal nations in using UNDRIP as advocacy and adopting UNDRIP as positive tribal law. E.g., The Implementation Project, The Tribal Guide to Implementing FPIC in the Context of Conservation and Development (2025); Tribal Implementation Toolkit (2020).

Tribal nations have begun to adopt laws asserting rights under UNDRIP. For example, the Hopi Cultural Preservation Office adopted the Protocol for Research, Publication and Recordings: Motion, Visual, Sound, Multimedia and other Mechanical Devices in 2021. Muscogee (Creek) Nation citizens have translated the UNDRIP into the Mvskoke language. The Navajo Nation Human Rights Commission has recommended that UNDRIP be made a part of Navajo law.

At times, tribal courts have looked to other international law principles. In Satiacum v. Reagan, 10 Indian L.Rep. 6009 (Puyallup Tribal Ct.1982), a tax protester's suit against the President of the United States, the tribal court declined to dismiss the suit at least in part on international law grounds. Citing numerous authorities, the court concluded, "The cases relied on by the United States to support its motion to dismiss are inconsistent with tribal policies of self-determination, with principles of international law, and are inconsistent as among themselves from the perspective of clarity and precedent." Id. at 6011. The court however noted that the plaintiff had already sued the United States in federal court raising the same claims, so the court invoked the federal judiciary's *Colorado River* doctrine of abstention and dismissed the suit.

B. INDIAN CIVIL RIGHTS ACT

In 1968, largely because the United States Constitution does not apply to tribal government activity, Talton v. Mayes, 163 U.S. 376 (1896); Colville Confederated Tribes v. Wiley, 22 Indian L.Rep. 6059, 6061 (Colville Tribal Ct.App.1995), Congress enacted the Indian Bill of Rights, a federal law that requires tribal governments to guarantee due process and equal protection to persons under tribal jurisdiction, codified as amended at 25 U.S.C. § 1302(a)(8). Congress listed most other rights equivalent to the federal Bill of Rights in ICRA as well. § 1302(a).

In 1978, the Supreme Court held that persons seeking to enforce those federal rights may do so in tribal forums only; federal and state courts are unavailable. Santa Clara Pueblo v. Martinez, 436 U.S. 49 (1978). Moreover, the Court held that tribes may choose to interpret the meanings of "due process" and "equal protection," to name two examples, in line with tribal laws, including customary laws. Id. at 71–72; Menominee Tribal Housing Authority v. Tucker, 18 Indian L.Rep. 6131, 6135 (Menominee Tribal Ct.1991) ("The legislative history of the Indian Civil Rights Act indicate that the courts have wide discretion in the application of due process and equal protection vis-à-vis tribal custom and tradition."); Billie v. Abbott, 16 Indian L.Rep. 6021, 6024 (Navajo Nation S.Ct.1988) ("Due process under the ICRA and the NBR [Navajo Bill of Rights] must be interpreted in a way that will enhance Navajo culture and tradition. * * * When

Navajo sovereignty and cultural autonomy are at stake, the Navajo courts must have broad-based discretion in interpreting the due process clauses of the ICRA and NBR, and the courts may apply Navajo due process in a way that protects civil liberties while preserving Navajo culture and self-government."). But see, e.g., Works v. Fallon Shoshone-Paiute Tribe, 1997 WL 34704273, at *2 (Nev. Inter-Tribal Ct.App. 1997) (holding that "the substantial and intended effect of the ICRA is that, if the tribe has enacted laws which conflict with the ICRA, the local laws must yield to the mandates of the ICRA").

Since the advent of the self-determination era of federal Indian law in the 1970s, tribal nations have adopted constitutions that also guarantee individual rights, often using the same or substantively similar language as federal law does. E.g., Grand Traverse Band of Ottawa and Chippewa Indians, Const., art. X., § 1(h) ("equal protection" and "due process"); Pokagon Band of Potawatomi Indians, Const., art. XVI(h) (same); Sault Ste. Marie Tribe of Chippewa Indians, Const. and Bylaws, art. VIII ("equal protection" and "rights or guarantees enjoyed by citizens under the Constitution of the United States"). Other tribes have adopted more bespoke individual rights statutes. E.g., Navajo Nation Bill of Rights, 1 Navajo Nation Code §§ 1–9 (enacted prior to the Indian Civil Rights Act).

Despite the opportunity to interpret the due process and equal protection clauses in accordance with tribal customs, however, tribal courts have usually applied (or modified) federal precedents to such claims. Given the practical nonexistence of court precedents and legal scholarship on Anishinaabe legal customs and traditions until recently, the reliance on the precedents of the colonizers was inevitable.

1. DUE PROCESS AND EQUAL PROTECTION

Due process and equal protection are vital because they protect individuals from unfair government actions by guaranteeing fair procedures in legal proceedings and ensuring all people are treated equally under the law, respectively. Due process safeguards life, liberty, and property through procedural safeguards like notice and a hearing, while equal protection prevents discrimination by ensuring laws are applied consistently to everyone in similar circumstances. Together, these principles foster a just society where fundamental rights are protected, and government power is limited to prevent arbitrary or discriminatory treatment.

By voluntarily adopting and applying these principles, tribes demonstrate their commitment to fundamental fairness, which strengthens their inherent right to self-government. Upholding due process and equal protection fosters trust in the tribal court system, encouraging greater participation and confidence among all who interact with it. These principles are essential for the fair administration of justice, ensuring that tribal courts are seen as legitimate and equitable forums for resolving disputes and enforcing laws. These rights serve as a crucial safeguard for both tribal members and non-Indians against potential abuses by tribal governments.

a. Federal Law and Political Theory

Due process and equal protection are foundational constitutional rights guaranteed to individuals in their relations to federal and state governments. In short, government cannot strip individuals of liberty and property without due process. Const. amend. V; Const. amend. XIV, § 1. Neither can government treat similarly situated persons differently. Const. amend. XIV, § 1. These are core principles of American government.

The due process clause is embedded in the Fifth Amendment to the Constitution. The language is tied to the prohibition on the government's arbitrary taking of a vested property interest without compensation for the loss of that property interest. American Indian people can justly feel that the due process clause has almost no teeth, given that Congress confiscated hundreds of millions of acres of tribal lands, most notably during the allotment era, without consent or meaningful compensation. For example, Lone Wolf v. Hitchcock, 187 U.S. 556 (1903), enabled Congress and the Department of the Interior to abrogate treaty-protected tribal lands without compensation or meaningful judicial review, a decision one tribal court called, "gut-wrenching[ly] legalistic[ ]." Board of Trustees of the Sisseton-Wahpeton Community College v. Wynde, 18 Indian L.Rep. 6033, 6034 (Northern Plains Intertribal Ct.App.1990). Later, the Supreme Court enabled the confiscation of tribal property by denying that Indian people possessed a vested property right in their aboriginal lands. Tee-Hit-Ton Indians v. United States, 348 U.S. 272 (1955). It is difficult to enforce the due process requirement when the judiciary rejects the premise that an individual possesses a legally protected interest.

The equal protection clause originated in the Fourteenth Amendment, one of the Reconstruction Amendments designed to eradicate the legal basis of slavery and to remedy the badges and incidents of racial discrimination. The Supreme Court has ensured that the equal protection clause does little or nothing to remedy past discrimination. Gratz v. Bollinger, 539 U.S. 244 (2003). Instead, the Court held that it only bars intentional discrimination. Washington v. Davis, 426 U.S. 229 (1976). More recently, the Court has imposed a colorblindness standard on the equal protection clause, eradicating any governmental effort to promote the goals and purposes of the Reconstruction Amendments and generally working only to protect white persons from "reverse discrimination." Students for Fair Admissions, Inc. v. President and Fellows of Harvard College, 600 U.S. 181 (2023).

These principles derive from an understanding and expectation—a philosophy—of relentless contradiction and even cynicism. The notion of federal and state sovereignty, borrowed from European nations, emphasizes a hierarchy of elite individuals (some elected, some not) that exercise enormous power over individuals and entities within the jurisdiction of government. The underlying philosophy is that a sovereign entity is necessary for peace and security. This philosophy understands humanity to be violent, competitive, selfish, and superior to all other creatures and things on earth (and some humans superior to others). Without a sovereign employing a monopoly on violence, human life would be nasty, brutal, and short, in the words of Hobbes. But naturally, such power consolidated by the Constitution in the sovereign potentially leads to abuses, which necessitates constitutional protections for individuals facing the might of the sovereign. These protections include due process and equal protection.

It is far from clear that the due process and equal protection clauses of the Fifth and Fourteenth Amendment do much to protect individual rights of underprivileged persons in the United States. Poverty, inequality, incarceration, and other social ills remain intractable in the United States.

b. Tribal Law and Indigenous Political Theories

Although it is fraught to generalize, Indigenous legal principles derive from philosophies and ways of being and knowing that originate from a much different understanding than American laws. The original difference is that Indigenous Peoples do not understand humans to have the power and obligation to exercise dominion over the earth and its creatures. Instead, humans are lesser creatures whose obligation is to ensure harmony. The great gift of the lesser creatures known as humans is imagination and creativity, important skills helpful toward fulfilling our obligation to promote harmony. Indigenous philosophies do not presume the need for a sovereign entity. In fact, if the theories undergirding American legal structures were empirically true, there might never have been organized groups of humans anywhere in history.

Understanding the philosophical difference between American and Indigenous law is helpful to theorizing how tribal courts interpret law, even the laws of the colonizer. Consider "due process." The notion of due process originated with the concerns of the American founding generation, exclusively represented by landed, wealthy white men, many of whom were slavers or slavery-enablers and competitors for Indian lands, if not outright Indian killers (the first American President, George Washington, was all those things, as were later presidents like Andrew Jackson). Those concerns primarily involved worries that government would act to confiscate their private property or strip them of their freedom. These men believed that government should be able to do either of those things, but only for good reason and by following a fair process. In these proceedings, which were and are adversarial, winners and losers emerged.

In tribal nations where individual Indigenous people and families possessed robust property rights, there was little or worry about a sovereign government. Indigenous nations governed according to kinship systems would meet periodically to address issues of governance. Every voice was heard. Debate was free and respectful. Ceremonies were sacred and ceremonies provided the process. If an Indigenous family disputed a hunting territory with another, for example, the entire tribal nation would meet to discuss how to ensure harmony, peace, and justice.

The Supreme Court's decision in *Martinez* placed the interpretation of the Indian Bills of Rights squarely in the hands of tribal courts and, to a more oblique extent, tribal legislatures. Most tribal courts since *Martinez* have relied heavily on federal precedents to interpret ICRA's due process and equal protection clauses, but some judges have questioned that reliance. E.g., Sells v. Espil, 17 Indian L.Rep. 6102, 6112 (Navajo Nation S.Ct.1990) (analyzing equal protection claim in light of the Diné common law principle of the "reciprocal obligation" that is "required of Navajos [to the broader community of relatives,] summed up in the saying used to describe someone who has misbehaved: 'He acts as if he had no relatives.' "); Ponca Tribal Election Board v. Snake, 17 Indian L.Rep. 6085, 6088 (Ponca Tribe Ct. of Indian Offenses Ct.App.1988) ("[W]e conclude that we must look to the tribal law of the Poncas, not vague notions of federal or state due process, to determine not only the source of a right to sue but ultimately what process is due to the plaintiffs in this matter.").

c. Due Process and Equal Protection Under Tribal Law

Tribal courts are beginning to assess what the due process requirement means in the contemporary context. For example, the Sault Ste. Marie Tribe of Chippewa Indians Court of Appeals expressly incorporated *Mino-Bimaadiziwin* into its analysis: "[T]he notion of due process emanates from the concept of achieving harmony in life, to live in balance with all of creation, otherwise known to the Anishinaabe as *mino-bimaadiziwin.*" Payment v. Election Commission, 2022 Sault Ste. Marie Chippewa App. LEXIS 1, at *9 (Sault Ste. Marie Tribe of Chippewa Indians Ct.App.2022). The court invoked several additional principles as well: "Our Anishinaabe teachings of *nibwaakaawin* (wisdom—use of good sense), *zaagi'idiwin* (practice absolute kindness), *minadendmowin* (respect—act without harm) as well as *ayaangwaamizi* (careful and cautious consideration) must guide this Court's decision-making." Id. The court added that Anishinaabe people "are no stranger to listening to the position of all interested persons on any important issue. To be sure, one only need to look to the Seven Grandfather Teachings of the Anishinaabe to understand that Indian nations did not learn 'due process' and 'fairness' from Anglo-American cultures." Id. at *10. The court analogized the talking circle, the process and structure by which Anishinaabe people participate in governance, to due process:

> [T]his Court is called upon to consider the last time its members participated in a talking circle—we think of the order of the circle as it exists in our traditional ways, the importance of the talking stick or eagle feather as the object that enables respectful discussion as well as demands respectful listening. We also think of expected outcomes and finality of the decisions made that result from the open, honest and respectful discussion. It could be said that the application of the Ojibway talking circle principles speak to the essence of due process—a governmental respect for all individuals subject to its authority. Like other Indian communities, this respect can be pragmatically translated in legal proceedings to mean notice and the opportunity to be heard when the deprivation of property or liberty is at stake.

Id. at *11. Compare a talking circle to the adversarial procedures that dominate judicial and administrative process. American due process is no more than the bare minimum. Indigenous due process stretches toward balance and harmony.

Similarly, the Navajo Nation Supreme Court has fleshed out the meaning of "due process" under Diné common law:

> The Navajo principle of *k'e* is important to understanding Navajo due process. *K'e* frames the Navajo perception of moral right, and therefore this court's interpretation of due process rights. *K'e* contemplates one's unique, reciprocal relationships to the community and

> the universe. It promotes respect, solidarity, compassion and cooperation so that people may live in *hozho*, or harmony. *K'e* stresses the duties and obligations of individuals relative to their community. [This is a part of the broader Navajo traditional principle of freedom with responsibility. An individual has much freedom in Navajo society, but that freedom must be exercised with respect for self, family, clan relatives, and the community at large. The importance of *k'e* to maintaining social order cannot be overstated. In light of *k'e*, due process can be understood as a means to ensure that individuals who are living in a state of disorder or disharmony are brought back into the community so that order for the entire community can be reestablished.

Atcitty v. Window Rock District Court, 24 Indian L.Rep. 6013, 6014 (Navajo Nation S.Ct.1996) (footnote omitted). The court invoked a theory of Navajo distributive justice in interpreting "due process" in the context of government benefit entitlements:

> Traditional Navajo due process encompasses a wider zone of interest than general American due process. In cases concerning entitlement to governmental benefits, Navajo due process protections would extend to outcome, making it very relevant. The Navajo doctrine of distributive justice underlies this reasoning:
>
> > Distributive justice is concerned with the well-being of everyone in a community. For

> instance, if I see a hungry person, it does not matter whether I am responsible for the hunger. If someone is injured, it is irrelevant that I did not hurt that person. I have a responsibility, as a Navajo, to treat everyone as if he or she were my relative and therefore to help that hungry person. I am responsible for all my relatives. This value which translates itself into law under the Navajo system of justice is that everyone is part of a community, and the resources of the community must be shared with all. [Yazzie, Life Comes From It: Navajo Justice Concepts, 24 N.M. L. Rev. 175, 185 (1994).]

Distributive justice requires sharing of Navajo Nation resources among eligible applicants. It has its roots in Navajo traditional concepts of community progress through sharing. This is part of Navajo egalitarianism. If the respondents are eligible for receiving governmental benefits, and although they are mere applicants, they have a sufficient property interest under Navajo common law to assert due process claims under the Navajo Nation Bill of Rights. We hold that the respondents in this case have asserted due process rights which would permit them to sue the Navajo Nation.

Id.

Lakota tribal courts have also expressed a higher standard of due process located in tribal custom and tradition. In High Elk v. Veit, 6 Am. Tribal Law 73 (Cheyenne River Sioux Tribal Ct.App.2006), the court stated, "This Court has long recognized that basic Lakota concepts of fairness and respect as well as the federal Indian Civil Rights Act, 25 U.S.C. § 1302(8), clearly guarantees all parties who appear before the courts of the Cheyenne River Sioux Tribe due process of law." Id. at 78. The court tied fundamental fairness to Lakota tradition:

> Just as Lakota tradition requires the respectful listening to the position of all interested persons on any important issue, the legal requirement of due process of law requires that all persons interested in a matter receive adequate written notice of any proceeding that would implicate their personal interests, including their property or, as here, rent payments contractually owed to them, that they be made parties to any case or judgment that would affect those interests, and that they have a full and fair opportunity to participate as a party in any hearing on such issues.

Id. (quoting Cheyenne River Sioux Tribe Housing Authority v. Howard, 32 Indian L.Rep. 6165 (Cheyenne River Sioux Tribe Ct.App.2005)).

Now consider "equal protection." Equal protection as a legal concept originated in the aftermath of the American Civil War, when the American people amended the Constitution to require governments to treat persons equally. Those persons are not identified in the text of the Fourteenth Amendment (except by the euphemism "Three Fifths of all other persons"), but we know them to include formerly enslaved persons. The Fourteenth Amendment also introduced birthright citizenship to all persons born within the United States, but Indian people were excluded from that entitlement. It is now understood that the equal protection doctrine protects people based on their race, gender, religion, sexual orientation, and other immutable characteristics from governmental discrimination narrowly tailored to fulfill a compelling governmental interest. Generations of Indigenous Peoples know all too well that state and federal courts offered virtually no enforcement of the requirement that government ensure equal protection of the laws.

Tribal courts can infuse the equal protection analysis with Indigenous culture. In Wright v. Nottawaseppi Huron Band of the Potawatomi, 2022 Nottawaseppi Huron Band Supreme LEXIS 1 (Nottawaseppi Huron Band of the Potawatomi S.Ct.2022), the court began its interpretation of the equal protection clause in the tribal constitution with Anishinaabe legal principles:

> We view Article X's equal protection guarantee through the lens of *Mno Bmadzewen* and the *Noeg Meshomsenanek Kenomagewenen* [Seven Grandfather Teachings]. The concept of equal protection originates in the Fourteenth Amendment of the United States Constitution. It is a mandate to state governments for correction and repair, or in the parlance of American history, reconstruction and the eradication of the badges of slavery. The mandate imposed on a government to guarantee equal protection assumes the state of

> horrendous and unequal protection rooted in a racial caste system. What a sad state of affairs! Bodéwadmi people, in contrast, hope to achieve harmony by living life correctly, which is the essence of *Mno Bmadzewen*. * * * "Harmony" in Anishinaabe tribal governance starts with cooperation and mutual aid. * * *

Id. at *34–35 (citations and footnote omitted). The court identified the teaching of *Debanawen* [love] and its healing elements as the most relevant principle associated with equal protection:

> We believe the leading principle of the *Noeg Meshomsenanek Kenomagewenen*, the teaching that best encapsulates the goal of harmony in this community, is *Debanawen* (love). Debanawen "is the capacity for caring and desire for harmony and well-being in interpersonal relationships and with the environment." * * * *Debanawen* "transcends time and space; it links us inexplicably to our ancestors and future generations." * * * In times of great difficulty and even violence, Bodéwadmi people reacted with *Debanawen*, a great healing tool. Article X's guarantee of equal protection must be interpreted in light of the corrective and reparative principle of *Debanawen*.

Id. at *35–36 (citations omitted).

In Colville Confederated Tribes v. Davisson, 35 Indian L.Rep. 6023 (Confederated Tribes of the Colville Reservation Tribal Ct.2008), the court affirmed against an equal protection challenge a tribal statute placing a higher burden for proving self-defense if the defendant was charged with domestic violence. The court reasoned that tribal customs strongly opposed to domestic violence justified the rule:

> In the legislative findings, [Colville Tribal Code §] 5–5–2, the Business Council found that:
>
>> The Tribes, in accordance with the unique and distinct attributes and values of our culture, find that domestic violence is contrary to the interests of our people, our traditional values, and a sense of wellbeing and growth. In order to promote healthy communities within our Tribes, we need to understand and embrace our traditional understandings of familial relationships which do not condone violence. . . .
>>
>> Another manifestation of this is domestic violence, which detrimentally affects generations of members of our community.
>
> These are adequate grounds for treating crimes involving domestic violence different than crimes not involving domestic violence. Equal protection is satisfied.

Id. at 6026. See also id. ("The [due process] question is just the same as [the] equal protection [question.]"). On appeal, the appellate court largely affirmed the lower court's reasoning. Davisson v. Colville Confederated Tribes, 10 Am. Tribal Law 403, 414 (Confederated Tribes of the Colville Reservation Ct.App.2012).

In general, however, tribal courts tend to follow federal precedents teaching that due process requires notice and an opportunity to be heard and that equal protection prohibits intentional discrimination against discrete minorities. See Hopi Tribe v. Mahkewa, 21 Indian L.Rep. 6139, 6140 (Hopi Tribal Ct.1992) ("The ICRA was passed by the U.S. Congress to extend constitutional guarantees to Indian people in tribal courts. It subjects Indian tribes to the same limitations as those imposed on the federal government in the United States Constitution. In other words, the rights of defendants in tribal courts must be protected in basically the same way as they are in non-Indian courts."). For example, in Hall v. Tribal Business Council, 23 Indian L.Rep. 6039 (Three Affiliated Tribes of the Fort Berthold Reservation Dist.Ct.1996), the court ordered the tribal business council to consider appeals of grazing range unit applications and further ordered the council members with conflicts of interest to recuse themselves. The court reasoned that due process requires a fair and impartial tribunal, concluding that "tribal applicants for range unit leases are entitled to due process under the Indian Civil Rights Act of 1968. The lineaments of such due process include the basic elements of fairness, notice, and an appropriate balancing of individual and (tribal) government interests to determine the adequacy of the procedure provided." Id. at 6043.

In Swinomish Tribal Community v. Peters, 15 Am. Tribal Law 377 (Swinomish Tribal Ct.2018), a case involving the right of a criminal defendant accused of domestic violence to confront their accuser, a tribal citizen who asserted tribal custom and tradition to excuse her from testifying against her alleged perpetrator (he was later convicted, see 15 Am. Tribal Law 382 (Swinomish Tribal Ct.2018)). The prosecution argued that sworn statements should suffice in light of tribal customary law:

> The tribe cites the book "A Gathering of Wisdoms, Tribal Mental Health: A Cultural Perspective", Second Addition (2002) to inform the court of the culture and history of the Swinomish community. In sum, the tribe contends that one of the values of the tribal community is to "be loyal to your family members" and a traditional value of non-direct interference with other's behavior as opposed to direct confrontation. As a result, and put in terms of giving testimony at trial, a victim "may be unavailable to testify due to Swinomish societal norms, obligations and unspoken rules." (quoting the tribe's brief in support of the motion).

Id. at 380. The court rejected the argument, asserting, "The tribe's proposed rule would allow the testimony of *any* crime victim to be presented in writing, and not subject to cross-examination." Id. at 381 (emphasis in original). The court reasoned that the tribal government's choice to opt-in to the special domestic violence jurisdiction over non-Indians under 25 U.S.C. § 1304(d)(4) justified the adoption of the rule. The court reasoned that the tribal court was already a western-style court: "As established, and in practice, the Swinomish Tribal Court is modeled after the western court system." Id. The court concluded:

> Looking at the past, present and future, the Swinomish tribe has moved deliberately and clearly in the development of the court and the protection of defendant's right to due process. This court finds no basis to support the proposal that it should reject the clear intentions and movement of the tribe even if there were evidence that the U.S. Constitutional right of confrontation is in direct conflict with the tribe's historical culture and traditions.

Id. at 381–82.

Tribal banishment or exclusion actions often implicate due process and equal protection concerns. In Burns Paiute Indian Tribe v. Dick, 22 Indian L.Rep. 6016 (Burns Paiute Tribal Ct.App.1994), the court held that the tribal banishment ordinance was constitutionally overbroad, violating the equal protection and due process clauses of the Indian Civil Rights Act. The court noted that the banishment ordinance was written in a way that could lead to the exclusion of a nonmember for a simple parking violation. In Chehalis Indian Tribe v. Charles, 22 Indian L.Rep. 6018 (Chehalis Ct.App.1994), the court reversed an exclusion order for lack of evidence that the excluded individual was a threat to the health, safety, or welfare to the tribe. In Calflooking v. Tulalip Tribes, 13 Am. Tribal Law 491 (Tulalip Tribal Ct.App.2016), the court reversed a conviction for violating an exclusion order where the excluded person had never been served with the order.

Unrepresented parties present an additional difficulty. In True Clown v. Coast to Coast, 23 Indian L.Rep. 6055 (Cheyenne River Sioux Tribal Ct.App. 1993), the court reversed a judgment against an unrepresented party involving a debt owed to a reservation store. During the trial, the trial judge questioned the defendant, who was unrepresented. The trial transcript indicated to the appellate court that the trial judge questioned the defendant excessively about "whether the defendant had any just excuse for not paying the presumed debt." Id. at 6059. The questioning undermined the court's obligation to allow both sides to present their cases. In a case where one or more parties is unrepresented, the trial judge has additional obligations to ensure fairness:

> While the obligation to create a satisfactory record normally falls on professional legal counsel where the parties are represented by lawyers, that responsibility must be partially assumed by the trial judge in those cases where the parties appear without counsel before the trial court. Tribal trial judges therefore must be scrupulously fair in assuring that they afford an opportunity to hear both sides of the case, that they hear all relevant evidence the parties desire to present, that they protect the rights of opposing parties to cross-examine or otherwise question the evidence presented against them,

> and that the trial judge makes a clear record supporting and explaining its legal conclusions.

Id.

2. SPEECH

Freedom of speech is core positive right available to all persons in tribal communities, extensively protected by tribal constitutional or statutory provisions, tribal case law, and the Indian Civil Rights Act.

Tribal free speech cases generally follow federal law. For example, in Fort Peck Tribes v. DeCoteau, 2008 WL 9493376 (Fort Peck Ct.App.2008), the court affirmed the dismissal of a criminal case brought against a tribal citizen for using obscene language against a tribal police officer. The tribe had argued that the defendant's speech rights were limited by a prior precedent of the court, Fort Peck Tribes v. Red Fox, No. 001 (Fort Peck Ct.App.1986). In *Red Fox*, the court affirmed the conviction of Red Fox for criminal contempt of court after he had referred to the trial judge in a denigrating way. The *DeCoteau* court disagreed that *Red Fox* was controlling, persuaded by a United States Supreme Court decision that held the First Amendment prohibited a prosecution for making negative comments to police.

Tribal courts ordinarily analyze tribal ordinances regulating speech under the federal doctrine of prior restraint. See In re Melendez, 1999 WL 34995660 (Nev. Inter-Tribal Ct.App.1999), where the court reversed the criminal conviction of a juvenile member of the Reno Sparks Indian Colony for violating a tribal ordinance that prohibited clothing that demonstrated a gang affiliation. The appellate court held the ordinance as unenforceable due to the potentially limitless application to all forms of symbolic speech:

> The record reveals that the Reno-Sparks Indian Colony gang activity ordinance is directed at a wide variety of symbolic speech, much of which is not inherently gang related. The subject matter of the law's prohibitions is not merely broad, but open-ended and potentially limitless. The ordinance does not define, list, or explain what constitutes a "gang symbol" or "gang colors," it broadly defines "gang" in such a way that defies even a talented prosecutor to sustain his or her burden in proving up the conditions put forth in the ordinance. Further, almost any color combination may become gang colors and almost any symbol may be a gang symbol, words, "the list is endless." What is innocent today may become a gang symbol tomorrow according to the whim of the gangs themselves. Were a gang (however defined) to adopt red, white, and blue as its colors or the crucifix as a symbol, every school and church would be "flashing" gang signals.
>
> Additionally, while the ordinance prohibits gang members from wearing gang colors, emblems, and insignia, it also prohibits non-gang members from engaging in symbolic

> speech, which is protected by the first amendment (ICRA and the U.S. Const., amend. I). While we do not presume to say that the Indian Civil Rights act and the United States Constitution, are coextensive, both include protections, not only written or spoken words, but also a considerable amount of expressive conduct, often called "symbolic speech." Nonverbal conduct implicates the first amendment if the actor intends to convey a particularized message and it is likely the message will be understood by those who view it. In this regard the ordinance is unconstitutionally overly broad. We declare the ordinance invalid.

Id. at *5.

Like state and federal officials, tribal officials' right to speak can be limited by tribal statutes restricting the authority of officials to speak on behalf of the tribe. In LaPorte v. Fletcher, 2006 WL 6351711 (Little River Band of Ottawa Indians Ct.App.2006), the court held that a tribal ordinance restricting speech rights of employees acting in their scope of duties did not run afoul of the right to free speech. In Mayes v. Smith, 6 Am. Tribal Law 6 (Cherokee Nation Judicial Appeals Trib.2005), the Cherokee Nation's high court refused to protect individuals who falsely claimed to be officials of the Nation. In another case, Chase v. Mashantucket Pequot Gaming Enterprise, 2 Mash. Rep. 387, 1998 WL 35234940 (Mashantucket Pequot Tribal Ct.1998), the court held that an employee of the tribe could "gossip" about a non-employee outside of the work environment, but that the employee's speech rights on the job were limited where job performance was negatively affected.

Tribal courts have dismissed criminal cases brought against politically active tribal citizens where the timing of the prosecution appeared related to the citizen's speech activities. In Washoe Tribe of Nevada and California v. Biggoose, 1999 WL 34995881 (Nev. Inter-Tribal Ct.App.1999), the affirmed the dismissal of a criminal complaint where the defendant had engaged in political opposition against the tribal government:

> The Defendant argued in her Motion to Dismiss that the issues surrounding the refiling of the complaint against her raise the issue of vindictive prosecution due to her political activity after the complaint lay dormant for almost four months from the time it was dismissed without prejudice. Her political actions to have the Chairman of the Tribe recalled resulted in the refiling of the complaint against her by the prosecutor. Basically, that if she was not involved as the lead person of the Reform Peoples Group to the recall petition, the complaint probably would not have been refiled against her. Thus she alleges her constitutional rights of free speech are violated.

Id. at *2. The appellate court agreed with the trial court that the defendant's original case had been dismissed without prejudice and inactive for several months. During the interval, the defendant had spoken out against the tribal government. Refiling of the original charges followed soon after, leading the court to conclude there was "ample evidence creating an appearance of retaliation against the Defendant [that] would have the impermissible effect of chilling the exercise of free speech. . . ." Id. at *4.

On occasion, tribal courts draw from tribal customary law to either expand or restrict free speech norms. In Gardner v. Littlejohn, 9 Am. Tribal Law 431 (Ho-Chunk Nation Trial Ct.2011), the court recognized a warrior's or veteran's privilege that would immunize them from defamation claims. The plaintiffs invoked *woigixate*, which "requires that all people be treated with respect and compassion and that no one should be treated badly or demeaned because of their situation," Topping v. Ho-Chunk Nation Grievance Board, 11 Am. Tribal Law 388, 393 (Ho-Chunk Nation S.Ct.2010), to allege a defamation cause of action under tribal common law. The tribal court certified a question to a traditional court of elders about whether traditional *hocąk* law recognized defamation as a cause of action. The traditional court did acknowledge a modified defamation cause of action:

> The Traditional Court indicated that in the tradition and custom of the Ho-Chunk Nation defamation existed, meaning on occasion, individuals did publicly question the honor of another individual. Nevertheless, *hocąk* people generally spoke the truth. If someone said something that was a lie or a false statement about another person, then that person typically

> ignored the lie that was said about them, knowing that it will come full circle back to the lying party. In other instances, the person who uttered the lie or false statement would repeat it to that person face-to-face with tobacco, and the truth would reveal itself.

Gardner, 9 Am. Tribal Law at 439. The court then inquired with the traditional court about defenses available to veterans. The traditional court acknowledged a warrior privilege:

> * * * The Traditional Court indicated that a warrior maintained a privilege to speak his mind. Ho-Chunk people have distinctive cultural values, and one such value is their proud warrior tradition. Warriors embody strength, honor, pride, and wisdom, and a warrior's success depends on the aforementioned embodiments. Warriors return to their respective community with experiences that make them valued members of their society.

Id. Armed with these findings, the trial court dismissed the defamation action on the ground that the defendant was a veteran entitled to a warrior's privilege akin to legislative privilege. The tribal appellate court reversed on procedural grounds. Gardner v. Littlejohn, 11 Am. Tribal Law 400 (Ho-Chunk Nation S.Ct.2011).

In Navajo Nation v. Crockett, 7 Nav. Rep. 237, 1996 Navajo Sup. LEXIS 14 (Navajo Nation S.Ct. 1996), the court reversed the termination of tribal employees who had reported possible misconduct by their managers. The court recognized tribal common law of speech as incorporating mindfulness toward personal relationships:

> [S]peech should be delivered with respect and honesty. This requirement arises from the concept of *ke'*, which is the "glue" that creates and binds relationships between people. To avoid disruptions of relationships, Navajo common law mandates that controversies and arguments be resolved by "talking things out." This process of "talking things out," called *hoozhoojigo*, allows each member of the group to cooperate and talk about how to resolve a problem. This requirement places another limitation on speech, which is that a disgruntled person must speak directly with the person's relative about his or her concerns before seeking other avenues of redress with strangers.

7 Nav. Rep. at 241, 1996 Navajo Sup. LEXIS 14, at *9. Tribal employees must respect their supervisors and attempt to speak things out with them first:

> In the employment context, relationships are established according to the personnel policies, and other instruments. When an employee has a complaint about a supervisor, according to Navajo custom and tradition, he or she should first approach the supervisor and discuss the problem in a respectful manner. Moreover, under the Navajo common law concept of *nalyeeh*, the employee should not seek to correct the person by summoning the coercive powers of

> a powerful person or entity, but should seek to correct the wrongful action by "talking things out." The employee should not seek a remedy from a stranger, but should rather explain the problem to the person or one of his or her relatives and ask that "things be put right." If this method proves unsuccessful, then the employee also has access to an internal employment grievance process. Even in this formal, modern process for addressing grievances, the traditional rules of respect, honesty, and kinship apply.

Id. However, when the employee alleges supervisor mismanagement, an exception can be made for matters of "public concern." Id.

Speech rights can be implicated in banishment or exclusion matters. Tribal nations possess the power to exclude persons from tribally owned or controlled lands, like any landowner, but as sovereign governments, the exercise of that power may not infringe on human rights such as free speech. In Fort Peck Tribes v. Smith, 16 Am. Tribal Law 247 (Fort Peck Ct.App.2021), the court rejected a claim that the tribe's exclusion ordinance was void for vagueness. The ordinance read:

> Any person may be excluded from the Reservation for:
>
> (a) Conduct which substantially threatens the life, the physical health or the safety of an Indian or Indians residing on the Reservation.

> (b) Conviction in Tribal Court of at least three felonies or Class A Misdemeanors which involve acts of violence against persons under the laws of the Tribes.

3 Fort Peck Tribal Code § 701. The court explained the background of the void for vagueness doctrine as requiring enough certainty of individual acts that could lead to exclusion to provide adequate notice to persons subject to the ordinance:

> It is important to note however that in order to lawfully exclude a person an Indian tribe has to give notice to those persons whom may be subject to exclusion with clarity what may constitute grounds for exclusion. Ordinances that may have a chilling effect on the exercise of free speech or religious freedom rights, or those that attempt to punish conduct, must clearly define that conduct which may result in penalties being imposed, or rights denied, in order to satisfy due process of law. Otherwise persons are not put on notice of what behavior may result in the denial of their freedoms or rights. In addition, if no standards are laid out in the law persons may be subjected to arbitrary enforcement of the law based upon the personal predilections of each Judge that may hear a case. One Judge may feel, for example, that drug use is having such a deleterious impact on the tribal community that such use justifies banishment, while another may feel that such a remedy is an overreach for drug activity. It is therefore up to the Fort Peck Tribal Council to define for the

> Tribal Court when banishment would be appropriate to avoid conflicting value judgments. This doctrine is referred to as the "overbreadth" or void for vagueness doctrine. Although they are distinct concepts, overbreadth and vagueness challenges are closely related in the principles they vindicate, and courts often discuss them together.

Smith, 16 Am. Tribal Law at 251. The court concluded that the Fort Peck ordinance was specific enough to give adequate notice to the public of acts that could lead to exclusion.

3. RELIGIOUS FREEDOM

Citizens of tribal nations have lived through centuries of religious discrimination inflicted on them by colonizers. Tribal constitutional and statutory like, and the Indian Civil Rights Act, protect tribal members and others under tribal jurisdiction from religious discrimination. However, due to the reality that numerous tribal nations choose their leaders through a traditional process, most tribal nations do not bar the establishment of a particular religion. This is also reflected in ICRA, which does not include an establishment clause.

There are relatively few conflicts over religious freedom in tribal communities, but they do occur. For example, in Redman v. Birdshead, 10 Okla. Trib. 110, 2007 WL 9193014 (Cheyenne-Arapaho Tribes S.Ct.2007), the court was confronted with conflicting claims to religious authority and authenticity. The Arapaho Indians of the Cheyenne-Arapaho Tribes in

Oklahoma are sometimes known as the southern Arapahos. The Arapaho Indians of the Wind River Reservation in Wyoming are referred to as the Northern Arapaho Tribe. The Northern Arapaho Tribe sued Birdhead and Spottedwolf attempting to bar them from performing the ceremony on the ground that they had not received the approval of the northern Arapaho practitioners. The court noted that an earlier tribal constitutional provision on religious freedom invoked the Indian Civil Rights Act: "To the extent applicable, no person shall be denied by the tribes in exercising self-government those rights guaranteed in Title II of the Act of April 11, 1968 [ICRA], including freedom of speech, conscience, worship, and assembly." Cheyenne-Arapaho Tribes Const. [1975] art. III, § 1. The operative tribal constitutional provision at the time of the decision was more emphatic in its protection of religious freedom: "The government of the Tribes shall not make or enforce any law which . . . (a) infringes on religious or cultural beliefs or prohibits the free exercise thereof, including the right to possess and use peyote for religious purposes, nor any law which establishes religion . . . ." Cheyenne-Arapaho Tribes Const. [2006] art. I, § 1. The court concluded that the 2006 constitution prohibited the enforcement of any governmental order barring individuals from performing Arapaho ceremonies.

4. RIGHT TO PRIVACY

Probably because the United States Constitution does not include an explicit right to individual privacy, neither do the Indian Bill of Rights and many tribal constitutions. At least one tribal court has interpreted the Indian Bill of Rights and a tribal statutory provision mirroring the Indian Bill of Rights to include an implied right to privacy. In Tonasket v. Cipp, 20 Indian L.Rep. 6125 (Colville Confederated Tribes Administrative Ct.1992), the court followed the guidance of federal constitutional law to find a right to privacy in the "penumbra" of the tribal civil rights statute. The case involved a drug test of a tribal enterprise employee. The court held the test was reasonably related to the enhancement of public safety and therefore valid. Other tribal courts are reluctant to do so. E.g., Swinomish Indian Tribal Community v. Seward, 15 Am. Tribal Law 373 (Swinomish Tribal Ct.2014).

C. INDIAN CHILD WELFARE

In Anishinaabe novelist Angeline Boulley's newest novel, *Sisters in the Wind*, she draws upon a common metaphor to describe the paradigmatic difference between Indigenous and non-Indigenous families. Non-Indian family treats families like peas and Indigenous families are like onions. Peas come in a pod where everyone looks the same, where the nuclear family is compartmentalized. Indigenous families look rough on the outside but are sweet on the inside, with layer upon layer of extended family built up to protect the inner core, which are the children.

Under early American common law taken from the English tradition, children were property of their male parents. While children are no longer considered property, the vestiges of the common law remain. Under federal and state law, children under 18 are incompetents under the law, subject to the guardianship of their custodians. Conversely, Indigenous Peoples typically treated children as individuals with their own prerogatives, not property or mere wards to a guardian. E.g., Alonzo v. Martine, 18 Indian L.Rep. 6129, 6129 (Navajo Nation S.Ct. 1991) ("Navajos do not view children as property or possessions, but value them as individuals in a community."). While most tribal nations have adopted child welfare systems similar to state systems, many tribes have attempted to apply culturally appropriate policies.

1. THE EFFECT OF THE INDIAN CHILD WELFARE ACT

In the United States, some of the worst human rights abuse perpetrated by the colonizer upon Indigenous Peoples involved the forced removal of many thousands of Indian children from their homes. The federal government, assisted by private religious organizations, forced entire generations of Indian children into boarding schools far from their homes starting in the mid-19th century and continuing for decades into the 20th century. In the mid-20th century, federal policy continued this program by enabling and encouraging states to remove Indian children and adopt them out to non-Indian families far from their homes and families. From 1958 to 1967, government programs like the Indian Adoption Project and private agencies removed an estimated 25% to 35% of Indian children, placing them in non-

Native homes. In 1978, Congress enacted the Indian Child Welfare Act (ICWA), 25 U.S.C. § 1901, et seq., to slow the rate of Indian child removal.

In some respects, most notably in terms of reforming state child welfare systems and enabling tribal nations to develop their governmental capacity, ICWA has been enormously successful. But because Indigenous poverty in the United States remains a critical problem, ICWA has not been terribly successful in stopping Indian child removals by states. Even now, the vast poverty of many areas of Indian country causes many tribal nations to struggle mightily with issues arising from Indian children in abuse and neglect situations. Tribal nations dedicate a large percentage of their resources to child welfare matters, though often those resources are still too limited to respond to the need.

ICWA routes many state court child welfare cases into tribal courts, but it should be noted that ICWA itself does not govern tribal child welfare matters. E.g., C.B. v. Little Flower Freedom Center, 18 Indian L.Rep. 6121, 6122 (Northern Plains Intertribal Ct.App.1991) ("[T]he Indian Child Welfare Act of 1978 is not binding upon the Devils Lake Sioux Tribe unless adopted by tribal council."). Congress designed ICWA to enable tribal nations to assume jurisdiction over their own children, 25 U.S.C. § 1911(a), but also to inform child welfare decisions with Indigenous cultures and traditions in mind, e.g., § 1915 (requiring state courts to follow tribal placement preferences). Tribal self-determination contracting also enables tribal nations to establish their own child welfare programs, working alongside with tribal justice systems. And, because ICWA allows tribes to intervene in state court Indian child welfare proceedings, § 1911(c), tribal child welfare programs also work with state courts and state child welfare programs.

Child welfare cases, as understood here, tragically involve the removal of a child from their home because of abuse or neglect. Child abuse is a criminal act and is treated as such. Child neglect is the cause of the large majority of child welfare cases adjudicated in tribal courts. Neglect derives directly from mental health and addiction issues, both of which are caused by the poverty and trauma that are the consequences of colonization. Once the tribal government has removed a child, the tribal court will schedule a hearing to determine whether the government had probable cause to remove the child and to determine placement. Prior to ICWA's enactment in 1978, state actors would remove Indian children from their homes and conduct removal hearings without providing Indian custodians any notice or opportunity to be heard. Too often, Indian children taken by the state would never be heard from again by their families. Tribal courts take notice and other fundamental fairness matters very seriously. In Matter of A.P., 15 Am. Tribal Law 272 (Fort Peck Ct.App. 2017), the court recognized "the due process right to be notified and have an opportunity to participate in a child welfare case involving his/her child(ren)." Id. at 278.

Tribal nations legislate in light of the history of Indian child removal, incorporating explicit policies disfavoring removals and favoring reunification and invoking cultural and traditional values. The child welfare code of the Nottawaseppi Huron Band of the Potawatomi, for example, provides:

> The Nottawaseppi Huron Band of the Potawatomi believes all children deserve the following: a mother (*gashe*); a father (*noos*); identity with the traditional way of life (*mno bmadzewen*); to learn and speak their language (*Bodewewadmi*); to have a family (*mezodan*); know their relatives (*nwemagen*); to know the traditional laws, customs, and ceremonies of the people; a knowledge and understanding of the seven grandfather teachings; *Bwakawen* (wisdom), *Debanawen* (love), *Kejitwawenindowen* (respect), *Wedasewen* (bravery), *Gwekwadzewen* (honesty), *Edbesendowen* (humility), and *Debwewin* (truth); and the ability to live according to the practice of the traditional laws, customs, and ceremonies that govern their people.

Nottawaseppi Huron Band of the Potawatomi Code § 7.5–1(C). Some tribes recognize positive rights for children, such as the right to be free from removal and the right to government services in the event of removal. The Waganakising Odawa Tribal Code provides:

> A. Children have the right not to be separated from their parents forcibly or against their will, except when competent authorities

> subject to judicial review determine that such separation is necessary for their best interests and all legal requirements in this Code for removal of a child are met. Whenever such separations are necessary, children have the right wherever possible not to be separated from other members of their immediate and extended family.
>
> B. Children temporarily or permanently deprived of their family environment shall be entitled to special protection and assistance provided by the Tribe, which shall strive to ensure continuity in their upbringing and the maintenance of ethnic, cultural, religious, and linguistic heritage.

Waganakising Odawa Tribal Code § 5.103.

Tribal courts also acknowledge tribal common law traditions and customs, invoking them as interpretative rules in interpreting tribal child welfare laws. In Bahe v. Platero, 11 Am. Tribal Law 104 (Navajo Nation S.Ct.2012), for example, the Navajo Nation Supreme Court pointed out that decisions involving Navajo children must be assessed in light of "*Diné bi beenahaz'áanii*, which teaches that our children occupy a space in Navajo culture that can best be described as holy or sacred." Id at 107. That court also instructed Navajo parents to fulfill their obligations to their children:

> Parents have a moral and legal obligation to protect their children through their own careful decisions. Parents must confront the situations

> involving their children and look to their children's needs above the parents' own personal disagreements. Through "talking things out," *baa yáti'*, those in disharmony are brought back into *hózhó*. . . . Through participation in mediation, it is up to both parents, without animosity, to come together for the sake of the children and fully participate in talking out the issues. If properly done, the children can be human beings who are reliable, compassionate, and upright. *T'áá nihí ánóht'ę́ęgo éí díí ḱǫ́ǫ bee nihá bik'eh 'áhoolyaaígíí bik'ehgo hazhó'ó ałch'į́' yá łti', 'ahigą́ dóó ahididláásh t'áág'ééd, dóó hazhó'ó binaho'áago éí niha' áłchiní bohónée dzáágo dinóoyééł*. Parents need to heed these fundamental principles on parental duties.

Id. at 112 (citation omitted). Some tribal nations allow for tribal cultural adoptions, which may vary considerably from adoptions in state courts, including allowing for open adoptions. E.g., DuMarce v. Heminger, 20 Indian L.Rep. 6077, 6078 (Northern Plains Intertribal Ct.App.1992) (quoting Sisseton-Wahpeton tribal code provision on *Ecagwaya* or "Traditional Adoption").

Some tribal courts have acknowledged that customary international law principles may be consistent with tribal customs and traditions. For example, see In re the Custody of T.M., 3 Am. Tribal Law 485 (Navajo Nation S.Ct.2001), a case addressing whether and how the court should weigh the preferences of a child in a custody dispute. There, the court pointed to Article 12 of the Convention on the Rights of the Child, United Nations General Assembly Resolution No. 44/25 (November 20, 1989). The court noted that neither the United States nor the Navajo Nation had ratified this convention, but that the court could apply it as a matter of tribal common law:

> * * * [T]he provisions of Article 12 of the Convention on the Rights of the Child mirror Navajo common law. The Appellant correctly states that everyone has a right to be heard at a meaningful time and in a meaningful way. * * * The Appellant also correctly notes that Navajos have a right to speak for themselves. * * * The applicable maxim is, "it's up to him," meaning that the individual must be consulted before action affecting his interest can be taken.
>
> There is no question that Navajo common law grants a child, and in this case, the Appellant, a right to be heard, considering his maturity, in a case involving that child's custody.

TM, 3 Am. Tribal Law at 489.

In spite of their best hopes, tribal nations occasionally do have to remove children from their homes. The emergency hearing sets in motion several legal matters. First, the tribal court will make a decision on placement. If there was no probable cause to remove the child, the child will go home. If there is, the tribal court will make a foster care placement decision based on the placement preferences established by tribal statute. Social science research conclusively shows that removal from home is never good for children, but sometimes removal is the best possible option in a given situation. Tribal officials hope to place the child in a close biological relative's home or in a tribally licensed foster care home. The federal government funds foster care, at least for the first year or so, through state child welfare systems. Tribal courts are usually required to seek payment through the state system, following state rules, unless a tribe seeks and receives authorization to seek payment from the federal government directly.

In a foster care placement scenario, the tribal goal is always the reunification of the family. For example, the appellate court of the Grand Traverse Band of Ottawa and Chippewa Indians reminded foster parents of their role in seeking reunification of the family, citing to fundamental Anishinaabe teachings:

> The [foster parents] remain at this time the primary caregivers of the Anishinaabe Benodjehn. Appellants can and should be guided by the Seven Grandfathers. Above all, it is the role and duty of the foster parents to ensure that the children are in a home guided by *zaagidwin*, love. The foster parents also have an important role to play as protectors of the children from the legal storm that swirls around them, which requires *aakwade'ewin*, bravery. Understanding the shifting roles played by foster parents requires *dbaadendiziwin*, humility, and *nbwaakaawin*, wisdom; appellants' counsel has a role to play assisting appellants in that regard as well. Appellants' obligations to the Grand

> Traverse Band and to the citizenship of the Anishinaabe Benodjehn requires *mnaadendimowin*, respect, to the tribe and its traditions. Going forward, as this matter appears headed for the real work of pursuing a goal of reunification, the appellants must be patient (which perhaps should be an eighth grandfather teaching). It is very true the biological mother and the Anishinaabe Benodjehn have been separated for many years. Reunification may be a difficult process, and all parties must be bound to *gwekwaadiziwin*, honesty, and to *debwewin*, truth.

In re Donn, 2017 Grand Traverse Band App. LEXIS 1, at *15 (Grand Traverse Band of Ottawa and Chippewa Indians App.Ct.2017).

Tribal nations dedicate a far greater proportion of government resources to child welfare than state governments do, though tribal resources are far more limited. States typically seek the termination of parental rights after a year or so once federal foster care money runs out. Children in state systems are then available for adoption and those not adopted remain in state foster care, wards of the state until they turn eighteen. Tribal nations have often moved away from the termination of parental rights, recognizing that the rehabilitation of families can take longer than a year. Tribes typically allow for open or cultural adoptions to occur after foster care money expires, opting for a less permanent termination of parental rights. Some tribal nations acknowledge a child's positive right to know where they come from. For example, the Navajo Nation Supreme Court acknowledges that right:

> Our common law takes as a right that it must be known precisely from where one has originated. . . . Knowing one's point of origination . . . is extremely important to the Navajo People, because only then will a person know which *adoone'e* (clan) and *dine'e* (people) the person is. Those precepts are essential to a Navajo's identity and must be known for Navajo religious ceremonies. One must know them to seek *hozho* (harmony and peace). When applied to a child, they are necessary for the child's emotional, physical, and spiritual well-being.

In re A.M.K., 9 Am. Tribal Law 191, 201 (Navajo Nation S.Ct.2010) (citations and quotation marks omitted).

At the removal, placement, and termination stages, and every other critical moment in a child welfare case, the tribal court must make a determination of the best interests of the child after a fact-finding hearing, typically called a best interests hearing. Those determinations are made in light of tribal laws; the Yurok Tribe's code is representative:

> Parents have the responsibility to make decisions and perform other parental functions necessary for the care and growth of their minor children. In any proceeding between parents under this chapter, the best interests of the child shall be the standard by which the Tribal Court

> determines and allocates parental responsibilities. The Tribe recognizes the fundamental importance of the parent-child relationship and that the relationship between the child and each parent should be fostered unless inconsistent with the best interests of the child. The interests of the child are served by a parenting arrangement that best maintains a child's emotional growth, Tribal and cultural ties, health and stability, educational needs, and physical care. The best interests of the child are ordinarily served when the existing pattern of interaction between a parent and child is altered only to the extent necessitated by the changed relationship of the parents or as required to protect the child from physical, educational, mental or emotional harm.
>
> A determination of the best interests of the child should include consideration of the rights of the child as a Yurok and the interest of the Yurok community and Tribe in retaining its children in its society; political membership in the Tribe and the attendant benefits such as hunting and fishing rights; the child's cultural heritage; and the opportunity to participate in the ongoing customary life of the Tribe and maintain the connection that each Yurok has with the Yurok territory and their extended family.

Yurok Tribal Code § 13.25.010. See also Colville Tribal Code § 5–1–108 ("The Court shall determine custody in accordance with the best interests of the child and, secondarily, the traditions and customs of the Colville Indian people.") (quoted in In re Guardianship of K.W.B., 33 Indian L.Rep. 5043, 6050 (Confederated Tribes of the Colville Reservation Tribal Ct.2006).

When tribal nations do move to terminate parental rights or remove children from their homes, the procedural protections afforded parents and guardians subject to a termination petition are robust. In E.C.D. v. D.B., 27 Indian L.Rep. 6001 (Cheyenne River Sioux Ct.App.1999), the court reversed an order terminating the rights of a parent that had consented to the termination by signing a document out of court before a notary. Tribal law, however, mirrored the best practices reflected in ICWA and required that the consent be "executed" before a judge with jurisdiction over the matter. See also In re Welfare of A.T. (Weber v. Children & Family Services), 32 Indian L.Rep. 6139 (Confederated Tribes of the Colville Reservation Ct.App.2005) (vacating order taking children into tribal governmental care violated due process in not explaining reasons for the removal); In re Welfare of J.L.V. (Valdez-Catalon v. Colville Confederated Tribes), 32 Indian L.Rep. 6142 (Confederated Tribes of the Colville Reservation Ct.App.2005) (vacating order assuming natural father was not acceptable placement because of he was a citizen and resident of Mexico). Cf. In Matter of L.C.M., 32 Indian L.Rep. 6032 (Pawnee Nation S.Ct.2005) (parent waived right to a termination hearing).

Matters involving children can become very complicated. In one case, In re Guardianship of K.W.B. (Wilder v. Boozer), 33 Indian L.Rep. 6043, 6050 (Confederated Tribes of the Colville Reservation Tribal Ct.2006), the case started as a child custody action arising from a marriage dissolution. But the mother walked on, leading the maternal grandparents to file a guardianship petition designed to prevent the non-Indian father from assuming custody. The court invoked the history and tradition of grandparent participation in childraising in concluding that grandparents can have visitation rights, despite the fitness of the father to parent the child. Importantly, the court made a determination that in that particular case, the application of custom and tradition was appropriate given the close connection the child and their family had with tradition Chinook culture:

> K.W.B. is an enrolled Colville tribal member. K.W.B. is Nez Perce and Moses (Finding of Fact # 118). Her maternal family is very traditional (Finding of Fact # 7). Traditionally, children were allowed to make their own decision about where to live (Finding of Fact # 8). Traditionally, children went to live with their father around the age of puberty (Finding of Fact # 9). K.W.B. sees Darlene Wilder as a mother figure in her life and there is a strong bond between them (Finding of Fact # 18, # 55). K.W.B. is involved in the longhouse tradition, digging roots, traditional plant identification, traditional powwow dancing, Chinook dances, Native American flute and is learning her own songs

> and Native American language and give aways (Finding of Fact # 73, # 82, # 88). K.W.B. will become a matriarch of her family (Finding of Fact # 81). The Court finds that K.W.B. is very strong and active in her Native American culture and traditions. The Court finds that Colville traditions and cultures have the same weight as state law and are given preference over state law and federal law.

Id. at 6053.

The appellate court reversed, holding that the trial court exceeded its jurisdiction to grant the petition for a guardianship. The court held that biological father was a fit parent and, once the court concluded as such, the matter should have ended. The court noted:

> We understand the cultural ramifications of our findings here. There is no question it can take Minor away from her Reservation and remaining Indian family. In our Courts we walk a fine line, however. It is not the role of the Judges or Justices to enter a judgment solely to protect a child's "Indianness." Minor has two parents, one Indian and one not. Nothing in our traditions and customs would support that one culture is better for a child than the other. She is a child of both. Nothing precludes Appellant from raising Minor to know of both her heritages. It is the role of a parent to make that decision, not the Court systems'. It appears from the record that the trial judge used "culture" as

> a super-factor in her analysis as the one factor that trumped a fit parent's right to child.

Boozer v. Wilder, 34 Indian L.Rep. 6023, 6024 (Confederated Tribes of the Colville Reservation Ct.App.2007). See also Boozer v. Wilder, 381 F.3d 931, 937 (9th Cir.2004) (ordering exhaustion of tribal remedies and concluding, "There is no evidence that the Tribe is not competent to handle the dispute, will not offer Boozer a fair opportunity to regain custody of K.W.B., or will not act in the child's best interests.").

Tribal child welfare commissions, where they exist, advise tribal child welfare executive officials on removal, placement, and termination decisions. For example, the Child Welfare Commission of the Little Traverse Bay Bands of Odawa Indians licenses foster care providers and advises tribal officials on case-specific and non-case-specific child welfare matters. Waganakising Odawa Code § 5.204(A). Most tribal nations already have or hope to move away from the adversarial child welfare model toward family wellness courts or other similar structure.

Finally, tribal court jurisdiction over child welfare proceedings often comes into contact or conflict with state court jurisdiction. ICWA acknowledges exclusive tribal court jurisdiction over Indian children domiciled on an Indian reservation. 25 U.S.C. § 1911(a). ICWA acknowledges presumptive jurisdiction in tribal court in other cases, requiring transfer of state ICWA cases to tribal court in the absence of good cause to the contrary or the declination of a tribal court to accept jurisdiction.

§ 1911(b). See In re C.M., 15 Am. Tribal Law 437 (Cherokee Ct. of the Eastern Band of Cherokee Indians 2019), where the court accepted the transfer of a state court ICWA case involving tribal member children domiciled on the reservation. For more than five years after the transfer, the tribal court did not move to accept jurisdiction. Once the tribe had the capacity to act, it moved to initiate proceedings in tribal court. The trial court dismissed that action on procedural grounds. Three years later, the tribe again attempted to initiate proceedings. The Cherokee Court granted the motion, concluding that under ICWA the tribal court was the exclusive forum for child welfare matters arising on the reservation.

2. CHILD CUSTODY AND SUPPORT MATTERS

Child custody and support matters are not generally considered child welfare matters covered by ICWA. Jurisdictional overlap in these areas unfortunately is common, with dueling marriage partners seeking marriage dissolution in both tribal and state courts at the same time. All both courts can do in such circumstances is to make independent determinations about their own jurisdiction. For example, see In re the Custody of Boehme, 12 Am. Tribal Law 310 (Tulalip Tribal Ct.App.2015), where the court vacated a trial court decision to decline jurisdiction over a proposed modification of a child custody plan. The trial court had declined because the other parent had filed first in state court. The appellate court pointed to tribal code provisions that required the judiciary to take into consideration tribal public policy: "It shall be the policy of the

Tulalip Tribes to promote the distinct and unique culture and heritage of the Tulalip Tribes, *and to ensure that Native children have a meaningful opportunity to experience their culture on a permanent basis. All actions authorized by this code shall be taken with due consideration of this policy.*" Id. at 313 (quoting Tulalip Tribal Code § 4.20.010) (emphasis in original).

Tribal custom and tradition may help define the scope of tribal authority in this area. In Helper v. Perkins, 13 Indian L.Rep. 6011 (Sitka Community Assoc. Tribal Ct.1986), the court asserted an Alaska tribal nation's retained inherent authority to exercise jurisdiction over child custody matters. The court petitioned a council of elders for guidance with respect to jurisdiction, which responded as follows:

> This court, having considered the question of tribal and clan jurisdiction over children born to the female descendants of members of the several clans comprising the Sitka Community Association Indian Tribe, finds:
>
> Under traditional Indian law of Southeast Alaska there is no question as to jurisdiction and responsibility for children of female clan members. Traditional law holds "children of female members of a clan are children of the clan regardless of where or under what circumstances they may be found. Clan membership does not wash off, nor can such membership be removed by any force, or any distance, or over time. Even in death clan

> membership continues, and in re-birth is it renewed."
>
> Therefore, this Court holds that children of female members of the several clans of this Tribe never leave the jurisdiction of this Court, and that the responsibility of the clans for the children of the clans comprising this Tribe shall remain under all circumstances, and further, that clan membership can neither be changed or removed, even in death.

Id. at 6016.

Tribal courts will look to tribal cultural traditions for guidance in determining jurisdiction. For example, see In re K., 2013 Nottawaseppi Huron Band Tribal LEXIS 4 (Nottawaseppi Huron Band of the Potawatomi Tribal Ct.2013), where the court was confronted with whether it possessed jurisdiction over a minor child who was eligible for enrollment but not enrolled and who did not reside on the tribe's trust lands. Looking to the tribe's cultural traditions as articulated in the tribal constitution, the court assumed jurisdiction:

> The NHBP Constitution states that its actions are to be done in a manner that is "consistent with our Bode'wadmi traditions and cultural values" with the care of its children a specific constitutionally mandated responsibility. The NHBP Constitution also states that "[t]he Band's jurisdiction shall also extend beyond its territory whenever the Band is acting pursuant to jurisdiction that is created or affirmed by

> rights reserved or created by treaty, statutes adopted by the Tribal Council in the exercise of the Band's inherent sovereignty, Federal statute, regulation or other federal authorization, or a compact or other agreement entered into with a state or local government under applicable law." To determine whether to include minor children as defined in the ICWA and the MIFPA [Michigan Indian Family Preservation Act] in the Code, the Court must take many factors into consideration including, but not limited to: the definition of an "Indian child" in the ICWA and MIFPA; the provision in the MIFPA that requires the state to transfer cases to the appropriate tribal court when an Indian child is involved; the leadership role the NHBP took in the passage of the MIFPA; the consistent and ongoing commitment of the NHBP in exercising its right to participate in state cases involving minor children enrolled at the NHBP or eligible for enrollment; and the constitutionally mandated responsibility to expand jurisdiction beyond trust lands to exercise the Band's inherent sovereignty. It is clear based on all of these factors that accepting jurisdiction over a guardianship case where the minor child is eligible for enrollment, but does not live on trust lands is appropriate. Most importantly, accepting jurisdiction in this case honors the Bode'wadmi values, traditions and beliefs as articulated in the NHBP Constitution.

Id. at *15–16.

Tribal court jurisdiction is often crucial for the protection of a tribal nation's interest in maintaining connections over their children. In Tafoya v. Ghashghaee, 25 Indian L.Rep. 6193 (Pueblo of Pojoaque Tribal Ct.1998), the court assumed jurisdiction over a tribal citizen child of a mixed marriage domiciled off the reservation. The non-Indian father, who was from Mexico, had threatened to take the child there, a threat the court took very seriously:

> Based on past actions, the tribal court and the Pueblo of Pojoaque must take any such threat as potentially injurious to ties between the child and the Pueblo. The Pueblo enjoys a rich historical tradition, through marriage and family relationships, with Mexico. At least two enrolled Pueblo children over the last three years have been removed by their Mexican national parent to Mexico. In this case, the father's threat may be attributed to the passion of the moment. However, there is no guarantee that such volatility may not reappear. Testimony was received that the father has not left the United States over the past seven years. However, such testimony merely reflects a pattern that may be weakened over time by parental emotions.

Id. at 6195. The court noted that the Pueblo and the court had experience with mixed Pojoaque and Mexican families, justifying tribal court authority:

> The tribal court is uniquely suited to safeguard the essential tribal relations between

> the child, the Pueblo and the non-American father. The Court and the Pueblo officials are routinely petitioned by guardians and parents of enrolled minors traveling to Mexico. The Court and the Pueblo officials accept testimony and prepare documentation to safeguard the return of the children to the Pueblo. Such services would be available for the father of A.E.G.

Id.

3. TRIBAL HEALING-TO-WELLNESS COURTS

Tribal Healing to Wellness Courts are tribal justice programs that address alcohol and drug abuse within a community by providing a holistic, team-based approach to treatment and rehabilitation. These courts incorporate cultural and traditional healing methods, using judicial supervision, frequent testing, and a combination of incentives and sanctions to hold offenders accountable while promoting individual and community well-being. They are a form of restorative justice that operates as a problem-solving court focused on achieving abstinence and altering criminalized behavior.

Programs integrate alcohol and drug treatment with community healing resources and traditional practices to address the physical and spiritual needs of participants. A team including a judge, prosecutors, defense counsel, treatment specialists, law enforcement, and community leaders work together to create a comprehensive plan for recovery. Culturally-specific components, such as talking circles and traditional ceremonies, are incorporated into the treatment and rehabilitation process. These courts emphasize healing for both the individual offender and the community, aiming to reduce substance abuse and related crime within the tribal community.

The Lac du Flambeau Band of Lake Superior Chippewa Indians has established the Zaagiibagaa Healing to Wellness Court. This court provides a combination of substance abuse treatment, education and supervision to hold participants accountable to the court, to themselves, to their family and to their community. The program incorporates cultural principles in order to reduce crime, restore individual health, and honor traditional values.

Examples of tribal codes establishing healing to wellness courts include without limitation Choctaw Nation of Oklahoma, Council Bill CB-96-24; Stockbridge-Munsee Tribal Code, Tribal Court Code § 06.01; Swinomish Tribal Code § 3–09.030; Ute Indian Tribe, Law and Order Code § 13–4–152.

INDEX

References are to Pages